Vietnamese
Anticolonialism
1885-1925

This book is sponsored by the Center for South and Southeast Asia Studies

THE CENTER FOR SOUTH AND SOUTHEAST ASIA STUDIES of the University of California is the unifying organization for faculty members and students interested in South and Southeast Asia Studies, bringing together scholars from numerous disciplines. The Center's major aims are the development and support of research and language study. As part of this program the Center sponsors a publication series of books concerned with South and Southeast Asia. Manuscripts are considered from all campuses of the University of California as well as from any other individuals and institutions doing research in these areas.

PUBLICATIONS OF THE CENTER FOR
SOUTH AND SOUTHEAST ASIA STUDIES:

Eugene F. Irschick
Politics and Social Conflict in South India: The Non-Brahman Movement and Tamil Separatism, 1916–1929   (1969)

Robert L. Hardgrave, Jr.
The Nadars of Tamilnad: The Political Culture of a Community in Change   (1969)

Angela S. Burger
Opposition in a Dominant-Party System: A Study of the Jan Sangh, the Praja Socialist Party, and the Socialist Party in Uttar Pradesh, India   (1969)

Briton Martin, Jr.
New India, 1885: British Official Policy and the Emergence of the Indian National Congress   (1969)

James T. Siegel
The Rope of God   (1969)

David G. Marr

Vietnamese

ANTICOLONIALISM

1885–1925

University of California
Berkeley, Los Angeles, London
1971

University of California Press
Berkeley and Los Angeles, California
University of California Press, Ltd.
London, England
Copyright © 1971, by
The Regents of the University of California
First Printing 1971
First Paperback Edition, Fall 1971
ISBN: 0–520–01813–3 cloth
   0–520–02046–4 paper
Library of Congress Catalog Card Number: 75–129611
Printed in the United States of America
Designed by Ikuko Workman

To My Wife, Ai

Contents

Abbreviations

AOM	—	Archives Nationales de France, Section Outre-Mer (Paris)
BK	—	*Bach Khoa* (Saigon)
CD	—	Tung Lam, *Cuoc Doi Cach Mang Cuong De* (Saigon)
CMCD	—	Tran Huy Lieu, *et al.*, *Cach Mang Can Dai Viet-Nam* (Hanoi)
CXL	—	Tran Van Giau, *Chong Xam Lang* (Hanoi)
DKNT	—	Nguyen Hien Le, *Dong Kinh Nghia Thuc* (Saigon)
HT	—	Vu Dinh Lien, *et al.*, eds., *Hop Tuyen Tho Van Viet-Nam (1858–1930)* (Hanoi)
JSEAH	—	*Journal of Southeast Asian History* (Singapore)
LT	—	Tran Van Giap, *et al.*, *Luoc Truyen Cac Tac Gia Viet-Nam*, vol. 1 (Hanoi)
NB	—	Phan Boi Chau, *Phan Boi Chau Nien Bieu* (Hanoi)
NCLS	—	*Nghien Cuu Lich Su* (Hanoi)
NTT	—	*Nguc Trung Thu* (Saigon)
SD	—	*Su Dia* (Saigon)
TP	—	Phan Boi Chau, *Tu Phan* (Hue)
VHNS	—	*Van Hoa Nguyet San* (Saigon)
VNDN	—	Nguyen Huyen Anh, *Viet-Nam Danh Nhan Tu Dien* (Saigon)
VT	—	Dang Thai Mai, *Van Tho Phan Boi Chau* (Hanoi)
VTCM	—	Dang Thai Mai, *Van Tho Cach Mang Viet-Nam Dau The Ky XX* (Hanoi)

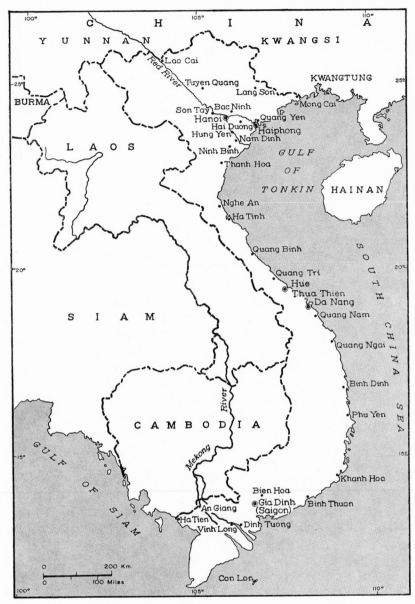

Map 1   The Provinces of Vietnam Around 1900

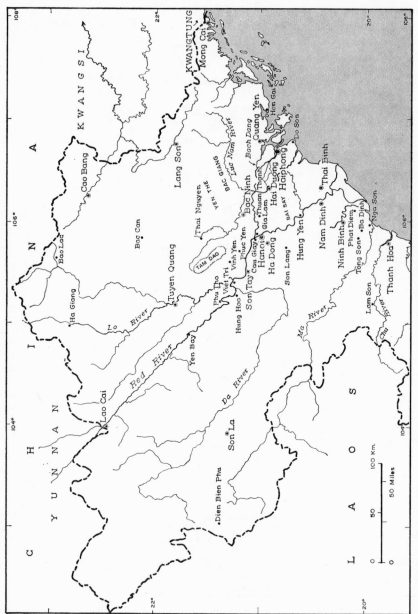

Map 2   North Vietnam

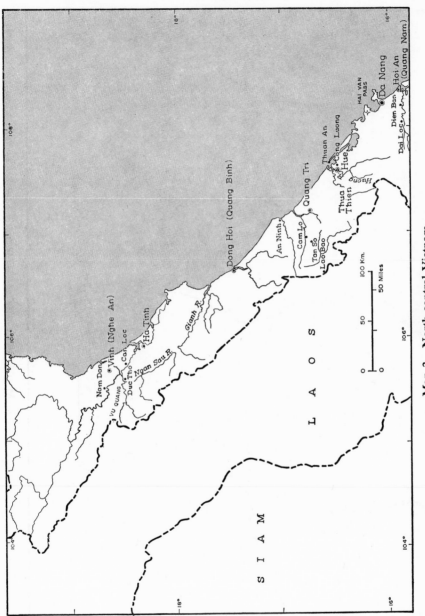

Map 3 North-central Vietnam

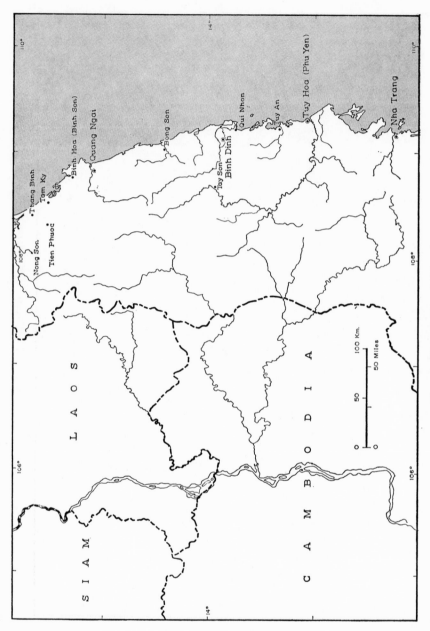

Map 4 South-central Vietnam

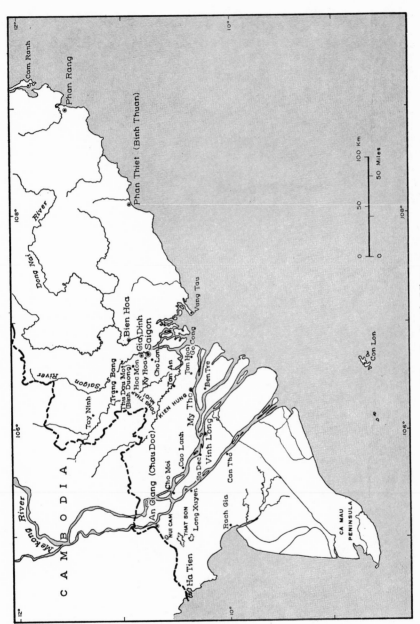

Map 5   South Vietnam

Preface

Events of the past five or ten years in Vietnam understandably have transfixed the world and sent many of us, in some fashion, to the barricades. For all our concentration on the present, however, even cursory examination serves to reveal how much we are prisoners of the past as Vietnamese and foreigners both act out roles delineated many years ago.

This study centers on certain political events at the turn of the century in Vietnam, a time when France had seized the entire country and was consolidating her rule for purposes of long-term exploitation. I make no pretense of writing a comprehensive political history of this period, particularly in regard to various collaborateur elements. Rather, my attention here is almost entirely devoted to those Vietnamese who resisted, to one degree or another, French colonial actions.

The fundamental assumption, therefore, is that one cannot understand resistance efforts in Vietnam in more recent times without going back at least to 1885. Yet, to date in the West, the focus has been almost entirely on the Indochinese Communist party, the Viet-Minh, and the National Liberation Front (more properly known as the National Front for Liberation of South Vietnam). In part this is because the study of Vietnamese anticolonial movements has been largely the preserve of the political scientist, the practicing journalist, and the intelligence specialist. Simply considering the course of events since 1945, their emphasis may appear justified. But what happens, for example, when someone asks, why did "communists" succeed in Vietnam and fail in places like India, Burma, Malaya, Indonesia, and the Philippines? More precisely, why did "noncommunist" groups lose out so decisively in Vietnam? The last few decades do not hold the basic answers to these questions—or to many others, for that matter.

One of the historiographical aims of this book is to demonstrate that the time has come to take Vietnamese-language (*quoc-ngu*) sources quite seriously. The bulk have come out since 1954, in an effort to make up for all the decades when Vietnamese publishing suffered under strict French controls. A fair proportion of these newly available publications are in fact valuable translations or transliterations of primary historical materials. For the specific period under scrutiny, a number of proclamations, poems, and essays survive—surprising, considering the obvious personal dangers involved in retaining them through the years. Since many activities were clandestine, not much remains of party records, but we are fortunate that several key resistance leaders went to the trouble of writing autobiographies, and that other individuals, who survived into the 1940s, related their stories to a new generation of anticolonialists. Since extreme secrecy and pre-modern communication limited each participant's knowledge of the total picture, such sources must be cross-checked intensively. In general, they cannot stand alone.

French sources also have been utilized here, particularly the Archives Nationales (Section Outre-Mer) and certain published collections and studies that have appeared in the past fifteen years or so. Given the wealth of books in French on the culture, general history, and colonial policies of Vietnam, it is surprising at first to discover how little was written for publication before 1945 on Vietnamese anticolonial activities. The exceptions are due to certain French admirals, diplomats, and merchant-adventurers who in the late nineteenth century not only wrote proudly and expansively on their colonialization efforts, but also provided occasional detail on those Vietnamese who chose to resist them. After that, a distinct reticence set in, betrayed only by French administrators and security officials in their detailed, confidential reports to the Minister of Colonies in Paris.

Unless otherwise noted, all translations are mine. I have felt an obligation to list Vietnamese sources in the footnotes and bibliography as liberally as possible, since others may well wish to pursue the same or similar subjects in the near future. Some readers may feel that I have relied too heavily on publications from Hanoi. This is mainly because scholars in North Vietnam have moved far ahead of their contemporaries in the South in the patient collection, annotation, and publication of primary data on anticolonial activities. Nevertheless, wherever possible, I have compared primary data published in both North and South, occasionally coming up with interesting discrepancies. In secondary or interpretive works, historians in Hanoi appear to have been somewhat more attentive to modern scholastic practices, while those in Saigon often have proved to be superior in capturing the "sense" of the period, empathizing more perhaps with traditionalist attitudes and values. None of this is to say, of course, that writers in either the North or the South have necessarily solved a number of basic problems in historical interpretation, particularly in their treatments of the late nineteenth century.

Technical matters, questions of terminology, translation, diacritical marks and the like, are dealt with in the footnotes and in the Glossary. Several points, however, deserve immediate mention. The country's name, for our purposes, is "Vietnam," not just because it is today's term and because others rouse resentment, but also because it has been acceptable to most Vietnamese since 1804. Before that there were obvious variations on the same theme, such as Nam-Viet, Dai-Viet, Dai-Nam, not to mention the colloquial "nuoc Nam" which carries through in poetry to the present day. While "An-Nam" traditionally was the Middle Kingdom designation for Vietnam, and while the French also found that term to be of some convenience, at no time did the Vietnamese really regard it as an appropriate appellation. For regional designations, I have generally used north, central, and south Vietnam, since, again, the equivalents to these in Vietnamese were used most commonly by people during the period of French colonial rule. Central Vietnam is taken to include the provinces from Thanh Hoa to Binh Thuan, with the northern and southern regions being the proverbial "baskets" on each end of this "carrying pole."

Individuals' names and titles may be more of a problem. With few exceptions, the name by which a person was known publicly as an adult is used here, all known pseudonyms being mentioned in the notes. Each portion of the name has been capitalized and hyphens excluded, a simplified usage increasingly acceptable within Vietnam. A more delicate problem arises in deciding how to refer to a person in the text. In ordinary conversation the Vietnamese use given names even for strangers, but this is not the case when they refer to esteemed historical figures—perhaps because it may sound too offhand or familiar. Using the entire name circumvents the issue, but clutters the text. Hence, I have stayed with surnames except where confusion is likely, as with the ubiquitous Nguyen. Once more, this is in line with general practice in Vietnamese history texts, except that I have tried to avoid excessive subjectivity by choosing to employ surnames for the apparent villains as well as the obvious heroes. Finally, there is the matter of whether the Vietnamese monarch's royal prefix should be Emperor or King. Fortunately the question is not central to the subject, since an answer would involve unraveling some extremely subtle cultural attitudes and the court diplomacy of three countries—Vietnam, China, and France. Except in direct quotes, I have used King, since the Vietnamese people on all but formal occasions seem to have referred to their monarch as *vua* rather than *hoang-de* (Emperor).

The more one studies a topic like this, the more one realizes the serious need to delineate process and structure in Vietnamese history, to step back and provide something of an abstract picture, to integrate and compare as well as simply to describe. A bit of this has been done by the better Marxist historians, both in Hanoi and in Paris. Their admitted perceptiveness on economic and social issues, however, has not yet carried over, in my opinion, to the intellectual, psychological, and cultural spheres. In any case, it is almost certain that not enough scholars are in the field yet, not enough monographs have been written, to enable real deductive conceptualization and analysis. This is all a roundabout apology, perhaps, for the high proportion of simple narration in this book—so much that is "new" by way of people, publications, ideas, and actions deserves preliminary treatment.

More people provided crucial assistance in the development of this study than I can possibly mention. First thanks go to those Vietnamese who patiently taught me their language during 1961 and 1962. Then there are the Vietnamese teachers and students who graciously offered advice and, in many cases, loaned or gave me source materials of great value. During most of 1967 a Fulbright-Hays research grant provided the means for me to seek out and work on materials in Vietnam, Hong Kong, and Japan. The Center for Southeast Asia Studies at the University of California, Berkeley, assisted me while I put those materials in dissertation form and also supported me in a research trip to Paris. Sincere appreciation is extended to Professor Frederic E. Wakeman, Jr., for his careful reading of two earlier drafts: some of his comments will keep me working far beyond the bounds of this book. Professors Milton E. Osborne of Monash University, John K. Whitmore of Yale University, Nguyen Cong Binh of the University of Hanoi, Truong Buu Lam of State University of New York at Stony Brook, and the late Professor Joseph R. Levenson of the University of California at Berkeley were also kind enough to comment in some detail. I am grateful to the Southeast Asia Program, Cornell University, and to Mrs. Tazu Warner for assisting in the typing of the final manuscript. Judith Quinn of the University of California Press provided extremely valuable editorial advice in the final stages of this effort.

There are almost certain to be errors of fact or interpretation; for them I am solely responsible. In some cases I have chosen to court criticism by including unverifiable data, appropriately noted. Two reasons for this can be offered. First, to exclude all apparent myth in Vietnamese anticolonial movements is to ignore the fact that myths have a way of affecting later events, particularly through the popular oral medium. If, as I implied previously, we are interested in seeing how anticolonial movements of these early years relate to later, historically more "decisive" movements, then it is essential that some attention be given to these communications. Second, what better way is there to proceed amidst generally uncharted surroundings than to set others to challenging the data and conclusions included here? In this respect, I fully expect—indeed, hope— that my work here will be rendered largely obsolete within the decade. Considering the barren starting point, that is not as bad a fate as some might imagine.

Vietnamese
Anticolonialism
1885-1925

Introduction

Today practically every city, every provincial town, in Vietnam, North and South, has major streets named for anticolonial patriots. In Saigon, Phan Dinh Phung Street runs through a tree-lined, upper-class remnant of colonial grandeur. In Hue, Phan Boi Chau Street pierces the heart of the jumbled precolonial market area, just outside the walls of the citadel. Da-Nang's Phan Chu Trinh Street cuts across the back of town, sprinkled with comfortable brick buildings and snack shops. Almost invariably there also are streets named for Hoang Dieu, Ham Nghi, Hoang Hoa Tham, Tran Quy Cap, Luong Ngoc Quyen, and others who dominate this narrative.

Street names are not always significant. Nevertheless, when hundreds of thousands of persons choose to fight and—inevitably—to die in struggle against a colonial ruler, particularly one that has the temerity to name Vietnamese streets after such "great colonizers," as La Grandier, Paul Bert, and Gallieni, then one may surmise that the *renaming* of streets upon independence will carry deep symbolic value.

And it is the creation and nurturing of symbols, above all, that I am concerned with in this study. More precisely, I hope to convey something meaningful about the origins and communication of anticolonial myths in Vietnam, orienting the question around the Vietnamese sense of their identity as a people. In one sense at least, *all* is myth, since all human thought is subjective. Here, however, I am talking about man's eternal need to formulate, for his own emotional satisfaction and with little reference to objective, verifiable "truth," potent reasons for this existence. As long as man finds it impossible logically to encompass himself and the world around him (which is to say, the foreseeable future) he will have to create myths to ease his path, to justify his torments. A goodly portion of these myths can be expected to deal with his senses of personal and group identity, the more so whenever this identity is being gravely threatened.

When practicing their craft, whether dealing with the question of identity or something else, historians often are asked to balance the elements of continuity in their story against the elements of change, to delineate the persistence of traditional symbols and attitudes from the apparent acceptance or development of new concepts and values among the people being studied.

Without doubt, the continuity in Vietnamese anticolonialism is a highly-charged, historically self-conscious resistance to oppressive, degrading foreign rule. Possessors of a proud cultural and political heritage, many Vietnamese simply refused to be cowed. In attempting as non-Vietnamese to understand this phenomenon, each of us must first ask himself some angry philosophical questions, the import of which extends far beyond Vietnam. What are the nature and causes of man's terrible inhumanity toward his fellow men? How do the strong treat the weak? More significantly, how do the weak react? Who, in the last analysis, are really the weak ones; who, the strong? We may never answer these questions, but, as we wind our way through a narrative strewn with exotic settings and strange-sounding names, they should never be far from our consideration.

While the Vietnamese people, then, had a proud, almost haughty, tradition, it was not enough to keep the French imperialists from seizing their country and beginning the process of bending the Vietnamese to their will. Hence it was that from 1885 (perhaps earlier in the South) the Vietnamese identity came under critical and sustained challenge, first felt by the scholar-gentry and eventually experienced by the miniscule bourgeoisie, the artisans, and, most important, the bulk of the peasantry. The scholar-gentry generation that came to political maturity around 1900 was haunted by the image of *mat nuoc*, of "losing one's country" not merely in the political sense, but more critically in terms of their future survival as Vietnamese. They struggled desperately to bring new meaning and ethnic salvation (*cuu quoc*) out of a developing sense of loss and despair. From this struggle came major changes in the world view and tactics of the Vietnamese anticolonialists.

The commonest causal interpretation of changes in this period in Vietnam emphasizes economic or material aspects. I cannot agree. It is true that most of the people I deal with here were members of the scholar-gentry (*si-phu*) class, whose families were openly threatened in the material sense by the French penetration and eventual control. But the French were most content to leave the scholar-gentry a fair portion of their material privileges—providing they collaborated politically. Indeed, after 1885 a majority of the scholar-gentry seem to have done precisely that, leaving the others, the prime subjects of this study, to reject collaboration on essentially spiritual or psychological grounds.

After 1919 it can be argued rather convincingly that economic transformation was indeed the most important factor in setting the course and tone of anticolonial activities, until at least 1939. World depression after 1929 gave the entire endeavor an air of economic desperation, something that had been anticipated by the scholar-gentry two decades before, but never as their prime motivation.

Parallel to the growing fear for ethnic and cultural survival was an ideological debate that began around 1900 and reached general exposition by 1907 or 1908. For, if the subjects of this story were members of the last generation of scholar-gentry, they were also the first Vietnamese to try to deal seriously with the strange, momentous questions of modernization and Westernization. What was Vietnam's future in a world of competing nation-states? Was there an East Asian "racial solidarity" that could prove meaningful in the Vietnamese quest for deliverance from French oppression? And how was the progressive character of history—an idea which these Vietnamese now accepted—to be interpreted and used to advantage in subsequent decades? It was a debate which in itself represented the first essential step toward developing an ideological position worthy of twentieth-century challenges. There would be further tortuous testing and elaboration, but the strategic and tactical guidelines had been set.

There may be some argument over my use of the term "anticolonial" to describe the movements of this period. Others may regard "anti-French," "resistance," or "nationalist" as more precise or meaningful. "Anti-French" may strike an appropriate note for much of what happened from 1858 to 1898, in the same way that "antiforeign" and even "antimodern" do in certain contexts. After that time, those men whom I define as activists continued to use highly derogatory, xenophobic terms for the French (hairy, smelly, big-nosed, white-eyed) in their propaganda; but the fact that they also came around to expounding favorably on Montesquieu, Voltaire, Rousseau, and Napoleon makes it evident that they considered some big-nosed types better than others. More important, those I define in this generation as reformists would never have described themselves as anti-French, since they were publicly willing to accept a French-led administration if it approximated their radically altered blueprint.

The same arguments apply to "resistance," which in Vietnam may be considered the broadest term, conveying an image of basically traditional response to foreign intervention. It is certainly appropriate to Vietnamese efforts relative to the Mongol, Ming, and Ch'ing incursions, and it is used herein for all movements against the French before King Ham Nghi's flight into the hills in 1885. After that, however, it is increasingly an anticolonial form of resistance I am talking about. Certainly by 1902 the colonial regime was *the* fact of life in Vietnam—powerful, grim, seemingly eternal. Those still choosing to struggle by then can best be defined as fundamentally opposed to that regime. And it is important to recognize that this included the reformists, who, while not opposed to the French presence per se, were openly, publicly, antagonistic to the particular colonial structure that was spread before their eyes. When they attacked the feudal system and the collaborationist court in Hue, they were attacking an essential part of that colonial structure—which is why most of them ended up in jail.

Finally, why not call them nationalist movements? In terms of both substance and mere definition, this is an extremely complex question, deserving of much future discussion among Vietnam specialists.[1] For the moment I have avoided the terms national or nationalist, largely because the nearest Vietnamese equivalents, *quoc-gia* and *quoc-dan*, carry unpardonable contemporary loads of political controversy and bitterness. The term *dan-toc* is more appropriate and acceptable, but that really has developed from the centuries-old Vietnamese sense of "peoplehood," which is involved more with ethnic and cultural-linguistic factors than with national and territorial ones. It is only in the 1920s that we see young petit bourgeois intellectuals really beginning to absorb the modern concept of nation-state, inclusive of ethnic minorities and, occasionally, operative in a positive, dynamic, ideological sense.

1. For arguments in favor of "nationalism" as the proper term for traditional Vietnamese resistance—to the Chinese, as well as the French—see Truong Buu Lam, *Patterns of Vietnamese Response to Foreign Intervention: 1858–1900* (New Haven, 1967), pp. 29–34.

Chapter One

Dẫu cường nhược có lúc khác nhau,
Song hào kiệt đời nào cũng có.

Although we have been at times strong,
at times weak,
We have at no time lacked heroes.

(Nguyễn Trãi, *Bình Ngô Đại Cáo,* 1428)

The Nature of Vietnamese Identity

What did it mean to be Vietnamese in the nineteenth century, just before the French colonial penetration? This question needs to be asked if we are to understand the attitudes and actions of subsequent anticolonialists, as they attempted with only the meagerest resources to sustain or regenerate a meaningful concept of identity.

Paradoxically, group identity may be understood best in terms of group differentiation. In other words, groups seldom ponder their commonality actively until faced with internal cleavage or the menace, overt or implied, of outside intervention. Perhaps most members of a particular group feel little reason to express their dependence on each other until such difficulties arise. At any rate, whether these observations deserve generalized application or not, the historian of Vietnam is repeatedly struck by the degree to which the Vietnamese have tended to define themselves in terms of their neighbors.

A glance at the complex ethnic situation on the Indochina subcontinent can tell us much. For many centuries the Vietnamese have both shared and contested this area with Tai, Mon-Khmer, Malayo-Polynesian, and Sinitic peoples of diverse origins and levels of development. Mentally the Vietnamese have tended to set themselves apart most sharply from the various highland residents, the so-called Montagnards, perhaps because the Montagnards did not share the Vietnamese passion for wet rice cultivation in the deltas and coastal lowlands of the region. While differing life styles did not rule out measured interaction, the relationship was not an easy one. Each endured the other because neither had sufficient reason or strength to alter the situation radically.

Such attitudes of differentiation from the Montagnards were probably common to all classes of Vietnamese, being as relevant to the poor peasant or tenant farmer as to the local and court elites. One may imagine, for example, a Vietnamese peasant squatting carefully beside his village gate, eyeing Montagnard families trudging along the paths to market carrying cinnamon bark, wild herbs, or animal hides. What did the two have in common, the peasant might ruminate, other than territorial propinquity and a healthy fear of each other? Of course they did sometimes share the same market, but their languages, costumes, house structures, and general modes of survival were extremely different.

On the other hand, the same peasant, who conceivably never left his home district, could easily come in contact also with ethnic Vietnamese of distant provinces, be they peddlers, fortune-tellers, garrison troops, or mandarins. Making comparisons, if he chose, he could perceive major similarities of life style. Each attuned himself, for example, to the annual cycle of rice cultivation. Together they knew that paddy fertility and techniques of paddy irrigation were essential to their survival. And they spoke to each other with this in mind.

Such dependence on rice was also shared, however, with other neighboring groups like the Khmer (Cambodians) and the slightly more distant Lao. In these cases group differentiation had little to do with economics and nothing to do with altitudes of settlement, since all three peoples were concerned with wet rice cultivation and preferred the lowlands. Yet there still existed profound differences in their choices of house structure, familial and village organization, and forms of religious observance, to name only a few. Once again one may suppose that it did not require a particularly elitist or educated mind to perceive these differences. During the nineteenth century such considerations were important, especially in the Mekong delta, where quite a few Khmer chose to remain, even though the area was increasingly subject to domination by Vietnamese immigrants from the north.

If the question of Vietnamese identity involved only differentiating them from the Montagnards, the Khmer, and the Lao, there would be little reason to spend much time on the subject. In Vietnamese eyes, relationships with these groups and with the by then largely exterminated Cham people, had always been relatively clear-cut and seldom were subject to dispute.[1] Rather, it was their giant neighbor to the north—the Middle Kingdom, the ubiquitous Han—that preoccupied the Vietnamese and provided their major identity problems. China was so much more powerful in terms of population, resources, and the degree of social mobilization that some concern

---

1. This is not to say that the Vietnamese did not borrow extensively from the Cham, Khmer, Lao, or even the Montagnard groupings, but only that they subjectively perceived their differences from these peoples as being preeminent and hence the form and degree of contact as less subject to concern.

was certainly understandable. However, it was more than this. The difficulty comes in conveying the subtle interplay of resistance and dependence
which appeared often to stand at the root of historical Vietnamese attitudes
toward the Chinese. This difficulty is multiplied by the fact that, in contrast
to their shared outlooks on the Montagnards, the Khmer, and so on, the
attitudes of elite and nonelite elements of the population were significantly
different.

Ngo Si Lien, a fifteenth-century Vietnamese historian, argued that the
Viet people sprang from Shen-nung, one of China's legendary "divine
rulers," but in a hereditary line quite distinct from the Chinese.[2] This may
have been the ideal Vietnamese image of their relationship to the Chinese:
dependent on the same sources, the same roots, yet with an independent
history that implicitly gave China no right of political hegemony. Indeed,
four centuries earlier, in 1077 A.D., the Vietnamese ruler of this small kingdom to the south had set the precedent by styling himself "Emperor" (*De*;
in Chinese, *Ti*) and declaring that his country's separate destiny had been
recorded in a celestial book.[3]

It has become fashionable recently in the West to point out, in praise
and seeming wonder, the ability of the Vietnamese people to maintain
some sort of separate identity during one thousand years of Chinese rule
and then to cast off the foreign yoke and for the next nine hundred years
thwart repeated Chinese attempts to turn back the clock.[4] Actually, although archaeological research provides a fairly clear idea of the types of
people settled in Vietnam before the imposition of Chinese rule in 111
B.C.,[5] the subsequent relationships of these groups to the Chinese and to
each other have barely been touched upon.

Doubtless, one important time frame encompasses much of the first half
of the first century A.D. Immediately following the Wang Mang usurpation
in China (9–23 A.D.), significant numbers of Chinese fled south to the Red

2. Ngo Si Lien, *Dai Viet Su Ky Toan Thu* (Hanoi, 1967) vol. 1, pp. 17, 59. One
is immediately reminded of Japan's imperial myth, with its similar concern for a
chronology as venerable as that of the mighty Middle Kingdom.

3. Hoang Xuan Han, *Ly Thuong Kiet*, pp. 299–300. Tran Trong Kim, *Viet-Nam
Su Luoc*, p. 108. The Ly dynasty (1010–1225 A.D.) monarchs, and others after
them, also co-opted such Chinese imperial reign names as Thai-to (Chinese: T'ai-
tsu), Thai-tong (T'ai-tsung), and Thanh-tong (Sheng-tsung).

4. For example, see M. Coughlin, "Vietnam: In China's Shadow."

5. Some of the pioneer archeological work appears in English in O. Janse, *Archeological Research in Indochina,* 3 vols. (Cambridge, 1947 and 1941; Bruges, 1958).
For an introduction to French materials, see L. Finot, "L'Archéologie Indochinois,
1917–30," *Bull. de la Commission Archéologique de l'Indochine* (Paris, 1931).
The most recent findings are available in NCLS.

River delta and coastal plains. Simultaneously, the Chinese governor of the region shifted away from a policy of association with the loosely knit native aristocracy to one of outright cultural and political assimilation—i.e., Sinicization. There is reason to believe that this was the primary cause of a short-lived rebellion (40–42 A.D.) led by the famous Trung sisters and aimed at sustaining local aristocratic privilege. The renowned Chinese General Ma-Yuan reacted by pillaging and burning aristocratic properties and leaving survivors the choice of either intermarrying with the Chinese settlers or fleeing southward into the hills. Over the next few centuries a hybrid elite seems to have developed, drawing heavily on Chinese culture and political precedent, yet also prone to defending its own interests rather than those of the faraway Chinese court. The relationship of the elite to the mass of local people, the rural peasants, unfortunately remains largely unexplored.[6]

The next crucial period, in terms of understanding the development of a distinct Vietnamese identity, probably extends over the tenth and eleventh centuries A.D. The question may be phrased more or less as follows: What happened at that time, what transformation occurred, to enable the people of the Red River area not only to overthrow their Chinese administrators (which had happened before, to no lasting avail) but, more important, to allow them to build a domestic system that could withstand repeated external challenges, both from the Chinese in the north and from the Cham kingdom to the south? In the broader sense, how does one explain the fact that the seemingly irresistible surge of the Han people southward was effectively halted from this point onward, with the Middle Kingdom stabilizing the frontier north of the Red River rather than taking in further monsoon territories appropriate to wet rice cultivation?

Again, much research remains to be done before these questions can really be answered. One eminent commentator has suggested that the people of the Red River area had borrowed so assiduously from the Chinese, particularly in the economic and bureacratic realms, that they were able at last to turn their acquisitions against their benefactors to critical effect.[7] While this may have been the case, it tells nothing about motivations— about why the local people felt it necessary and desirable to break away permanently. After all, if one had assimilated Chinese ideas and outlooks sufficiently, one would not lightly have wished to renounce one's cultural

6. For general treatments of the period of Chinese rule, see Tran Trong Kim, *Viet-Nam Su Luoc*, pp. 45–81; and Le Thanh Khoi, *Le Viet-Nam, Histoire et Civilisation* (Paris, 1955), 98–134, 136.

7. Henri Maspero, "L'expédition de Ma Yuan," *Bulletin de l'Ecole Française d'Extrême-Orient*, vol. 18, no. 3, pp. 27–28.

father and one's position amidst the stellar galaxy that revolved around the "true emperor" to the north.

At any rate, after the establishment of the Ly dynasty (1010–1225 A.D.) in the Red River delta and the north-central plains, the outlines of identity are relatively clear, and we have no trepidation at labeling the people "Vietnamese." For all the supposed impact of a millennium of Chinese rule, Ly society in Vietnam strikes the observer as essentially non-Confucian, if Confucianism is taken as the rather routinized, official type so well entrenched in China by that time. The system in Vietnam was openly robust, ruthless, and politically decentralized, with a surprising degree of informality at court. Ly monarchs rewarded loyal followers with large estates, complete with prisoners of war or families of criminals to develop and work the land.[8] Body tattooing, betel chewing, and teeth lacquering were still prevalent, although these practices must have caused Chinese administrators to blanch in disgust during previous centuries. The observance of Buddhism, which had been in part an import from the south (and not via China), was widespread, and Buddhist clergymen wielded considerable political influence.

It may be argued that by the late Ly and early Tran (1225–1400 A.D.) dynastic periods, some of these distinctive characteristics were under challenge from within. Tattooing was ruled unacceptable, first on the body of the king and then within the army. The Buddhist clergy was subjected to increased surveillance and repression. The manners of China's Sung dynasty were gradually adopted at court, insofar as the Vietnamese were able to secure reliable data and advice on such matters. Confucian ideology gained adherents steadily. There was an increase in learned discussions on the concept of righteousness (*nghia*) and the proper way to show concern for the public weal. Nevertheless, it is significant that such trends were rather abruptly, if temporarily, halted by the development of new threats from the north, this time the Mongol armies of Kublai Khan. In the subsequent struggle, it is possible to sense once again a high Vietnamese pride in martial skills and battlefield allegiances, both distinctly alien to the official Confucianism of the time.

The battle with the Mongols produced Vietnam's first real culture hero, if we take that to mean not only one who is revered widely but also one whose personality and historical actions are well enough known for him to be remembered by subsequent generations as much more than a mere repository of generalized symbolism and disembodied ideals.[9] Tran Hung

8. Le Thanh Khoi, *Le Viet-Nam,* p. 146.
9. Earlier individuals, such as the Trung sisters or Ly Thuong Kiet, also are obviously historical figures, uniquely meaningful to the Vietnamese; yet so little

Dao[10] was undoubtedly one of Vietnam's great strategists and—equally important—sensitive and shrewd enough to seek out as lieutenants several tacticians of considerable daring and combat ability. His written proclamation to his officers, serving as a preface to a longer work titled *Binh-thu yeu-luoc* (Résumé of Military Tactics), is a masterpiece of virile, martial patriotism. It opens with some standard classical precedents for loyalty to king and country, but then quickly sets these aside in favor of concrete, almost contemporary examples of prolonged struggle between Sung and Mongol. Tran Hung Dao does this, he says, because his officers have been "brought up in the military tradition," without literary backgrounds. For the same reason he praises the military skills of the Mongols, perhaps also to feed the pride of his men in taking on such renowned adversaries. But in case anyone is thinking of appeasement, he reminds them sharply of the crude pressures which have been exerted by the Mongols on Vietnam for almost thirty years:

> We have all grown up in difficult times. We have seen the enemy's ambassadors stroll about in our streets with conceit, using their owls' and crows' tongues to abuse our court, flexing their goats' and dogs' bodies to threaten our ministers. Simulating the orders of the Khubilai, they have demanded precious stones and embroidered silks to satisfy their boundless appetite. Using the title of the Prince of Chen-an[11] they have extracted silver and gold from our limited treasures. It is really not different from bringing meat to feed hungry tigers; how should we avoid catastrophe in later times?[12]

Tran Hung Dao then reminds his officers of previous shared dangers and pleasures, of all the personal favors he has done for them, of the clothes, food, horses, promotions, and allowances that have been theirs. Now they have gotten soft, however, sitting around shamelessly watching their master and their country humbled. He chastises them for enjoying cock fights,

---

really is known about them as people that they are overshadowed to a much larger degree than Tran Hung Dao by the events and environment of which they were a part.

10. His original name was Tran Quoc Tuan, but he is known historically by this name from his title of *Hung Dao Vuong* (Tran Trong Kim, *Viet-Nam Su Luoc,* p. 134.)

11. Toghan, Khubilai's son, who was commander-in-chief of the expedition against Vietnam and Champa.

12. This and the following translated extract from the proclamation are from Truong Buu Lam, *Patterns of Vietnamese Response to Foreign Intervention: 1858–1900,* pp. 49–54. A Vietnamese translation is available in Tran Trong Kim, *Viet-Nam Su Luoc,* pp. 136–139.

for gambling, for whiling away time in their gardens, for indulging themselves with their wives and children, for absorbing themselves in hunting,
and for liking good wine and love songs. Then he declares:

> Should the Mongol army invade our country, the cock spur shall not
> pierce the enemy's armor, nor can the gambler's artifice substitute for
> military tactics. Then, though you possess many gardens and ricefields,
> you will not be rich enough to pay the ransom for your life in thousands
> of [pieces of] gold. Furthermore, of what usefulness will you be in mil-
> itary matters when you are pushed around by your wife and dragged
> hither and thither by your children? Your wealth, even when abundant,
> will not buy the enemy's head. Your hunting dogs, though they are very
> strong, cannot chase the enemy. It is neither possible for good wine to
> intoxicate the enemy to death nor for melodious songs to mellow him.

> At that time, you and I will be made prisoners. How painful it will be!
> Not only will my fief go, but your salaries too will be in the hands of
> others. Not only will my family be dispersed, but yours also will be
> enslaved by others. Not only will my ancestors' altars be discarded, but
> your parents' tombs too will be excavated. Not only will I be humiliated
> in this life, not only will my name be tarnished for a hundred years to
> come and my reputation remain soiled forever, but you too will not be
> spared the shame of defeated generals. Will you then be able to enjoy
> your life according to your desires?

Those who capitulated would see shame descend on them for thousands of
generations. But if, on the contrary, officers trained their men well and
there was victory, then their fame would be "registered in the books of
history."

After some maddening setbacks and much bloodshed, the Vietnamese
were victorious. The royal court returned to the capital, and primary consideration immediately shifted to developing diplomatic contacts. The goal
was an acceptable tributary relationship with the Yuan dynasty in China,
with adequate precedents, we may presume, in the extensive Ly-Sung dia-
logue of the late eleventh century.[13] Through much of the fourteenth cen-

---

13. For an authoritative discussion of the Mongol invasions, see Yamamoto Tat-
suro, *Annanshi Kenkyu* (A Study of the History of Annam), pp. 45–261. NCLS
has numerous articles also, listed here by author and NCLS issue number: Dao
Duy Anh 42: 16–20. Nguyen Van Di and Van Lang 43: 27–36 and 39: 37–45.
Tran Ha 46: 60–66. Tran Huy Lieu 50: 1–6. Nguyen Ngoc Thuy 63: 36. Van Tan
66: 2–7 and 67: 39–45. For some indication of Tran Hung Dao as a culture hero,
see the cult figures reproduced in Maurice Durand, *Imagerie Populaire Vietnamienne*, Publication de l'Ecole Française d'Extreme-Orient, vol. 47 (Paris, 1960), pp.
230, 232, 234.

tury, Vietnam turned its attention southward, where Champa presented both a distinct threat and an opportunity for territorial aggrandizement.

When the Yuan were overthrown in China and the Ming dynasty was established in 1368, the Vietnamese court was careful to seek new tributary contact that very year. By 1384, however, the Hung-wu Emperor was showing excessive interest in "An-Nam," and Vietnam's Tran monarchs were in no position to resist external pressures. In any event, they succumbed to the plots of their own prime minister, Ho Quy Ly, who set himself up as emperor in 1400.[14] This in turn provided the pretext for Ming intervention, allegedly in support of the Tran. Their Chinese armies defeated the Ho forces without difficulty, after which they quickly cast aside their Tran collaborators and proceeded to a policy of heavy-handed assimilation akin to that of General Ma Yuan, almost 1400 years earlier.

The Ming ordered altars erected in each district and forced the Vietnamese to sacrifice to Chinese deities. They forbade Vietnamese men to cut their hair, as had been the practice, and made the women wear Chinese-style costume.[15] Chewing of betel nut and blackening of teeth were declared illegal. Local historical records and literature were collected and shipped to China. Studies for the mandarinate were restricted and strictly supervised by the Chinese. A pao-chia (neighborhood security) net was organized, beginning with compulsory carrying of identification papers. The land tax was altered to conform to Ming procedures, a salt tax imposed, and large numbers of peasants rounded up for the opening of mines and cutting of timber in the mountains. But what may have cut the Vietnamese most deeply, both then and later, was the fact that the Ming could rely on a significant contingent of native mandarin collaborators to maintain the foreign presence while the foreigner himself simply set policy, supervised implementation, and retained a military force-in-being in the event of disorder. As a contemporary source remarked bitterly:

> The mad Ming, stealthily awaiting every opportunity, took advantage of the situation to pour poison onto our population, at the same time that a group of scoundrels who longed for treason prepared to sell out our country.[16]

14. Le Thanh Khoi, Le Viet-Nam, pp. 193–204.
15. Interestingly enough, even after the Ming were driven out many Vietnamese men kept their hair long and some of the women retained the Chinese-style trousers. But this was probably more a product of sumptuary edicts from Vietnam's subsequent Le monarchs than an example of popular regard for Chinese customs.
16. Nguyen Trai, Binh Ngo Dai Cao (Proclamation on the Pacification of the Wu), 1428. Translation from Truong Buu Lam, Patterns, p. 56.

Disorder was not long in coming, from the direction of Thanh Hoa and organized by a local leader named Le Loi. Beginning with his own kin and neighbors and then gaining the support of village elders and district brigands, he set up a mountain base and, in 1418, declared himself Binh-dinh-vuong (Pacification King). After he nurtured his position on the periphery for eight years, Le Loi's armies were at last able to penetrate the Red River delta and score several significant victories. The next year he began promulgating edicts and organizing administrative echelons. Collaborator mandarin families were allowed to buy their way back from annihilation. Strict troop discipline and the imposition of martial law served to stabilize conditions in the countryside. In the end it may have been these essentially political efforts that were decisive, providing guidance to the delta population, and a new orientation amidst general disorder, thus permitting Le Loi to move smoothly from his role as military "pacifier" to that of founder of a new dynasty.

After another victory in early 1428 over Ming reinforcements which entered Vietnam from Kwangsi, Le Loi, like his predecessors vis-à-vis the Sung and the Yuan, proceeded to make extremely pious, deferential overtures to the emperor of the Middle Kingdom. Doubtless unwilling to send yet another expeditionary force, the Ming condescended to receive Le tributary delegations every third year. Le Loi's famous proclamation of 1428[17] in vigorous, aggressive prose, reestablished for domestic purposes Vietnam's separateness from China. Yet the same proclamation also incorporated most Chinese classical and imperial symbols as implicit legitimization by Le Loi of his own founding of a new dynasty—another example of the curious, important dichotomy permeating the Sino-Vietnamese relationship.[18]

During the Le dynasty (1428–1788), and partly as a result of such heavy emphasis on Chinese forms, governmental bureaucracy was elaborated beyond Vietnam's needs and, eventually, beyond the ability of the peasantry to support it. Long before that, however, the systematic adaptation of Chinese systems and concepts aided the Vietnamese greatly in accelerating their thrust to the south. It gave them the ideological continuity,

17. It was actually composed by Nguyen Trai, his prime scholar-advisor. For articles on Nguyen Trai, see NCLS as follows: Editors of NCLS 42: 1–7. Van Tan 44: 9–16; 53: 11–15; 54: 2–9. Hai Thu 65: 7–13. Thanh Ba 69: 34–38.
18. An English translation of this proclamation is available in Truong Buu Lam, *Patterns*, pp. 55–62. Chinese and *quoc-ngu* versions: Tran Trong Kim, *Viet-Nam Su Luoc*, pp. 224–232. For an excellent study of the early Le dynastic period, particularly neo-Confucian reform efforts, see John K. Whitmore, "The Development of Le Government in Fifteenth Century Vietnam."

the political apparatus, and, not least, the tax base to support their destruction of Champa (essentially complete by 1471) and to start their equally relentless push against the Khmer. This expansion produced the oddly shaped country that is the Vietnam of more recent times, with all its obvious difficulties for communications and central control. Soon powerful families emerged to attempt either outright usurpation (the Mac) or dual government (the Trinh). The latter, bearing resemblances to Japan's shogunal system of the same general period, prevailed as the dominant phenomenon until the late eighteenth century.[19] Nevertheless, the ideal of a unified Vietnam apparently remained alive and meaningful during this period of "seigneurial rule,"[20] with the monarchy simply becoming more a spiritual and ceremonial institution, less a temporal one.

The mideighteenth century saw major social and economic changes in Vietnam. One consequence was the emergence of the peasant-oriented Tay-Son movement. The Tay Son succeeded in destroying the balance of power among seigneurial families, and then overturned the Le dynasty entirely and provided the preconditions for new political unity. A strictly derivative aspect of this momentous domestic upheaval, the Tay Son defeat of Chinese invaders in 1788 and 1789, concerns us especially here, since this resistance provides the last historical precedent for the scholar-gentry groups almost a century later who also attempted to foil the foreigners.

As in 1406, the entreaties of representatives of a defunct Vietnamese dynasty—in this case the Le—provided sufficient pretext in 1788 for Chinese armed intervention. After all, argued those at the Ch'ing court who favored intervention, what did the tributary system mean if China did not meet her obligations to her vassals?[21] Somewhere along the way, however, the aging Ch'ien-lung, emperor and his expeditionary commander, Sun Shih-i, overestimated the remaining domestic strength of the Le and gravely underestimated the potential of the Tay Son to mobilize local elders, peasants, and tenants in resistance. Nguyen Hue, youngest and most dynamic of the three Tay Son brothers, took the opportunity to declare himself emperor under the name of Quang Trung. Unexpectedly striking both Ch'ing and Le units on the third night of Tet (Lunar New Year) observances, Nguyen Hue subsequently used his elephant brigade to plunge

19. Tran Trong Kim, *Viet-Nam Su Luoc*, pp. 250–285. Le Thanh Khoi, *Le Viet-Nam*, pp. 231–241.
20. The term is used in Milton Osborne, "The Vietnamese Perception of the Identity of the State," p. 10.
21. Hoa Bang, *Quang Trung*, pp. 156–157 (for a Vietnamese translation of Ch'ien-lung's edict on the subject; p. 203. Tran Trong Kim, *Viet-Nam Su Luoc*, pp. 374–375.

through enemy defenses and drive quickly into the capital. Sun Shih-i barely had time to flee across a pontoon bridge spanning the Red River. His panic-stricken troops behind him overloaded the structure, and it snapped, causing heavy losses. Tay Son units pursuing Sun Shih-i captured a file of Ch'ing staff documents; and insights gained there were quickly put to use by Nguyen Hue in setting a strategy for consolidating his victories through diplomacy. By the summer of 1789 Ch'ien-lung had declared his willingness to recognize Nguyen Hue, and the Le family remnants were quietly sequestered in Peking.

Nguyen Hue was another of Vietnam's great generals, perhaps second only to Tran Hung Dao in the pantheon of Vietnamese heroes. Nevertheless, unlike most dynastic founders, he neglected the long-term solidification of his family position. Although he had helped to lead a movement that in certain respects altered the nature of Vietnamese society, Nguyen Hue's role, like his military command, remained personal, not institutional; his reforms remained merely ideas, not accomplishments. And he had the particular misfortune to die in 1792, only three years after defeating the Ch'ing, at the age of forty when his son and successor was only ten years old. When the court split into factions and began fighting for spoils, the way was open for a few remnants of the defunct Nguyen seigneurial family to reconstitute a base in the Mekong delta and, with key French technical and military assistance, to move slowly northward to domination of Vietnam in 1802.[22]

Moving away from the chronological record, I shall attempt a tentative characterization of the Vietnamese relationship to the Chinese as it bears on the question of Vietnamese identity. I have emphasized the times in history when Vietnam and China experienced major strains in their relationship, not because this is the full story, but because it was at these points' that the senses of group separateness and of ethnic affiliation were put to the test and became subject to continuing creative definition. A more general account of Sino-Vietnamese contacts would certainly give attention to the many decades—even full centuries—when all was peaceful, and the benefits to the Vietnamese were quite considerable in such areas as commerce, tributary exchange, and educational, administrative, and technological acculturation.[23]

22. For the roles of the French, see Georges Taboulet, *Geste Française en Indochine,* pp. 240–263. For the Tay Son in general: Le Thanh Khoi, *Le Viet-Nam* pp. 304–313, and Jean Chesneaux, *Contribution a l'Histoire de la Nation Vietnamienne,* pp. 58–64. NCLS on Nguyen Hue and the Tay Son: HK 46: 21; Van Tan 58: 5–14; 59; 19–21; 60: 3–10; Nguyen Khac Dam 60: 35–38; Tran Van Giap 46: 4–20.
23. Whitmore, in "The Development," treats such a peaceful era in the fifteenth

The basic point here, however, is that the mass of Vietnamese probably had rather short memories regarding the foreign origins of much of their culture— not unlike Americans in more recent circumstances, I might add. If the average Vietnamese was at all aware of the debt he owed to China, he apparently was not particularly concerned about it. Certainly it seems not to have caused him to question his basic identity.

The best example of this phenomenon may be the Vietnamese language, which at various times has incorporated a wide range of Chinese terminology, modes of expression, and basic sentence patterns. While some of these linguistic accretions remained largely the property of the Vietnamese educated elite, it appears that much that was originally Chinese did end up well embedded in the spoken language of the peasantry. Such things as village and hamlet status arrangements and the rites, procedures, and obligations of even the lowliest peasant and tenant families, were phrased in essentially Chinese terms. Yet it is equally true that the Vietnamese language remained stubbornly particular and innerdirected. The use of the term "we" (ta), for example, was in curious fashion often limited to Vietnamese speaking among themselves, and was inappropriate to mixed conversations with foreigners or to foreigners using the Vietnamese language. When a Vietnamese spoke of "our" clothes, "our" food, "our" people, he used "ta" in the sense of belonging to Vietnam alone. Foreigners trying to speak of their *own* customs had to employ a circumlocution; "ta" was unacceptable, a contradiction.[24] The fact that much of what the Vietnamese labeled as "ours" was actually cultural baggage from the Chinese seems to have been either forgotten or ignored. It was fundamentally irrelevant.

It may be asked, nevertheless, why the Vietnamese became so hostile when the armies of their northern neighbor occasionally impinged on their existence. After all, if the Chinese soldier demanding a chicken or some greens from the peasant's back yard was culturally so akin to the peasant and to those Vietnamese soldiers who presumably requisitioned much the same things, why the special fuss? The answer, of course, was that the Chinese soldier was *not* perceived by the peasant as kin, for which there were many practical reasons. Again, most important was the spoken language: Vietnamese may have borrowed heavily from various Chinese dialects, but apparently never in such a way that oral communication could be effectively established. By contrast, people in each and every province of Vietnam could and did communicate with each other, with only the degree of

---

century, particularly the reforms of King Le Thanh Tong. Alexander Woodside, "Vietnam and the Chinese Institutional Model" is almost exclusively concerned also with the peaceful acculturation during the first half of the nineteenth century.
24. I am indebted to Mr. David Elliott for discussions that served to point up this interesting linguistic distinction.

accent and variation in vocabulary one might expect in a country of such geographical extension. In addition to language there were obvious differences in Chinese and Vietnamese costume, body fashion, and general physical bearing. There were popular Vietnamese cults that not only had no correspondence to Chinese cults, but that sometimes glorified resistance to the Chinese, as, for example, those dedicated to Tran Hung Dao and to the Trung sisters. If this was not enough, there was also the existence from the tenth century onward of completely autonomous dynastic traditions among the Vietnamese. Small temples dedicated to popular monarchs of the Ly, Tran, and Le were maintained in many villages, and it also was common to find their images on family and village altars, amidst the other deities.

What, then, of the elite, meaning particularly the scholar-gentry? Were they as confident as the mass of Vietnamese in distinguishing themselves from their Chinese counterparts? In many ways this is a more difficult question, even though far more materials for studying their situation historically are available.[25] The Vietnamese scholar-gentry were profoundly conscious of their cultural, intellectual, and moral debt to China and to Chinese models. More than that, most of them gloried in it, struggling to ensure that, from the level of personal demeanor up to that of statecraft, their attitudes and behavior corresponded to what they understood to be the case in the China of their choice—be it the Ch'ing, the Ming, the T'ang, the Han, or the distant epoch of the Sages.

Perhaps a tentative answer is implicit in this comment. The elite in Vietnam tended to detach Chinese thoughts and practices from their original contexts. Such idealization, among other things, allowed them to range across the full span of Chinese history, picking and choosing whatever met their fancy as Vietnamese, rather than simply aping the current dynasty in power to the north. And since the Chinese continually emphasized that their culture, their learning, were the common property of all civilized beings and not the Han people alone, educated Vietnamese had few reservations about developing specific, if not necessarily unique, interpretations of classical thought, providing of course they were larded well with appropriate citations and obeisances to the ancients.[26] Indeed, the Vietnamese sometimes felt qualified to bring their northern neighbors to task for back-

25. Woodside, in "Vietnam and the Chinese," uses such materials perceptively in dealing with elite attitudes toward China in the Ming Mang (1820–1841) era. See especially pp. 18–22, 56, 84, 123–155, 171–202.
26. King Gia Long in 1805 employed the hallowed term *trung quoc* (Middle Kingdom; Chinese, *chung kuo*) to refer to Vietnam, thus apparently altering the meaning to include any kingdom founded on the principles of the classics and surrounded by unlettered barbarians. *Ibid.*, p. 18.

sliding. One of King Minh Mang's (ruled 1820–1841) favorite intellectual themes, for example, was "decadent China and orthodox Vietnam"—especially true, he felt, with a barbarian dynasty, the Manchus, in control.[27]

This is not all the story. It also can be argued that the Vietnamese elite —sometimes unconsciously, often more openly—utilized Chinese learning as an effective weapon against the mass of their own people.. In structural terms this included adaptation of such things as China's intricate judicial hierarchy, their centralized tax system, the royal courier network, and the royal palace complex, with its massive gates, moats, bridges, pools, and audience halls which rendered king and court virtually inaccessible to the people. In the subtler and perhaps more significant areas of customs and ideology, the elite went to great pains to convince the rest of the people that the rigid hierarchical patterns of official Confucianism were the natural order of human existence. At times they would launch fervent orthodoxy campaigns, for example, upholding the proper "five social relationships."[28] They might demand further local expenditures on temples to Confucius or even call for the imposition of Chinese-style costume, hairdress, and personal mannerisms. Their heated denunciations of "heterodox" creeds and attitudes among the people doubtless were motivated in part by insecurity and the fear that somewhere in the villages things were going on, thoughts were being propounded, over which they exercised little control, either moral or coercive.[29]

Given such ambiguities, it is no surprise that at crucial points in Vietnam's history—above all, when the polity was fragmented and a royal dynasty disintegrating—some members of the elite chose to flee across the northern frontier and beg Chinese intervention on their behalf. This was the case to a minor extent in the Mongol invasions, and it also figured in the decisions of the Ming and later the Ch'ing to send armies into Vietnam. We may speculate that for such elite Vietnamese, knocking at the Chinese gate in this manner was simply an extension, albeit exaggerated, of their previous dependence on adapted Chinese systems and ideas in retaining their power and privilege.

Certainly this would help to explain why nonelite Vietnamese seldom participated to any great extent in such physical defections, much less, initiated them. Equally important, in the context of continuing internal

27. *Ibid.*, pp. 183–187.
28. In Vietnamese, *ngu-luan*: father-son, ruler-ruled, husband-wife, elder brother-younger brother, friend-friend.
29. The best example of this is the general hostility of the Vietnamese elite toward Buddhism, at least from the late Tran dynastic period onward. But their treatment of Catholicism, as well as some Taoist sects, also stemmed in part from elite insecurity.

disputes, a call for intervention by one elite Vietnamese group left the other with the one realistic alternative of banding together and mobilizing large numbers of Vietnamese peasants to resist invasion. There was no other major foreign power in the area of whom they could request aid sufficient to offset the Chinese. Lacking this possibility, the magnitude of the threat also demanded that they partially abandon their traditional coercive practices vis-à-vis the peasantry and instead depend on shared interests and attitudes to energize the alliance. In this respect, one of the most important messages of Vietnamese history seems to be that enough of the elite had enough in common with the mass of the peasantry to pool their talents at appropriate times in ultimately victorious struggle against a foreign invader. More than anything this is what it meant to be Vietnamese when the French arrived on the scene.

Chapter Two

> Trước làm nghĩa, sau cùng làm nghĩa,
> Trước sau cho trọn nghĩa vua tôi.
> Sống có danh, thác cũng có danh,
> Sống thác được thơm danh nhà nước.
>
> *In the beginning righteousness,*
> *in the end righteousness,*
> *From beginning to end behave as to carry*
> *out your moral obligations to your king.*
> *Life has fame, death too has fame,*
> *Live and die such that your fame will spread*
> *like fragrance to your families and your country.*
>
> (*Hịch Kêu Gọi Nghĩa Binh Đánh Tây*, 1864)

A Patrimony Lost

King Gia Long, leader of Nguyen seigneurial family remnants and founder of the Nguyen dynasty in 1802, in many ways rested his throne on shifting sands. He had relied on foreign assistance to achieve power, a debt which proved to be of little consequence to him, but which came back to haunt his great-grandson, King Tu Duc. Gia Long had faced and crushed a social movement, not merely a dynastic rival, yet he did little or nothing to assuage the bitterness or relieve the underlying grievances of the vanquished. Perhaps most important, Gia Long initiated in Vietam what can best be termed a policy of massive reassertion of Confucian values and institutions, continued with a vengeance by his successor, Minh Mang (1820–1841). While this retrieval in the short run may well have served the interests of the dynasty and the scholar-gentry, it happened at the moment when Vietnam was about to be challenged critically by a non-Confucian enemy for the first time in at least four hundred years. Ironically, it was also a time when Confucian orthodoxy was being subjected to increasing criticism in other parts of East Asia, particularly in Japan, but also in the Middle Kingdom itself. Hence, Vietnam's elite in some respects would come to view the Western threat from a more doctrinaire, ideologically conservative posture than even their supposed paragons to the north.

The fact that Gia Long would pursue this course after twenty-five years of intimate contact with non-Confucian traditions (Khmer, Thai, and French Catholic) bears testimony in one sense to the resiliency of Confucianism in Vietnam. As a corollary it probably involved Gia Long's perception that, after decades of civil strife and social upheaval in Vietnam, he and his family were sorely in need of some legitimizing accouterments. This reduced itself in practical terms to convincing the scholar-gentry that he was having nothing of heterodox Tay Son influences, indeed, that he was wiping the recent past from the history books in favor of a systematic return to the dynastic models.[1] Since the largest number of remaining scholar-gentry families were in the north, the location of continuing loyalist sentiments for the long-enduring Le dynasty, Gia Long's policy had a definite logic.

Court antipathy toward the defunct Tay Son and lingering uncertainty about the strength of the popular support for their government may also explain why Gia Long and Minh Mang devoted so much attention to the building of star-shaped Vauban-style fortresses in hitherto modest regional and provincial town and village centers. Admittedly Gia Long had learned of the strictly military effectiveness of these fortresses from his French military advisors. But certainly he—and, even more, his son Minh Mang—must have been aware that they also tended to mark off the provincial administration from the surrounding countryside and fostered a modest form of urbanization that ran counter to orthodox principles of rural agricultural supremacy. At any rate, the fortress mentality of the early Nguyen kings had long-term implications: militarily it bred generations of Vietnamese generals who believed in static defense at a time when European gunnery technology was advancing by quantum degrees in terms of increased power, range, and mobility; socially it imposed heavy new military induction and corvée requirements on the peasantry; and politically it helped to discourage any thoughts among the military or the court of following Tran, Le, and Tay Son dynastic precedents by moving out amidst the peasants in the event of serious threats from foreign invaders.

By and large, Gia Long allowed his military lieutenants, the men who remained closest to him until his death, to ignore the tactical and technological revolution under way in Europe during his reign. This is mildly surprising, since both Gia Long and his associates personally had mastered many aspects of eighteenth-century European warfare—in this respect differing markedly from their contemporaries cloistered in Peking. Did they never sense that a dynasty assisted to power by European expertise might

1. For example, the Nguyen court forbade its historians from compiling an account of the short-lived Tay Son dynasty (1788–1802), normally a routine function associated with maintaining for posterity chronological continuity from the distant past.

later be threatened by a more sophisticated expertise from the same source? Had they failed to grasp the progressive nature of events and allowed Confucian concepts of historical permanence and intellectual superiority to blind them during their prolonged exposure to change? Or was theirs simply a case of military obtuseness, of generals supremely confident that the next war was going to be like the one they had just gone through?

Whatever the explanation, several decades later in the 1830s the situation was even more acute. Not only did technological and organizational advances not reach the troops in the field, but in some cases eighteenth-century improvements previously introduced seem to have vanished without memory.[2] True, Minh Mang studied contemporary Chinese materials on Western warships and was well aware that their guns were superior. He also had a passion for steamships and had even purchased a small one in order to copy the engine. But when the first attempt failed, the court bought two more ships rather than continuing the investigations.[3]

In the last analysis, such efforts represented mere tinkering by an extremely intelligent but circumscribed monarch. The problem of ineffective response was increasingly systemic, not one of individual royal personalities, as events during the reigns of Thieu Tri (1841–1847) and Tu Duc (1847–1883) would amply demonstrate. Nguyen dynasts, in tandem with the scholar-gentry, were constructing a Confucian bureaucracy and physical superstructure that, once again, was going far beyond the needs of the society and, more important, beyond the abilities and desires of the peasantry to support it. Like the Le bureaucracy of the late fifteenth century, the Nguyen bureaucracy geared itself both for increased control and exploitation of Vietnam's village population and for expansion to the south, in this case Cambodia and possibly Siam.

Unlike the Le, however, there is reason to believe that the Nguyen dynasty never really succeeded in establishing its legitimate writ at the village level. Serious local uprisings broke out during Minh Mang's reign in both the north and far south, and the unrest grew progressively worse in the 1840s and 1850s.[4] In the crucial decade before 1858 and permanent French intervention, the court was burdened with almost continuous do-

2. Alexander Woodside, "Vietnam and the Chinese Institutional Model," p. 452, says that an 1838 Vietnamese handbook on coastal defense made no mention of what Gia Long had learned from his French advisors. Precedents cited went back no earlier than 1820.

3. *Ibid.*, pp. 453–454.

4. Nguyen The Anh, "Quelques aspects économiques et sociaux du problème du riz au Vietnam dans la première moitié du XIXe siecle." The author discusses unfavorable developments in the pricing and distribution of rice, as well as population increases, epidemics, and famines. See also Kieu Oanh Mau, *Ban Trieu Ban Nghich Liet Truyen,* for a Nguyen court history of antidynastic activities.

mestic distress, including tax protests, smallpox, tribal uprisings, drought, locusts, and—worst of all—repeated breaches in the Red River dike system often because of administrative neglect.[5] Not unrelated to these unsettled conditions was a continuing challenge from within the royal family regarding the legitimacy of Tu Duc's original accession to the throne. This led Tu Duc to execute his own elder brother in 1854 and then twelve years later to kill his brother's family (except for two daughters), as the direct consequence of an attempted palace coup and local uprising.[6] Among the people there circulated such despairing phrases as, "Since Tu Duc came to the throne there has been neither peace nor abundance" and "posterity will remember the miseries of the reign of Tu Duc."[7] Meanwhile, both civil and military mandarins found new ways to favor themselves and their relatives, sentiment for the long-departed Le persisted in the north, Catholic missionaries found significant lower-class response to their revolutionary doctrines, and Siam continued quietly to probe Nguyen control of the Mekong valley.

As I have implied, King Minh Mang and his immediate advisors were aware of a threat from the Western maritime powers, particularly with the opening of the Opium War in 1839. In restricted fashion they attempted to prepare for both change and military encounter:

> The dynasty . . . wanted and expected intercourse with the West but simultaneously feared Western military aggression and religious proselytization. More receptive than the Ch'ing court to the benefits of Western commerce, it was perhaps far less certain that it could withstand the undesired pressures that accompanied them. Hence it moved inconclusively between the two extremes of a closed country policy (chinh sach be mon toa cang, more literally, "close the gates and lock the harbor") on the one hand, and what were later to be called "bread and milk studies" (hoc banh tay sua bo)—i.e. the study of the culture of the Westerners, renowned for their milk drinking, on the other.[8]

Minh Mang and his immediate successors were caught in an almost hopeless dilemma by the very nature of the system they had built to protect themselves. The political inconclusiveness mentioned above was a product of this dilemma. Basically, they could not move to a long-term "Western studies" program without immediately undermining the patiently con-

5. Pham Van Son, "Xet-lai nguyen-nhan cua cac vu loan duoi doi Tu-Duc." Bui Quang Tung, "La Succession de Thieu-Tri."
6. Bui Quang Tung, "La Succession," pp. 29–51, 78–106.
7. *Ibid.*, pp. 53, 55, citing Nguyen Dong Chi and Ninh Viet Giao, *Hat giam Nghe Tinh* (Hanoi, 1962), pp. 23–25.
8. Woodside, "Vietnam and the Chinese," p. 423.

structed framework of Confucian orthodoxy that had endeared them to the scholar-gentry. On the other hand, at various times they did attempt a closed-country policy, but each time they found that Vietnam's coast was very long, its navy increasingly outmoded, and cooperation from seaside villages erratic at best.

What if the monarch and his court had dared to move out among the villagers to organize a protracted, decentralized resistance? After all, the capital of Hue was constrained geographically. It had little room around it for maneuvering; and, being only twelve kilometers from the sea, it was quite accessible by flat-bottomed naval craft, as the French in the end proved so decisively. Earlier dynasties had had no qualms about moving to more defensible locations in the face of enemy threats. While we have reason to believe that such proposals were made during Tu Duc's reign, there is no indication that they were given serious consideration. Beyond strategic myopia, there was the court's extreme Confucian conservatism which caused them to tarry over all the geomantic problems and disruptions of ancestral ceremony consequent to any such shift of location. And beyond conservatism existed the unspoken fear that leaving Hue for some place like Thanh Hoa would put all the court increasingly at the mercy of the local scholar-gentry and the peasantry, raising uncomfortable questions of dynastic challenge and survival. Most members of the royal family and high court figures considered dynastic preservation to be synonymous with preservation of the country, making their reluctance to move quite understandable, given the pervasive social and political unrest.

All in all there was a historical irony embedded in the half-century or so before 1858, when the French began attacking in earnest. As a new dynasty the Nguyen sat just firmly enough on the throne to retain stubborn confidence in their traditional Confucian system and values. However, as a dynasty of meager legitimacy with a predilection for alienating an ever-larger segment of the population, they almost inevitably maneuvered themselves into a deadly cross fire—hostile subjects challenging them on the one hand and French imperialists enroaching on the other. It was not until June 1885 that they moved out of this cross fire, far too late to prevent complete colonial take-over, but still soon enough to provide some enduring symbols for subsequent generations.

Some segments of the French population had retained a lively interest in "Annam" ever since the Bishop of Adran's abortive maneuvers at Versailles in 1787, on behalf of his client Nguyen Anh. Sixty years later, in 1847, Hue court actions against foreign Catholic proselytizers sparked the French navy's destruction of Vietnamese ships and its dismantling of fortifications in Da Nang harbor. Nevertheless, it was the 1848 revolution and the advent of the Second Empire that produced a coalition of interests—patriotic, religious, strategic, and commercial—sufficiently formidable to propel France into Vietnam on a long-term basis.[9] Admiral Regault de Genouilly, who had commanded a ship in the 1847 raid, was provided an invasion force by Napoleon III and in September 1858 met no difficulties as he again seized the Da Nang fortifications which were within close range of his shipboard guns. However, support from distant Catholic villages and Le sympathizers which had been rashly promised by some French priests was not forthcoming, and disease began to take a heavy toll of the French and Filipino troops.[10]

Somehow, despite King Tu Duc's repeated interference in Vietnamese military operations, General Nguyen Tri Phuong managed to maintain order among the tens of thousands of troops sent from the provinces and even succeeded in slowly advancing a ring of trenches toward the enemy positions. By January 1859 Admiral Genouilly perceived that even a general retreat of Vietnamese forces in the Da Nang area would probably lead to another stalemate farther north. Hence, leaving a small holding force at Da Nang, he sailed down to the Mekong delta and seized the Gia Dinh defense complex (present-day Saigon) with striking ease on February 17, 1859.[11] A huge booty of Vietnamese cannon, firearms, swords, sulfur, saltpeter, shot, and copper cash was seized; and a fire was set in the rice granaries which was said to have smoldered for three years.[12] Nevertheless, once again the French were unable to advance very far from their naval guns. By April Admiral Genouilly was back in Da Nang with part of his forces, trying, despite cholera, typhus, heat prostration, and increasing Vietnamese opposition to force Hue to accept an unequal treaty along the lines of settlements being "negotiated" with China at about the same time.[13]

Momentous events of this nature reduced the Nguyen court to total confusion. In part it was, I admit, a matter of royal personality. King Tu Duc

9. John T. Cady, *The Roots of French Imperialism in Eastern Asia* (Ithaca, 1954), pp. 87–102. C. S. Phillips, *The Church in France, 1848–1907* (New York, 1936).
10. Spain was also involved in this venture, largely for religious reasons. Nguyen Khac Ngu, "Nhung cuoc hanh-quan cua Phap o Trung va Nam-Ky," pp. 99–110. Georges Taboulet, *La geste française en Indochine* pp. 371–374, 378–418, 433–440.
11. Nguyen Khac Ngu, "Nhung cuoc," pp. 110–119. Vuong Hong Sen, *Sai-Gon Nam Xua*, pp. 55–60. The "old" Gia Dinh fortress, built along Vauban lines in 1790, had been destroyed in 1835 on Minh Mang's orders as retribution for one of the uprisings in that area. It was replaced two years later by a much smaller fortress which was much more vulnerable to enfilade bombardment from a nearby stream —another example of the declining military consciousness during this period.
12. Vuong Hong Sen, *Sai-Gon*, p. 56.
13. Taboulet, *La geste,* pp. 440–452. See Joseph Buttinger, *The Smaller Dragon,* pp. 404–405, n. 56, for a list of French eyewitness accounts and interpretations of this period in Vietnam.

had the historic misfortune of being a really accomplished Confucian scholar and poet with a more than average passion for traditional values and methods of reasoning.[14] Furthermore, he had no top-level advisor who might dare confront the dominant obscurantist party at court, supported openly as it was by his ultraconservative, domineering mother. If this was not enough, Tu Duc was beset by physical ailments, and this often led him to posit a moral relationship between such personal deficiencies and the misfortunes of his patrimony.[15] More than once he had flashes of grim insight into the fate awaiting his country, at which time he would ponder the situation furiously, gather his advisors, fire off a royal edict to the bureaucracy—and await results that never came. A prisoner of Confucian idealism, so in love with words, Tu Duc was capable of savoring the logic of the reform memorials submitted to him, of marking them with obvious approval, and of then putting them down on the table for some, often unspecified, subordinate to take action on.[16] Significantly enough, the lack of action on reform memorials stood in stark contrast to officialdom's generally rapid implementation of Tu Duc's brushed comments on memorials ordering the quelling of popular uprisings, of which there were many in those years.[17]

Personality was important, but not crucial. A Gia Long or a Minh Mang might have suffered much the same experience. Always in the background was the contradiction between the essentially private interests of the royal family and the interests of the mass of Vietnamese. From afar Tu Duc tried persistently to order units and commanders around, not because he prided himself as an amateur strategist but because by theory and custom that was the way a dynasty kept the throne. Alternatively, if military commands had been decentralized and weapons distributed to the villagers, they might have been able slowly to harass French forces into withdrawal. But wherefore the dynasty in such an arrangement? If the monarch had abandoned Hue, which was obviously vulnerable to attack from the sea, and moved the capital to a safer location, he would have been following valid historical precedents, and he might have been able to formulate a prolonged struggle. But he would also have been far more subject to the needs and demands of the people at large. Finally, and perhaps most telling, if observers and emissaries had been dispatched overseas to gain better

14. LT, pp. 430–431.
15. Truong Buu Lam, *Patterns of Vietnamese Response to Foreign Intervention: 1858–1900*, pp. 19–20. In all likelihood he also bore guilt for the execution of his brother and his brother's family. Bui Quang Tung, "La Succession," pp. 88–95.
16. CXL-2, pp. 109–111.
17. Le Van Hao, "May net ve hoi song Viet-Nam giua the ky thu XIX." Phan Khoang, *Viet-Nam Phap Thuoc Su,* pp. 83–115.

comprehension of this alien, amorphous threat, they might well have provided critical intelligence on French political vulnerabilities and advised
the court on necessary reforms. But they might also have brought back
heretical doctrines which could undermine the very foundations of the
Vietnamese political system. When educated Vietnamese did go overseas
on their own and return with sweeping suggestions, they were treated with
ill-disguised suspicion or hostility.[18]

In short, the Nguyen dynasty was strong enough to contain domestic
dissent and retain power for itself, but worried enough about its under-
pinnings—its sources of support—to be unwilling to take really appropriate defensive measures. In this crisis the mandarins, who had been consistently cultivated and favored by the Nguyen monarchs, might have been
expected to provide initiative. Yet they, too, faltered.

With the ending of hostilities in China in 1860, France was able to move
major sea and land reinforcements into Gia Dinh. The key battle came in
late February 1861 at Ky-Hoa (now Chi-Hoa), a defense complex developed with great care by General Nguyen Tri Phuong just outside the
city. The Vietnamese forces, rather too large (22,000) to be controlled
properly, seem to have held their ground stubbornly; but their artillery was
hopelessly inferior to the French mobile guns, and the end was a bloody
retreat northward to Bien Hoa.[19]

After the battle of Ky-Hoa it is possible to delineate a progressive degeneration of formal, organized Vietnamese defense and a rise in the Mekong delta of popular, regional resistance—mostly under the leadership of
local scholar-gentry who refused to follow Hue's cautious attempts at seeking a compromise peace with the barbarians.[20] Admirals Charner and Bonard, successive French expeditionary commanders, pursued a strategy
similar to that used against Peking. That is, they forced concessions from
the court, tied them down solemnly in treaties, and then proceeded if necessary to "safeguard" the Nguyen from popular wrath, favoring them as

18. The best example is Nguyen Truong To, a Catholic with classical training, who
traveled to Europe in 1858 or 1859 and returned by 1862, submitting memorials
until 1871. Phan Khoang, BK 71 pp. 19–25 and BK 72, pp. 15–22. Chuong Thau
and Dang Huy Van, NCLS 25: 57–71. Hoang Nam, NCLS 29: 34–40. Ho Huu
Phuoc and Pham Thi Minh Le, NCLS 31: 60–62. Editors, NCLS 33: 8–16. A
complete list of Nguyen Truong To's memorials is in LT, pp. 425–426. For translation into English and brief commentary on several of his memorials, see Truong
Buu Lam, "Patterns," pp. 89–103.
19. Nguyen Khac Ngu, "Nhung cuoc" pp. 131–142. Taboulet, *La geste,* pp. 457–463.
20. An interesting comparison could be made with the situation in and around
Canton in the decade or two after the Opium War. See Frederic E. Wakeman, Jr.,
Strangers at the Gate. It remains to be seen, however, whether enough primary
documentation has survived in Vietnam to enable such an intensive social history.

locally constituted authority for maintaining the new status quo.[21] This was the first in a long series of French attempts both to cow and to "prop up" the Nguyen, which ended after 1885 in subservience on all essential matters by those Vietnamese who chose to remain in Hue. It was an unholy alliance that would preserve many aspects of Vietnamese court obscurantism into the twentieth century.[22]

Meanwhile, a fair proportion of the population in the Mekong delta had taken matters into its own hands. Among other things, this meant ambushing French rivercraft, denying food to French bases, assassinating collaborators, and sending plainspoken messages to court representatives to take the field against the enemy. It is a measure of the court's dilemma, caught between superior French military power and increasingly bold and resolute patriots, that they tried simultaneously to make peace and to encourage resistance, in the end doing neither effectively. Irregular resistance was pervasive enough in late 1862 and early 1863 to force French units to withdraw from outlying points and concentrate defensively while awaiting reinforcements. At this time Napoleon III apparently considered making some concessions to Hue; but the growing colonial party in Paris and—particularly—the Navy men and priests on the spot could argue with some basis in fact that Hue had lost control in the south. The mandarins were "vanishing"; "bandits" roamed at will! Hence in large part the "need" for French direct rule in the Mekong delta grew out of local resistance efforts, almost irrespective of the diplomatic desires of Napoleon's government in Paris.

At least one southern resistance leader is worth discussing in some detail, since he proved to be the most important man of his type in the south before the 1920s and 1930s. Truong Dinh (also known as Truong Cong Dinh) was born in 1820 in central Vietnam,[23] the son of a military mandarin. As a young man he accompanied his father south when the latter was made military commander of Gia Dinh province. When his father died there unexpectedly, the normal thing for the youthful Truong would have been to return to his home area. However, he had married into a wealthy southern family[24] and apparently had decided to make his fortune there

---

21. Leopold Pallu, *Histoire de L'expédition de Cochinchine en 1861*, pp. 212 ff. Taboulet, *La geste,* pp. 477–487.

22. Jean Chesneaux, *Contribution à l'histoire de la Nation Vietnamienne,* p. 106. Professor Chesneaux goes even further to conclude that intervention "retarded" Vietnamese adjustment to the modern world, rather than advancing it as had been the presumed French intention.

23. Binh Son *huyen* (district), Quang Ngai *phu* (prefect), Quang Nam *Xu* (region); at that time Quang Ngai was part of Quang Nam.

24. In the area of Tan-An, Dinh Tuong province.

on the frontier.[25] Perhaps the turning point in Truong Dinh's life was King Tu Duc's order in 1854 granting General Nguyen Tri Phuong permission to organize southern levies under the local *don-dien* (military colony) system. Utilizing the money of his wife's family, Truong Dinh helped organize a don-dien in Gia Dinh province and received in return a rank of deputy regimental commander from the mandarin authorities. Soon he had a reputation beyond Gia Dinh as an efficient, skilled military organizer, having perhaps a thousand tenants and peasants armed with spears and swords, trained and on call as necessary.[26] He is also alleged to have treated his tenants better than most, trying at least to insure that they had enough to eat and something to wear.[27]

When Admiral Rigault De Genouilly moved south in February 1859 to attack the Gia Dinh fortress, Truong Dinh brought his local levies into the fray. As mentioned previously, however, Gia Dinh fell quickly, with both royal troops and local levies regrouping in the countryside. Other local armed groups began to arrive, including those led by Tran Thien Chanh[28] and Nguyen Huu Huan.[29] In the February 1861 battle of Ky-Hoa these irregulars were all under the command of Nguyen Tri Phuong, the king's chosen general. Nevertheless, when the bulk of the royal Vietnamese troops retreated north to cover Bien Hoa, Truong Dinh moved his forces southwest to Tan-Hoa, not far from his wife's family home.[30] Almost a year later, he was joined by several court representatives; but friction apparently developed rather quickly over whether to attempt regular aggres-

25. Nguyen Thong, "Ky Xuyen Van Sao," in Bao Dinh Giang and Ca Van Thinh, *Tho Van Yeu Nuoc Nam Bo,* pp. 162–167. See also SD 3 (1966), an issue devoted to materials on Truong Dinh. CMCD-1, pp. 48–56 has a discussion of Truong Dinh, largely taken from eyewitness French accounts. For one such account, see Paulin Vial, *Les premières années de la Cochinchine, colonie française.*
26. Nguyen Dinh Chieu, "Van te Truong Dinh," in Bao Dinh Giang and Ca Van Thinh, *Tho Van,* pp. 56–61. Pallu, *Histoire,* pp. 295–296, 300–301. For a brief discussion of the don-dien system, see Dang Phuong Nghi, *Les Institutions Publiques du Viêt-Nam au XVIIIᵉ Siècle* (Paris, 1969), pp. 85–86.
27. Bao Dinh Giang and Ca Van Thinh, *Tho Van,* p. 162.
28. A cashiered *tri-huyen* (district magistrate) in Binh Duong.
29. Better known as "Thu Khoa" Huan (a *cu nhan* graduate of the regional examinations in 1852). He had since held the position of *giao thu* (educational officer) in Kien Hung prefect, Dinh Tuong province. Bao Dinh Giang and Ca Van Thinh, *Tho Van,* pp. 214–219. For a knowledgeable discussion of the education and examination system during the Nguyen dynasty, see Woodside, "Vietnam and the Chinese," pp. 265–357.
30. This was also a good place to sustain contacts with new resistance groups led by Nguyen Trung Truc, Tran Xuan Hoa, and others in the Go-Cong and My-Tho regions; yet it was within striking distance of the strategic Gia Dinh area. See Map 5.

sive sorties from Tan-Hoa (Truong Dinh's strategy) or simply to utilize this place as a base in which to husband forces, awaiting events.[31] This difference naturally assumed more serious proportions after the Hue court's plenipotentiary, Phan Thanh Gian, put his brush to the highly concessionary and heavily criticized Treaty of June 5, 1862.[32] On the one hand the court now ordered Truong Dinh to disband his forces and accept a high position in An Giang province. On the other hand, however, Truong Dinh's lieutenants and followers pressed him to remain, for fear that they faced extermination at the hands of "the Westerners."[33]

Claiming that his followers would not let him leave, Truong Dinh took a dangerous chance and refused his appointment to An Giang, instead adopting the exalted title of Binh-Tay Sat-Ta Dai Tuong (Western Pacifying, Antiheresy General). He continued his harassment of French patrols and the terrorizing of those Vietnamese families who chose to cluster around French posts.[34] Among the populace there circulated the now famous eight-character epithet: "Phan-Lam mai-quoc; Trieu-dinh khi dan" (Phan and Lam sell out the country; the court doesn't care for the people).[35] French commanders nevertheless were convinced that Truong Dinh remained in secret contact with Hue and had Tu Duc's sanction for his resistance, as proved, they said, by a bronze seal of office in his possession.[36] The best one can conclude at this point is that a distinct ambiguity had developed in local feelings of loyalty towards the monarchy:

They [the partisans] drew a careful distinction between the person of an individual king and the moral principle of loyalty to the monarchy. Anxious to resolve any moral contradiction inherent in their behavior, they again and again pledged loyalty to the king. "King" did not always mean the actual incumbent of the throne but rather a ruler who would be worthy of that title. The monarchy was therefore an idealized institution not tarnished by any accidental deviation from the ideal. Even

31. Bao Dinh Giang and Ca Van Thinh, *Tho Van*, p. 163.
32. See Taboulet, *La geste*, pp. 472–476, for text and commentary on this treaty. Phan Khoang, *Viet-Nam*, pp. 138–170, may have the most detailed description of the court confusion leading to the treaty.
33. Bao Dinh Giang and Ca Van Thinh, *Tho Van*, pp. 163–164.
34. Most of these families were probably of Catholic background. Vuong Hong Sen, *Sai-Gon*, p. 145, says there were 27,000 native Catholics in Saigon in 1859.
35. "Phan" naturally is Phan Thanh Gian, while "Lam" is Lam Duy Hiep, who also signed the 1862 treaty.
36. Most French historians also have seen the relationship this way. Some Vietnamese writers now dispute it. For example, Ho Huu Tuong, SD 3 (1966): 115–129, argues that Truong's basic allegiance was to the people and not the Nguyen monarchy, more or less in the tradition of the Tay Son against the Le and their Ch'ing backers.

against royal orders, the partisans would fight to avenge the insults the monarchy had borne.[37]

In the strategic sense, Truong Dinh seems to have understood clearly both the possibilities and the limitations of armed resistance, in contrast to many of his scholar-gentry compatriots, who were lacking in military experience. Truong hoped to bleed the French slowly, speaking, for example, of the role of malaria, his "special ally," which would help compensate for his people's obvious inferiority in general weaponry.[38] More fundamentally, he doubtless hoped to maintain a living alternative to the political and military structure which the French admirals at that moment were extending to the district towns by force of arms.[39] Unfortunately even these objectives required a high degree of multiregional coordination and constant spiritual encouragement to the people, functions that in those days could only be provided by the throne or its duly constituted representatives. There was also that weakness which would plague resistance and anticolonial movements well into the twentieth century: the almost total lack of political and economic intelligence about the enemy, especially in his homeland. Truong Dinh as a result could never know the best thrust, the best strategy for a chosen moment. Even more, he could never sustain his followers with the knowledge of just how politically precarious France's Indochina adventure was at repeated junctures.

By late February 1863, Admiral Bonard had sufficient reinforcements to attack and seize Truong Dinh's main strongholds in the Tan Hoa/Go Cong area, with the Vietnamese suffering heavy casualties and retreating in disorder. Truong then reorganized his units, purchased a few more firearms via the local Chinese, and resumed his harassing tactics. He also seems to have devoted more attention to rousing support over a broader geographical area, for example, by distributing leaflets (which appeared in Saigon and My Tho) calling upon *nghia quan* ("righteous armies" or partisans) of other provinces to join him in common struggle.[40] But now

37. Truong Buu Lam, "Patterns," p. 10. It should be remembered that the throne, at least during the Nguyen dynasty, combined political and spiritual functions, so that the distinction quite rightly pointed out by Professor Truong Buu Lam was in all probability bred of immediate adverse conditions and not the product of a long tradition.
38. Truong Ba Phat, SD 3: 31. See also, Tran Van Giap, "Tai-lieu moi ve Truong Cong Dinh (1821–1864)."
39. For a perceptive discussion of these initial French efforts, see Milton E. Osborne, "Rule and Response," pp. 102–143. A more admiring account is Pham Cao Duong, "Mot vai khia canh dang chu y trong duong loi cai tri cua nguoi Phap o Nam-ky tu 1861 den 1967." Also Taboulet, *La geste*, pp. 521–552.
40. One source indicates that Truong Dinh even tried to link up with a Khmer lead-

the French were able to keep him and the other remaining resistance leaders constantly on the move, aided by a growing number of local informants
and the more sophisticated pacification policies of Bonard's successor,
Admiral La Grandiere. Additionally, what in 1862 had been only a threat
of famine became a reality in 1863, with the result that resistance leaders
often were unable to find provisions for their followers. And the court in
Hue showed no indication whatsoever of providing more practical support,
which was undoubtedly disheartening to the remaining nghia quan and a
boon to the French, who therefore could practically ignore court forces in
Binh Thuan and concentrate on destroying the local resistance.

The end came for Truong Dinh in August 1864, when he was betrayed
by one of his former associates. His son, Truong Quyen, then twenty years
old, attempted with moderate success to carry on the struggle. A new base
of operations was set up in the Tay Ninh region, more advantageous in
terms of maneuvering space, but still dependent in part on food and supplies from old supporters in Tan Hoa, well to the south. Some efforts were
made to recruit participants among the Stieng and Mnong minorities and
contact was maintained with nearby Khmer insurrectionaries. The major
actions occurred in Tay Ninh during June and July 1866, with the word
quickly spreading throughout the delta and other nghia quan again taking
the field. Nguyen Trung Truc[41] was active in the Rach Gia area; Nguyen
Huu Huan revived efforts in Tan An and My Tho.[42] Such continued resistance contributed heavily to the French decision to seize the remaining
three delta provinces to the southwest (Vinh Long, An Giang, and Ha
Tien) in 1867.

Following the Treaty of 1862, King Tu Duc had been trying through
diplomatic means to persuade the French that they should give back the
first three provinces they had seized. Because of a combination of Vietnamese diplomatic inexperience and French duplicity, Hue did not understand until 1865 that the chances of this were negligible. At that point,
fearing further French aggression, Tu Duc sent as viceroy to the three remaining provinces the man the French were most likely to trust, the one
who had been subject to Vietnamese condemnation for his signature of
the 1862 treaty, Phan Thanh Gian. Knowingly or not, Phan entered an
impossible position, facing on one side continuing delta resistance, breakdown of mandarin rule, and complete demoralization of regular Viet-

---

er, called in Vietnamese Thien Ho Duong, who had a separate effort under way in
the Dong Thap Muoi area. To Minh Trung and Nguyen Xuan Huy, *Binh Tay Dai
Nguyen Soai Truong Dinh,* pp. 48–51.
41. He was also known as Chai Lich, Quan Chon, and Quan Lich. VNDN, pp. 231–
233. Son Nam and Ngoc Linh, *Nguyen Trung Truc.*
42. To Minh Trung and Nguyen Xuan Huy, *Binh Tay,* pp. 60–73.

namese troop units, and on the other side French demands that either he put an end to "bandit" harassment or they, the French, would seize the area by storm. On June 20, 1867, Admiral La Grandiere did precisely that, luring Phan Thanh Gian from the Vinh Long fortress for discussions and detaining him while French forces carried out a quick, bloodless assault. This procedure was replayed the following day at the An Giang (Chau Doc) fort and two days later at Ha Tien—final testimony to how demoralized and impotent the official Vietnamese structure had become in the south.[43]

The impact on the court, the scholar-gentry, and the general populace of Vietnam was of momentous significance. In the narrowest sense, King Tu Duc's peace policy was reduced to shambles. Except for lashing out briefly at those mandarins directly implicated, Tu Duc mostly seems to have tried to ignore the new annexations, perhaps hoping to wish them away with even further increments of righteous will power. The greatest significance of 1867, however, was psychological. Among the partisans in the south it may at first have meant the loss of base camps and of free movement on rivers and streams.[44] But it really also meant a loss of hope, a cracking of morale that led quickly to the movement's disintegration and the relapse of most delta people into postures of nonviolent resignation. Most of the scholar-gentry who had not been killed now chose to flee the delta permanently. For the village notables and canton chiefs it was a time to begin, under French colonial domination, to think of salvaging something for themselves and their families. Until 1867 only a handful of educated people had collaborated with the French. They had been on the psychological defensive, cowed and apologetic before their peers.[45] After 1867 more coherent, positive arguments were being advanced, for example, in favor of accepting a subordinate role under foreign masters in the "higher interests" of economic and technical development.

---

43. Truong Ba Can, "Phan Thanh Gian voi viec mat ba tinh mien Tay." Taboulet, *La geste,* pp. 512–517.

44. Truong Quyen, for example, was at first confined to the Trang-bang area and then was driven well north of Tay Ninh into the mountains. Upon hearing of a rising by Phan Thanh Gian's two sons far to the south, Truong tried to move his small force down and across the Mekong. He was killed in an engagement en route in August 1867. To Minh Trung and Nguyen Xuan Huy, *Binh Tay,* pp. 72–73. For information on the forced exile of Phan Thanh Gian's sons to France, see AOM, A–50 (2) carton 22.

45. The best known collaborator before 1867 was Ton Tho Tuong, whose apologetic attitude in a famous literary exchange with Phan Van Tri illustrates this point. Nguyen Ba The, *Ton Tho Tuong 1825–1877.* Nhat Tam, *Phan Van Tri.* The important parts of this exchange are translated in Truong Buu Lam, "Patterns," pp. 81–86.

Proponents of this view included such men as Truong Vinh Ky, Huynh Tinh Cua, Tran Ba Loc, and Do Huu Phuong. The first two were noted for their efforts to mediate between French and Vietnamese cultures, although they were certainly a part of the political life of the colony of Cochinchina as well.[46] The latter two, on the other hand, served as adminstrative instruments of the French in extending control down to the villages of the colony.[47] People like this represented a slowly growing but significant new elite in Cochinchina that found collaboration psychologically acceptable. Their attitudes and those of their sons, students, and disciples, continued to predominate in the south until at least the 1920s, making the situation there radically different from that which developed in north and central Vietnam.

While admitting the influence of the collaborators in Cochinchina, one should not be misled into inferring that they went unchallenged in their own time among their own people. They held the limelight, but in the shadows were others who denigrated collaboration and who attempted to sustain the ideals of Truong Dinh and his contemporaries. Their usual medium was poetry, increasingly in *chu nom* (demotic characters) rather then *chu nho* (Chinese characters)—a reflection of their desire to circulate their ideas widely among the people. Their moods ranged from covert but biting character assassination[48] to hagiographies of those who had only recently lost their lives in battle with the French.[49]

46. Truong Vinh Ky (1837–1898) was the best known collaborator. He received missionary training overseas, served as interpreter in Phan Thanh Gian's abortive delegation to Paris in 1863, and helped train early French administrators in Saigon. Osborne, "Rule and Response," pp. 87–88, 204–209; 278–280. Milton E. Osborne, "Truong Vinh Ky and Phan Thanh Gian." Khong Xuan Thu, *Truong Vinh Ky (1837–1898)*. NCLS articles on Truong by the following authors: H. H. 56: 13–23; Nguyen Anh 53: 17–27, 38; Mai Hanh 58: 15–28; Nguyen Khac Dam 59: 33–42, 46; To Minh Trung 59: 43–46; Man Quoc 60: 39–45; Hoang Van Lan and Dang Huy Van 61: 16–30; Ho Song 61: 31–34; Chu Quang Tru *et al.* 62: 27–29. Tran Huy Lieu 64: 29–31. Complete data on these articles is in the Bibliography.

Huynh Tinh Cua was significant for his participation in the early *quoc ngu* (romanized script) newspaper *Gia Dinh Bao*, for his translation efforts and for his compilation of Franco-Vietnamese dictionaries. Osborne, "Rule and Response," pp. 203–204.

47. Osborne, "Rule and Response," pp. 89, 177–178, 184–186, 280–287.

48. For example, at a ceremony honoring the entry into colonial officialdom of Tran Ba Tho, the son of Tran Ba Loc, someone presented him with an inscription bearing characters that could be interpreted both as a laudatory reference to his grandfather and as a cursing implication of Tran Ba Tho as a "dog," a lackey of the colonials. Bao Dinh Giang and Ca Van Thinh, *Tho Van*, p. 13.

49. The best example is Nguyen Thong, *Ky Xuyen Van Sao*, portions of which are in Bao Dinh Giang and Ca Van Thinh, *Tho Van*, pp. 159–170.

The best known literary opponent of collaboration in the south was Nguyen Dinh Chieu, born in Gia Dinh province in 1822 of gentry parentage.[50] In 1846, while in Hue awaiting the opening of the metropolitan examinations (he had passed the regional exams three years earlier), Nguyen Dinh Chieu had received news of his mother's death. Leaving immediately for his faraway home, he contracted an eye disease en route and was soon totally blind. Nevertheless, he opened a small school in Gia Dinh and soon was much in demand both as a teacher and as a medical practitioner.[51]

When the French attacked Gia Dinh in 1859, Nguyen Dinh Chieu fled to Ben Tre. While his blindness kept him from participating directly in the subsequent guerrilla-style efforts of Truong Dinh and others, it undoubtedly led him to channel his frustration and anger at the foreigner into vivid, highly proficient *nom* poetry, which circulated widely in the south, largely by word of mouth. Later, after overt resistance had died down and the colonial regime had banned much of his poetry, Nguyen Dinh Chieu remained with a small circle of students in Ben Tre, demonstrating by his attitude and mode of living that he would have nothing to do with the new system.[52] His poetical commemoration of Truong Dinh and other resistance figures, his condemnations of Catholicism and his upholding of traditional Vietnamese values, even his bittersweet allegories on Chinese history, continued to circulate in the Mekong delta well into the twentieth century, ultimately providing a thread of continuity for resistance groups of much different background and intellectual persuasion.[53]

Several contemporaries of Nguyen Dinh Chieu also deserve mention for their anti-French literary efforts. Phan Van Tri[54] differed from most of his compatriots in his long-standing, barely concealed hostility to Vietnam's Nguyen dynasty and its entire mandarinate.[55] He is best known for his

---

50. Nguyen Dinh Chieu's father was a native of Thua Thien, near Hue; but as an official his father traveled south to serve General Le Van Duyet and there took a second wife, who bore him four sons. Thai Bach, *Nguyen Dinh Chieu (1822–1888)*, pp. 9–10.

51. *Ibid.*, p. 11.

52. When a French official offered him back the land confiscated from him in his home village, Nguyen Dinh Chieu is said to have replied sardonically, "When our common land, our country has been lost, how is it possible still to have individual land?" Bao Dinh Giang and Ca Van Thinh, *Tho Van*, p. 50.

53. *Ibid.*, pp. 51–82.

54. Born in 1830 in Gia Dinh province, he passed his regional exams at twenty, but apparently never attempted the higher exams or accepted official appointment. Nhat Tam, *Phan Van Tri*, pp. 5–6.

55. He advised a friend who held the position of *doc hoc* (provincial education commissioner) as they were walking down a dusty road together, "Don't stand

sardonic capping of the verses of Ton Tho Tuong, an early collaborator, but his other short poems on such seemingly innocent subjects as dogs, cats, crabs, buffalo, ants, lice, and mosquitoes also represent devastating attacks on those who would chase after the foreigner, exploit the people, and "sell out their heritage."[56]

Nguyen Thong[57] abandoned his mandarin position in Vinh Long when the province fortress was seized by the French in 1867. Like many other officials, he left the south but continued to hold a variety of positions under King Tu Duc until 1880. Perhaps his most important contribution was in compiling hagiographies of southern resistance figures, which in some cases are the only firsthand accounts in writing to survive into the twentieth century. His poems of homesickness and yearning for his southern homeland also reveal the bitterness of the dilemma men in his position faced at that time.[58]

Others whose poems circulated long after their demise included Bui Huu Nghia, Huynh Man Dat, and Nguyen Van Lac.[59] Perhaps the attitude of most of these remnant southern scholars was summed up best when Nguyen Van Lac in Saigon chanced upon the funeral cortege of Huynh Cong Tan, the man who had betrayed Truong Dinh in 1864 and who later had risen to prefect under the colonial regime.

THE FLOATING DOG'S CORPSE

In life you snatched meek rabbits and listened to them squeak in pain,
In death your rotting carcass drifts down the river,
The colors on your hide jumbled yet still clear,
The smell infamous and penetrating to the core.

Only a gang of shrimps lingers as cortege,
Bustling to greet the circling crows and falcons.
Along comes the wind and the splash of a wave,
See how your bones and flesh scatter![60]

For Vietnam as a whole, however, the overriding tone in 1867 was set neither by the Southern collaborators nor by the remnant southern literati.

---

around wasting time and energy; walk along, and as you go urinate the outlines of a dragon [the imperial symbol]." Bao Dinh Giang and Ca Van Thinh, *Tho Van,* p. 84.

56. *Ibid.,* pp. 87–88, 94–96, 100, 103–105.

57. Born in 1827 in Gia Dinh province of poor, nonscholar parentage, Nguyen Thong was assisted in his studies by relatives and passed the regional exams at age twenty-three. He failed his metropolitan exams apparently because of an ink smudge on the paper, but by 1862 he was *doc hoc* of Vinh Long province. *Ibid.,* pp. 126–127.

58. *Ibid.,* pp. 138–170.

59. *Ibid.,* pp. 171–213.

60. *Ibid.,* p. 209.

Even in death, Phan Thanh Gian held center stage. Writing a final memorial to his king and returning with it the twenty-three royal awards given him over the years and his full mandarin regalia, he accepted total blame for the disastrous loss of the remaining three Mekong provinces and committed suicide. Even among those scholar-gentry who had openly opposed his peace policies, Phan seemed the personification of Confucian righteousness and personal morality. Hence his death, in this manner and in such an emotionally charged atmosphere, was in some respects the death of an ethos throughout Vietnam.[61] The Nguyen dynasty, embodiment of official response to foreign incursions, would not again command local allegiance on its own initiative until king and courtiers at last broke pattern in 1885 in one final, terribly delayed attempt to reestablish contact with the people.

With considerable logic some modern Vietnamese historians have argued that there was still time after 1867 for major reformation, given the limitations of the French economy, the tensions in her polity, and above all the temporal opportunities provided for Vietnam by France's defeat by Germany in 1870.[62] The loss of all six southern provinces was as much of a shock to Vietnam's government as the 1863 destruction by Western warships of the Shimonoseki forts in Japan was to the Tokugawa shogunate or the burning of the Summer Palace in 1860 was for the Ch'ing dynasty in China. Yet it failed to provoke anything similar to the series of events in Japan that led to the Meiji Restoration. Like China, Vietnam faltered. Differences in response of this magnitude are too complex to be analyzed at this point and should be the object of serious future research. Nevertheless, it should be stated in passing that there was no lack of high-level Vietnamese proposals for reform in Vietnam, from the development of port facilities to the introduction of a phonetic writing system (citing Japan's *kana*), from formation of semipublic corporations to ill-disguised attacks on Confucian historicism in general.[63] By and

61. Nam Xuan Tho, *Phan Thanh Gian (1796–1867)*. Nguyen Phut Tan, *A Modern History of Vietnam*, pp. 227–240, has almost verbatim (but uncited) English translations of portions of the Nam Xuan Tho book. For an English translation of one of Phan's final writings, see Truong Buu Lam, "Patterns," pp. 87–88. Taboulet, *La geste*, pp. 517–520. LT, pp. 317–318. VNDN, pp. 282–287. For a series of articles assessing Phan, see NCLS: Dang Huy Van and Chuong Thau 48: 12–23; Dang Viet Thanh 49: 27–31; Nguyen Anh 50: 29–35; Nguyen Khac Dam 51: 29–34, 48; Chu Quang Tru 51: 35–39, 48; Nhuan Chi 52: 38–46; Tran Huy Lieu 55: 18–20. Titles of NCLS articles are in the bibliography.
62. See especially CXL-2, pp. 11–35.
63. Phan Khoang, *Viet-Nam*, pp. 117–130. The proposals of Nguyen Truong To again deserve special mention: Truong Buu Lam, "Patterns," pp. 89–103; HT pp. 173–185.

large, reform proposals even at this late date were dismissed by the court with elaborate Confucian rationales, perhaps an indication that the dominant conservatives sensed the revolutionary implications and were unwilling to take the chances involved.

The next hammer blows from the French came between 1872 and 1874 at the opposite end of Vietnam, with the audacious adventures of the freelance agents Jean Dupuis and Francis Garnier, discreetly supported by Admiral Jules-Marie Dupre in Saigon.[64] Dupuis, a consummate bluffer, totally contemptuous of the Vietnamese authorities, wanted to supply salt and weapons to a Yunnanese general by way of the Red River. Backed up by hired ruffians from Hong Kong and receiving intelligence from French missionaries and local Chinese merchants, he completely outmaneuvered Hue's representatives and, with timely assistance from Captain Garnier and his soldiers, seized the massive citadel of Hanoi. Garnier's gunboats then began to roam the rivers and tributaries of north Vietnam, creating panic and collecting booty at each provincial fortress. This marauding ended only with the surprise killing of Garnier by some well organized Chinese units just outside Hanoi.[65] The whole affair caused serious arguments to break out in France regarding colonial policy, a controversy of which Hue remained generally ignorant.

Admiral Dupre, embarrassed politically, ordered a French diplomat to travel north with a Hue official in order to restore previous administrative arrangements. But the situation could never again be the same: the Nguyen were now discredited in the north as well as the south, and local bands were organizing to take terrible vengeance on those who had openly collaborated with the foreigners, particularly the Vietnamese Catholics. King Tu Duc, by acquiescence expressed in the Treaty of March 15, 1874, moved substantially closer to the French and away from the sentiments of his own people.[66]

After 1874 the conglomeration of forces in north Vietnam became incredibly complex, reflecting a general breakdown of the established order, and an increasing antidynastic sentiment, in contrast to the situation in south Vietnam only a decade earlier. Along with the gradual emergence of district and provincial nghia quan, led mostly by scholar-gentry, there were sizable Taiping and Heaven and Earth Society remnants from China, some in the erratic pay of Hue, others subsidized by the French.

64. Jean Dupuis, Le Tonkin de 1872 a 1886 histoire et politique (Paris, 1910), pp. 367-375. M. Dutreb, L'Amiral Dupre et la conquete du Tonkin (Paris, 1924).
65. Truong Buu Lam, "Patterns," pp. 107-108, has a translation of a Vietnamese mock funeral for Garnier.
66. CXL-2, pp. 36-84. Phan Khoang, Viet-Nam, pp. 199-247. French text of the 1874 treaty in Taboulet, La geste, pp. 743-747.

There were also Ch'ing border forces, French consulate troops, armed Vietnamese Catholic units, Le dynasty pretenders, rebellious mountain tribes, and, finally, some royal units around the strategic position of Son Tay, still taking orders from the court.

King Tu Duc, not unaware of ambitious self-strengthening efforts by officials in China, and in any event unwilling to face the French again militarily, now directed more and more attention to securing help from Peking.[67] As I have mentioned, monarchs of earlier Vietnamese dynasties had done this when in imminent danger of losing their patrimony. While Tu Duc was a man who knew historical precedent, if anything, this time it was not simply a domestic upheaval that threatened the throne. It was a combination of internal disintegration and multipronged attacks from a second major foreign power, for which the history books held few if any models or remedies.

As it was, the French were not about to stand by idly while Hue and Peking collaborated to box them out of north Vietnam.[68] In April 1882 Captain Henri Riviere moved toward the same Hanoi citadel that had been taken by Garnier eight years earlier. Hoang Dieu, the general commanding Hanoi, had previously urged Tu Duc to approve a strategy of prolonged struggle in the mountains, rather than one of holing up again in the fortresses. He and a few other leaders had come to appreciate the French navy's capacity for dominating Vietnam's coast and river system. Together these men were the forerunners of a psychological reorientation of the Vietnamese inward toward the mountains which would characterize most overt resistance efforts for the next eighty years. Hoang Dieu, however, had seen his request denied, and, after seven hours of French naval bombardment, a shot at last found the powder magazine of the citadel. French soldiers quickly scaled the walls in the ensuing chaos. Rather than escaping out the back with the bulk of his troops, Hoang wrote a farewell message to his king and hanged himself on a nearby tree.[69]

It is a measure of the court's increasing provincialism that its most resolute action after the fall of Hanoi involved strengthening the fortifications of Thuan An just outside its own capital city of Hue. The general charged with the defense of the north, Hoang Ta Viem, was ordered to

67. Tu Duc between 1874 and 1882 also made perfunctory attempts at meaningful relations with Italy, England, Siam, and Spain. However, a combination of court disinterest and French maneuvers to limit Hue's foreign contacts torpedoed each effort. Phan Khoang, *Viet-Nam*, pp. 252–261.
68. Taboulet, *La geste*, pp. 674–730. For a detailed study of Chinese policy formulations on the issue, see Lloyd Eastman, *Throne and Mandarins*, pp. 33–205.
69. Taboulet, *La geste*, pp. 765–777. Truong Buu Lam, "Patterns," pp. 102–112 (Hoang's message, translated). CXL-2, pp. 140–146. Tran Huy Lieu, NCLS 39: 1–4.

move remaining units out of sight of the French. Hoang at that point disobeyed his king, but he and other vociferous members of the "war party," mostly in Hue, were basically putting all their hopes for deliverance on a Chinese entry and not on the resistance of their own people. If and when those hopes died, most of the high-ranking officials would cease struggling.

At this point in the north the only well organized units facing the French were commanded by a former Chinese Triad leader, Liu Yung-fu (in Vietnamese, Luu Vinh Phuc), the man responsible for Garnier's demise. He sought refuge across the border in Vietnam in 1865 with several hundred followers after the defeat of the Taipings. His ranks swelled over the years until he in fact controlled the administration of the upper reaches of the Red River. His units, often called the Black Flags (*Co Den*), contained a hodgepodge of Vietnamese, Chinese, and tribal contingents, fighting mostly for booty and survival but also from hatred for the Westerners and occasional feelings of class consciousness.[70] They showed particular toughness between 1882 and 1884, partly because Liu realized that French domination would put an end to their semi-autonomous existence.

Regular Ch'ing troops had crossed into Vietnam from Kwangsi in August 1881 and from Yunnan in July 1882. After protracted negotiations, the French countered in March 1883 with seizure of the prized Hongay coal mines and the Nam Dinh fortress, the latter move cutting off normal communications between central and north Vietnam. In May 1883 Captain Riviere felt confident enough to attempt a surprise thrust west from Hanoi on the road to Son Tay. But Black Flag units, acting on information from a Vietnamese interpreter traveling with the French, caught Riviere in ambush at Cau Giay. Riviere and thirty-two other Frenchmen were killed.[71]

The Cau Giay defeat—and, above all, the triumphant parading of Riviere's severed head from village to village—may have been France's most serious loss of face in Indochina before their encounters with the Japanese in 1940. Actually, the French National Assembly had voted the money for substantial reinforcements before hearing of Riviere's death. Nevertheless this incident added the element of popular outrage that would give the minority pressure groups—military, commercial, bureaucratic, and religious—all the leverage they had been seeking for years. The strategy of striking directly at the Vietnamese court was revived; in

70. For an interesting debate on the role in north Vietnam of Liu and the Black Flags, see NCLS: Van Tan, 34: 7–15; Chuong Thau and Minh Hong, 36: 7–14, 27; Dang Huy Van, 37: 15–19, 25; To Minh Trung, 38: 31–34; Dam Xuan Linh, 40: 48–52; 41: 8–22; Tran Huy Lieu, 42: 21–25, 38; Nguyen Van Nhan, 42: 26–29. Full titles in bibliography.
71. CXL–2, pp. 177–182. Taboulet, *La geste,* pp. 786–797.

August 1883 French units landed at Thuan An and stormed the forts there without particular difficulty.[72] They then found several mandarins willing to sign a harsh new protectorate agreement, while all the time keeping a military noose around Hue.[73]

Meanwhile, King Tu Duc had expired in July. The court then became the scene of a tragi-comical power struggle, complete with petty palace coups, poisoned monarchs, and heavy-handed manipulations by resident French diplomats. By early 1884 Ton That Thuyet, a tough military mandarin and sworn enemy of the French, emerged on top and secret instructions went out to local officials to begin manufacturing weapons and planning for the requisition of local boats and supplies. However, Ton That Thuyet dallied for another year and a half before doing what might have been obvious decades before—namely, withdrawal of the king from Hue into the mountains and proclamation of a countrywide movement of resistance. But it was too late. By that time, the French had found a significant party of mandarin collaborators at court, had smashed the remaining royal forces at Son Tay in the north, and had forced the Chinese to cease combat and drop their claims of suzerainty in Vietnam. In Chinese engagements with French units it is significant that local, irregular bands of Vietnamese had assisted the Chinese, or sometimes had risen independently to ambush the French, even though some Chinese units had displayed a tendency to ignore Vietnamese sovereignty and ethnic sensitivities.[74] But the French also had begun to organize native colonial units for use in the north, drawing them from the Catholics and from the peasants of Cochinchina. In the end, for many Vietnamese the deepest psychological agony would stem from a realization that the French from this point onward succeeded in consolidating their power largely by the use of some Vietnamese to destroy other Vietnamese.

72. An eyewitness description appears in Auguste Thomazi, *La conquête de l'Indochine*, pp. 165–166.
73. This is the so-called Harmond Convention, August 25, 1883. French text, Taboulet, *La geste*, pp. 807–809.
74. CXL–2, pp. 232, 235, 238. Such low-level relationships developed independently of high-level Chinese policy, wherein their negotiators were willing at several points to carve the area north of the Red River into permanent Chinese and French protectorates. Eastman, *Throne and Mandarins*, pp. 58–60, 110–112.

Chapter Three

The Can Vuong Movement

The Nguyen rulers and their representatives attempted to meet the barbarian threat in the only ways they knew—namely, by exclusion of Westerners, repression of Catholicism, antiquated military defense from within citadels and breastworks, and, when all this failed, negotiation from positions of abysmal weakness, perhaps hoping to stall or perhaps unconsciously envisioning a simple "shifting of tribute" from Peking to Paris. In the 1860s and 1870s, however, as the tragedy worked itself out, a few mandarins began to leave office in disgust, while literati who did not hold office began to find more and more reason simply to stay in their home villages and avoid involvement. As in the south, these people remained loyal to the monarchy as an idealized institution but became increasingly hostile toward those who were conducting state policy.

When events came marching to their doors, however, all were forced to take stands. They were expected as scholar-gentry to provide guidance and leadership. Yet, though no figures are available, we can surmise that a numerical majority chose passive resistance, an angry but nonviolent withholding of services and support. Traditionally, this was an acceptable form of scholar-gentry protest to a new dynasty, but it had never achieved much respectability as a tactic against foreign invaders. We may wonder whether this time the bulk of the villagers—the peasantry—found it to be an acceptable form of "leadership," as French patrols began to enter the very bamboo hedges around the villages and to disrupt their existence entirely.

In the long run, it would be the minority of the elite that would put the heaviest imprint on modern Vietnamese history, in this case those obdurate, militant, idealistic scholar-gentry who "knew the proper way of dying" for a person of their status in society. It is important to understand what this meant, since the message was lost on most French contemporaries and even to this day has been misinterpreted by most writers not familiar with the ethos of the period. In an objective sense, the violent actions of these men forced the French after 1885 to intrude more directly and comprehensively into the affairs of north and central Vietnam than was wise in a "protectorate," exposing the fist of foreign de facto control down to the district level and thereby undercutting the effectiveness of court and mandarin collaborators. Even more significant was the subjective impact. By their armed resistance, seemingly hopeless by any rational criteria, they sustained an alternative ethic to those being presented in Hue and Saigon, an ethic deeply rooted in Vietnam's previous experiences with foreign intervention. It was this ethic, nurtured on a day-to-day basis by the slights and savageries of French colonial rule, that was successfully passed on to subsequent generations, providing what I believe is one of the real keys to an understanding of anticolonial movements in Vietnam.

I have made passing reference already to the breakdown well before 1882 of official authority in the north. The origins of this lie far back in the long Trinh/Le domination of the north and in the recurrent popular risings of the nineteenth century which made that area the most difficult to control for each Nguyen ruler.[1] When Garnier stormed Hanoi in 1873, making Hue's impotence perfectly obvious, he met little or no locally organized resistance. This was partly because the events happened so fast, including Garnier's death and the consequent withdrawal of most French forces from the scene, but also because people in the north were already demoralized and directionless, having been subjected to raids and extortion from every imaginable source.[2]

With the return of French forces to the Red River delta in 1882 and the second fall of Hanoi, northerners were just about through with any hopes of concrete royal leadership. They organized more and more without reference to Hue. We know from the backgrounds of some later resistance leaders that villages already were being organized for self-protection, were establishing their own ties outside the district, and were obtaining firearms from China via a wide range of Chinese, Vietnamese, and tribal intermediaries in the hills. Royal court records of this period were filled with messages from district mandarins to the effect that the people were

1. For example, when conscripting soldiers the Nguyen are said to have taken one recruit for every three village tax registrants in the center and south, whereas in the north they limited it to one in every seven. This probably reflected both a desire to gain favor in northern villages and a lack of trust in their troop levies. J. B. Alberti, *L'Indochine d'autrefois et d'ajourd'hui* (Paris, 1934), pp. 55–60.

2. CXL–2, pp. 59, 65–68, does try to provide evidence of organized popular resistance in the 1873 and 1874, including the destruction of a French powder magazine and random shootings on French gunboats. But the paucity here, compared with later years, seems only to reinforce my point.

asking to fight, wanting to fight. And Riviere's messages praised certain Hue representatives for "helping quiet" the people in and around Hanoi.[3] After the August 1883 agreement was signed in Hue, a French diplomat accompanied a group of mandarins northward to order general observance of the new, harsh provisions. But they were avoided or refused outright in many places; some local mandarins turned in their seals of royal patent and headed out to recruit resistance forces, and a few committed suicide—several trying to kill a Frenchman personally before killing themselves.[4] Perceptive Frenchmen had reason to compare the situation with the grand fiasco of Napoleon III in Mexico, guerrilla resistance and all. There was major resistance, but it would come too late, with no central direction, and—perhaps most important—with the depressing knowledge that Vietnam after 1885 was without allies, since China would not influence events in anything like the manner of the United States in Mexico.

The poor showing of remaining royal units during the French attack on Son Tay December 14, 1883, put a final cap on northern alienation from Hue (see Map 2). One leaflet circulated at the time spoke of the royal officer who opened the Son Tay gates to the French as a "God-cursed traitor who acted like a worm in one's bones." "Imperial edicts reach us in bitterness," the leaflet grumbled, and court officials are "cowards excessively anxious to save their lives." The writer significantly found his heroic symbols in pre-Nguyen times:

> We possess our life, but we must know how to give it up.
> Shall we remain silent and thereby earn the reputation of cowards?
> As long as there exist people on this earth, we shall exist.
> As long as there is water, we must bail it out.
> We must read the Proclamation on the victory over the Wu.
> We shall follow the example of those who exterminated the Mongols.[5]

During 1884 there were numerous local attacks on French units, in direct violation of orders from Hue. Some former mandarins began to achieve fame as resistance leaders well beyond their home districts, for example, Nguyen Thien Thuat (Hai-Duong, Quang Yen provinces), Ta Hien (assisting Ch'ing forces in Bac-Ninh province), Nguyen Quang Bich

---

3. *Ibid.*, pp. 150–151.
4. *Ibid.*, pp. 220–221, 212–214.
5. HT, pp. 110–111. Translation from Truong Buu Lam, *Patterns of Vietnamese Response to Foreign Intervention: 1858–1900*, pp. 113–115. The "Proclamation on the victory over the Wu" refers to Le Loi's edict following defeat of the Ming (see Chapter 1).

(with Liu Yung-fu in Tuyen-Quang province), and Nguyen Cao (Bac-Giang province).[6] French operational timetables for pushing the Chinese out of Vietnam toward Kwangsi and Yunnan were repeatedly upset by the necessity of retaining or shifting large numbers of troops in rear areas as defense against "bandits."[7] A striking Ch'ing victory at Lang-Son in March 1885 raised local Vietnamese hopes. As the Chinese were making preparations for new attacks against Bac-Ninh and Hung-Hoa, however, word arrived of a Sino-French armistice, and Vietnamese spirits plummeted accordingly.

With the withdrawal of Ch'ing troops being essentially complete by the end of May 1885, the French could turn full attention to emasculating the lingering war party in Hue and to crushing all centers of local resistance. General Roussel de Courcy, the new French commander-in-chief and plenipotentiary, was almost a caricature of the arrogant colonialist, convinced that he could solve all France's remaining problems in Indochina by humiliating and destroying the regent Ton That Thuyet and his slightly more moderate associate, Nguyen Van Tuong. For all that, however, it may be a measure of Ton's self-serving character that it took de Courcy's personal thrusts, which virtually forced him into a corner, to set him at last to resolute action—namely, a surprise attack on the French garrison at Hue and, failing there, the escorting of King Ham Nghi into the mountains.[8]

There should be no hesitation in marking July 5, 1885, the date of Ham Nghi's flight from the capital, as a turning point in the history of Vietnam's response to foreign intervention. First, it brought central Vietnam into the resistance struggle with a vengeance for the first time, no small factor if we recall the active historical role of this area in struggles against Mongol, Ming, and Ch'ing. Particularly by providing leaders, imagery, and psychological sustenance, the center was destined to be in the forefront of Vietnamese resistance from 1885 right up to the present.[9]

Next, this date marked the termination of all remaining vestiges of Hue's sovereignty and the imposition of the final structural elements of French colonial rule on Vietnam—without a native monarch to sanction these acts. This does not mean that the French neglected to place an

6. CXL–2, pp. 226–227, 262–264.
7. *Ibid.,* pp. 272, 274–275.
8. CXL–3, pp. 60–68. Pham Van Son, *Viet-Nam Cach Mang Can Su, 1885–1914,* pp. 26–37. For a detailed if romanticized biography of Ham-Nghi, see Marcel Gaultier, *L'étrange aventure de Ham Nghi, empereur d'Annam.*
9. CMCD–1, pp. 69–82, has a rough list of resistance centers in north and central Vietnam during the Can Vuong period. Computation reveals that thirteen of thirty-two (42 per cent) "risings" occurred in the three central provinces of Thanh-Hoa, Nghe-An, and Ha-Tinh, alone.

alternative to Ham Nghi on the throne in Hue: King Dong Khanh, the brother of Ham Nghi, went through the necessary rituals in September 1885. Collaborator mandarins could and did argue for his legitimacy. Indeed, no less a figure than Tu Duc's widow wrote wistfully that under the protectorate there could again be high mandarins, and they would "recover and govern as in the past."[10]

On strictly legalistic grounds, particularly among those who put survival of the dynasty ahead of all else, such a position was not illogical. Nevertheless, the realities of serving a puppet king could hardly have been lost on these sophisticated students of political power.[11] Vietnamese mandarins choosing thenceforth to collaborate with the French had no reasonable monarchist ideal to defend: they were tools of foreign rulers, and they knew it. But mandarins choosing to fight—even those who perceived the hopelessness of their situation—retained the monarchist ideal and something more—the confidence that they were neither betraying their forefathers nor leaving a besmirched reputation for their descendants to live down. In many cases they had to make agonizing Confucian choices between staying behind to protect family tombs and elderly parents and sallying forth to defend king and country, a choice that in itself would advance the development of modern patriotic norms.

Finally, and perhaps most important, the significant numbers of scholar-gentry and peasants who had been pursuing local resistance efforts in previous years without traditional royal sanction must have been tremendously relieved and elated to find the king and some of his highest mandarins moving out among them, depending on them, and calling in the most emotive terms for a final struggle to throw out the foreign barbarians. For the young king, the mandarins, and some of their families, such an existence would be new and physically trying in the extreme—all the more reason for followers to empathize and develop an even more venomous hatred for the French. It has been easy for some observers, particularly those who cannot sense the Vietnamese people's agressive pride in themselves and their history, to dismiss this loyalist movement as simply the last stand of an outmoded, obscurantist ideal. Yet there is a continuity,

---

10. Alexander Woodside, "Vietnam and the Chinese Institutional Model," p. 166. Truong Buu Lam, "Patterns," pp. 24–25.
11. Any doubts about popular attitudes on the subject would have been removed during Dong Khanh's abortive tour of the provinces. While hoping to rally support, the royal entourage, with a heavy French escort, was instead each night subjected to some form of local attack. After getting laboriously to Dong Hoi (Quang Binh), it was decided to discontinue the tour and return to Hue by sea. Charles Gosselin, *L'Empire d'Annam* (Paris, 1904), pp. 266–267.

an unbroken thread tying this antiquated resistance to more successful efforts in the twentieth century.

For more than a year before the flight from Hue, Ton That Thuyet had been storing weapons, rice, gold, and copper cash in several mountain strongholds, particularly one named Tan-So which was situated above Cam-Lo in Quang Tri province. By the time the entourage reached this location, however, a good portion of the royal family had decided to turn around and take their chances with the French in Hue. That initiative seems to have come from Tu Duc's old mother, probably encouraged by Nguyen Van Tuong, who had by then split completely from Ton That Thuyet. Then, with the hotly pursuing French troops cutting off the road north and seizing Cam-Lo in the valley below, Ton realized that Tan-So was more of a trap than a stronghold. So he proceeded to escort the king and his greatly diminished retinue westward in a long, perilous swing up into north-central Vietnam. Much of the gold and cash was captured by Hue mandarins who were accompanying the French.

The major accomplishment up to that point lay in the promulgation and distribution to all corners of Vietnam of the Can Vuong (Loyalty to the King) Edict, which gave the resistance movement its name and which deserves translation in its entirety here:

> The Emperor proclaims:
> From time immemorial there have been only three strategies for opposing the enemy: attack, defense, negotiation. Opportunities for attack were lacking. It was difficult to gather required strength for defense. And in negotiations the enemy demanded everything. In this situation of infinite trouble we have unwillingly been forced to resort to expedients. Was this not the example set by King T'ai in leaving for the mountains of Ch'i and by Hsuan-tsung when fleeing to Shu?[12]
>
> Our country recently has faced many critical events. We[13] came to the throne very young, but have been greatly concerned with self-strengthening [tu-cuong] and sovereign government [tu-tri]. Nevertheless, with every passing day the Western envoys got more and more overbearing. Recently they brought in troops and naval reinforcements, trying to force on Us conditions We could never accept. We received them with normal ceremony, but they refused to accept a single thing. People in the capital became very afraid that trouble was approaching.

12. King T'ai refers to Chou T'ai-wang, who left his country under barbarian threat, and yet saw his whole people follow after him as a measure of their respect for his qualities as a ruler. T'ang Hsuan-tsung fled during An Lu-shan's uprising.
13. *Tram* (the royal *We*).

The high ministers sought ways to retain peace in the country and protect the court. It was decided, rather than bow heads in obedience, sitting around and losing chances, better to appreciate what the enemy was up to and move first. If this did not succeed,[14] then we could still follow the present course to make better plans, acting according to the situation. Surely all those who share care and worry for events in our country already understand, having also gnashed their teeth, made their hair stand on end, swearing to wipe out every last bandit. It there anyone not moved by such feelings? Are there not plenty of people who will use lance as pillow,[15] thump their oars against the side,[16] grab the enemy's spears,[17] or heave around water jugs?[18]

Court figures had best follow the righteous path, seeking to live and die for righteousness [nghia]. Were not Ku Yuan and Chao Tsui of Chin, Kuo Tzu-i and Li Kuang-pi of T'ang men who lived by it in antiquity?[19]

Our virtue being insufficient, amidst these events We did not have the strength to hold out and allowed the royal capital to fall, forcing the Empresses to flee for their lives.[20] The fault is Ours entirely, a matter of great shame. But traditional loyalties are strong. Hundreds of mandarins and commanders of all levels, perhaps not having the heart to abandon Me, unite as never before, those with intellect helping to plan, those with strength willing to fight, those with riches contributing for supplies—all of one mind and body in seeking a way out of danger, a solution to all difficulties. With luck, Heaven will also treat man with kindness, turning chaos into order, danger into peace, and helping thus to restore our land and our frontiers. Is not this opportunity fortunate for our country, meaning fortunate for the people, since all who

---

14. The surprise attack against the French garrison.
15. A literary allusion to Liu Chu of Chin, who rested on his lance and at dawn awoke to fight the enemy and save his country.
16. A reference to Su Ti of Chin, who waited until his forces were in midstream to beat his oars and cry out: "If I don't destroy those bandits, I shall never recross this river."
17. Allusion to a T'ang general who three times in a row grabbed his opponent's weapon. HT, p. 301, n. 3. Or to Vietnamese General Tran Quang Khai who in a poem mentioned his grasping of Mongol spears. Truong Buu Lam, "Patterns," p. 119, n. 5.
18. Reference to T'iao K'an of Chin who hardened himself for combat by lugging water jugs out of his home in the morning and back at night.
19. The former two helped Ch'ung Erh, son of Duke Hsien of Chin, to regain his throne in the seventh century B.C. The latter two helped defeat the Turfans in 763 A.D. so that the T'ang emperor could return the next year to his capital.
20. Tu Duc's mother and Tu Duc's wife.

worry and work together will certainly reach peace and happiness together?

On the other hand, those who fear death more than they love their king, who put concerns of household above concerns of country, mandarins who find excuses to be far away, soldiers who desert, citizens who do not fulfill public duties eagerly for a righteous cause, officers who take the easy way and leave brightness for darkness—all may continue to live in this world, but they will be like animals disguised in clothes and hats. Who can accept such behavior? With rewards generous, punishments will also be severe. The court retains normal usages, so that repentance should not be postponed. All should follow this Edict strictly.

By Imperial Order

Second day, sixth month, first year of Ham-Nghi[21]

(July 13, 1885)

It should be evident, even in translation, that this was a resistance edict in the classical tradition, appealing above all to the scholar-gentry, but not without emotional impact if read or interpreted to the people in general. We do know that copies reached the major provincial centers of the north and even penetrated the Mekong delta; and undoubtedly the message spread by word of mouth to practically every village and hamlet in Vietnam.[22] In subsequent days more detailed edicts were sent to specific provinces and commanders, calling either for direct assistance to King Ham Nghi in central Vietnam or granting belated royal "permission" for local anticolonial uprisings.[23] Royal sanction was thus squarely behind popular resistance—too late for any temporal success, but still of great importance in sustaining resistance through its most barren years. With the flight of the monarch, indignation could no longer turn against him and therefore focused increasingly on the French.

Without the prospect of reinforcements from France in the immediate future, General de Courcy was disturbed enough by the popular response

21. The original was in Chinese, a copy of which can be found in Shao Hsun-cheng *et al.*, eds., *Chung-Fa chan-cheng* (Shanghai, 1957), vol. 7, p. 474. A Chinese transliteration is in HT, pp. 298–299. Vietnamese translations in HT, pp. 300–301; CXL–3, pp. 69–71; Pham Van Son, *Viet-Nam*, pp. 45–46. Truong Buu Lam, "Patterns," pp. 117–120, provides another English translation.

22. For example, in the far south the aging and blind poet, Nguyen Dinh Chieu, is said to have been deeply moved by the news of the Can Vuong Edict. Nguyen Ba The, *Nguyen Dinh Chieu (1822–1888)* (Saigon, 1957), p. 98.

23. CXL–3, p. 71. Pham Van Son, *Viet-Nam*, pp. 46–47. The latter author seems to be drawing almost verbatim from the former, although credit is not given.

to their edict to propose to the Minister of Foreign Affairs a partial or even general troop withdrawal from the north in order to concentrate on quieting the center.[24] As it turned out, this was a pessimistic appraisal. Enough high-ranking members of the royal family proved willing to collaborate and enough high mandarins were found to set up a new Secret Council (*Co-mat Vien*) to begin to counter the influence of Ham Nghi and Ton That Thuyet in the provinces. With the enthronement of Dong Khanh as a pliant, unassuming replacement for Ham Nghi, the French at least could feel a bit more in control, even though Hue meant less each month as a physical symbol for the Vietnamese at large. Dong Khanh was the closest the French would come to having an eager collaborator king (of a total of five until 1945), but his premature death four years later nullified their ambitious plans for royal tutelage and manipulation.

While such activities in Hue were becoming a matter of mere derisive interest to more and more Vietnamese, there is considerable evidence that emotional, idealistic monarchism was about to enjoy a last burst of glory which centered on Ham Nghi until his capture in 1888, and then somehow continued without a monarch for six or seven years more. After the Can Vuong movement had been crushed totally, the activists of the next generation still felt the need for a royal pretender, until new symbols began to emerge after 1911.

To the degree that the Can Vuong was a disembodied monarchism, it was not within the mainstream of Vietnamese tradition, which empowered the physical king with both temporal and spiritual functions.[25] Nevertheless, certain ideals would be nurtured by the Can Vuong and passed on without break to subsequent generations, including a deep sense of reciprocal leader-follower responsibility, violent resistance in the face of hopeless odds, ruthless self-denial, and glorification of death in service to a principle.

Lest we ourselves engage in idealization of this traditionalist phenomenon, it was important to remember that the scholar-gentry of the nineteenth century were closely rooted to the soil, specifically the soil of their home villages and districts. Only a scant few were born and raised in the cities, which is in effect to say Hue or Hanoi. Even these cities should in no way be thought of as approaching in size, grandeur, or functionality such contemporary East Asian metropolises as Peking, Canton, Kyoto, or Edo. For example, Hue had a rather modest court, an oversize citadel, and a satellite town clustered along the river—all surrounded by an ocean of

24. CXL–3, p. 72, quotes de Courcy's dispatch, but with no date.
25. This may help to account not only for the ultimate demise of the Can Vuong but also for the twentieth century failure of the puppet kings in Hue to fulfill spiritual roles left to them by their foreign overlords.

ricefields and hamlets. It was a place to which scholar-gentry at various times in their lives came and went, but they spent most of their existence far from court and close to the annual harvest cycle, teaching, writing, or serving in district and provincial positions. In short, it was the ricefields that provided them, as well as the peasants, a reason for being and sealed the contract between man, the soil, and the sky.

Thus the scholar-gentry could and did communicate regularly and easily with the mass of the populace, an advantage that subsequent more urban elites shared less and less over the decades. However, this also rendered them highly provincial: in many cases their regional loyalties paralleled or bisected countrywide loyalties, depending on conditions at the time. As I have argued, Vietnamese scholar-gentry did share a firm sense of ethnic identity with the lower classes. The scholar-gentry themselves were held together by their common educational backgrounds, by sharing across Vietnam the same elitist values, by the contact maintained among exam graduates of the same year, and, of course, by traveling much more than the average person. In the end, however, scholar-gentry leaders of the resistance after 1885 would find it more difficult each year to maintain effective liaison with their counterparts in other provinces and regions, and much more so to develop any overall political or military strategy. The situation would get much worse before it got better, with no anticolonial organization until the 1930s even coming close to surmounting the problem.

The only way that the Can Vuong movement can be rendered coherent in detail is to describe it along essentially regional lines. Almost all the scholar-gentry leadership had, as we shall see, followings drawn substantially from their own villages, districts, or provinces. In the short term this gave backbone to local resistance. In the long term, however, it enabled French and native colonial units to partition the movement gradually, crushing one segment at a time. Lack of a central command, lack of a common strategy, and even the breakdown under stress of elitist bonds of loyalty proved more important in defeating the Can Vuong warriors than the more obvious geographical hindrances and technological deficiencies.

The first area worth describing centers on the province of Quang-Binh, with overlap into Nghe An and Ha Tinh to the north and including the nearby mountains of Laos (see Map 3). After Ham Nghi's flight, the French moved quickly to seize the forts at Dong-Hoi and Vinh, but patrols found nearby villages practically deserted and rice going unharvested.[26] Soon the heart of resistance became the lateral spur of hills dividing

26. Gosselin, *L'Empire*, p. 247.

Quang Binh and Ha Tinh, quite heavily populated in the upper reaches of the Ngan-Sau and Gianh rivers and connected with provinces to the north by numerous footpaths which skirted the vulnerable coastlands. It was to this area that Ham Nghi and his diminished retinue eventually retired. French units coming down from Vinh moved into the hills in December 1885 and again in January 1886. Each time, however, they lacked the resources to stay in the area, while several successful ambushes against them raised the popular prestige of local partisans (nghia quan) to the point where Ton That Thuyet was allegedly turning back volunteers.[27]

There was a weakness to this particular region, nevertheless, which the French would quickly learn to exploit. Of an estimated fourty thousand residents in the Gianh River valley itself perhaps one-fourth were practicing Catholics. Considerable blood had already spilled between Catholic and non-Catholic villages before 1885. Now Ton That Thuyet did nothing to discourage the destruction of churches, and French units hardly intervened when local Catholics burned pagodas. Memories of the killing, raping, and pillaging of this period would still be alive in the middle of the twentieth century. After a while, the French had no difficulty in persuading whole Catholic communities to move and cluster at key lowland junctions, where small forts could be erected, colonial troop units could be trained, and terror or counterterror expeditions could be organized. In February 1886 French units, striking by surprise with the aid of an informer, almost caught Ham Nghi in a pagoda where he had been residing for some months. Ham Nghi fled west into the mountains, but the destruction and demoralization wrought by this enemy sortie seems to have convinced Ton that his only long-term hope was once again to "knock at the gates" of the Middle Kingdom. Leaving his two sons as personal guardians of the king, he set off for the border to request assistance.[28]

In the meantime, however, uprisings in north Vietnam induced the French to shift some of their units up there again. This gave Quang Binh resistance units under Le Truc, the former governor of Hanoi, the opportunity to roam the coastal lowlands almost at will until late in 1886. After that the net tightened perceptibly, with the French even managing to establish a fort square in the midst of Le Truc's home area. Replying to French letters offering lenient surrender terms, Le Truc castigated the French policy of turning Vietnamese Catholic (giao) against non-Catholic (luong) by using priests to lead invasions and spread religious turmoil.[29]

27. CXL–3, p. 90, Gaultier, L'étrange, pp. 111–122.
28. CXL–3, pp. 89–91. Gaultier, L'étrange, pp. 123–145. AOM, A–50 (10) carton 23, has information on Ton That Thuyet's activities in 1888 and 1889.
29. CXL–3, pp. 93–95 (quotes from Le Truc letters). VNDN, p. 118.

During the Tet holidays of 1887 a French patrol was led by an informer to the hideout of one of Le Truc's prime mandarin associates, Nguyen Pham Tuan.[30] His death and the increasing viciousness of French and Catholic terrorism in local villages marked the beginning of the end in Quang Binh. Spies were everywhere, demoralized resistance units fell prey to nighttime attacks (in one of these Le Truc's wife and children were captured), and Ham Nghi let himself be gradually boxed in rather than leaving for other areas to the north.

Ham Nghi had the additional problem in his upper mountain retreat of being heavily dependent on villagers of the Muong tribal minority, a people who had not been treated kindly under the rule of his royal predecessors. In the end the French developed a complex plot with a Muong follower of Ham Nghi, whereby the king would be betrayed for some opium and a minor military title. In these more and more desperate circumstances, some of the youngest resistance leaders turned out to be the most fanatically determined and loyal. Ham Nghi (then sixteen years old) was finally surprised and captured in November 1888 but not before Ton's sixteen-year-old son, Ton That Thiep had been slain at his feet. Ton's eldest son, Ton That Dam (twenty), upon hearing the news at a nearby defensive position, instructed his followers to disperse, wrote a letter of apology to Ham Nghi, and committed suicide in a pagoda.[31] Ham Nghi, sounded out by his French captors to see whether he would "cooperate," refused to answer to his name or to express any willingness to meet his relatives in Hue. He was subsequently put aboard a ship for a life of exile in Algeria.[32]

The next resistance area to the north included most of Ha Tinh, Nghe An, and Thanh Hoa, all cordoned off from points south by concentrations of French troops, although liaison was maintained by the mountain footpaths. First to recruit local forces in support of Ham Nghi was a young Ha Tinh man named Le Ninh (often known as Am Ninh), one of the few Can Vuong leaders without civil examination credentials, but nevertheless of rather wealthy parentage. Moving swiftly, he and his band stormed the Ha Tinh provincial seat and executed a mandarin who had declared his opposition to the Can Vuong Edict. Word of this exploit having stimulated his recruiting, Le Ninh set up headquarters in his home village of Trung-Le. However, attacks on several Catholic villages failed, and fortune turned against Le Ninh. His entire village was wiped from the face of the map, the survivors being either jailed or resettled. Le Ninh

30. HT, pp. 288–289.
31. CXL–3, pp. 99–102. Gaultier, *L'étrange,* pp. 146–193.
32. Diep Van Ky, personal recollections, printed in *Cong luan,* 1933, and cited in CXL–3, p. 100. Pham Van Son, *Viet-Nam,* pp. 88–98.

himself managed to flee to the hills, where he died of illness the next year.[33] His followers soon entered the ranks of the more sophisticated organization of Phan Dinh Phung.

A man of different status led early Can Vuong efforts in Nghe An province. Nguyen Xuan On (1825–1889), often called Nghe On, had achieved *tien-si*[34] rank in 1871 and served as prefect (*tri-phu*), provincial education commissioner (*doc-hoc*), and provincial judge (*an-sat*) before turning in his seal of office to go recruit resistance forces in his home province.[35] In December 1885 his concerted attack on the French garrison at Vinh was thwarted by reinforcements from Ninh Binh. In December 1886 and January 1887 Nguyen Xuan On did whatever he could to take enemy pressure off Thanh Hoa and the Ba-Dinh defense complex, causing the French to divert at least one unit south to Vinh to curtail his attacks. Weapons and ammunition, particularly sulphur for gunpowder, seem to have been at a premium in the area.[36] In May 1887 the French captured one of his bodyguards and forced the man to lead a surprise assault on Nguyen Xuan On's headquarters. Nguyen was captured, refused entreaties to collaborate, was transferred to Hue in a cage, and died in jail two years later.[37] He left behind a volume of poems, one of which I attempt to translate here:

Cam Tac (Touching Impressions)
Wherefore our land of perpetual trouble?
Half is Heaven's doing, half is man's.
The barbarians could terrorize the Chin[38]
Yet three clans could also overthrow the Ch'in.[39]

33. Phan Boi Chau, *Viet-Nam,* p. 13. Le Thuoc, "Chuyen cau am Ninh khoi nghia," *Tri Tan* 156. HT, pp. 286–287.
34. A successful candidate in the metropolitan exams, usually translated as "doctor."
35. For a brief discussion of administrative structures under the Nguyen, see Roy Jumper and Nguyen Thi Hue, *Notes on the Political and Administrative History of Viet-Nam, 1802–1962,* pp. 26–35.
36. Tran Thanh Tam, "Mot so tai lieu bang chu viet vua moi tim duoc ve may cuoc khoi nghia o mien nui Nghe-Tinh," p. 52, reprints a written order by Nguyen Xuan On for special expeditions to purchase sulphur, since there were no local sources apparently.
37. CXL–3, pp. 112–113. LT, pp. 501–503. HT, pp. 262–272.
38. Reference to the five northern tribes in the third century A.D. that repeatedly attacked China's short-lived Chin dynasty.
39. In China the aggressive state of Ch'in took over the state of Ch'u, but three clans refused to be subdued and eventually helped overturn the Ch'in. This two-line apposition provides concrete historical evidence in support of the previous line.

Peace offerings of jade and silk simply made things worse.
Yet how many have dared to thump oars,
brandish spears to kill the enemy?
How odd: from old mandarin cap and gown,
To all those people running around in savage
barbarian clothing![40]

In the first three years in central Vietnam by far the most important
Can Vuong effort centered in Thanh Hoa province, particularly around
the village bastion of Ba-Dinh, adjacent to the road connecting the central
and northern parts of the country (see Map 2). In essence this was a
carefully planned, well executed position defense of three integrated villages, aided by the surrounding maze of swamps, mud flats, and high
bamboo thickets. As such, it was bound to fail, given complete French
superiority in artillery and naval gunfire. Still, there are aspects of this resistance which deserve more than passing mention. First, there was the
precise, studied manner in which scholar-gentry from throughout the
province—not just the local district—agreed on Ba-Dinh as the most
defensible position, selected a scholar-gentry commander-in-chief, and
parceled out jobs to units in other villages. They then devoted several
months to directing the construction of fortifications, for which they drew
supplies and labor from villages many miles away. For example, each village in the districts of Nga-Son and Tong-Son contributed thirty large
wicker baskets, one hundred bamboo poles, and ten shoulder-pole loads
of straw.[41] Thousands of peasants dug a moat around the entire complex
and piled the mud up to make a wall, using straw as the strengthening
agent. Behind this, one or more shorter defense rings were constructed.
The wicker baskets took the place of sandbags; they were filled with dirt
and used in the construction of firing embrasures. Most of the bamboo
poles formed multiple rings of spikes around the position, many of them
under water.[42]

The commander-in-chief, an 1884 cu-nhan[43] graduate and doc-hoc

40. The last line obviously tied in the barbarians referred to in a Chinese cultural
context to the French as they were then affecting Vietnam. HT, pp. 266–267, taken
from Nguyen Duc Van and Ha Van Dai, *Tho Van Nguyen Xuan On* (Hanoi, 1961).
41. CXL–3, p. 115.
42. CXL–3, pp. 113–116. Hoang Tuan Pho, "Tro lai van de Ba-Dinh," pp. 42–43.
Detailed map in Thai Vu, "Tim hieu ve cu-diem Ba-Dinh," p. 64.
43. A scholar passing all four portions of the triennial regional exams, often translated as "licentiate" or "masters." For an excellent discussion of the educational and
exam system under the Nguyen, see Woodside, "Vietnam and the Chinese," pp. 265–
357; also Takeda Ryoji, "Gencho kakyo seido no ikko-satsu," *Tohogaku Ronshu
Nukizuri* (July 1, 1962).

named Pham Banh, was wise enough to know his military limitations: he delegated all tactical authority to Dinh Cong Trang, a nonmandarin from outside Thanh Hoa, with considerable guerilla experience and a small, tough band of his own. While skirmishes occurred from October 1886 onward, the French only moved in seriously in December, first cutting off access routes and forcing in Vietnamese outposts, and then launching a major assault on December 18. Several units did penetrate the outer defenses, but they were pinned down and isolated and their officers killed or wounded. Hasty withdrawals finally were executed under cover of 81 millimeter cannon fire. French forces then marked time while distant reinforcements were called on, building up by early January 1887 to some fifteen hundred French and one thousand native colonial troops, plus four gunboats and five thousand coolies recruited from the Catholic villages of Phat-Diem.[44]

Their next full-scale assault, on January 6, proved to be even more disastrous for the French. Using explosives to clear holes in the bamboo hedges, several units again penetrated the outer defenses and again were isolated and forced to retreat under artillery cover. Reluctantly settling then for classic seige tactics, the French built their own impressive counterfortifications closer and closer to the Ba-Dinh resisters, bombarding incessantly and even using oil slick fires in the moats and swamps to destroy the bamboo hedges and force back snipers. Captain J. J. C. Joffre (later a marshal) commanded the engineer units which undertook most of these seige efforts, even as pressure was building from higher authorities to finish the campaign before political repercussions occurred in metropolitan France.[45] At this point Dinh Cong Trang sent word out to other resistance units in Thanh Hoa, particularly to one of about two thousand men a half-day's march away, calling for major actions to divert some of the French seige force. The best response he got was some ineffectual light harassing fire from the outside. Informal cooperative arrangements had been adequate in the planning and preparation stages, but in actual engagement there was no substitute for a unified area command.

By this time both sides were suffering the ill effects of the scores—perhaps hundreds—of unburied bodies strewn around the defense works. Cholera was beginning to spread rapidly. On the night of January 20 Dinh ordered his troops to break out at all costs and head for another carefully chosen defense position to the west, this one on high ground and

---

44. CMCD-1, pp. 88–89. CXL-3, p. 119, by contrast indicates that nineteen hundred native colonials may have been involved.
45. In January, 1922—exactly thirty-five years later—Marshal Joffre revisited the Ba-Dinh site and dedicated a memorial. It was partially destroyed after the August 1945 revolution. Hoang Tuan Pho, "Tro lai," p. 42.

protected on several sides by a deep, rapidly flowing river. It was a bloody escape, however, and the French gave them no time to rest or regroup. The new position was hit February 2, forcing resistance remnants to retreat southward several days later. Pham Banh surrendered to gain release of his mother and his children and then immediately committed suicide. Dinh Cong Trang escaped to Nghe-An, where he was killed later in 1887. The three villages of Ba-Dinh were ordered razed and their names removed from government maps. Physically, nothing remained of Ba-Dinh but a hump of earth amidst overgrown fields; but spiritually—that was another matter.[46]

Whereas resistance in central Vietnam from Quang-Binh northward was widespread and occasionally systematic, the action from Quang-Tri all the way south to Binh-Thuan appears to have been episodic, allowing the French to delegate most pacification duties to their mandarin collaborators. Catholic enclaves in Quang Tri were the scene of some acrimonious encounters in September 1885, as local scholar-gentry circulated copies of the 1883 royal ordinance urging village logistical support of the resistance and then took the provincial fortress without opposition and distributed the weapons and ammunition to their followers. This was apparently the signal for partisans throughout Quang Tri to move against the nearest Catholics, pillaging and burning houses and killing those who did not recant or flee to their churches. In several cases the churches themselves were set afire, with hundreds of persons being burned alive. Native Vietnamese priests were captured and forced, sometimes under torture, to admit that they had "called the French into their country." The seminary at An Ninh, overflowing with four thousand refugees, managed to defend itself against perhaps three thousand partisans employing cannon and desultory seige tactics. In reaction to this, General de Courcy marched up from Hue and quickly reoccupied the fortress, but it was almost a month before he had enough troops to relieve such Catholic outposts as An Ninh. Subsequent retributions against non-Catholics were equally bitter, and memories of this episode also continued to haunt the people of Quang Tri well into the twentieth century.[47]

The strongest sustained effort south of Quang Binh may have been in Quang Ngai and Binh Dinh, but even there the defection of a prime scholar-gentry leader and some of his following exposed the other scholar-gentry to rapid extermination.[48] In Quang Nam the Can Vuong leaders in the end came to question each other's loyalty, which led, among other

46. CMCD–1, pp. 90–98. CXL–3, pp. 117–130. LT, pp. 447–448. VNDN, p. 254.
47. M. Tabouille, "Une page de l'histoire du Quang-Tri: Septembre 1885," *Bulletin des Amis du Vieux Hue,* November/December 1923.
48. Phan Boi Chau, *Viet-Nam Vong Quoc Su,* pp. 11–12.

things to the killing of the father of Phan Chu Trinh, one of the prime leaders of the next anticolonial generation. In Binh Thuan the French employed the services of the infamous native pacification expert from Cochinchina, Tran Ba Loc, to destroy and pillage all suspected villages.[49]

When looked at from the French side, the decade after 1887 in central Vietnam was one of gradual but definite progress in the consolidation and rationalization of colonial rule. By this time the bulk of the royal family and a fair proportion of the scholar-gentry had reluctantly accepted foreign domination as a fait accompli, a fortunate thing for the French, since there is some doubt that they could have financially sustained a top-heavy system of direct rule in the center like that imposed on the south. Until 1895 there would still be a substantial, if manageable, financial drain for the training and maintaining of military forces in their efforts to wipe out the last major pockets of resistance. Increasingly, however, the French were able to rework the local tax structure so that not only did Vietnamese kill other Vietnamese for the foreigner, but they bore the financial costs of the operation as well.

Thanh Hoa, after the collapse of the resistance centered around Ba-Dinh, was seemingly quiescent until early 1889. At that point Tong Duy Tan, a tien-si and former doc-hoc in his own home province of Thanh Hoa, as well as an early Can Vuong mountain base commander, returned from hiding and roused the scholar-gentry of several districts to dig and supply another major fortified position. The first colonial patrol sent to investigate was ambushed October 8, 1889, suffering heavy casualties. A larger force returned after several days, but had to withdraw under fire. This brought a French colonel with one hundred and eighty-five French troops, who on October 22 forced the resistance units to flee their fortifications. However, word of these exploits had spread, causing risings and even some sustained assaults on French camps and posts from December through March 1890 in other parts of Thanh Hoa. Propaganda leaflets were distributed among Vietnamese serving in colonial units, implying imminent assistance for the anticolonials in north Vietnam from China and Germany and appealing for an end to Catholic/non-Catholic fratricide in the common cause of throwing out the foreigner. If soldiers did not feel they could actively join the resistance, then they were advised to return to their families and turn over their weapons to those who had joined, in exchange for cash.[50]

On both sides of this new Thanh Hoa conflict, however, the numbers of participants never seem to have approached those in the Ba-Dinh effort. By April 1890 the French were able to mount a long series of counter-attacks and succeeded in smashing or scattering the main resistance units

49. For Tran Ba Loc's career, see Osborne, "Rule and Response", pp. 280–283.
50. Full text in CXL–3, p. 205, and CMCD–1, p. 121.

by the end of that year. Tong Duy Tan and his prime associate, Cao Dien, held together a force of perhaps one hundred men and fifty rifles until 1892, at which time Tong was captured and executed and Cao forced to flee to north Vietnam, where he was caught in 1896.[51]

In Nghe An and Ha Tinh the French crushing of the initial risings and capture of Ham Nghi in 1888 had deeply stunned the scholar-gentry. On the one hand, this tended to stimulate significant new defections to Hue. On the other hand, however, it set the minority to developing a more sophisticated, long-term concept of resistance. The soul of this resistance would be Phan Dinh Phung, the highest ranking court official after Ton That Thuyet to take part fully in the Can Vuong movement. The muscle, the élan, and the tactical expertise of this effort, would above all reside in Cao Thang, a young bandit leader of decidedly nongentry background, whom Phan's brother had protected from royal troops ten years earlier.[52]

Phan Dinh Phung was born in 1847 in Dong-Thai village, La-Son district, Ha Tinh province. Dong-Thai village had a reputation for producing high mandarins far back into the Le dynasty, and the Phan family could boast successful examinees and mandarins in each of twelve generations before Phan Dinh Phung. All three of Phan's brothers who lived to adulthood passed exams and became mandarins. Phan himself gave early indications of a real distaste for classical learning. Nevertheless, he was determined to follow the traditional route, passing the regional exams in 1876 and then receiving highest honors in the metropolitan exams of the following year. Finally, in the court exams King Tu Duc asked a specific question about the reasons behind the West's rapid military progress; Phan is reputed to have cited Japan as an Eastern country already demonstrating clearly what Vietnam could do if she had the will. There was no reason, he argued, why the West should keep a monopoly on military skills.[53]

For all his scholastic success, Phan would never be known for his literary ability. It was his reputation for courage and stiff integrity that raised him quickly to the top and kept him his devoted following unto the very end in 1895. In his first position as a district mandarin in Ninh-Binh province, Phan saw fit to punish a native Catholic priest, who allegedly had terrorized local non-Catholics with implicit support from the French. Amidst the subsequent diplomatic furor, Phan is said to have avoided blaming the hated alliance between local Catholics and French on the nature of Catholicism itself, feeling rather that this collaboration had developed out of the military and political weakness of Vietnam's central

51. CXL–3, pp. 201–208. CMCD–1, pp. 115–126. For several of Tong Duy Tan's poems, see HT, pp. 259–261.
52. Dao Trinh Nhat, *Phan Dinh Phung (1847–1895)*, p. 96.
53. *Ibid.*, pp. 5–17, 111–112.

government. Nevertheless, the end result was a bowing by Hue to French pressure and the removal of Phan as district mandarin and his reassignment to the court as a member of the censorate (*Do-Sat-Vien*).[54] There Phan earned the enmity of many but the trust of his king by revealing to Tu Duc that virtually all court mandarins were making a mockery of royal orders to engage in periodic rifle practice.[55] After this Tu Duc sent Phan on an inspection trip to north Vietnam, and his report led, among other things, to the king's cashiering the viceroy for that entire area.[56]

Despite his prominence in the last years of Tu Duc's reign, it is not clear from the evidence just where Phan Dinh Phung stood on the overriding court questions of "attack, defense, or negotiation" with the French. Given subsequent events, we might assume that he stood in the "war party" with Ton That Thuyet. Yet he almost lost his head—literally—just after the death of Tu Duc for trying to oppose Ton's palace coup which set aside Tu Duc's will of succession. Phan was lucky merely to have been imprisoned and stripped of his positions; and he eventually was allowed to leave Hue for home.[57] There Phan seems to have avoided public recriminations with Ton, for example, accepting secret responsibility for building up mountain bases in Ha-Tinh long before Ham Nghi's flight from Hue. Rather than sharing Ton's lingering hopes for another Ch'ing intervention, Phan toyed with ideas of major assistance from Siam, recalling a sister of King Gia Long who long before had married the king of that country. But the most that ever came of this, much later, was several pack trains of guns and ammunition.[58]

In the first period of Can Vuong activity after July 1885 Phan used his home village as nerve center, setting up a small weapons factory and using local scholar-gentry as troop commanders. Their first serious attack was aimed at two nearby Catholic villages. French troops arrived some hours later and chased them all the way back to their home village, where retribution naturally was heavy. Phan Dinh Phung escaped, but his elder brother was later captured by his old enemy, the cashiered viceroy of north Vietnam, who by this time was serving the French as governor of Nghe-An. The device used against Phan was classic, the pressing of an old friend and fellow villager into writing an impassioned, deeply Confucian appeal to

54. For a brief discussion of the censorate under the Nguyen, see Woodside, "Vietnam and the Chinese," pp. 101–106.
55. Tu Duc himself hunted with Western rifles and even deigned to wear Western high rubber boots in the swamps and paddies. Dao Trinh Nhat, *Phan Dinh Phung*, p. 30.
56. *Ibid.*, pp. 18–26.
57. *Ibid.*, pp. 38–40.
58. *Ibid.*, pp. 72–75.

Phan to surrender himself to save his elder brother, his family's tombs, and —indeed—his entire village. Phan is said to have told his lieutenants:

> From the time I joined with you in the Can Vuong movement, I determined to forget questions of family and village. Now I have but one tomb, a very large one, that must be defended: the land of Vietnam. I have only one brother, very important, that is in danger: more than twenty million countrymen. If I worry about my own tombs, who will worry about defending the tombs of the rest of the country? If I save my own brother, who will save all the other brothers of our country? There is only one way for me to die now.

After this he is reported simply to have written his former friend, "if anyone carves up my brother, remember to send me some of the soup."[59]

This incident helps illustrate why Phan Dinh Phung became important to later generations of anticolonial leaders for his apparent identification with a countrywide cause, far removed from questions of family and region. It would be too much to conclude that Phan was expressing a revolutionary ethic, since this problem of competing loyalties, of particular versus universal values, was also a theme in traditional Confucian literature. Whatever the wellsprings, however, no one can deny that Phan's actions and the statements attributed to him came to symbolize the highest personal standards of Vietnamese patriotism.

In 1887, considering his efforts up to that time to be ill-conceived, Phan ordered Cao Thang and other subordinates to cease open conflict and concentrate on building a solid network of base camps, food caches, intelligence agents, and peasant supply contacts. He himself set out for north Vietnam, hoping to coordinate strategy with scholar-gentry leaders there.[60] While Phan's mission ended in failure, Cao Thang in his absence achieved wonders, carefully reorganizing a main force of one thousand men equipped with five hundred firearms. Interestingly enough, besides possessing a variety of older firearms, Cao Thang captured several model 1874 French rifles, disassembled them personally, and then supervised the

---

59. Both are quoted in *ibid.,* p. 86, but with the original source not indicated. Dao Trinh Nhat in 1925 wandered through Ha-Tinh and Nghe-An collecting data, so we may assume that he picked up many of his "quotes" from the local people at that time. I have included the quotations nevertheless because, even if they are eventually proved unreliable, we still must recognize that the "myth" of Phan's statements clearly passed into the mainstream of popular folklore and had an objective, verifiable impact on subsequent anticolonial sentiments.
60. A letter and several poems by Phan Dinh Phung, written in Nghe-An en route north (March 1887), survive in the original. Le Thuoc, "Mot van kien cua cu Phan Dinh Phung vua moi phat hien."

manufacture (by Vietnamese artisans kidnapped for the purpose) of perhaps three hundred and fifty copies. According to French officers who captured some later and sent them home for analysis, these copies were pro-
ficiently done in every detail except for the tempering of the springs, which
were made from umbrella spokes, and the lack of rifling in the barrels,
which naturally cut down their effective range and their accuracy.[61]

Phan Dinh Phung and Cao Thang had in fact picked the only area in
central Vietnam where prolonged resistance was feasible after 1888. The
mountainous western borders of Ha-Tinh, Nghe-An, and Thanh Hoa were
redolent with the history of dynastic and antiforeign struggle. We may
surmise that Phan thought of himself in a role somewhat akin to that of
Le Loi, more than four centuries earlier. In much the same area, both
of them attempted to build small, disciplined guerrilla forces that offered
political alternatives to collaboration. Both patiently endured the worst
trials, waiting for the proper moment to strike into the lowlands, gain local
gentry support, and then sweep north or south to ultimate victory.

Small remnants of risings in other locations did gravitate to the leadership of Phan Dinh Phung and Cao Thang. A command headquarters was
established at Vu-Quang, and fifteen other bases were strung along the
mountains, each with a subordinate commander and one hundred to five
hundred men. A sophisticated balance of centralized command and unit
dispersion undoubtedly was one reason that this resistance lasted so long.
For much of the time a land tax in both silver and rice was levied by the
movement, local bases essentially being supported by nearby villages and
any excess going to Vu-Quang. Cinnamon bark was collected and sold,
while lowlanders gave whatever steel, iron, and brass they had to help in
the production of weapons.[62]

Upon Phan Dinh Phung's return from the north in 1889, the first order
of business was to track down the Muong betrayer of King Ham Nghi and
behead him. This accomplished, there commenced a series of inconclusive
small-unit engagements lasting through the summer of 1890, with the
French mostly relying on district and provincial colonial units (kho-xanh)
to man their ever-expanding string of local forts, each usually under the
command of a French lieutenant. In late 1890 there was an ineffective

61. Gosselin, L'Empire, p. 313. Dao Trinh Nhat, Phan Dinh Phung, pp. 101–109.
62. CMCD–1, pp. 128–137. CXL–3, 214–217. Dao Trinh Nhat, Phan Dinh
Phung, pp. 129–134. While Phan Dinh Phung's organization is said to have extended
into Thanh-Hoa, where Cam Ba Thuoc, a former member of the Hanlin Academy,
was the commander, there apparently was not much open activity from 1889
onward. See Tran Tranh Tam, "Mot so tai lieu," for quoc-ngu translation of a con-
gratulatory citation issued by Cam Ba Thuoc to village elders of Gia-Hoi (today a
part of Nghe An).

French effort to move into the villages and isolate them from the mountain bases. A major French sweep in the spring of 1892 in Ha-Tinh failed however, and in August Cao Thang mounted an audacious counterattack on the province seat of Ha-Tinh, freeing compatriots in the jail and killing a large proportion of the native colonial defenders. This apparently led the French to conduct a counteroffensive during the remainder of 1892, pushing resistance units back into the mountains and forcing them to abandon two mountain bases. While still unable to pin down resistance units, steady French pressure from that time onward did begin to snap covert resistance links with lowland villages, thus compounding the problems of securing food, supplies, intelligence data, recruits, and so on. A ring of enemy forts kept tightening around the remaining base camps. The only bright aspect was the rather plentiful supply of gunpowder, brought in by pack train from Siam under the direction of a resourceful female member of the resistance.[63] This enabled them to mix foreign and local powder on a fifty-fifty basis, compared with the previous weak twenty-eighty mixture.[64]

At this point Cao Thang, either wearying of guerrilla conflict or sensing the ultimate decline of their movement, proposed to Phan Dinh Phung in open council a full-scale attack on the provincial seat of Nghe An and the surrounding posts. His plan included diversions to the south and the training of almost two thousand men in conventional military maneuvers. The troops were eager, but Phan seems to have approved the scheme much against his better judgment. Even though Le Loi's successful attack on Nghe An in 1425 represented an obvious precedent, Phan must have known that the chances this time were slim. After overcoming several small posts en route, their main force was pinned down in an attack on the key fort of No on September 9, 1893. Leading a desperate frontal assault with one hundred and fifty men, Cao Thang fell mortally wounded along with his brother, and the troops retreated in total confusion. Cao Thang had simply been unable to control and sustain the momentum of such an ambitious attack. His relationship with his men had always been personal, not structural, and his previous successes had come from a combination of meticulous planning and small-unit surprise.[65]

Phan Dinh Phung quickly perceived the significance of this loss, as is revealed in his eulogy and funeral oration for Cao Thang.[66] From as early

---

63. For the legendary exploits of this woman, known only as Miss Tam, see Dao Trinh Nhat, *Phan Dinh Phung*, pp. 150–170. Truong Buu Lam, *Patterns*, p. 128, has a translation of one of her songs.

64. Dao Trinh Nhat, *Phan Dinh Phung*, pp. 168–170.

65. *Ibid.*, pp. 180–188.

66. CXL–3, pp. 230–232. Dao Trinh Nhat, *Phan Dinh Phung*, pp. 189–192. While the eulogy was in Chinese, the oration was recorded in *nom*.

as 1889 there is reason to believe that Phan had clearly understood both the advantages and the limitations of prolonged resistance. Although he may have doubted that he or anyone else could evict the French in his lifetime, he still saw certain long-term advantages both in threatening them and in maintaining a viable alternative to the defeatism and venality emanating from Hue. Now, however, he was unlikely even to present a threat to the French anymore. All that remained, thus, was the symbolism of demonstrating to his contemporaries and to subsequent generations a total unwillingness to accept servility, whether physical or spiritual.

French administrators may not have perceived Phan's intent. But high mandarin collaborators did—and none of them better than Hoang Cao Khai, viceroy of Tonkin and member of yet another prestigious scholar-gentry family from Phan Dinh Phung's village of Dong-Thai in Ha-Tinh province. It was Hoang who then became a prime sponsor of all-out efforts to crack Phan's resistance campaign once and for all, by using every political, psychological, and economic device available. By late 1894 suspected supporters in the lowlands and relatives of participants in the resistance had been thoroughly terrorized, several more resistance commanders had been killed, and their communications had been broken. No base area was secure. The Phan family tombs had been dug up and all available relatives jailed.

One of those relatives was selected to carry a long message from Hoang Cao Khai to Phan Dinh Phung. Rather surprisingly, Phan sent a written reply, so we are extremely fortunate in having a last highly charged, yet subtle exchange between traditional mandarin paragons.[67] Hoang's letter recalled their common origins and promised intercession with Governor General J. M. A. De Lannessan and other French officials. He credited Phan with selfless dedication, righteousness, and loyalty toward the monarch:

> But now the situation has changed and even those without intelligence
> or education have concluded that nothing remains to be saved. How is it
> that you, a man of vast understanding, do not realize this? But I seem to
> perceive your reasoning. You are determined to do whatever you deem
> righteous. You give all your efforts and talents to the cause you consider
> just. And yet, although it is in a man's power to undertake any enter-
> prise, its outcome depends upon the will of Heaven. All that matters

67. Chinese texts in Le Xuan Giao, "Anh hung dan toc, Luoc khao ve than the va su nghiep vi anh hung dan toc la cu Phan Dinh Phung." *Minh Tan*, New Series no. 33 (Saigon [?] 25 January 1966), pp. 63–79. Vietnamese translations in Dao Trinh Nhat, *Phan Dinh Phung*, pp. 202–209. English translations below, excerpted from Truong Buu Lam, *Patterns*, pp. 122–127.

indeed is the giving of one's life to one's country. No one therefore can deter you from your goal.

The subject I should now like to introduce is the suffering imposed upon our country. . . . I have always been taught that superior men should consider the care of the people as fundamental; who has ever heard of men who were loyal to their King but forgot the people's aspirations? . . . I would understand your resistance, did you involve but your family for the benefit of a large number! As of now, hundreds of families are subject to grief; how do you have the heart to fight on? I venture to predict that, should you pursue your struggle, not only will the population of our village be destroyed but our entire country will be transformed into a sea of blood and a mountain of bones.

Phan Dinh Phung's reply was a classic in savage understatement, utilizing standard formalism in the interests of propaganda, with deft denigration of his opponent. Recalling Vietnam's struggles against Han, T'ang Sung, Yuan, and Ming, he asked why even China, sharing a common border and "a thousand times more powerful than Vietnam," could not succeed in swallowing the Vietnamese. "It was surely because the destiny of our country has been willed by Heaven itself." Implicitly, the French, coming from much farther away, would discover this for themselves.

To Hoang's statements about popular grief and suffering, Phan retorted that responsibility for this must rest with the French, who "acted like a storm," forced the king to flee, and cast the country into disorder.

Our rivers and our mountains have been annexed by them at a stroke and turned into a foreign territory. *These events affected the whole country, the entire population. It is not any particular region or any particular family alone that has suffered this trial.* [My emphasis.]

After reviewing his personal actions and stressing the loyalty of his followers as a factor in continuing the struggle, Phan concluded with a stinging rebuke to Hoang and all collaborators:

If our region has suffered to such an extent, it was not only from the misfortunes of war. You must realize that wherever the French go, there flock around them groups of petty men who offer plans and tricks to gain the enemy's confidence. These persons create every kind of enmity; they incriminate innocent persons, blaming one one day, punishing another the next. They use every expedient to squeeze the people out of their possessions. That is how hundred of misdeeds, thousands of offenses have been perpetrated.

Quite clearly, Hoang's particularistic appeals had been countered with an appeal to history, a demand that blame for death and destruction rest with the foreign intruder, and an important raising of the stakes, above family and village to the entire country and people. The arena was not Dong-Thai village or Ha-Tinh province, but Vietnam itself.

Hoang Cao Khai translated both letters into French and presented them to De Lanessan with the recommendation that it was time for final "destruction of this scholar-gentry rebellion." In July 1895 French area commanders brought together three thousand troops to tighten the noose around three remaining base areas. Several times, resistance units succeeded in executing skillful ambushes and night withdrawals, but Phan was by this time wracked with dysentery and had to be carried when his unit moved every three or four days. A collaborator mandarin named Nguyen Than, with previous pacification experience in Quang Ngai and Quang Nam provinces, was brought in to cut the last links with the villages and to attempt to buy off Phan Dinh Phung's subordinates.[68] The men were now living on roots and occasional handfuls of dried corn and were desperate for salt; their shoes were rotted out, and most were without blankets. A few committed suicide. Phan himself died of dysentery, probably on January 21, 1896; later, twenty-five followers who surrendered were taken to Hue and executed. Nguyen Than, following traditional precedent for "bandits," managed to find Phan's grave, burn the corpse, and fire the ashes out of a cannon.[69] The soul of resistance to the protectorate was gone, said the triumphant report submitted by the governor general to the Minister of Colonies in Paris.[70]

Can Vuong efforts in north Vietnam, while different in approach from those of the center, were nonetheless just as important in sustaining the resistance ethic and in setting specific precedents for future generations. In contrast with people in most of central Vietnam, people in the north had been living amidst war and chaos for some years already. Conflict in north Vietnam immediately after Ham Nghi's flight from Hue in July 1885 was hard to separate from French efforts to terminate the Sino-French conflict and consolidate their hold in a few key areas. Promulgation of the Can Vuong Edict merely signaled another round of deadly conflict. This time, however, the moral climate was more invigorating. Confusion bred by Hue's decades of indecisive diplomacy was swept

68. Dao Trinh Nhat, *Phan Dinh Phung*, pp. 211–263.
69. CXL–3, pp. 232–238. Dao Trinh Nhat, *Phan Dinh Phung*, pp. 264–282.
70. Governor General Foure's report, dated January 31, 1896. AOM, A-30 (104) Carton 21.

away. Popular resistance was now legitimate. It was either fight or collaborate—with no room in the middle.

In general, Can Vuong command relations in the north were even less structured than were those in central Vietnam, because newly energized royalist scholar-gentry had to place themselves in a more intimate and even dependent relationship with those forces, antidynastic and otherwise, which had been active well before 1885. Leaders of those forces already possessed an appreciation of the strategic significance of mountainous areas along the Sino-Vietnamese border. Even for groups choosing to resist in the Red River delta, it was a great advantage to receive the small but steady flow of arms and supplies from across the Chinese border, until about 1894 when the Ch'ing authorities finally moved to cut off such traffic. In the north there also was considerably more room to maneuver, and it took the French a much longer time to extend their strings of forts up the main valleys and along the frontiers there than in the central provinces. When in 1896 the French succeeded in neutralizing the Yen-The area and bringing some last mountain commanders to heel, it was the end of the entire Can Vuong movement.

The man selected by Ham Nghi and his advisors to coordinate all resistance in north Vietnam was a tien-si from Nam-Dinh province named Nguyen Quang Bich.[71] Nguyen's earlier career had included holding positions as *an-sat* (provincial judge) of Son-Tay province, where in 1873 and 1874 he had worked closely with Liu Yung-fu's Black Flags, and as governor of Hung-Hoa, where failure in defending the local fort had led him to organize local militia bands for sustained resistance. Now as Ham Nghi's representative he twice traveled into Yunnan seeking new Ch'ing assistance, on one occasion at least bringing back six hundred firearms, sixty boxes of ammunition, and two thousand catties of opium as convertible currency.[72] Later he received substantial arms shipments from Ton That Thuyet, who had failed to persuade the Ch'ing to intervene again but who was still able for some years to coordinate supply shipments from China across the frontier.

In fact, China's empress dowager, Tz'u-hsi, had decided to abandon all semblances of traditional tributary relations with Vietnam. The Sino-French treaty signed June 9, 1885, reaffirmed the French protectorate and specified that Vietnam was to conduct its relations with other countries only through the intermediary of France.[73] However, either Vietnam's

71. 1830–1890. His original family name was Ngo, hence he also appears as Ngo Quang Bich.
72. CXL–3, p. 149.
73. Eastman, *Throne and Mandarins*, pp. 200–201.

Can-Vuong resisters failed to understand the significance of Peking's acquiescence or they deliberately tried to influence China's Ch'ing-i clique to bring about another change of face in Peking. In 1886 a group of northern Vietnamese scholar-gentry sent a petition to the Chinese governor general of Yunnan and Kweichow for transmission to the emperor. As with Nguyen Quang Bich and Ton That Thuyet, this was in the immediate sense a desperate call for military assistance. But it also played heavily on the Middle Kingdom's sense of responsibility toward its vassals and sought to prevent China from reaching any permanent understanding with France that would jeopardize Vietnam. It explained why King Ham Nghi had been forced to flee the capital and denigrated, by name, the mandarins who had subsequently collaborated with the French in installing Dong Khanh:

> Assuming a heavy responsibility toward his country, our King has decided to resist and to seek a solution to his difficulties rather than remain quiet and await the catastrophe. Wherever is our King, there is our country. The other King, established by the French, is rather our enemy. How can he appropriate temples and command the loyalty of the gods and the people?[74]

The Can Vuong generation, steeped in idealistic respect for traditional Confucian morality, never quite recovered from the Middle Kingdom's final abandonment of Vietnam into barbarian hands. It was left to the next generation to draw their own sobering conclusions.

Nguyen Quang Bich never tried seriously to organize a central command for north Vietnam, and it is doubtful that he could have. He did maintain regular liaison with resistance leaders in at least six provinces, but this does not appear to have produced much coordinated activity. The French tried to buy Nguyen Quang Bich off and, failing this, jailed his mother. Nevertheless, his resistance efforts continued until his death of natural causes in 1890.[75] Following are portions of his letter answering the French offers, which doubtless are representative of Can Vuong political thinking:

> You [Frenchmen] came to look our country over, displaying good techniques, clever skills and a well-trained army. And on this basis it seems that more than half of our people have left brightness and righteousness

74. Truong Buu Lam, *Patterns*, p. 135. Complete Chinese text in Shao Hsun-cheng, et al., eds., *Chung-Fa*, pp. 484-486.
75. HT, pp. 245-256, for a selection of his extensive writings. LT, pp. 467-468. Kieu Huu Hy, *Tho van Nguyen Quang Bich* (Hanoi, 1961), as cited in Truong Buu Lam, *Patterns*, p. 131.

in order to follow you. This land of long civilization, of countless mandarins and proper ceremony has just about become French property. This being the case, you may consider us extremely foolish for not having measured our strength realistically, instead courting disaster by gathering some hundreds of scholar-gentry [*than-si*] and several thousand exhausted soldiers to oppose you. But we think repeatedly of the tie between monarch and subject in this world, not shirking temporal responsibilities that are as clearly defined as the waters of the Ching and the Wei rivers[76] and we do not dare forget our obligations. It is simply this tie that we must live up to.

When you first came to our country, you first talked of peaceful relations, then of protecting us. But these were no more than the diversionary tactics of a thief, subsequently allowing you to seize our fortresses, drive out our King, his generals, and then on your own volition enthrone Dong Khanh. Political authority is now completely in your hands. Civilian as well as military officials have been detained and put under your control. How could you have been more heartless? Calling it peaceful relations, calling it protection, and then having it work out like this?! . . .

As long as you continue to boast about your strength, your skills, we will continue to refuse to give up our failures, our weaknesses. Then, if we happen to win, to live, we will be the court's righteous men [*nghia-si*]. If we are unlucky enough to lose and die, we will still be supernatural devils [*qui-thieng*] for killing bandits. Better to endure punishment from you than ever think of punishment from our monarch. Better to be sentenced once than be sentenced for eternity.[77]

In the Red River delta the most sustained resistance occurred in Hung-Yen, Hai-Duong, and Bac-Ninh provinces (see Map 2), with the main base in Bai-Say (Plain of Reeds)—an area in Hung Yen that had been well cultivated until the dikes had broken repeatedly during Tu Duc's reign, turning it into a bandit's lair.[78] There the early leader was Nguyen Thien Thuat, a native of Hung-Yen and a former mandarin, who had departed angrily for China when Hue put pressure on him to observe the treaties with France. Upon hearing of the Can Vuong Edict, he returned and quickly organized forces to threaten several enemy communication routes, the emphasis always on mobile, small-unit attacks rather than defense of fixed positions. Up through 1887 the French were too occupied in central Vietnam to threaten Bai-Say, but in 1888 they

76. Two rivers in Shensi province, the Ching being clear (white) and the Wei muddy (black).
77. I have not been able to find the original Chinese. Vietnamese translation in HT, pp. 254–256, and Kieu Huu Hy, *Tho van Nguyen Quang Bich,* pp. 280–282. Alternative English translation: Truong Buu Lam, *Patterns,* pp. 129–131.
78. CMCD–1, p. 104.

organized a special native colonial force under Viceroy Hoang Cao Khai to mount attacks on nearby villages and slowly to isolate the regular resistance units. Nguyen Thien Thuat now turned command over to his younger brother and another deputy in order to return to China in search of help from Liu Yung-fu and his Black Flags. Fighting was bitter and widespread through 1888, but by 1889 the noose was drawn tight, and a number of Vietnamese leaders had been captured or had surrendered. Remnants managed to flee to Yen-The, where Hoang Hoa Tham was just beginning his fight.

Between 1885 and 1889 the French were vaguely aware that pacification of the Tonkin lowlands depended ultimately on controlling the surrounding hills and mountains. Without this control small resistance units could always slip out for rest and regroupment and then filter back with new weapons and supplies. Perhaps more important, as long as resistance continued in the hills, the vast bulk of Vietnamese in the delta would have adequate psychological rationale for refusing to accept colonial rule as ultimate, final, and without alternative. Up through 1890 the French lacked the means to control these hills and instead merely seized strategic points along the frontier (Mong-Cai, Lang-Son, Cao-Bang, Bao-Lac, Ha-Giang, Lao-Cai) and tried to keep open the main communication routes out of the delta (the Red, Da, and Lo rivers and Lang-Son road). The only exception I know of was their early moves to control the Tam-Dao spine of hills, which points like a knife deep into the delta.[79]

Thus, in 1890 most of north Vietnam's midlands and highlands were essentially autonomous, containing a fantastic conglomeration of ethnic Vietnamese, remnant Chinese, Nung, Thai, Muong, Meo, and other tribal groups—none owing firm allegiance to anyone above the district or provincial level. It was not an easy period for anyone—above all, the more peaceful peasants trying to make a living in the valleys and the less warlike of the tribal villages on the slopes. Guns were the primary "instrument of communication," and stability existed only where various small armed bands had worked out temporary arrangements with each other.

Such armed bands have come down in French history books as *pirates* and *rebelles,* while more recent Vietnamese historians generally have hailed them as patriots and righteous armies (nghia-quan). Without wishing to get involved in this semantic quarrel, for which there is a voluminous history, it should be stated in passing that the French had little justification for calling the kettle black, for labeling someone else as *pirates,* considering the manner in which they took over all of Vietnam

79. Emmanuel P. G. Chabrol, *Opérations militaires au Tonkin,* pp. 41–67. *Histoire militaire de l'Indochine de 1664 a nos jours* (Hanoi, 1922), p. 121.

and the spurious attitudes they developed toward the people of the area.[80] On the other hand, present-day Vietnamese historians should be prepared to recognize that most of the leaders of these mountain bands operating after 1890 had motives which differed in degree, if not in kind, from representatives of the traditional elite like Pham Banh, Tong Duy Tan, Phan Dinh Phung, and Nguyen Thien Thuat.

Perhaps the best way to illustrate this is to outline the career of one of the most colorful and certainly the longest surviving of these mountain leaders: Hoang Hoa Tham, better known as De Tham, the "tiger of Yen-The."[81] De Tham apparently was a peasant from Hung-Yen, where his father had found reason in the early 1840s to join an antidynastic group in the nearby mountains of Son-Tay. There De Tham's father and mother were both captured by Nguyen forces in 1846, she being executed on the spot and he allegedly committing suicide en route by biting his tongue, a traditional method. A paternal uncle raised the only son, the future De Tham, by fleeing to the Yen-The area and changing the family name from Truong to Hoang.[82] Yen-The was host to local bands, Black Flags, and vigilante units well before the first French penetrations of north Vietnam in 1873 and the Sino-French hostilities between 1883 and 1885. Serving in a variety of groups for an unspecified time, De Tham eventually became a minor leader with an increasing reputation for bravery and cunning. As other leaders were killed or bought off by the French, and particularly as the failures of scholar-gentry campaigns in the populated lowlands sent remnants into the hills, De Tham and a handful of other autonomous leaders took on greater stature. Also, as local French authorities appropriated land in the valleys, some peasants gathered around De Tham because he promised them restitution and showed a general willingness to aid the poor.[83] It was largely this constant reservoir of armed men in the Yen-The area that allowed De Tham to recoup and reform his resistance after repeated setbacks.[84]

80. Nguyen Van Trung, *Chu Nghia Thuc Dan Phap o Viet-Nam*, pp. 15–119. In French, of course, *pirate* has the wider meaning of "lawless person" or "outlaw."

81. AOM, A–50 (11) carton 23. AOM, A–50 (17) carton 23. AOM, A–50 NF 595. See also Nguyen Duy Hinh, *De Tham: Con Hum Yen-The* (Saigon, 1961); and Paul Chack, *Hoang Tham Pirate* (Paris, 1933)—popularizations from Vietnamese and French points of view, respectively.

82. This account is from Hoai Nam, "Ve goc tich cua Ong De Tham." The author located distant relatives of De Tham who still possessed a family register (*gia-pha*) detailing his ancestry. However, this evidence, if correct, makes De Tham at least fifteen years older than all other sources would seem to indicate.

83. Dinh Xuan Lam, *Hoang Hoa Tham va phong trao nong dan Yen-The* (Hanoi, 1958), as cited by Truong Buu Lam, *Patterns*, p. 45.

84. CMCD–2, pp. 5–8. CXL–3, pp. 246–247.

Yen-The saw its first really serious enemy penetration between November 1890 and January 1891, with French forces building up to a total of thirteen hundred troops and forcing resistance units to retreat farther into the mountains. More weapons and ammunition were secured from China, using cattle and lumber as exchange. But the French hit hard again in early 1892, employing overwhelming artillery fire to crack a key mountain fortress and seize fifteen thousand kilograms of corn and rice. Relentless pressure brought some resistance bands to surrender and others to work out live-and-let-live arrangements with the French. By December 1893 the famous Colonel Joseph Gallieni (later a general) was in charge of a high-priority political/military plan to eliminate or at least neutralize De Tham and his remaining allies.[85] Considerable friction developed at this point between French civilian and military echelons, the former willing to make local deals with the "bandits" so that they could concentrate on their primary interests, which were the seizure of land for plantations and the completion of the Lang-Son railroad.[86]

A great amount of plotting and counterplotting ensued among the Vietnamese, those leaders who had gone over to the French trying to assassinate the holdouts and vice versa. Meanwhile, Gallieni was carefully constructing a web of forts and supply posts around the area, plus a series of military roads penetrating it. Each time he drove his enemy out of a valley, he would have a fort constructed and try to persuade the local people, by force or otherwise, to break all links with the resistance. Since men like De Tham hardly had the scholar-gentry image of a Phan Dinh Phung, or even the multigenerational ties that most scholar-gentry resistance leaders had with surrounding villages, it is no surprise that Gallieni enjoyed considerable success in the political aspects of dividing, penetrating, and expanding his control of areas—which he called his "oil-spot approach." His success was temporarily halted, nevertheless, in September 1894 by De Tham's counterplay of attacking trains on the Lang-Son line and kidnapping a very influential colon for ransom and a military truce. To Gallieni's chagrin, De Tham succeeded in making a settlement with the French civilian administrators and proceeded to reconsolidate a little quasi-feudal domain in the Yen-The area.[87]

For all that, however, by late 1895 the civilian administrators were again dissatisfied with arrangements, particularly in view of De Tham's attempts to infiltrate native colonial units and to extend his alliances to

85. Georges Taboulet, La geste française en Indochine, pp. 894-899. Joseph S. Gallieni, Gallieni au Tonkin (1892–1896) (Paris, 1941). H. Deschamps et P. Chauvet, Gallieni pacificateur (Paris, 1949).
86. Nguyen Duy Hinh, De Tham, pp. 29-39. CXL-3, pp. 248-259.
87. CMCD-2, pp. 9-21. Nguyen Duy Hinh, De Tham, pp. 40-51.

other localities. Gallieni, who had seen to it that complete political and military intelligence was maintained on the Yen-The situation, convinced Governor General Paul-Armand Rousseau that he could resolve the problem with a short, inexpensive operation, which in fact did force the surrender of some resistance units and the dispersal of most others into adjacent provinces. Nevertheless, random skirmishes in 1896 and an inconclusive sweep of the area in 1897 demonstrated that a permanent solution had eluded the French. Another deal was worked out, this one considerably less advantageous to De Tham, yet at least allowing him to continue for fifteen more years of plotting uprisings and assassinations and occasionally providing aid and comfort to a later generation of anti-colonial leaders. After 1897 French military and political supremacy in the pragmatic, "rational" sense made men like De Tham seem anachronisms. But in the realm of popular mythology his cunning against such a mighty foe became nothing short of supernatural. Young, angry intellectuals came to study his tactics and admire his gall, if not his outdated politics. He was something of a missing link, by his mere existence reminding proud Vietnamese of martial values that the French would have had them forget.[88]

There were other areas of resistance besides Yen-The after 1890, as the French and their mandarin collaborators slowly penetrated the upper valleys and mountain ranges. Along the Da River after 1889 resistance seems to have increased with the arrival of new weapons from Ton That Thuyet and the defection of some Vietnamese from colonial units. As contact with the delta diminished, however, resistance units were forced to rely more and more on the Muong people who made up the majority in the lower Da valley. There being no particular policy for altering the traditional Muong attitude of suspicion toward the Vietnamese to a new spirit of alliance, it is not surprising that French commanders were able to exploit the situation. By the middle of 1892 the prime remaining leader, Doc Ngu, was substantially isolated. In August 1893 his assassination was accomplished by Muong mercenaries.[89]

Until 1894, much to the anger of the French, it was still relatively easy to cross and recross the Sino/Vietnamese frontier. From China Ton That Thuyet still managed to harass the French in Cao-Bang, while Vietnamese and Chinese partisans attacked the coal mines and outposts along the coast and inland to the Luc-Nam River. With the outbreak of the Sino-Japanese War, however, Peking gave strict instructions to her mandarins along the southern frontier to avoid irritating the French at any cost. Re-

---

88. CXL-3, pp. 260–263. Nguyen Duy Hinh, *De Tham*, pp. 51–96.
89. CXL-3, pp. 263–271.

sistance units retreating into China were not allowed to return, and Ton That Thuyet was ordered to shift his residence to the vicinity of Canton.[90] By the time Governor General Paul Doumer arrived in Indochina in February 1897, the Can Vuong movement was a thing of the past. His massive administrative and financial reforms would coincide with the emergence of a new generation of anticolonial leaders.

Taken collectively, what was significant about the Can Vuong? From our vantage point eighty years later, it obviously was doomed to failure, if success is taken to mean ejection of the French and the revival of a strong monarchist ethic amidst modernizing conditions. The Can Vuong movement was never national in scope, even among the scholar-gentry class alone. It was a mass movement only at times and in rather restricted locations. Elitist leaders mobilized the local peasantry more for common soldiering and logistical backup than for the provision of comprehensive intelligence on the enemy or impressive political response and support. There was no thought of generating anything that could be labeled revolutionary. In short, this apparent minority of the scholar-gentry acted as their idealistic ethic instructed, and some peasants loyally followed, as they had in resistance against the Chinese in previous centuries. But the French were not the Chinese. Since the Can Vuong leaders were not irrational mystics, most of them, after the first barrages from modern French cannon and rifles, appreciated that the balance of forces was completely against them.

Yet they did fight on to eventual death or capture. In the material sense their struggle was rather foolish. And certainly very few Frenchmen ever quite understood what it was all about, to their ultimate misfortune. The Can Vuong movement provided crucial moral and spiritual continuity to the long struggle against this new foreign invader. Many of the more sensitive Can Vuong leaders, acutely aware that they almost surely would die violent deaths long before their country was liberated, paid self-conscious attention to their personal images as patriots in the eyes of the people—including the yet unborn. The patriotic poems, anecdotes, and narratives that spread during their resistance and after their deaths were in many ways historical reality in themselves, quite apart from their objective truth or falsity. The impact of poetry in particular was more real than anything conveyed by this page. And as we shall see, the next generation came to maturity amidst this turmoil. Whether later they were sympathetic to or skeptical of Can Vuong efforts, the positions they argued and the actions they took were in large part conditioned by the tactical failures and the spiritual successes of their predecessors.

90. CXL–3, pp. 274, 285, 293.

Chapter Four

Người sao làm chủ hoàn cầu
Ta sao nô lệ cúi đầu làm tôi?

Why do they rule the world,
While we bow our heads as slaves?

(*Cáo Hủ Lậu Văn*, 1905)

A Generation of Lasts and Firsts

As Can Vuong leaders one by one acted out the last proud scenes in a traditional drama of loyalty and resistance, their sons, nephews, and younger cousins were growing up in a world increasingly dominated by the French provincial administrator, or résident, his local French police and military lieutenants, and his bevy of ingratiating mandarins. This more than anything else set them apart from their elders. By 1900 the French colonial government considered the "pacification of Indochina" accomplished, according to official plan. "Administratively," as one French commentator has stated, "Vietnamese patriotism was dead, and those who rose against us were mere 'outlaws.' "[1]

For all the massive alterations in political environment, changes in basic Vietnamese living patterns and attitudes, came much more slowly and selectively. The new generation, born largely between 1860 and 1885, was raised on the traditional Confucian Four Books and Five Classics (Tu-Thu Ngu-Kinh), aspired to the traditional success in examinations, and intended also—at least initially—to pursue careers in the mandarinate.

I have alluded already to the educational system crafted with such care by the Nguyen dynasty before 1885. In north and central Vietnam this system was hardly touched by the French before the first decades of the twentieth century. For their initial training young men there continued to rely on their fathers and relatives, and then later perhaps on nearby literate landlords, teachers, and retired officials. After five or ten years of studying basic classical forms, the most promising students were funneled into official district, prefectural, and provincial schools.[2] There, under

1. Pierre Dabezies, *Forces Politiques au Viet-Nam,* p. 117.
2. Unlike in China, independent gentry and clan schools do not seem to have played

the stern eyes of the appropriate educational mandarin, teen-age Vietnamese students would patiently memorize up to a thousand poems (tho), a hundred or more poetic essays (phu), and perhaps fifty dissertations or commentaries (van sach). If a student was particularly industrious, he could seek out quotations from highly rated contemporary scholars, such as the poetry of the late King Tu Duc. Given the strains of quick recollection, (as opposed to comprehension), it apparently was not uncommon for candidates to smuggle into their examination tents scraps of paper containing phrases likely to be of use no matter what questions might be specified by the proctors.[3]

Such official schools received their teaching materials from the court, which, in turn, acquired most of its original texts from China. At least, this had been the case while Vietnam was recognized as a vassal of the Middle Kingdom; indeed, one of the functions of the periodic tribute missions had been to solicit prized texts of one kind or another.[4] After 1885, however, there were no more tributary missions. While Chinese merchants appear to have filled the continuing demand for Chinese texts, we may presume that the court at Hue exercised much less control over this traffic than it once had. This fact assumes more importance when one comes to assessing the impact of reformist writings imported from China at the turn of the century, writings potentially subversive in content and destined to spark major intellectual changes in Vietnam.

South Vietnam (Cochinchina) provided a partial but significant deviation from the patterns described above. Elite families choosing to remain there after 1867 had to prosper or perish by forming new economic relationships with their foreign overlords, usually in land development, the colonial civil service, or urban commerce. With traditional exams discontinued and good Confucian teachers extremely scarce, those families with continuing classical inclinations and the necessary money generally imported teachers for their children from central or north Vietnam. For example, Nguyen Quang Dieu (1880–1936), a southern activist in the Dong Du movement after 1907, studied Chinese with his father until he was ten, shifted to *quoc-ngu* (romanized script) until he was fifteen, and

---

significant roles in elite education. Alexander Woodside, "Vietnam and the Chinese Institutional Model," p. 234.

3. VT, pp. 29–30. The author also mentions that Phan Boi Chau, whom I follow subsequently in some detail, was punished at one examination because a friend of his, knowing Phan had not memorized certain texts, slipped a few sheets of paper into the folds of his rolled-up tent.

4. Woodside, "Vietnam and the Chinese," pp. 171–173, 369–370. The author argues that this general reliance on official book traffic may have been one reason why the scholar-gentry in Vietnam seldom got wind of major literary debates under way in China.

finally undertook serious classical studies after that with a *tu-tai*[5] recipient brought in from the north. He did not drop his traditional studies until he became an activist in the Dong Du movement.[6]

Such efforts to sustain traditional learning were significant and appear to have continued in numerous Mekong delta localities until at least the first decade of the twentieth century. By then, the raison d'être of such study was unclear even for the most traditionalist and monarchist of southern Vietnamese. The result was an educational vacuum, Chinese and *nom* (demotic) characters losing their significance but not yet being replaced by either the French language or even *quoc-ngu* until after World War I.[7] Together with a serious decay of village social organization in south Vietnam, this lapse in rural education and moral guidance would provide fertile ground for the development of various messianic and chiliastic movements.

The necessity here of positing the south as an exception to the remainder of the country points up one of the overwhelming tragedies confronting this younger generation as the nineteenth century came to an end. Vietnamese society was moving rapidly from a traditional regional separation (north, center, and south) evidenced mainly in varied linguistic accents and settlement patterns to a new, more rigid foreign-enforced separation based above all on economic advantage to the colon and political expediency for the French administration. After 1867 it was quite difficult for Vietnamese to circulate in and out of south Vietnam. Until the *Duy Tan Hoi* (Reformation Society), after 1903, made herculean efforts to reestablish contact with elements of the southern elite, there was an increasing dichotomy and mutual ignorance, with two segments of an entire generation of Vietnamese being cut off from each other. Then, between north and central Vietnam after 1885 the same thing began to develop, although it never approached the extent of the separation from the south. Governor General Doumer took the decisive administrative step in 1897 when he abolished the office of viceroy of Tonkin, a Vietnamese mandarinal position, and made the French résident supérieur in Hanoi the sole "representative" of the Hue court in the north. Adminis-

5. A scholar who had passed three of four portions of the regional exams, often translated "bachelor."
6. Nguyen Van Hau, *Chi Si Nguyen Quang Dieu*, pp. 27–34.
7. In and around Saigon *quoc-ngu* took hold three or four decades earlier, being used especially by the Catholic community, native civil servants, and others doing direct business with the French. Milton E. Osborne, "Rule and Response," pp. 252–253, quotes an 1886 election pamphlet in *quoc-ngu*, worked up by a candidate for the Colonial Council. At first sight this might indicate a broad reading audience for *quoc-ngu*, until we remember that the Colonial Council had an extremely limited, essentially elitist constituency.

trative distinctions arranged by the French between Tonkin, Annam, and Cochinchina eventually altered Vietnamese social, economic, political, and educational patterns greatly, something this new generation was the first to sense—and to fear.

In passing, it should be pointed out that all the divisive restrictions, all the subsequent worry about retaining ethnic unity, ironically, affected the foreigner as much as the Vietnamese in the end, in that the foreigner actually came to believe in the divisions and argued his legitimacy on that basis. The French would dwell lovingly, for example, on the supposed quaint backwardness, the natural simplicity of the "Annamite" as contrasted with the suave sophistication of the Saigonese or the oxlike toughness of the Tonkinese. Such myths of differentiation became increasingly important as native political challenges to colonial rule intensified in the twentieth century. They were a prime rationale for sustained French presence, for the job of "mediating" regional differences, of providing the necessary order among implicitly divisive native principalities.[8] Long after events had established otherwise, the foreigner would continue to insist on his responsibility to save the Vietnamese from themselves.

What sorts of new political differentiation did the Vietnamese face by the turn of the century? In terms of laws, financial manipulations, economic and commercial development, and the like, there is an extensive literature in Western languages.[9] Cochinchina was dominated by the Colonial Council, surely one of the most overt instruments of private aggrandizement any colony has ever seen.[10] Doumer's reforms put a crimp in the council's prerogatives, but really did little to check the increasing power of a small set of French functionaries, planters, and merchants in Cochinchina. Meanwhile, in Annam and Tonkin around 1900 the most startling feature was the drastic new tax and corvée system instituted by Doumer, first to eliminate the colony's heavy budgetary reliance on Paris and later to enable construction of modern railroads, roads, bridges, harbors, and hydraulic works. It is here ironic, yet somehow fitting, that Paul Doumer, the man who "rationalized" Indochina's financial and administrative system, by the very same acts also sowed the seeds of eventual mass peasant participation in anticolonial movements. This last scholar-gentry generation would see and write vividly about the impact on the

8. See for example, Albert Sarraut, *Grandeur et servitude coloniale* (Paris, 1931), p. 266.
9. See in particular Paul Isoart, *Le phénomène national vietnamien*, pp. 126–139, 165–209. Joseph Buttinger, *Viet-Nam*, pp. 3–43, 56–62. Charles Robequain, *The Economic Development of French Indo-china.*
10. Paul Doumer, *L'Indo-Chine française: Souvenirs* (Paris, 1903), p. 85. Philippe Devillers, *Histoire du Viet-Nam de 1940 à 1952* (Paris, 1952), p. 33.

Vietnamese peasant of Doumer's drastically widened monopolies of the production and sale of salt, alcohol, and opium, his expansion of local customs tariffs, and the increasingly arbitrary utilization of corvée for public-works projects.[11]

Of more than passing importance also to that scholar-gentry generation was the virtual revolution in patterns of land ownership. I have already mentioned that many landowners in the south returned to their villages after 1863 or 1867, only to find Frenchman or French-protected Vietnamese in irreversible custody of their property.[12] After that the entire land development operation in south Vietnam was rigged in favor of French concessionaires and the wealthiest Vietnamese collaborators. In north and central Vietnam after the collapse of the Can Vuong movement there were similar rude shocks to many, both resister and refugee, as they filtered back to their home villages, although the total impact did not seem as great in these regions because the expropriation occurred at different times in different provinces. And, when French or native colonial units pursued De Tham and the various Chinese bands operating in Yen-The and the upper Red River valley, masses of peasants either fled or were forced, as part of the French pacification strategy, to leave their home districts. Failing even with this to put an end to the resistance, the colonial administration encouraged European planters to take over ownership of the vacated lands and bring in contract laborers from distant towns and provinces. By 1898 there was a land-grabbing rush in the midlands of Tonkin, the governor general again taking advantage of traditional Vietnamese royal land prerogatives to parcel out vast permanent concessions to private Frenchmen, based on French private land law.[13]

In less spectacular but equally significant manner, the degeneration of royal administrative and judicial authority at the district level in north

11. Whether the public works projects that Doumer instituted were of much benefit to the mass of Vietnamese peasants has been the subject of an extended polemical debate, important to an understanding of political attitudes after 1920, but not of direct relevance here. See Robequain, *Economic Development,* Anh Van and Jacqueline Roussel, *Mouvements Nationaux et Lutte de classes au Viet-Nam,* pp. 17–32. Jean Chesneaux, *Contributions à l'histoire de la Nation Vietnamienne,* pp. 159–182. Buttinger, *Viet-Nam,* pp. 26–43. Pham Cao Duong, *Thuc Trang cua gioi Nong Dan Viet-Nam, duoi thoi Phap thuoc,* pp. 171–227.
12. Pham Cao Duong, *Thuc Trang,* pp. 53–56. Le Thanh Khoi, *Le Viet-Nam, Histoire et Civilisation* (Paris, 1955), p. 409.
13. The traditional Vietnamese ideal had been one of temporary private usage of public lands. Pham Cao Duong, *Thuc Trang,* pp. 57–70. For an ambitious plot to eject the French in late 1897 of Vietnamese plantation workers, led by a young student returned from France, see Do Thien, "Phong trao Ky-Dong nam 1897." Also AOM, A-50 NF 599.

and central Vietnam after 1885 allowed the more ambitious Vietnamese families—and even strangers—to grab public lands in and around hundreds of villages, often in league with local mandarins or local Catholic priests. As public lands moved gradually into private hands (often on an unwritten basis in order to avoid the occasional French investigations and the rare attempts to halt this development), the poorer peasant landowners found themselves going increasingly into debt and, almost inevitably, into the status of full or partial tenants.[14] This process was only beginning in 1900, but the new generation of anticolonial leaders quickly sensed what was happening. By 1906 and 1907 some of them were launching open political attacks on such take-overs.

For all the above, there was something else that stabbed at the vitals of this generation more than any apparent material considerations. The scholar-gentry, while obviously wielding considerable economic power at the local level, was a traditional elite that conceived of itself primarily in intellectual and moral terms. The crucial issue to divide this new generation would be their proper relationship to French colonial rule. The majority of the young elite would react to the colonial threats to their social status and economic position, to French legalism and rigid tax collection procedures, by actively collaborating with the foreigner, as had many of their elders. And their political powers as local mediators, as molders of local attitudes, often were not immediately decreased by such a posture. Among themselves, on the other hand, they had extreme difficulty in rationalizing their collaboration in terms of their proud intellectual and moral heritage. This problem was heightened by the relative political sophistication of Confucianism, which is to say that serious students of the classics only with great difficulty could retain illusions about who really held power in Vietnam in the last years of the nineteenth century. Hence scholar-gentry collaborators were extremely vulnerable to savage intellectual and moral attacks from the minority of their peers who were willing, to a greater or lesser degree, to jeopardize their immediate positions in favor of some future goal, some dream that allowed them above all to retain their self-conceptions of individual purity. For this minority, certain traditional maxims would assume ever more poignant significance: "risk death to do a man's work"; "sacrifice life to defend righteousness"; "in such conditions, if we don't act, who will?"[15]

These men, who are the special objects of the remainder of this study (as distinct from the larger number of scholar-gentry that privately sympathized with them and the members of other classes who participated

14. Pham Cao Duong, *Thuc Trang,* pp. 74–83.
15. VT, pp. 10–11.

actively only on occasion) probably never numbered more than several hundred. Nevertheless, they had two extremely powerful weapons: individual moral principle which existed as a political force and the Vietnamese heritage of resistance to foreign servitude. They were acutely aware that, while their material positions might be destroyed in the process of anticolonial endeavor, their status, both among their peers and among the people, could hardly suffer, since they were operating from a time-honored, sanctioned position of the morally righteous. This implied moral covenant, not mere deference to political or economic position, was the basis for whatever trust and respect the peasantry offered the scholar-gentry. Particularly in times of great crisis, the people looked to the scholar-gentry as the "soul" (*linh hon*), the spiritual locus of society.[16] If they lived up to their demanding stipulations, fine; if not, their legitimacy was quickly suspect. Those who were seen to place their own prerogatives ahead of the common interest found their moral authority draining away. By the time the anticolonial minority of the scholar-gentry had grown old and given way to others, they had succeeded—at the very least—in demolishing among the people the lingering sense of respect and legitimacy granted to collaborating scholar-gentry. Given France's continuing need for native elite participation in the colonial system, this in itself was a momentous accomplishment.

By and large, members of this generation were making their personal decisions between the majority and minority positions from 1900 to 1905. What influenced them? The following brief descriptions of the early lives of certain minority figures may provide a few clues.

Phan Boi Chau (1867–1940)

Towering above all is the figure of Phan Boi Chau, born in 1867 of relatively poor scholar-gentry parents in Nghe-An province.[17] His first three years were spent in his mother's village of Sa-Nam, whose history dated back to the T'ang period. After that the family all was able to live in his father's village of Dan-nhiem, Nam-Dan district. His *tu-tai* father often being away teaching in other villages, however, it was Phan's mother who was careful to instill in him the Confucian virtues; she apparently

---

16. VTCM, pp. 24–25.
17. VNDN, pp. 267–271. LT, pp. 508–509. Originally he was named Phan Van San and was often called Giai San after he passed the regional exams with highest honors. Later he used the pseudonyms Phan Sao Nam, Phan Thi Han, and was given the courtesy name of Hai Thu. For a recent translation into French of TP and NB, see Phan Boi Chau, "Mémoires," *France-Asie/Asia* 194–195, pp. 3–210. Translation, annotation, and indexing by Georges Boudarel.

provided a high degree of parental devotion until her death in 1884 when Phan was seventeen. By age five Phan was being allowed to attend his father's classes, using banana leaves in place of paper to practice the *Three-Character Classic* (*San-tzu ching*; in Vietnamese, *Tam-Tu Kinh*) and *Analects* (*Lun Yu*; *Luan Ngu*). In his autobiography Phan admitted to not having understood much of the meaning in early years, but at the age of six he was literate enough to get a thrashing from his father for scribbling a little parody of his fellow pupils.[18]

In 1874 Phan and his young classmates, observing local scholar-gentry resistance to Tu Duc's current peace policies, themselves constructed "guns" of bamboo in order to participate in "driving out the Westerner." Hue was sufficiently shocked by scholar-gentry attitudes and activities in Nghe-An and Ha-Tinh to move in troops to crush all hints of local mobilization.[19] While Phan's family was spared direct harm, the young boy was deeply moved by the whole affair. By the time Phan was thirteen his father wanted him to shift to a more prestigious teacher. Lacking money to send Phan any distance, he arranged for Phan to study with a local *cu-nhan* who was able to borrow a range of books from wealthier families in the area. Word of new French attacks and general disorder in north Vietnam in 1883 led Phan to compose an anonymous proclamation calling for mobilization of local units to send against the French, which he posted at various points along the main road. To his chagrin, nobody paid much attention, and in a few days the proclamations had been torn down. The next year his mother died, and Phan began helping his father with the teaching chores.

July 1885 was a month to change all lives in Nghe-An, what with Ham Nghi's flight from Hue, the proclamation of the Can Vuong Edict, the mobilization of local scholar-gentry, and the quick arrival of the first French units in that province. Phan and sixty other young men studying for the exams organized a "candidates' corps" (*Thi-sinh-quan*), sought out an older *cu-nhan* graduate as commander, and had just reached the point of collecting money and materials for weapons when a French patrol arrived and blasted the village. Almost all the members of the candidates' corps panicked completely, while Phan's father ordered him to run to the commander and ask that membership rolls be destroyed. From

18. TP, pp. 19–20.
19. Dang Huy Van, "Ve cuoc khoi nghia cua Tran Tan va Dang Nhu Mai nam Giap Tuat o Nghe An va Ha Tinh." Also Truong Buu Lam, *Patterns of Vietnamese Response to Foreign Intervention: 1858–1900*, pp. 106–107, for translation of an outspoken scholar-gentry memorial from Nghe-An/Ha-Tinh, drawn from Dang Huy Van, "Them mot so tai lieu ve cuoc khoi nghia nam Giap Tuat (1874) o Nghe An va Ha Tinh," pp. 13–14.

these early experiences Phan says he learned: (1) people don't listen to those without a scholastic degree and (2) the largest part of bravery is in the long, slow nourishment of a scheme, not the final, bold action.[20]

The experience must indeed have been unsettling, since Phan admits to having avoided anticolonial activism for another twelve years. More important to his inactivity perhaps was the practical fact that he was the only male heir in a family that had suffered this hereditary misfortune for four generations. With his father ill and requiring support, and he himself lacking heirs for the moment, it would have been surprising for him to follow any other course. His primary loyalties were still in many ways particular—father, family, degree—and these all dictated that he would not—could not—involve himself in open resistance. Nevertheless, during the years of study and teaching, he did seek out and copy ancient Chinese and Vietnamese books on military strategy and quietly selected from his many students a couple whose anticolonial sentiments seemed to run especially deep. He savored the tales of occasional Can Vuong visitors and passed them along to his students—particularly those stories concerning Phan Dinh Phung.[21]

From the time he was young, Phan Boi Chau loved folk singing, especially the form of semicompetitive, extemporaneous rounds (*phuong vai*) that were exchanged between groups of men and women. Many of these concerned simple amusement and village courtship, but themes of glory and patriotism were certainly not lacking. Indeed, the Nghe An and Ha Tinh people felt themselves on intimate terms with history and the ghosts of bygone struggles.[22] Some of their heroes had fought victoriously— perhaps more had left their blood on the land. Each, however, had received a shrine and some commemoration in song. Phan's later literary efforts would be deeply influenced, both in content and in form, by this local heritage.[23]

In several unspecified years Phan appears to have failed the regional

20. TP, pp. 21–23.
21. Although reading was directed primarily at preparing for exams, Phan's students also probably gave attention to the works of such historic Vietnamese luminaries as Nguyen Trai, Le Thanh Tong, Nguyen Binh Khiem, Le Quy Don, Doan Thi Diem, Nguyen Huy Tu, Nguyen Du, Ho Xuan Huong, and Nguyen Cong Tru. VT, p. 48.
22. There is a regional saying: *Thanh cay the, Nghe cay than* (Thanh Hoa relies on worldly events, Nghe An relies on spirits of the past). In other words, Thanh Hoa was the land of kings and princely ambitions, while Nghe An (and Ha-Tinh, long a subordinate part) lived on memories, perseverance and, implicitly, orthodox idealism. As one example of how this worked, some aging scholar-gentry of Nghe An in the first decades of the twentieth century were still referring to Ham Nghi's reign period for their calendar dating. VT, pp. 39, 44.
23. VT, pp. 54–56.

exams (*huong-thi*). Perhaps for this reason, in 1897 at the age of thirty he traveled to Hue to teach, to "improve his contacts," and to receive some special training before trying again. At Hue he made friends quickly, including Dang Nguyen Can (Thai Son)[24] and Nguyen Thuong Hien (Mai Son)[25] who would be associated with him for the remainder of their active political existence. Nguyen Thuong Hien, in fact, introduced him to the unpublished writings of the Vietnamese reformist Nguyen Lo Trach.[26] This was Phan's first exposure to the proposals for self-strengthening, made during Tu Duc's reign, and his first intellectual contact with major political and military developments in the modern world beyond Vietnam.

Returning to Nghe An in 1900, Phan passed the regional exams with highest honors (*giai nguyen*). Several months later his father died at the age of sixty-nine, and Phan felt sufficiently released from his familial obligations to embark, along with several of his students, on the one-way road of covert anticolonial activism.[27] This was also the time—specifically, from 1901 to 1904—that Phan sought out and read copies of works by the Chinese reformist Liang Ch'i-ch'ao, including *Wu-hsu cheng-pien, Chung-kuo hun,* and issues of the periodical *Hsin-min ts'ung-pao.*[28]

Phan Chu Trinh (1872–1926)

Next in stature after Phan Boi Chau stands Phan Chu Trinh,[29] born in 1872 to a wealthy scholar-gentry family of Tay-Loc village, Tien-Phuoc district, Quang Nam province. Phan's father studied for the exams but apparently never passed, instead becoming a fairly high-ranking military official. Phan's mother died soon after bearing him, the last of three boys. His early education seems to have been erratic, partly because his father did not arrange it smoothly, partly because Phan displayed little interest

24. 1867–1923. LT, pp. 505–506. VNDN, pp. 49–50.
25. 1865–1925. LT, p. 487. VNDN, pp. 225–226.
26. 1852–1895. Strongly influenced by the memorials of Nguyen Truong To and the self-strengthening literature of China, he wrote along similar lines from 1877 to 1892, rather too late to have done much good at court but still of considerable influence on the next generation. Anh Minh, ed., *Nguyen Lo Trach.* HT, pp. 186–190. LT, p. 500.
27. TP, pp. 23–29.
28. TP, p. 50. Later, in a 1905 letter of self-introduction to Liang Ch'i-ch'ao, Phan wrote that he had been reading Liang's works for a decade. This is most likely poetic license. TP, p. 52. Chuong Thau, "Anh huong cach mang Trung Quoc doi voi su bien chuyen cua tu tuong Phan Boi Chau," pp. 13–14. To Minh Trung, "Gop y kien voi ong Chuong Thau ve bai 'Anh huong cach mang Trung-quoc voi su chuyen bien tu tuong cua Phan Boi Chau," p. 52.
29. Sometimes written Phan *Chau* Trinh. Later pseudonyms of Hi Ma and Tay Ho. VNDN, pp. 271–273. LT, p. 479.

in the Chinese classics. In early 1885 his father started him on a training program in the military arts (*vo*), and, with Ham Nghi's flight to the mountains some months later, Phan found himself at the age of thirteen helping his father prepare the defense of a fort in Tam-Ky district of his home province. Within a short while, they too were forced to flee into the mountains, where his father was killed by fellow Can Vuong participants under suspicious circumstances.[30]

Now an orphan and deeply affected by the disastrous events around him, Phan Chu Trinh in 1887 left the hills where his father had died and returned to find their house burned down and their belongings destroyed. Fortunately, one of his elder brothers took matters in hand and started Phan on a four-year basic program of Chinese studies with a local scholar. He seems to have learned very rapidly, moving on to more advanced teachers at the age of twenty and again the next year. His late introduction to the Chinese classics may be one reason that he read them critically, favoring the *Analects* and Mencius and discarding just about everything else except perhaps the *Spring and Autumn Annals* (*Ch'un Ch'iu*; *Xuan Thu*), *Book of History* (*Shu Ching*; *Thu Kinh*), and *Book of Poetry* (*Shih Ching*; *Thi Kinh*). Beyond this instruction there was the influence of foreign commercial activity in nearby Da-Nang, which made all of Quang-Nam an intellectually more stimulating, contradictory place than Phan Boi Chau's home province of Nghe-An.

Phan Chu Trinh attempted the regional exams at twenty-two and at twenty-five, each time failing and returning to study with well known teachers. In 1899 he was allowed to prepare at the provincial academy, which apparently altered his fortunes, since he graduated third in the 1900 regional exams and in the next year passed the metropolitan exams (*hoi-thi*) on the second roster (*pho-bang*).[31]

Successful metropolitan scholars were normally next expected to spend several leisurely years in the various court ministries, ingratiating themselves with their superiors and forming political links which might last a lifetime. Those young men most successful in this polite but intense infighting were likely to be picked early as district magistrates (*tri-huyen*),

30. The Nguyen, *Phan Chu Trinh*. The author indicates than Phan's father was killed by other Can Vuong leaders, but does not elaborate. To Minh Trung, "Chu-nghia cai-luong Phan Chu Trinh," p. 31, states that Phan's father was killed as a suspected traitor. If so, this may help account for Phan Chu Trinh's later refusal to ally with remnant Can Vuong elements, not to mention his lifelong antipathy to violence and his general position as a loner rather than an organization man. Huynh Thuc Khang, *Phan Tay Ho Tien Sinh Lich Su*, pp. 9, 11. This may be the most reliable source on Phan's early life, but it does not explain the death of Phan's father.
31. Huynh Thuc Khang, *Phan Tay Ho*, p. 12. The Nguyen, *Phan Chu Trinh*, pp. 12–15.

positions admittedly of decreased political power after 1885 but still with some social prestige and definite economic benefits for the lucky families involved. It was at this point, however, that Phan Chu Trinh and a whole set of contemporaries decided to break out of the pattern—not simply in the traditional fashion of retreating to one's village to teach, but instead by launching a full-scale political assault on the mandarin system. For Phan this shift took several years. He began, interestingly enough, by refusing to participate in the innovative French-language study program at the new Quoc-Hoc college, pleading that he was overage. Assigned to some meaningless position at court, he went for months without showing up at his office. Then his elder brother died, causing Phan to return home for one year. Coming back again to Hue in 1903 at the Ministry of Rites (*Le Bo*), his way was clear for full-scale introduction to Western learning through the medium of Chinese reformist sources and a decision in 1904 to break completely with the mandarin system.[32]

Following men of Phan Boi Chau's and Phan Chu Trinh's stature are several score scholar-gentry who can be readily identified by name, but for whose activities prior to 1903 data is sadly lacking at present. As a means of rounding out the picture of this generation in its formative stages, however, I will introduce information on seven other individuals whose early lives are at least not complete ciphers.

Nguyen Thanh (1863–1911)

One of the oldest on the list was Nguyen Thanh,[33] born in 1863 in Thanh-My village, Thang-Binh prefecture (*phu*), Quang Nam. His father was a high mandarin during Tu Duc's reign. Nguyen Thanh in reality represents something of an intergenerational figure, since he was on his way to take his regional exams in 1885 when the fighting in Hue preliminary to Ham Nghi's departure led him to join a local resistance group.[34] Later in 1885 he was one of Ham Nghi's military appointees (with Nguyen Duy Hieu) for the Quang Nam/Quang Ngai area and is said to have fought hard enough for several years to gain the grudging respect of even his French and collaborator enemies.[35] He was permitted by the infamous Nguyen Than to return to his home village. Never resuming his

32. Huynh Thuc Khang, *Phan Tay Ho*, pp. 13–14. The Nguyen, *Phan Chu Trinh*, p. 16.
33. Also known as Nguyen Ham. Later pseudonyms of Triet Phu and Tieu La. VNDN, p. 216.
34. CMCD-1, note pp. 79–80. The Nguyen, "Chi Si Viet-Nam: Nguyen Thanh," p. 37, says that Nguyen Thanh dropped his studies in 1880 and joined a resistance group then. This seems unlikely for central Vietnam's scholar-gentry.
35. The Nguyen, "Chi Si Viet-Nam," p. 37.

quest for a scholastic degree, Nguyen Thanh instead very slowly developed contacts with the younger anticolonialists. Unlike most Can Vuong remnant figures, he would become part of the new inner circle of young militants, influencing it in a conservative direction for the first few years and remaining a member of Phan Boi Chau's apparatus until his death in prison on Con-lon island in 1911.[36]

Tran Cao Van (1866–1916)

Still another figure of significance from Quang Nam was Tran Cao Van,[37] born in 1866 in Phu-Cu village, Dien-Ban prefecture, also the home area of General Hoang Dieu, who was to die defending the Hanoi citadel in 1882.

His father apparently was of scholar-gentry background but never passed the exams, busying himself instead with supervising the raising of silkworms and rice. The first son of his father's first wife (of three wives), Tran Cao Van began formal studies at nine and was reputed by thirteen to be the village's best "capper" of parallel sentences. In 1882 his life was changed by the news that Hanoi had fallen and Hoang Dieu's body was being brought back to a nearby village for a full-dress funeral, which Tran attended. With anti-French and anti-Catholic feeling again sweeping the province, Tran by 1885 had decided that the examination path was meaningless; he took leave of his family and entered a Taoist mountain temple in Dai-Loc district. In 1888 family pressure seems to have brought him out of the temple to take the regional exams, but he failed and returned to his mountain.[38]

During all this time Tran appears not to have been only meditating, however. He used the temple as a meeting place, while a scholar friend circulated from district to district seeking contacts. One result was the arrival at his temple in 1891 of a colonial inspection party, after which Tran left for Binh-Dinh province to teach traditional geography. He was quick to acquire a local reputation for geomancy and a following of anti-French mystics and Buddhist monks. In 1898 Tran was involved in an unsuccessful local rising, fleeing westward into the hills as villages were burned by local colonial troops. Some time after that he returned quietly to his home in Quang Nam, where he was seized in 1908 as an alleged instigator of local tax protests.[39]

36. Ngo Thanh Nhan, *Ngu Hanh Son Chi Si*, pp. 50–51.
37. VNDN, pp. 321–323.
38. Hanh Son, *Cu Tran Cao Van*, pp. 9–22.
39. *Ibid.*, pp. 23–49. The author obtained much of his information from Tran Cao Van's wife.

Huynh Thuc Khang (1876–1947)

Next to Phan Boi Chau, the man we now know the most about as an individual is probably Huynh Thuc Khang,[40] mainly because he lived so long and left some autobiographical writings. Born in Thanh-Binh village, Tien Phuoc district, the same district of Quang Nam as Phan Chu Trinh, his name would be closely linked with the latter until at least 1911. Huynh's ancestors had emigrated from the north four generations earlier, his grandfather being considered a wealthy peasant and reaching the status of village elder. His father had aspired to scholastic status and married his prestigious teacher's daughter, but he nevertheless failed the exams repeatedly, finally returning to till the land and encourage his five sons in their studies. All but Huynh Thuc Khang died before reaching their prime, leaving Huynh to carry the family colors alone. This he did in admirable fashion, having begun formal studies at the age of seven (1883) and followed his two older brothers as they were taught by first one teacher then another.

Events from 1885 to 1887 had a dramatic impact on Huynh's village and family, his elder brothers fleeing back from Hue where they had been preparing to take exams, and his maternal grandfather turning down repeated scholar-gentry appeals to accept leadership of the local Can Vuong effort. Instead the old man taught the Chinese *Book of Poetry* to his grandchildren.[41] To no avail, however, since colonial troops on operations against the Can Vuong in 1887 chose to ruin his house anyway. The bulk of Huynh's family had fled into the nearby hills, while their grandfather had elected to remain in the lowlands and was hence suspected of collaboration; he seems to have escaped punishment from Can Vuong leaders only because so many of them had been his pupils. Returning from several months in the hills, Huynh's family first survived near-starvation, only to be felled in province-wide epidemics of plague and smallpox. Huynh lost an older brother, an older sister, a younger sister, and a brother-in-law. As can be imagined, he would recall this period with particular poignancy in his autobiography fifty years later.[42]

Amidst this turmoil, traditional patterns nevertheless reasserted themselves, and Huynh was soon deeply engrossed in classical studies. It was what his family wished, and we may assume that it was a source of humdrum order and comfort to a boy increasingly troubled by evidence of change beyond his village hedges. In his autobiography he recalled warmly the backgrounds and reputations of each of his teachers, as he worked

40. Pseudonyms of Minh Vien and Su Binh Tu. VNDN, p. 89.
41. Huynh Thuc Khang, *Tu Truyen*, pp. 9–13.
42. *Ibid.*, pp. 13–17.

his way toward the regional exams. Often he watched the ritual of candidates' signing up for local exams. At the tender age of sixteen he was himself screened and permitted to travel to take regional exams in Hue, achieving momentary fame by passing all but one section. Soon he became a close friend of Phan Chu Trinh and other lifelong associates, while studying under the same teachers and traveling to take exams at the same time. He was married in 1895 and remembered the years between 1896 and 1899 at the provincial academy with a real fondness, emotionally and intellectually stimulating, yet in retrospect the end of an era, the last stand of an entire way of life. Huynh particularly recalled that from 1894 to 1900 none of his contemporaries, or even any of the court mandarins he met, ever mentioned or seemed aware of the Sino-Japanese War, a clear indication of their isolation.[43]

In 1900, at the age of twenty-four, Huynh scored highest among the forty-two who passed all portions of the regional exams. By then it had become normal procedure to order young *cu-nhan* graduates to Hue for French-language studies, but Huynh's father opposed this successfully in favor of his remaining home to prepare for the metropolitan exams. That same year, however, his father died; and this, plus a half-year of his own serious illness, postponed Huynh's candidacy until 1904. A resounding success, he scored first in the metropolitan exams and fourth in the palace exams (*dinh-thi*).[44] It was not until 1904 that Huynh gained access to several books by the Chinese reformists Liang Ch'i-ch'ao and his mentor, K'ang Yu-wei—an intellectual confrontation that would change his life.[45]

Ngo Duc Ke (1878–1929)

Ngo Duc Ke[46] was born in Trao-nha village, Can-loc district, Ha-Tinh province, the son of a high court mandarin and heir to a long family tradition of wealth and leadership. Nevertheless, after passing his metropolitan exams in 1901 he elected to return home directly to teach and to study some contemporary Chinese modern learning (*tan-hoc*) texts he had acquired in Hue. He appears to have had some early contact with Phan Boi Chau, most likely through their mutual friend Dang Nguyen Can, but it was the ideas of K'ang and Liang that would make him one of the most passionate advocates of the reformist (as distinct from the activist) position, particularly in connection with educational change and

---

43. *Ibid.*, pp. 17–25.
44. His close friend Tran Quy Cap placed second at the palace (see Chapter 7).
45. Huynh Thuc Khang, *Tu Truyen*, pp. 25–26.
46. Pseudonym, Tap Xuyen. LT, p. 481. VNDN, p. 150.

scholar-gentry initiative in the opening of Vietnamese commercial enterprises.[47]

Nguyen Thuong Hien (1865–1925)

Nguyen Thuong Hien[48] would be the most prominent northerner of this generation of scholar-gentry anticolonialists. He was born in 1865[49] in Lien-bat village, Son-lang district,[50] Ha-Dong province, the son of a court minister. While still in his teens, he was married to the daughter of Ton That Thuyet. In 1884 he passed his regional exams and the next year was apparently successful in the metropolitan exams, but he was unable to take the palace exams before his father-in-law's abortive attack on the French garrison and the king's flight from the city. Nguyen Thuong Hien fled to Thanh Hoa, returning in 1892 to place second (*hoang giap*) in the palace exams—rather surprising, considering the outlaw status of his in-laws. At that time, he became quite close to the Vietnamese self-strengthener Nguyen Lo Trach, reading all of the latter's materials and participating in quiet small-group discussions with others of similar outlook. His first position, an appointment in the Historical Bureau (*Quoc Su Quan*), also probably gave him access to even more immediate Chinese works. Later he was appointed doc-hoc (education commissioner) of Ninh-Binh, then again to the same position in Nam-Dinh province. Nguyen Thuong Hien met both Phan Boi Chau and Phan Chu Trinh at a rather early date; it was he, as I have mentioned, who showed Phan Boi Chau the writings of Nguyen Lo Trach. Yet, while he undoubtedly shared some of their sentiments, it was not until the removal of King Thanh Thai by the French in 1907 that he resigned his position and escaped to join Phan Boi Chau and Cuong De in Japan.[51]

Nguyen Quyen (1869–1941)

Born of scholar-gentry parentage in Thuong-tri village, Thuan-thanh district, Bac-Ninh province, Nguyen Quyen[52] is mainly remembered for his having been principal of the Dong Kinh Nghia Thuc School in 1907. He was ranked *tu-tai* in the regional exams and subsequently appointed *huan-dao* (education officer) of Lang-son prefecture. Vi Van Ly, seventy-

---

47. HT, p. 551.
48. Pseudonyms, Mai Son, Dinh Than. Also known as Doc Nam, from his position as *doc-hoc* of Ninh-Binh and Nam-Dinh provinces. LT, p. 487. VNDN, pp. 225–226.
49. Some sources say 1868.
50. Now Ung-hoa district.
51. HT, pp. 472–474, 495. Anh Minh, ed., *Nguyen Lo Trach*, pp. 9, 48–51.
52. Sometimes known as Huan Quyen, for his position as *huan-dao* (educational officer of a prefecture) of Lang-Son. VNDN, p. 212.

year-old scion of a Chinese immigrant family with long hereditary authority in that area bestowed by the Nguyen dynasty, had requested a huan-dao via the French résident, but, since the highlands had very few students preparing for exams, it must have been more for the prestige than anything else. As it turned out, the lack of things to do led Nguyen Quyen to spend most of his time reading. Lang-Son being very near the border, he quickly came upon Chinese translations of Western works and the publications of K'ang Yu-wei and Liang Ch'i-ch'ao. In an interview much later in life, he particularly recalled reading *Chung-kuo hun* and *Ch'un chi chuan chieh lun* and becoming quite excited, sometimes forgetting to eat or sleep in his passion to read further:

> The more I read the more I became aware that the things we studied, our examination system, were wrong—indeed the real reasons for our having lost our country. From that point on I was determined to seize upon our country's literature and on modern learning to awaken our citizenry.[53]

Shortly after this, probably in 1903 or early 1904, Nguyen Quyen met Tang Bat Ho, who had recently returned from extensive travels overseas, listening in fascination to his stories of the modernization efforts well under way in Japan. In late 1904 he met Phan Boi Chau, then en route to Japan. But Nguyen Quyen had already decided in his own mind that the development of popular education should come before all schemes of violent uprising. Soon he would be in contact with Luong Van Can, Le Dai, and other men of similar persuasion.[54]

Nguyen Than Hien (1856-1914)

Nguyen Than Hien[55] should be regarded as the most important southerner in this generation of anticolonialists, even though he was somewhat older than the rest. His family was of considerable renown in Ha-Tien province; in the last years of Nguyen dynastic control in the south his father served as a district magistrate in Vinh-Long and then as governor (*tuan phu*) of Ha Tien. According to a still extant family register (*gia-pha*), Nguyen Than Hien was a quick student of the classics and by the age of twenty was considered to be of examination caliber. But that was already nine years after the fall of his home province to the French: taking the traditional exams meant nothing unles one was prepared to leave the south permanently for Hue or some other town to the north. Instead,

53. Dao Trinh Nhat, *Dong Kinh Nghia Thuc*, p. 9.
54. *Ibid.*, pp. 7–14.
55. Pseudonyms, Hoang Xuong, Hoi Dong Hien; the latter refers to a position he once held on a local colonial commission.

Nguyen for a time accepted appointment to one of the local colonial commissions, then resigned to develop a pepper plantation in Ha Tien. Later he moved his family to Can-Tho and developed rice fields which eventually encompassed ten hamlets in three districts.

Yet, for all his obvious involvement in the French-directed change in Cochinchina, there is abundant evidence that Nguyen Than Hien, along with many other wealthy southern landowners, retained a fierce sentimental attachment to the Nguyen dynasty, intensified perhaps by enforced separation and related historically to the extended tribulations and ultimate successes of Nguyen Anh (Gia Long) in the area one hundred years earlier. By 1900 Nguyen Than Hien had quietly forged links with men of substance and similar sentiments in other parts of western Cochinchina. He wrote a poem dedicating the remainder of his life and all his fortune to his country—signifying specifically an attempted monarchist revival throughout Vietnam.[56] Hence, one of the anachronisms of early-twentieth-century anticolonial ideology: those participants who had grown up under direct "enlightened" French colonial rule—the "Cochinchinese"—proved to be the most militant and steadfast monarchists, who in many cases clung to the idea of kingship long after it had been supplanted by the idea of republicanism among central and northern activists.

As I have mentioned, data on the early lives of other resistance individuals is extremely sparse, often being limited to year and place of birth, years in which examinations were passed, and first indications of sustained contact and cooperation with other men of anticolonial beliefs. Nevertheless, we do know that each individual spent many years in classical studies. Most attempted the exams at one time or another, the majority reaching at least *tu-tai* or *cu-nhan* status. Exceptions occurred among the younger participants, men born in the late 1870s or early 1880s, who generally spent their teens in classical studies and then broke the pattern after 1900, most of them by going overseas.

Not all the families from which this generation emerged were wealthy. A few even approached discreet poverty. But all were willing, somehow, to spare one or more sons from daily chores, to buy the ink, borrow the books, and find a string of teachers for the many years of serious scholastic preparation. Actually, more significant than economic position was the pattern of a fierce family pride that emerges in a study of these early lives, a tradition in the family of leadership, of social and political

56. Nguyen Van Hau, "Nguyen Than Hien, mot lanh tu trong yeu trong phong-trao Dong Du Mien Nam," BK 124: 9–13.

responsibility that was to be upheld by the sons and grandsons. Except in Cochinchina, parents up to the end of the nineteenth century simply assumed that the examinations were a necessity, a prerequisite to occupying significant leadership roles. Not the least of their sons' major accomplishments would be the effective denigration and destruction of the entire exam system, mostly by holding it up to public ridicule.

Why this radical change in intellectual attitude after having obeyed family instructions and followed traditional learning patterns into adulthood? After all, we have seen in the above background sketches that currents of modern thought did not really reach this generation, by and large, until after 1900, when their formative years were essentially behind them. Study of the French language was actively avoided until well into the first decade of the twentieth century, when the boredom of jail provided the final personal impetus for many. "Modern learning" would for this generation come via the Chinese language and would have tremendous impact. But what was it that made these men so receptive? What set them up in advance? Their Can Vuong predecessors had treated French penetration into their land simply as a repetition of Vietnam's historical experience with the Chinese. An entire generation of scholar-gentry had reacted according to a centuries-old scenario, whether they chose collaboration, withdrawal, or die-hard resistance. They remained smugly secure —or at least they gave that impression—that foreign domination for one or more generations, although it might involve loss of political sovereignty, was still not an ideological or cultural loss. Confucius was alive, regardless of what the barbarians said or did.

But something did change, and I think that change was perceived by the new generation in their formative years. There was an increasing awareness—often an ill-defined fear—that the French seizure involved not just the sovereignty of Vietnam, but its very soul. During their youth the chief source of this awareness was increasing public evidence of servility among the Vietnamese people at large, or more precisely the development of a subtle master-slave mentality, among both French overlords and Vietnamese subjects. Ironically, many swashbuckling French military commanders of earlier years had shown grudging respect for their Vietnamese antagonists, if only because they fought and died well, even in futility. Those early Frenchmen had been replaced, however, by more sedentary types, by garrison commanders, clusters of stuffy bougeois administrators, political hangers-on, and money-minded plantation owners, all of whom came to view the contemporary passivity of most Vietnamese as evidence of an inferior or "childlike" character. Animal or savage images began to dominate colon language regarding the Vietnamese, as for example, they started calling simple groups of people "bands" or "hordes," comparing the language with cats' meowing, and measuring the strength of peasants against that of water buffalo.[57]

However, what really hurt these young Vietnamese, these inheritors of a proud cultural tradition, was not the apparent or alleged attitudes of the French. Many of them (particularly the activists) retained an implicit image of the French as barbarians and, indeed, would have been perplexed if barbarians had not acted according to role. Rather, it was the manner in which men of their own class, the collaborator mandarins, and eventually the royal family, seemed to fall into slavelike behavior, pandering and groveling at French doors. Bad enough for interpreters, camp followers, and servants to fawn over their foreign masters, but scholar-gentry . . .! A number of those older mandarins who had resigned in disgust after 1885 retreated to their home villages and wrote poetry that was strikingly vivid in its ridicule of collaborators, in its sneering at their slavish mannerisms.[58] We know that such poems circulated far and wide, and we can assume that they were known to most members of the new generation.

As I will have occasion to point out further, the primary intellectual theme of this new anticolonial generation may be succinctly expressed in one Vietnamese compound: *mat-nuoc*. Superficially it means to lose one's country.[59] But there are at least three levels of significance, ranging from the simple loss of sovereignty, to the much more serious loss of one's ethnic identity or "soul" (which, however, may be "regained"), to the ultimate and most tragic deprivation—the physical extermination or absorption of an ethnic group.[60] I believe that this scholar-gentry generation's desperate concern with this problem and its subsequent efforts to reassert Vietnamese identity originated in the concussive events of the 1870s and 1880s, first in the physical attacks of the foreigner and their impact on individual families, but then just as substantially in the increasing evidence of moral degeneration among the majority of their own class. In this respect it is not completely accidental that six of the nine men introduced above were from central Vietnam, where the heavy shock of foreign penetration had been put off longest, but where it hit finally with

---

57. Nguyen Van Trung, *Chu Nghia Thuc Dan Phap o Viet-Nam*, pp. 63–70.
58. See, for example, certain poems of Nguyen Khuyen (1835–1909), who had previously placed first in all three levels of exam competition. He had withdrawn to his home village in 1883. HT, pp. 319–341. LT, pp. 475–476. See also the works of Nguyen Thien Ke, particularly his slashing ridicule of a district magistrate in Son-Tay who felt obliged to carry the wife and children of the French résident piggyback across a flooded area. HT, pp. 368–372. LT, pp. 497–498.
59. The Sino-Vietnamese compound is *vong-quoc*.
60. Ly Chanh Trung, "Suy nghi ve hai chu 'mat-nuoc.' "

devastating psychological effect in the Can Vuong years, during the child-hood or youth of most of them.

It should be obvious that classical Confucian pedagogy and exam preparation was not the regime most conducive to a "soft entry" into the twentieth century. The very depth of the traditional Confucian commitment intensified the trauma of adaptation or transformation. Nevertheless, we should remember and emphasize that this indoctrination was at least conducive to basic political perception, Confucianism being perhaps the most politically oriented of any historic world doctrine. Man's strengths and weaknesses as a political animal were abundantly evident to readers of the classics. In this context I have already remarked on the degree to which Can Vuong scholar-gentry gauged power realities after 1885, understanding just how marginal their chances were in temporal terms. The generation emerging after 1900 had the same basic education and hence the political sophistication that enabled them to cut through profuse French and collaborator verbalisms to a perception of where power resided, who exercised it, and how. They saw the French successfully institutionalizing the colonial presence, and they were deeply upset.[61] With servitude staring them in the face, they began searching actively outside their own traditions for alternative methods and ideas, a process that was startlingly open-ended and that has continued in many ways to the present day.

To date, most Western discussions of Vietnam's anticolonial movements have stressed either economics or ideology as prime change-producing elements. Yet, it seems evident that simple economics should have led the generation introduced here into collaboration rather than resistance. Their contemporaries who did collaborate were generously rewarded. As for ideology, access to new, unsettling foreign conceptual structures came only after these men had proceeded through the traditional learning process and had reached maturity, and also after they had been conditioned by foreign humiliations to embark on a path most of them knew to be dangerous—even deadly. New ideas would be extremely important, but they could never have been received so eagerly and have taken root without the emotional humiliation, the self-doubt that preceded them. Out of disgust and self-denigration arose in these Vietnamese a mood of critical inquiry and hopefulness.[62]

61. VTCM, pp. 43–44.
62. VTCM, pp. 48–49; 82–83.

Chapter Five

Hồn xưa dòng dõi Lạc Long,
Con nhà Nam-Việt, người trong giống vàng.
Chi-na chung một họ hàng,
Xiêm-la, Nhựt-bổn cùng làng Á-đông.

Our soul is descended from distant Lac Long,
We are children of the Vietnam house, men of
the yellow race.
China is part of the extended family,
Siam, Japan are part of the village of East Asia.

(NGUYỄN QUYỀN, *Kêu Hồn Nước,* 1907)

Phan Boi Chau's First Trip to Japan

As might be expected, the prestige of the Ch'ing dynasty suffered a rad-ical decline among the Vietnamese after 1885. France had forced the Middle Kingdom to abandon its historic suzerain/vassal relationship with Vietnam. Can Vuong pleas for assistance had been officially ignored by China, although covert support continued into the 1890s on a limited basis near the border. In the intellectual sphere we have seen that self-strength-ening proposals were advanced at Tu Duc's court, but with negligible results. In China, too, the self-strengthening movement lapsed into irre-mediable compromise with the inherited system. By the 1890s it had been replaced by the reform movement, led by men who were convinced that if their country were to survive, there was no alternative to recasting the institutions of China along the lines of the nation-states that were threatening its existence. The impact of reformist ideas on Vietnam's scholar-gentry, however, was very much delayed. This may have been due in large part to the general lapse of normal, time-honored communi-cations from the north after 1885.

Data now available is not helpful about precisely when Chinese re-formist writings first entered Vietnam. News of the precipitous rise and fall of the reformists in Peking in 1898 seems to have reached Vietnamese ears quickly, but that does not necessarily mean that they had access to the more substantial writings of men like K'ang Yu-wei and Liang Ch'i-ch'ao. I have mentioned Nguyen Quyen and Nguyen Thuong Hien in this respect, both of whom apparently had read K'ang and Liang earlier than others—probably in 1901 or 1902. By 1903 and 1904 however, evidence is definite that numerous reformist texts were available. For example, a scholar in Hue named Dao Nguyen Pho is known by that time to have purchased contemporary Chinese books, including Liang's *Wu-hsu cheng-pien* and *Chung-kuo hun*.[1] A study in Chinese of the Meiji Restoration titled *Jih-pen san-shih nien wei-hsin shih* (History of Japan's Thirty Years of Reform), apparently translated from Japanese, was also widely available.[2] And reports by Chinese scholars after inspection trips to Japan in 1902, describing in some detail that country's educational and cultural progress, had reached Vietnam, where they were painstakingly recopied.[3]

Furthermore, a number of Vietnamese sources indicate the quick availability of Liang's *Hsin-min ts'ung-pao* (The Renovation of the People), which began in Tokyo as a bimonthly periodical in 1902. Phan Boi Chau said that he read copies before leaving Vietnam in February 1905.[4] Huynh Thuc Khang remembered copies of *Hsin-min ts'ung-pao* at Dao Nguyen Pho's house in 1904 being read along with many new books by a cluster of eager young scholar-gentry, including Phan Chu Trinh.[5] Articles by Liang in 1902 issues, criticizing absolutist government, arguing for an awakening of the Chinese people's consciousness for the general advance into the modern world, and advocating development of a strong conscript army, are all known to have been recopied by the Vietnamese and, we must surmise, circulated among scholar-gentry.[6]

All such activity represented a sweeping change in intellectual and educational initiatives. As I have mentioned, the court in Hue had traditionally monopolized book traffic from China. Inside Vietnam strict restrictions had been maintained on printing and publishing. In addition, it had been common for educational mandarins at various levels (province, prefecture, district) to husband jealously the texts allotted them,

1. Huynh Thuc Khang, *Tu Truyen*, p. 26.
2. *Ibid.*, p. 26.
3. Wada Hironori, "Matsumoto Nobuhiro kyoju shorai no Betonamu shahon sanshu ni tsuite," *Shigaku*, vol. 35, no. 4 (1963), pp. 93–96. Professor Wada's careful researching of volumes at Keio Gijuku University establishes that reports of the 1902 trip by Wu Chih-fu and Ch'en T'ing-t'ai were recopied by ((unknown) Vietnamese and bound with documentary fragments of a work relating to forced labor in the thirty-fifth year of Tu Duc (1882). It has not been possible to establish the exact date of recopying, but it seems unlikely that it would be later than 1905, when Phan Boi Chau was himself in Japan sending home first-hand reports that circulated widely.
4. TP, p. 50. NB, p. 52.
5. Huynh Thuc Khang, *Tu Truyen*, p. 26. Huynh Thuc Khang, *Phan Tay Ho Tien Sinh Lich Su*, p. 14.
6. Wada Hironori, "Matsumoto," pp. 94–95. Again, dates of recopying cannot be established directly. However, it is almost certainly before Phan Boi Chau's first return from Japan (August 1905), since he brought back more current printed issues.

seldom permitting them to circulate among the local scholar-gentry.[7] Now, both the court and the educational mandarins were being impudently bypassed. A contemporary Chinese work would make its way into Vietnam, often via the local Chinese community, and it would then be assiduously transferred, copied, and recopied from province to province. Within a year or two scholar-gentry throughout north and central Vietnam had access, if they chose, to the "latest" modernizing currents among their counterparts in China. Naturally the process was not without its imperfections, as we shall see. But it remains extremely significant that, given a choice between accepting Western ideas directly from their French overlords and receiving them indirectly by way of China, these scholar-gentry figures without exception opted for the latter.

The intellectual and social implications of this Chinese Reformist thought in Vietnam will concern us more later. But I mention its infusion into Vietnamese life here before taking up the origins of the Duy Tan Hoi (Reformation Society), because it is evident that activists like Phan Boi Chau and Nguyen Thanh were also respectful readers of "modern" or "new learning" (hsin-hsueh; tan-hoc) and were influenced by it, though in ways quite different from those which K'ang and Liang might have intended.[8] When K'ang borrowed from the doctrine of Social Darwinism and spoke of the struggle for survival of the fittest among nations and ethnic groups, when he presented the Ottoman Empire and colonial India as dire examples of China's probable fate if she did not reform herself, he was penetrating to the heart of Vietnamese scholar-gentry fears, as well as giving a contemporary explanation for Vietnam's tragedy. When he suggested Peter the Great and Emperor Meiji as exemplary figures and the restructuring of political institutions as an essential prerequisite for salvation, he was helping Phan Boi Chau understand why Tu Duc had failed and why ignoring Nguyen Truong To's self-strengthening proposals had spelled doom for Vietnam. However, Phan Boi Chau and other Duy Tan Hoi activists did not share the Chinese reformists' aver-

7. Alexander Woodside, "Vietnam and the Chinese Institutional Model," pp. 294–297.
8. Vietnamese references here to "modern" or "new" learning (tan-hoc) appear to be limited to the works of K'ang, Liang, and others of their generation at the turn of the century. This should not be confused with "modern learning" (chin-wen) as a doctrinal school of Confucianism, which extended back to the Han dynasty. At this point we have no evidence on whether the Vietnamese scholar-gentry of this generation or the previous one read the Kung-yang commentary to the Spring and Autumn Annals or knew of the nineteenth-century revival of chin-wen/ku-wen debates in China. This would be an important subject for future research, aiding considerably our understanding of the intellectual antecedents to tan-hoc advocacy in the first decade of the twentieth century.

sion to violence or their continuing hopes of influencing the wielders of power at the top of their contemporary systems. Vietnam was long since under tight foreign colonial rule, not just threatened by it. Desperation was already in the air.

Phan Boi Chau's success in the regional exams and the death of his father, both in 1900, left him free to devote all his energies to planning and organizing future resistance.[9] With Dang Thai Than,[10] his most dedicated and sympathetic pupil, and a few other close comrades, Phan formulated an early three-point strategy:

1. Contact Can Vuong remnants and assorted mountain bands willing to participate in future violent efforts to expel the foreigner;
2. Seek out a titular leader (*minh-chu*)[11] among members of the royal family, and with his assistance develop secret ties at high official levels; and
3. If it becomes warranted, send persons out of the country to seek foreign assistance in restoring independence to Vietnam.[12]

None of these points was particularly original; Phan himself commented ruefully in his autobiography that there was no ideological depth behind them. And until 1903 only the first point received consistent attention, with Phan particularly using his friendship with Dao Tan, the governor (*tong doc*) of Nghe An, as an effective cover for unrestricted travel in both central and northern Vietnam.

In 1903 Phan shifted emphasis to Point 2, using the excuse of preparing for the following year's metropolitan exams to move down to Hue and sound out certain court factions and elements of the royal family. Finding most of them cowed by the French authorities, Phan traveled on to Quang Nam for his first face-to-face contact with Nguyen Thanh—a man known by his CanVuong reputation who was destined to exert tremendous influence on the tenor of the new generation's anticolonialism. Nguyen Thanh quickly proposed a royal associate of his, Ton That Toai, for consideration as titular leader. Phan, however, found him uninspiring and returned to Hue to scout the royal family again. This time he followed Nguyen Thanh's advice to concentrate on direct descendants of King Gia Long, since this line still commanded the warmest sympathy among

9. TP, p. 29. NB, p. 33.
10. Pseudonym, Ngu Hai; home village, Hai-Con, Nghi-loc district, Nghe-An. LT, p. 506. VNDN, p. 51. A 1905 poem by Dang is reprinted in VTCM, p. 260.
11. More precisely, *minh-chu* may be defined as "the person who administers an oath."
12. NB, p. 33. TP, p. 29.

wealthy Mekong delta landowners, among whom they hoped to raise the bulk of their war chest.[13]

By March or April 1903 they had come up with an excellent and willing choice—Prince Cuong De, direct descendant of Gia Long's eldest son, Canh, who had been crown prince until his death of smallpox in 1801. Custom normally would have made Canh's eldest son the next crown prince, but Gia Long eventually settled on his own fourth son, who took the name of Minh Mang upon acceding to the throne in 1820. Prince Canh's line, however, never had reconciled themselves to this. Throughout the nineteenth century and right up to the time of Cuong De, it is possible to trace a thread of court intrigues and punishments stemming from Gia Long's decision. Cuong De's father, for example, had been approached by representatives of the high-ranking anticolonial leader Phan Dinh Phung after the French capture of King Ham Nghi, in the hopes that another popular individual could be advanced as alternative to the puppets Dong Khanh and Thanh Thai. Cuong De's father had demurred, citing his excessive age, but in 1894 he apparently did offer Cuong De (then twelve years old) in his place, the plan falling through with the death of the intermediary and that, in January 1896, of Phan Dinh Phung himself.[14] Nevertheless, Cuong De states that this event did change the course of his life; henceforth he directed his studies toward history, geography, economics, and the like, dreaming of the exploits of such patriotic heroes as Tran Hung Dao and Ly Thuong Kiet in Vietnam, Chang Liang and Chu-ko Liang in China, Toyotomi Hideyoshi and Saigo Takamori in Japan, and Cavour, Bismarck, Washington, and Lincoln in the West.[15]

With this valuable royal addition to their coterie, Phan Boi Chau felt his chances of rousing mandarin support had improved. He proceeded to write *Luu Cau Huyet Le Tan Thu* (Ryukyu's Bitter Tears), an essay in traditional form appearing superficially to deal with the loss of sovereignty to the Japanese by the Ryukyu islands, but in reality, of course, treating the fate of his own country.[16] His corrective program still was phrased

13. NB, p. 37. TP, p. 33. As indicated, Gia Long had managed to use the Mekong delta as a base for his slow march northward to victory. His primary wife was also from the south, and her family tombs were carefully maintained by the dynasty until the fall of the delta in 1867.

14. CD, p. 10. This book is a Vietnamese translation of a Japanese text, not now available, apparently all based on a series of interviews by the author (Matsubayashi?) with Cuong De in 1943. Cuong De seems to have had access to his personal papers when interviewed, judging from the abundant detail of his account, but the background of this book should be investigated more thoroughly.

15. CD, pp. 10–11.

16. NB, pp. 38–39. TP, pp. 34–35. In both of these Vietnamese translations of Phan's second autobiographical effort, he clearly indicates that he wrote *Luu Cau*

strictly in the tradition of Mencius and the self-strengtheners, emphasizing "popular zeal" (*dan-khi*), "popular intellect" (*dan-tri*), and the cultivation of "talent" (*nhan-tai*), with a conclusion aimed at stirring the passions of others like himself to patriotic action. A copy was circulated within the various court ministries, and a few high officials called Phan in for private discussions. But the general reaction was highly defensive, and even his most sympathetic contact, the mandarin for whom he had really written the book, could only exclaim; "At the time when we might still have done something, nobody worried about it; now, when there is not an ounce of freedom, what further can be said?" At any rate, ministry subordinates apparently did transcribe more copies of *Luu Cau Huyet Le Tan Thu*, which made their way to certain scholar-gentry in other provinces. We know, for example, that this book was read by men like Phan Chu Trinh, Tran Quy Cap, and Huynh Thuc Khang.[17]

Nguyen Thanh, at this point the prime strategist of the group, now advised Phan Boi Chau to travel south into the Mekong delta to relay word of Prince Cuong De's decision and line up permanent associates. A passport was purchased covertly,[18] and by January 1904 Phan was circulating through the six provinces (*luc-tinh*) of the south, seeking out the remaining elderly followers of Truong Dinh and urging the formation of a new anti-French movement. With Phan's status as a top-ranking regional examinee (*giai nguyen*), he was bound to gain a hearing. As I've indicated, a significant number of persons in the south simply refused to accept the French as permanent overlords. They demonstrated their sentiments in such small but meaningful ways as continuing to wear their hair long, quietly reciting snatches of Nguyen Dinh Chieu's poetry, joining politico-religious associations, and sneering at those who had discarded traditional forms and "become enamored of French wine." A few stalwarts even refused to use modern soap because it had been introduced by the hated Westerner.[19]

Such attitudes reflected a larger temporal distinction. Whereas in northern and central Vietnam it was the modernizing elements of the

---

Huyet Le Tan Thu in 1903 before traveling south. On the other hand, his first autobiography, NTT, pp. 23–25, says that *Luu Cau* was written in April 1904, shortly *after* returning from the south. For a Vietnamese translation of what is probably a portion of this work, see Le Thuoc, "Co phai day la bai *Luu Cau Huyet Le Tan Thu* cua Phan Boi Chau khong?" VT, pp. 64–65, discusses this text briefly.

17. Huynh Thuc Khang, *Phan Tay Ho*, p. 17, and *Tu Truyen*, p. 26.

18. The French strictly limited Vietnamese movement in and out of Cochinchina, and Phan Boi Chau did not want them to know of his travels. A poem written by Dang Nguyen Can apparently as a send-off to Phan on this southward journey is reprinted in VTCM, p. 253.

19. VTCM, pp. 44–47.

population—the "haircutters" as the French labeled them—who were beginning to take the initiative against both colonial overlords and court traditionalists, in the south for at least the next fifteen years the reverse remained true, modernizers mostly being within the civil service of Cochinchina, and traditionalists holding forth, insofar as possible, in the countryside. As we shall see, however, there were interesting exceptions in both areas, persons who somehow bridged modern and traditional worlds. The situation was eminently transitional, as traditionalists everywhere became increasingly anachronistic. But even if Phan Boi Chau in 1904 had perceived the major historical trends, it would have provided small comfort, occupied as he was with trying to weld a truly countrywide anticolonial movement immediately.

One of Phan's earliest and best contacts during this trip was with Tran Nhut Thi,[20] a Buddhist priest in the Seven Mountains (*That Son*) region of Chau Doc province. While not much is known of Tran himself except that he sustained a lifelong antipathy for the French, we do have a reasonable amount of information on other southern priests of similar persuasion, including several in Chau Doc.[21] For example, Cao Van Long, better known as Bay Do, found funds in 1904 to begin building an ambitious pagoda on Cam mountain in this province. Long before it was completed, people were discreetly congregating on the mountain to contemplate, to hear Bay Do expostulate on the few available Chinese-language texts, to practice martial exercises (*vo*), and to receive assorted amulets, seals, and brevets.[22]

Priests like Tran Nhut Thi and Bay Do traveled widely in the Mekong delta, practicing medicine, raising money, preaching deliverance, and maintaining informal liaison among diverse groups at the village level. People turned to such Buddhist and Taoist priests in part because the representatives of Confucian authority, the royal mandarins, had long deserted them.[23] Absentee landlordism and tenancy were growing pre-

20. Referred to as Tran Thi in NB, p. 39, and TP, p. 35.
21. This data is largely the by-product of harsh French repressions and investigations following episodes in Cochinchina between 1913 and 1916. The main published source is Georges Coulet, *Les Sociétés secrètes en terre d'Annam*. Although the author infers it is a study of all Vietnam, in fact, most of the book is concerned with Cochinchina. Numerous dossiers in the French archives also treat the "troubles" in Cochinchina. See especially, AOM A-50 NF 28(1); AOM A-50 NF 28(2); AOM A-50 NF 450(2); AOM A-50 NF 606 carton 51.
22. Coulet, *Les Sociétés*, pp. 90–96; 158–167; 181–187.
23. Coulet, *Les Sociétés*, pp. 120–123, briefly discusses the apparent Buddhist revival in the south after 1867, particularly as represented by the Dao Lanh (Good Religion) sect.

cipitately. Village administration was undergoing profound alterations.[24] Anyone who seemed able to explain such disturbing events in the context of traditional symbols and beliefs was highly prized.

Tran Nhut Thi was also able to provide Phan Boi Chau with introductions to wealthy landowners in Sadec and Can-Tho—most important, to Nguyen Than Hien and his associates.[25] Two months after his departure from Hue, Phan was back, relieved that the mandarinate apparently had been unaware of his absence.[26] Results of this trip were significant. Members of the southern landowning group would provide the bulk of the finances and the largest number of young students for the Dong Du (Eastern Study) movement. But they were also the most cautious, conservative element in subsequent anticolonial efforts, in general acting as a brake on more militant, progressive elements in central and northern Vietnam.

In April 1904 Tran Nhut Thi joined Nguyen Thanh and Phan Boi Chau in Quang Nam for discussions and then traveled up to Hue for an audience with Cuong De. While Tran returned south to raise money, Phan quickly headed up the coast to make contact with followers in the north, interestingly enough, relying on a Catholic friend to talk their way past suspicious checkpoint functionaries. Within weeks Phan was back in Quang Nam, for the first formal meeting of what soon would be labeled the Duy Tan Hoi. Nguyen Thanh, Cuong De, and twenty other key men were present. Traditional precautions for secrecy were employed, such as not maintaining personnel rosters, passing instructions by word of mouth, and referring to each other only in the elder brother-younger brother form (*anh-em*) rather than by any rank or position. Tasks such as recruiting new members, raising money, and writing propaganda were divided among the whole group, whereas planning and preparing a quest for overseas aid were delegated to Nguyen Thanh and Phan Boi Chau, in order to maintain strictest secrecy.[27]

There is no indication that the group attempted any fundamental ideological reassessment during this crucial formative stage, a fact that probably influenced Phan Chu Trinh and other reformist scholar-gentry subsequently to avoid participation in the group. At this point in time there was little to differentiate the Duy Tan Hoi from earlier Can Vuong

24. For an informed discussion of rural Cochinchina at the turn of the century, see Osborne, "Rule and Response," pp. 296–315.
25. Nguyen Van Hau, "Cu Phan Boi Chau va vai hoat-dong chinh-tri trong chuyen 'Nam Hanh' nam Qui Mao."
26. NB, p. 41. TP, p. 37.
27. NB, pp. 42–44. TP, pp. 38–40.

"groups of devoted men," pledging sacred oaths of loyalty and vengeance. The Confucian concept of fidelity or faithfulness (*trung*) continued to dominate their thinking. An ardent love-hate (*yeu-ghet*) dichotomy suffused their poetry, with righteous scholar-gentry and followers on one side, foreign intruders and collaborators on the other.[28] The only difference—significant but not yet crucial—was this leadership's insistence on trying to organize and coordinate actions on a countrywide basis. The leadership in addition already may have gained some new knowledge of and respect for French technical and institutional powers. But they had yet to devise ways to communicate this coherently to their eager, ambitious followers.

For centuries the place for dispossessed Vietnamese political elements to seek aid had been China. But in 1904 Peking's general failure to protect her vassal from France was still fresh in Vietnamese minds and, besides, it had been increasingly obvious after 1895 that China was having a hard time protecting even herself. Nguyen Thanh's new choice was Japan, first, because the Japanese were of the same race as the Vietnamese and, second, because their reform effort had enabled them to defeat China and, at the moment of this decision, seemingly was giving them amazing strength against the Russians. Nguyen Thanh felt Phan Boi Chau was the man to send, and he had even found the perfect guide, a Can Vuong follower named Tang Bat Ho who had fled the country some years before, traveling through such places as Kwangsi, Kwangtung, Taiwan, Japan, and Siam.[29] A third man, Dang Tu Kinh, was selected as liaison to keep Nguyen Thanh and others in Vietnam informed about proceedings overseas.

Hoping to tighten up organizational lines before his departure, Phan made a final swing through north and central Vietnam, returning to Hue at the end of 1904 to develop an alibi about retreating to his home village to await the next metropolitan exams (he apparently took and failed the 1904 series of exams). Another meeting with Nguyen Thanh (the last time they would see each other), an audience with Cuong De, a few

28. VTCM, p. 137.
29. There are many popular stories about Tang Bat Ho's travels and exploits. For example, he and Nguyen Thien Thuat (see Chapter 3) are reputed to have served in the Japanese armed forces against the Russians and thus they attended a military reception given by the Meiji emperor, at which time Nguyen Thien Thuat petitioned the emperor emotionally for aid to their enslaved country. Phuong Huu, *Phong Trao Dai Dong Du*, pp. 7–8. This is conceivable, but unlikely: Japanese sources make no reference to this early contact, and we know that Tang Bat Ho was back in Lang-Son many months before joining Phan Boi Chau in 1904. Dao Trinh Nhat, *Dong Kinh Nghia Thuc*, p. 10. Since the Russo-Japanese War began February 8, 1904, Tang would have been required to do all his fighting and traveling very quickly.

days in his home village to attend to the family tombs and observe Tet, and Phan Boi Chau was on his way north out of the country, using a water and land route well known to Tang Bat Ho. En route Phan scribbled a poem that included the lines:

> My job is for one lifetime
> Future tasks will be taken by those yet to be born.[30]

Up to this point we do not know whether the French colonial security service, the Sûreté, was at all informed on the activities of the Duy Tan Hoi. Phan Boi Chau did mention being called before the résident supérieur in 1904 to explain certain police reports, but he found them to be merest rumors and had little trouble accounting for his movements.[31] Phan also referred to a number of mandarins, both in Hue and in the provinces, who were either actively covering for the Duy Tan Hoi or silently aware of what was transpiring. We may thus conclude that as of 1903 and 1904 there were still channels of communication among the highest native elite, both oppositionist and collaborator, not yet tapped by the Sûreté. Between 1904 and 1912, however, this ambiguity of political conduct disappeared and anticolonialists learned through bitter experience precisely how efficient a French police apparatus could be in turning apparent allies into informers.

Stopping off in Hong Kong, Phan Boi Chau showed the conspiratorial style that would awe his compatriots for the next eight years or more. He plunged into things with total dedication. He always managed also to pursue multiple courses, soberly aware that in the business of conspiracy against a great colonial power, many promising leads would dry up along the way. Tang Bat Ho was sent out to make contact with Ton That Thuyet and other Can Vuong émigrés, while Phan spent some days walking around, assiduously observing the British colonial system in action and comparing it with that of the French. During this time he also befriended a young, lower-class Vietnamese who was working as cook and steward on a local steamer; this man, Ly Tue, would serve for many years as Phan's most important liaison agent, helping to transmit money and messages, to ferry out Vietnamese students, and to report on French countermeasures in the many ports he visited.[32]

Phan also sought out editors of Chinese newspapers in Hong Kong, quickly perceiving the political schism that had developed between China's

30. Chinese transliteration and Vietnamese translation available in HT, pp. 434–435. For two other poems written by Phan at about this time, see VT, pp. 111–113.
31. NB, p. 43. TP, p. 40.
32. Phan states in NB and TP that he met Ly Tue at this time. NTT, however, indicates it was 1906.

reform monarchists and "revolutionary" republicans. His own intellectual predilections favored monarchism, and this was even more true of most members of Duy Tan Hoi at home. But when Hsu Ch'in, editor of the monarchist newspaper *Shang-pao*, failed to receive him, Phan was quite happy to meet with Feng Tzu-yu of the republican periodical *Chung-kuo jih-pao*. Feng told Phan frankly that the Vietnamese could only expect substantial Chinese assistance after the revolutionaries had thrown out the Manchu. He rather paradoxically suggested Phan contact the Ch'ing governor general of Liang-Kwang, Ts'en Ch'un-hsuan, a Kwangsi man quite familiar with traditional Sino-Vietnamese tributary relationships.[33]

Phan Boi Chau made the attempt, writing Ts'en a letter in highly deferential, traditional manner. Ts'en's failure even to reply probably swept away whatever nostalgia Phan may have had for the Ch'ing dynasty, but his letter deserves study as Phan's earliest, rather naïve attempt at foreign "diplomacy." Opening with numerous classical references serving to idealize historic Sino-Vietnamese relations, Phan then drew a sharp, bitter contrast with Vietnam's contemporary status as a French protectorate:

> [The French] treat our people like garbage, in the beginning using terror to chase them, in the end pushing them into the trap like cattle. The meek are made into slaves, the strong-minded are thrown into jail. The physically powerful are forced into the army, while the old and weak are left to die! Externally the French speak of their 'protectorate' in order to deceive the world powers. Internally they squeeze every last drop, every ounce from the people. The common people see the blade and block before them and are paralyzed with fear. The land is splashed with blood. The whole country has a tragic hue.

Phan also mentioned the earlier failures of Ham Nghi, Phan Dinh Phung, and Nguyen Thien Thuat. Then he shifted abruptly to the international balance of power, arguing that France was incurring increasing trouble in her alliance with the enfeebled Russians and from the German diplomatic offensive against French jurisdiction in Morocco.[34] He made a concrete request for a secret staging area along the Sino-Vietnamese

33. NB, pp. 51–52. TP, pp. 49–50.
34. The latter refers to the dramatic speech by Kaiser William II in Tangier in March 1905, proclaiming Germany's determination to uphold Moroccan independence. This was followed by German demands for a conference of the powers. The ensuing crisis did force the resignation of French Foreign Minister Delcasse, but the Germans pushed their advantage too far and ended up isolated and outvoted at the Algeciras Conference of January–March 1906. Raymond J. Sontag, *European Diplomatic History 1871–1932* (New York, 1933), pp. 103–111.

border and concluded by pointedly stressing the real danger to Kwangtung and Kwangsi if France was allowed to keep Vietnam perpetually.[35]

Moving on to Shanghai, there was a wait of one month until the end of Russo-Japanese hostilities, at which time Phan Boi Chau and his two associates boarded a Japanese merchant ship for Yokohama. There were also forty Chinese nationals aboard: the Vietnamese quickly made friends with the overseas students among them and took up Chinese aliases when that appeared the safest course, a pattern they would continue for some years. En route to Shanghai Phan had been delighted to discover that Liang Ch'i-ch'ao was residing in Yokohama. Nevertheless, Phan's closest contact among the Chinese sailing to Japan was a follower of Sun Yat-sen, and Phan knew enough by now of émigré politics not to ask for an introduction to Liang from him.[36]

Instead, upon arrival in Yokohama, Phan took a chance on writing a letter of self-introduction to Liang and going directly to his office. This approach proved successful, and several extended conversations followed, both men using the writing brush liberally rather than attempting verbal interpretation through Phan's guide, Tang Bat Ho. Basically, Liang advised Phan to put his real emphasis on educating and awakening his own people to the multifold challenges of the modern world. Only when this had borne fruit, he counseled, would external assistance prove meaningful. More precisely, Liang warned against letting the Japanese military into Vietnam, recommending instead that he try simply to cultivate relations with the Japansese government to the point where they might be the first major power to grant diplomatic recognition to Vietnam when independence eventually was achieved. The idea was not to try to force independence through outside aid, but rather to prepare the people so that all would be in readiness when the right chance came—specifically, an almost certain showdown between France and Germany, as Liang envisioned it. As for weapons, perhaps when the time came they could be supplied by Kwangtung and Kwangsi, although Liang apparently considered it beneath his intellectual dignity to spell this out.[37]

All this was instructive to Phan Boi Chau, as it showed the world to be much more complex than it must have appeared previously from within Vietnam. Already he was impressed by Japan's modern facilities and, more than that, by the individual discipline and apparent political responsibility of the Japanese citizenry. As a classical scholar he had no trouble

35. Phan Boi Chau, "Hai van-kien ngoai-giao dau tien cua Phan Boi Chau," pp. 61–63. Translation and comments by Chuong Thau.
36. NB, pp. 52–54. TP, pp. 51–52.
37. NB, pp. 54–55. TP, pp. 52–54.

equating popular awareness with governmental power; but seeing the Japanese in action gave him his first rueful insight into just how far the Vietnamese people would have to move in this quest. Nevertheless, he had been sent by the Duy Tan Hoi to request concrete assistance in over-throwing the French. Liang explained that acquiring weapons or aid from the Japanese government itself was most improbable, but he was willing to introduce Phan to Kashiwabara Buntaro, secretary of the Dobun Shoin (Common Culture School) and parliamentary assistant to party leader Inukai Tsuyoshi.

Just what sort of political environment was Phan Boi Chau entering in Japan? As Professor Marius Jansen has demonstrated in his book *The Japanese and Sun Yat-sen,* Japan's Asian policy before 1905 was an ill-coordinated but honest hodgepodge bred of idealism, opportunism, and chauvinism. Contact between "liberal" party leaders like Okuma Shig-enobu and Inukai, and chauvinist leaders like Toyama Mitsuru or Uchida Ryohei, reflected a common annoyance at the "low posture" adopted by the Meiji oligarchs in relation to the Western powers. Instead of accepting the implications of international balance-of-power diplomacy, both civil-ian politicians and chauvinists showed a special concern for neighboring China and a desire to hold Western imperialism at bay in Asia. These two groups shared this objective—but not much else—with yet another group, the "professional" Japanese revolutionaries like Miyazaki Torazo, Oi Kentaro, and Kayano Chochi.[38]

Arriving in Japan, a foreign nationalist or anticolonialist looking for help could get shelter and some money from Toyama and his Kokuryukai (Amur River Society), on the basis of feudal chivalry, if nothing else. Then he might well be able to persuade Toyama to mediate in contacts with Japanese military, political, or financial figures. This had been the case, for example, with Mariano Ponce when he arrived in Japan in 1898 as a representative of the Filipino Revolutionary Committee.[39] After that, Sun Yat-sen had managed via the chauvinists to get promises of aid from the highest Japanese army and navy sources for the Waichow uprising of 1900, although Ito Hirobumi, then head of the Japanese Privy Council, had torpedoed the project, leaving Sun's Waichow activists to suffer a crushing defeat. As for K'ang Yu-wei and Liang Ch'i-ch'ao, their gentry backgrounds and high scholastic reputations had allowed them to bypass mere chauvinist intermediaries and engage in direct, intimate re-

38. Marius Jansen, *The Japanese and Sun Yat-sen,* pp. 34–58. Robert Scalapino, *Democracy and the Party Movement in Pre-war Japan,* pp. 76–81, 349–351. Hugh Latimer Burleson, "The Kokuryukai in Northeast Asia," pp. 24–28, 54.
39. Kuzuu Yoshihisa, ed., *Toa Sengaku Shishi Kiden,* vol. 1 (Tokyo, 1932), pp. 627–646.

lations with Inukai and Kashiwabara. K'ang and Liang were closely connected with the Toa Dobun Kai (East Asia Common Culture Society), and, in turn, Kashiwabara became executive secretary of Liang's Kao-teng ta-t'ung hsueh-hsiao (Great Harmony Secondary School).[40]

Liang and Sun Yat-sen apparently were personal enemies as early as 1900.[41] Until 1905, nevertheless, it was Liang who held general intellectual initiative within an entire Chinese student generation, brilliantly berating the scholar-gentry for not doing their moral duty and painfully dissecting Chinese society with conceptual tools borrowed from Smith and Spencer, Bentham and Burke. Meanwhile, Sun worked ever more closely with Japanese revolutionaries, plotted new uprisings, raised funds, and even managed to visit the French colonial exposition in Hanoi in 1903.[42] While personal and intellectual differences may have sparked the Liang/Sun feud originally, we can surmise that by 1905 it was the practical competition for student recruits and émigré finances that was forcing a showdown.[43] When Phan Boi Chau debarked in Yokohama, Sun's *Min-pao* and Liang's *Hsin-min ts'ung-pao* were already engaged in open journalistic warfare, crucial to the future course of Chinese nationalism.

At this same time, Japan's entire position in Asia was under-going momentous transformation, largely because of the initiative of those oligarchs so distrusted by most of the personalities mentioned above. By means of the Anglo-Japanese alliance of 1902, Britain had secured Japan's support in maintaining the imperialist treaty system in China and had forestalled any Russo-Japanese agreement to partition northeast Asia. Japan, in turn, had insured the isolation of Russia from potential Western allies in any subsequent conflict and had received the British blessing in organizing a dominant "special relationship" with Korea. The Russo-Japanese War of 1904–1905 and the Treaty of Portsmouth provided the conditions for Japan's triumphant entry into the arena of international power which was perfected two years later by a network of agreements between Japan, France, Russia, and Britain. Japan would now be an accepted member of the imperialist club in Asia, working to secure concessions from the decaying Manchu dynasty and rather above petty political intrigues with men like Sun Yat-sen. Popular consciousness of

40. Joseph R. Levenson, *Liang Ch'i-ch'ao and the Mind of Modern China* (Cambridge, Mass.: 1959), pp. 62–63. Jansen, *The Japanese*, pp. 32–34, 59–104.
41. Levenson, *Liang Ch'i-ch'ao*, p. 66.
42. Georges Soulie de Morant, *Soun Iat-senn* (Paris, 1931), pp. 112–117.
43. The number of Chinese students in Japan grew as follows: 1902, 500; 1904, 1,500; 1905, 8,000; and 1906, 13,000. The figures are based on analysis of *Japan Weekly Mail* by Roger F. Hackett, "Chinese Students in Japan, 1900–1910," *Papers on China*, vol. 3 (Harvard Regional Studies, Mimeographed, 1948), p. 142. Vietnamese students were probably included in these figures.

power—indeed, an increasing pleasure in exercising it—hardened the national self-esteem and rendered ever more slight the chances of substantial Japanese support for liberal or republican forces in Asia.[44]

For Vietnam the irony of this situation was sharp, indeed, although very few sensed it at the time. The Russo-Japanese War had stirred Vietnamese patriots to attempt to emulate Japan and Japan's patriots, precisely at the time when Japan herself was moving into acceptance of the Western imperialist credo and away from any possibility of anti-imperialist alliance with oppressed Asian peoples. Phan Boi Chau landed in Japan at the time when any sensitive Asian would have to have been most impressed by Japan's power and its political system, but also just when the Japanese were shifting their attitudes and outlook about their Asian neighbors. Almost four years passed before Phan and his group felt the real impact of this shift, to their ultimate dismay and misfortune.

Returning to my narrative, Phan Boi Chau seems to have made a good enough impression on Kashiwabara for the latter to contact Inukai, who encouraged Liang to bring Phan up to Tokyo in June for a full-dress meeting with Okuma Shigenobu.[45] One of Inukai's first questions for Phan, again transmitted by means of written Chinese, was whether his request for assistance had the support of members of the Vietnamese royal family. Phan quickly pulled Cuong De's photograph and identification papers out of his pocket, whereupon Inukai suggested that Cuong De be brought out of the country. After a huddle with Okuma and Liang, Inukai offered Phan unobtrusive Kenseihonto (Orthodox Constitutional party) support, but counseled patience in requesting any material assistance against the French. When asked if he could "await future opportunities," Phan says he retorted that his group would hardly have gone to the trouble of sending him to beg help if the situation weren't desperate already. Okuma apologized on the grounds that they had known nothing of Vietnam previously.[46] He advised Phan to encourage as many students

---

44. Jansen, *The Japanese*, p. 105. John K. Fairbank, Edwin O. Reischauer, and Albert M. Craig, *A History of East Asian Civilization*, vol. 2 (Boston, 1965), pp. 478–482.

45. The following conversation is in NB, pp. 55–57. TP, pp. 54–56. Since Phan wrote this autobiography three decades later, the conversation can hardly be considered literal. Nevertheless, upon cross-checking comments and statements throughout Phan's autobiography with independent sources, it becomes evident that Phan had a surprisingly accurate memory for distant events, perhaps cultivated through a life of clandestine activism that absolutely precluded the use of written files or records.

46. This statement is open to doubt, since Okuma most likely would have known of Sone Toshitora, a former Japanese naval intelligence officer and China adventurer who observed the Sino-French War (1883–1885) and afterward wrote a little book criticizing the Japanese government's indifference to the fate of Annam. Sone and his

as possible to leave the country, take up any positions they might find, and learn the ways of the modern world. To those who wished to come to Japan, he offered positions and money, adding that the Japanese were well known for their esteem of warriors and patriots. At this point in the conversation Phan focused his eyes on Okuma's face, overflowing with pride in Japan's accomplishments. While stomaching his own sense of shame, Phan fired back that it was somehow improper to sit in Japan while countrymen at home continued to suffer, and he personally doubted that Okuma would respect anyone who did this. Recalling this poignant confrontation in his autobiography three decades later, Phan seems to have perceived the impossible nature of his earlier position. It is doubtful, however, that he saw this in 1905.

Shortly after this exchange, Inukai's wife entered the room, bearing a fan for Phan to inscribe. He recalls brushing a line from the *Book of History*: "*Tu phuong phong dong duy nai chi huu*" (The people everywhere responding as if moved by the wind—this is your excellence), an apparent appeal to the Japanese sense of duty toward their racial and cultural brothers. This probably represented an end to serious business, but Phan recalls Kashiwabara's picking up the many sheets of "brush conversation" (*but-dam*) and remarking that it was all like reading an old warrior novel, since the distant Vietnamese had never before approached the scholar-gentry (*si-phu*) of Japan. Once again Phan was inwardly ashamed, wondering why earlier Vietnamese had been unable to think of making such contacts, leaving it instead to a time when the French were in tight control.

From a letter that Phan sent to Okuma shortly after this meeting, we know that Phan was becoming increasingly aware of Japan's fascination with international power politics. He aimed all his arguments to Okuma at Japan's pride and what he thought must be Japan's national interest, including some clever reproofs for being the strongest power in Asia and yet letting France and other non-Asian powers elbow in with such arrogance:

> Vietnam is not on the European continent, but the Asian. Vietnam is common to Japan in race, culture, and continental positioning, yet the French gangsters are left to spread their bestial venom without fear. Hence the French are unaware that Asia already has a major power, already has Japan. The strength of Japan has been felt in the Northwest, all the way to the Ch'ing and to the Russians. Why then has Japan allowed the French to trample over Vietnam without trying to help us?

---

associates allegedly plotted to assist the Vietnamese, but the Japanese government arrested them to avoid all possibility of an altercation with the French. See Kuzuu Yoshihisa, *Toa Sengaku*, vol. 2, pp. 816–817.

Phan then painted a grim picture of Russia and France working together to carve up China. He pointed to the French penetration of Yunnan and Kwangsi and inferred that the French might well have designs on Taiwan and the Ryukyu islands. Finally, Phan alluded to Okuma's great historical destiny—serving his emperor and guiding Japanese policy in an effort to neutralize the Western imperialists and make Asia safe for the Asians.[47]

Back in Yokohama, Liang invited Phan to his own extended strategy discussion. This time the emphasis was on the historical relationship of Vietnam with China, not Japan, with Liang speaking particularly of the French railroads in Yunnan and Kwangtung as "cancers in China's stomach" and promising Chinese military assistance as soon as China was strong. For the moment he counseled Phan to concentrate his energy on two fronts:

1. A serious literary presentation to the world of the plight of Vietnam in the face of France's policy of extermination, which hopefully would gather foreign sympathy that might later prove invaluable; and

2. Encouraging Vietnamese youth to study overseas, as a start to awakening popular consciousness and improving the general level of education.

It was this conversation, Phan indicated, that led him to a realization of how very complex his anticolonial efforts were likely to become and of how much he still had to learn about the world outside Vietnam.[48]

The first thing Phan did was to return to his room and begin writing *Viet-Nam Vong Quoc Su* (History of the Loss of Vietnam), which was quickly published by Liang, primarily for distribution among overseas Chinese but also for smuggling into Vietnam. This is one of the most important books to appear in the course of Vietnamese anti-colonial efforts. First, it may be considered "Vietnam's first revolutionary history book,"[49] in that it not only grieved over the Nguyen dynasty's feeble, tardy response to the foreign threat and presented vivid memorials to Can Vuong heroes, but also attempted a serious analysis of the oppressive French social and economic policies and argued for the establishment of a national, anticolonial front made up of seven classes or interest groups who had special reason to fight the oppressors.[50] Second, it was written in a new

47. Phan Boi Chau, "Hai van-kien," pp. 63–64.
48. NB, pp. 57–58. TP, pp. 56–57.
49. Chuong Thau, "Anh huong cach mang Trung Quoc doi voi su bien chuyen cua tu tuong Phan Boi Chau," p. 15.
50. Both the original Chinese and a *quoc ngu* translation are in *Dai Hoc Van Khoa,*

literary style, in large part borrowed from the writings of Liang Ch'i-ch'ao and his associates, which generally avoided flowery nuance and classical allusions in favor of a direct, hard-hitting prose that seems particularly effective in the analytical sections and in Phan's precise thrusts at the French. This was a precursor of a major alteration of literary style among Vietnamese scholar-gentry in general, extremely important to subsequent formulations of political concepts and to the permanent modification of the Vietnamese language.

Third and last, is the documented impact on people who read *Viet-Nam Vong Quoc Su*. It was printed for distribution in China at least five times, the first two appearances being in Liang's periodical *Hsin-min ts'ung-pao* and the bound edition mentioned above.[51] Liang himself contributed an introduction in which he warned the Chinese people of similar dangers they were now facing. An essay by an unknown Chinese, written in 1906 or early 1907, showed honest shock at Phan's description of French activities and concluded fearfully that China had better wake up, or within a decade she would share the same fate.[52] Unfortunately for Phan and his compatriots, other responses to his literary effort seem also to have been centered on China: instead of producing any measurable Chinese willingness to help Vietnam toward liberation in the near future, it only showed that most Chinese tacitly assumed that Vietnam was gone—lost.

Viet-Nam Vong Quoc Su was destined for a more positive impact at home. Phan Boi Chau and Dang Tu Kinh, leaving Japan for the first time in August 1905, carried in fifty copies which circulated throughout Vietnam, being recopied often in the process. We may surmise that Phan's blunt, nonallegorical style upset some traditionalists, but did make the book comprehensible to literate people lacking extensive training in the classics, who then passed the main ideas orally among even wider circles. One *quoc ngu* translator, Ta Thuc Khai, who was eight years old when copies first were circulated, wrote in 1960 of the excitement it had created in his home village.[53]

1959–1960 edition (Saigon, 1961), pp. 3–35. Japanese translation, Nagaoka Shinjiro and Kawamoto Kunie, eds., *Betonamu Bokokushi* (Tokyo, 1966), pp. 1–83.

51. Chuong Thau, "Anh huong cua Phan Boi Chau doi voi mot so to chuc cach mang Trung Quoc," p. 34, has the full publishing history.

52. This essay was used in 1907 by the Dong Kinh Nghia Thuc as teaching material. A copy is available at Central Scientific Library, Hanoi. Cited by Chuong Thau, "Anh huong cua Phan Boi Chau," p. 35.

53. *Dai Hoc Van Khoa*, translator's preface, p. 3. He also indicates that by the time he was old enough to read *Viet-Nam Vong Quoc Su*, copies were not available locally. His copy for this translation was finally obtained in Taiwan. A translation of the last section, "The Future of Vietnam," is also available in VT, pp. 114–123.

Viet-Nam Vong Quoc Su is divided into a short introduction and four main sections:

1. THE CAUSES AND TRUTH OF VIETNAM'S LOSS: Here Phan glorified the expansion of Vietnam southward and lashed out at the Nguyen dynasty for aping the Ming and Ch'ing and teaching only the classics, not to mention usually regarding public opinion as dirt under their feet. He quoted Mencius to reinforce his argument that the court, by their complete failure to educate or arouse the people politically, made it possible for the French to seize Vietnam. Catholic missionaries of the early nineteenth century were described as being under the political direction of the French government. Then came a painful recitation of disasters after 1847, with some deep cuts at the Ch'ing for their apparent inability or unwillingness to maintain their half of the historic suzerainty bargain. Considering that the essay was designed primarily for Chinese consumption, Phan also showed a surprising willingness to describe Vietnamese scholar-gentry schisms of the 1880s, in particular, presenting Nguyen Van Tuong as the prime traitor and the man responsible for sabotaging court attempts to procure British or German help against the French. Summarizing general court response to foreign penetrations, however, Phan quoted the popular saying: "When the rain is threatening, nobody worries; when it pours they curl up and sigh with regret."

2. BIOGRAPHIES OF PATRIOTS DURING THE TIME OUR COUNTRY WAS LOST: This may be the first modern Vietnamese hagiography, an obvious effort to preserve the memories of Can Vuong leaders for later generations.[54] Of the seventeen patriots discussed, nine were holders of the exalted *tien-si* degree, reflecting Phan's repeated stress on the position of top scholar-gentry as the moral fulcrum, the arbiters, good or evil, of popular attitudes and behavior. By the same token, those *tien-si* who "sold out" to the French were to be hated above all others, since they had violated the highest code of ethics. Patriotic scholar-gentry were pictured as absolutely scornful of death and always mindful of their debt to so-

---

54. See Truong Buu Lam, *Patterns of Vietnamese Response to Foreign Intervention: 1858–1900*, pp. 140–151, for a translation of an anonymous poem written about 1900 that in many ways shares this distinction, although nothing is known of its distribution or popularity. Original Chinese, plus *quoc ngu* translation is in NCLS 73: 21–29. Both of these works, with many others, serve to refute the statement by Joseph Buttinger, *Viet-Nam*, p. 123, that early resistance leaders "were almost unknown to the Vietnamese until the country . . . regained its independence." My own discussions with elderly and middle-aged Vietnamese also revealed that fathers took great pains, often as part of home education, to recite popular resistance stories of the Can Vuong period, even when the family was in fact tightly involved with the French colonial system.

ciety. But, in part unwittingly, Phan also pointed up some prime weaknesses of this leadership with his repeated stress on individual prowess, on the ties to parents and schoolmates as restricting factors, and on the CanVuong failure to coordinate efforts across the whole country. Phan's longest and most exemplary description was reserved for Phan Dinh Phung, stressing the latter's refusal to bow to Hoang Cao Khai's exploitation of traditional kinship and village vulnerabilities. In this case, Phan Boi Chau appeared to reach out consciously for examples of nonparticularistic loyalty, increasingly influenced, we may surmise, by his observation of the Japanese and their apparent identification with national symbols and ideals.

3. FRENCH POLICIES LEADING THE VIETNAMESE PEOPLE INTO IGNORANCE, ILLITERACY, WEAKNESS, AND MISERY: This is by far the longest section, pursuing a theme that would haunt Phan Boi Chau for the remainder of his life. After discussing the offhanded French treatment of Vietnamese monarchs and the French vengeance on scholar-gentry resisters or their families, Phan focused on the impact of colonial rule among the people. Above all were the taxes! Phan cited at least four taxes on salt (field, purchase, weighing, market) and six taxes on tobacco (field, weighing, transport, wholesale, retail, market), plus twelve other taxes that hit the people heavily and repeatedly. He argued that the traditional head tax had been levied on only a small minority, while the traditional land tax had reached only to those owners with large acreages.[55] Not only did the French reorient and intensify the tax structure, but, even more galling, they turned the proceeds to their own benefit and against the Vietnamese.

Phan then related the apocryphal but popular story of an extremely poor village which at tax time simply found itself without a thing to pay the collector. The village elders decided to take a chance and state their problem to the local French résident, whereupon they found him demanding that they sell their lands, homes, wives, and children to pay taxes. Crying out that all this had already been done, the elders pleaded that all they had left was the sky above their heads. With glee the Frenchman whipped out a paper for them to sign away the sky on—which they did, only to find a unit of soldiers barring the entrances when they returned home. After all, the French commander remarked, it was hardly possible for them to move around on the ground if it meant breathing air from the French-owned sky!

The rest of this section dealt with the noneconomic aspects of oppres-

---

55. Of course, this begs the question of whether these minorities passed the tax cost on to their tenants and subordinate relatives.

sion. Phan detailed French utilization of local mandarins collaborators and their clever recruitment of déclassé types as spies and policemen. He was outraged that the police attempted to extort payment from respectable single girls in the villages and towns, by threatening otherwise to force them to carry prostitutes' identification cards. Colonial education policy, Phan argued, was aimed at promoting mass ignorance and also at preventing Vietnamese from studying overseas. Finally, he mentioned villages which were being forced to buy the official newspapers and derided the government-organized press information centers in Hanoi, particularly for the use of "Dai Nam" in the title of the native center: "Vietnam is no longer a country, so how in blazes can they still talk of 'Dai' [Great]! Are the French trying to deceive someone, either on earth or in heaven?"

4. THE FUTURE OF VIETNAM: Now the ultimate assessment: Was Vietnam lost forever? Phan professed not to be sure. It all depended on the people of Vietnam, on their willingness or unwillingness to join together and possibly die together in final struggle against the "few thousand French devils [*con quy*]":

> If we look at overt indications, then in truth there is no longer anyone with a Vietnamese soul. But if we look at hidden, inner indications, then there is not a person lacking the soul of a Vietnamese. The Vietnamese do not bare their insides for all the world to see, and it is difficult to enter into them. Nevertheless, Vietnam is a country composed of human beings, not a country of animals, so let us operate on human premises and make a guess.

Phan then discussed seven categories or classes of people who had reason, he believed, to struggle against the French, if the proper conditions were to arise. First came the scholar-gentry, beneficiaries of past privileges who therefore bore a moral obligation to lead the anti-French struggle. Second, the lesser Can Vuong followers, whose families had suffered in defeat and who continued to nurse dreams of revenge. Third, the native Catholics, who had fared badly, Phan claimed, in recent years. This marked a significant departure from the CanVuong's rather indiscriminate hatred of the Catholic minority, a rather obvious attempt by Phan to envision a national movement transcending religious schisms. Fourth, there were the masses, who lived in constant fear and deprivation. Better to die for glory than to die like fish drying on the sand!

> Ten thousand Vietnamese can at least kill one hundred Frenchmen,
> One thousand Vietnamese can kill ten Frenchmen,
> One hundred Vietnamese can kill one Frenchman.

In this way four to five hundred thousand Vietnamese can wipe
out four to five thousand Frenchmen!
Those grey-eyed, heavily bearded people cannot live if Vietnam
is to live!

Fifth, Phan listed those people, anywhere, who would fight because they
were of yellow skin and the French were white. Sixth, interestingly
enough, came the mandarin collaborators, who Phan still maintained
would abandon the French when their rice bowls were not sufficiently
filled. Last, the native colonial troops, interpreters, servants, and so forth
who would see sooner or later that it was intolerable to live off the flesh
and blood of their parents, brothers, sisters, cousins, and neighbors.

More than anything else *Viet-Nam Vong Quoc Su* exemplified the
strong, continuing psychological or emotional undercurrent of anticolonial thinking. Events in later decades demonstrated that Phan Boi
Chau was both overly fearful, in his estimate of the Vietnamese people's
capacity for survival, and overly optimistic, in his hope to unify all major
classes against the French. Although every subsequent anticolonial organization would make such appeals for alliance on the basis of common
history, common ethnic stock, and common benefit, this was not enough.
It would take a lot more rigorous intellectual effort and a substantial reorientation of values before Phan's ideal of a united front bore fruit.

Phan's indictment of French rule was still patently traditional in
phraseology, but the emphasis had changed. Mencius was now employed
prominently for popular saction, while the call for a conservative rallying
around the banner of the monarch pretender was decidedly muted (partly,
it must be said, for the practical reason that Cuong De had yet to escape the country). The old ideology legitimized revolt. By contrast, Phan's
employment of Pan-Asian or racist themes was tentative, uncertain. What
was there never blossomed as a major theme in Vietnamese anticolonial
movements, largely because of Phan's subsequent disasters with the
Japanese and the Chinese.

Chapter Six

Hòn máu uất chất quanh đầy ruột,
Anh em ơi! Xin tuốt gươm ra,
Có giời, có đất, có ta,
Đồng tâm như thế mới là đồng tâm!

Blood is boiling in your heart,
Countrymen! Draw forth your swords,
There is Heaven, Earth, and Us,
That is what we call true unity!

(PHAN BỘI CHÂU, *Hải Ngoại Huyết*
Thư, 1906)

The Dong Du Movement

Phan Boi Chau's primary objectives in returning to Vietnam were to bring out Prince Cuong De with a first contingent of students and, implicitly, to report the substance of his Japanese discussions to the Duy Tan Hoi.[1] Speed was deemed essential because there was some indication that the French were aware of Phan's activities in Japan. Phan also knew that money would flow much more freely from wealthy Vietnamese once Cuong De was in Japan and thus established as a real alternative to Thanh Thai in Hue.

Beyond such immediate requirements, we may presume that Phan Boi Chau well understood the mystique connected with such clandestine comings and goings, a mystique not unimportant to the development and sustenance of popular anticolonial attitudes. From the hills, from beyond Vietnamese borders, a few men already were both demonstrating an alternative ethic and giving the colonial overlords occasional moments of worry:

> Liaison between these various patriots and the people, the country's youth at home, was never severed. Once in a while, from some remote base, from Siam, China, or Japan, a "rootless" individual would furtively return. In the midst of the night a shadow from afar would step into the house, cautiously assess the mood of relatives and friends, and remain on the lookout for the omnipresent informers of the enemy authorities. He

1. NB, pp. 58–60. TP, pp. 57–59.

would be around only a night, an instant, with whispered stories of perilous existence, of bravery among those not yet dead, those never willing to accept defeat. Sometimes there would be a letter, or a book from distant shores, providing a bit of information on "world conditions," or describing the courageous spirit of revolutionaries from other countries. A new vista was spread before the inquiring eyes of the young people.[2]

Back home, Phan discovered that orders were out for special area searches by police, although no one was sure of the reason. More seriously, there were signs among his associates of a developing difference of opinion between reformists and activists.[3] Phan's fellow Nghe-An friend, Dang Nguyen Can, was duly impressed by a handwritten note Phan had brought from Liang Ch'i-ch'ao, urging the establishment of commercial, agricultural, and educational societies. Dang soon joined with other scholar-gentry leaders like Ngo Duc Ke and Le Van Huan[4] to attempt precisely that. But, meanwhile, a number of Phan's other associates, especially within the Duy Tan Hoi, were decidedly disappointed by his failure to secure weapons and not particularly excited about his new overseas student project. While it should be remembered that the Duy Tan Hoi had provided for a division between secret and open activities—the latter often identical in appearance with associations and businesses just being started by reformist scholar-gentry—the basic priorities of this group were always activist, violent, even putschist, in character. Phan made major efforts to bridge these divisions, or at least to coordinate the strategies. Intellectually, Phan wanted to believe in both approaches, but emotionally and spiritually he repeatedly demonstrated a preference for heroic, violent destruction of colonial rule. Although to the end Phan remained able to communicate on warm, personal terms with reformist leaders like Phan Chu Trinh and Nguyen Quyen, after 1905 he was not really able to coordinate strategies with them effectively.

Fears of Phan Boi Chau's being seized by the police now haunted his closest associates, to the point where they urged him to leave the country again even before Cuong De's escape from Hue had been engineered.

---

2. VTCM, p. 30. The author of this vignette, Dang Thai Mai, was born and raised in Nghe An and was personally familiar with some of the scholar-gentry in their later years.
3. In Vietnamese these political tendencies are usually associated with the terms *bao dong* and *cai luong*, respectively. Alternatives are *kich liet* and *on hoa*. Technically, *bao dong* and *kich liet* are translated as "violence" or "violent," but "activist" is more descriptive in this context.
4. Pseudonym, Lam Ngu. From Trung-le village, Duc-tho district, Ha-Tinh, Le scored first in the 1906 regional exams, hence often was called *giai* Huan. HT, p. 595.

Taking three students with him,[5] Phan in October 1905 crossed back into Kwangtung, where he this time apparently had the opportunity to meet the aged Black Flag commander Liu Yung-fu and the Can Vuong leader Nguyen Thien Thuat.[6] Liu, now almost seventy years old, showed his sentiments by beating the table and yelling "Tso-Tso-Tso!" ("Heresy!"; in Vietnamese, "Ta! Ta! Ta!") every time the French were mentioned. And Nguyen Thien Thuat, so the story goes, was so moved by a reading of Phan's *Viet-Nam Vong Quoc Su*, that he smashed his opium pipe and swore off the habit.[7] Having waited more than a month for Cuong De, to no avail, Phan escorted his three students across to Yokohama and a meeting with Liang Ch'i-ch'ao. Hearing Phan's complaint that rich boys were afraid to go and poor boys lacked the money, Liang once again encouraged him to write pamphlets as a way of rousing domestic enthusiasm and financial support. The result was the short *Khuyen Quoc Dan Tu Tro Du Hoc Van* (Encouragement to Citizens to Contribute for Overseas Study), which Liang published without charge in more than three thousand copies.[8]

Whereas *Khuyen Quoc Dan Tu Tro Du Hoc Van* added little to *Viet-Nam Vong Quoc Su* in terms of substantive political conceptions, it did provide domestic readers with a much clearer idea of what Phan had in mind in attempting to take scores—perhaps hundreds—of students to Japan in what was soon to be called the Dong Du (Eastern Study) movement. In Phan's opinion, the independence secured from China a millenium earlier had been lost to the French and remained lost for two basic reasons: people were either ignorant (*ngu*), or they were cowardly (*hen*). Some might plead that Vietnam was too small in territory or population to defeat France. But this was silly. After all, was Vietnam smaller than England? Was its population smaller than that of Japan when they had decided to modernize? Japan had succeeded, Phan believed, because the Japanese people knew how to show compassion for each other, to live and die in common effort. In Japan's darker hours there had been only Yoshida Shoin, demanding resistance and preaching

---

5. Of these, apparently the only memorable one was Nguyen Thuc Canh, also known as Tran Huu Cong. Phan mentions that he was from Dong-chu, Nghe An (?), the eldest son of one of Phan's earlier teachers. NB, p. 60. TP, p. 59.
6. Phan's first autobiography, NTT, does not mention this meeting, but NB, pp. 60–61, and TP, pp. 59–60, have a detailed description.
7. Phan also records there that Nguyen Thien Thuat's eldest son was soon killed while serving with De Tham; another son and a younger brother died in prison on Con-lon island, and a grandson died of tuberculosis while studying at a Peking military school.
8. NB, p. 62. TP, p. 61, says the title was *Khuyen Quoc Dan Du Hoc Van*. Vietnamese translation, in VTCM, pp. 181–188.

Japan's development as a great power.[9] But after a while there were thousands, tens of thousands of Yoshida Shoins, yelling and clapping for the same objectives. Was Vietnam lacking in such spirit?

Phan Boi Chau's rather bluntly phrased solution was for the rich and the poor in Vietnam to conduct an exchange of services; in other words, for the "cowardly" to see fit to suport the "ignorant" in extended overseas study. By and large, he said, the wealthy were too elderly, cautious, or hidebound to change their ways significantly. Yet, many were patriotic and wanted somebody to act. The poor were often young and lacked the means to travel and study, but, if given the opportunity, they would get things moving. "The two groups," Phan urged, "will assist and complement each other, and no one will end up doing harm to anyone else."[10]

The cost of supporting one student for one year in a program of general studies was about 250 piastres and in the Japanese military academies, 300 piastres. It would take eight or nine years to get the best students all the way through the universities, while the others could graduate from lesser schools in two or three years. Hence, Phan argued, wealthy supporters at home would do well to pool their funds and use the interest for long-term assistance. In return, the young beneficiaries would cultivate a courageous attitude, refuse to be daunted by adversity, and foreswear entirely such "lustful" pleasures as singing girls, sex, liquor, and gambling. Above all, there was a need for everyone concerned to develop patience and not look for small advantages:

If we are rash, we will never reach our objective. If we only seek petty gains, we will ruin the whole larger effort.[11]

Before *Khuyen Quoc Dan Tu Tro Du Hoc Van* could be distributed, six more students had arrived in Yokohama.[12] Now the money problem really was acute, since all six had arrived with pockets empty. Tang Bat Ho moved to arrange for credit from the local Chinese rice and charcoal

9. Yoshida Shoin (1830–1859) was a junior samurai leader who early became interested in "Dutch learning" and established a school to preach the overthrow of the shogunate and the development of Japan as a great power. He was executed in 1859, but not before he had implanted his ideas in the minds of an important group of young disciples.
10. VTCM, p. 187.
11. VTCM, p. 187.
12. Most well known among these students subsequently were Luong Lap Nham, better known later as Luong Ngoc Quyen, and Nguyen Hai Than, the latter already a *tu tai*. Luong and his brother, Luong Nghi Khanh, who also went to Japan at this time, were the sons of Luong Van Can, a wealthy Hanoi silk merchant and subsequent principal of the Dong Kinh Nghia Thuc. VNDN, pp. 135–136.

merchants, did some dockside work, and then took a steamer to Kwang-tung to raise money through Liu Yung-fu and Nguyen Thien Thuat. But these were stopgap solutions. Soon the Vietnamese in Yokohama saw their first snow; it was the beginning of a difficult winter. Too proud to borrow money, Phan did borrow many books from Liang for all to read. Finally, Luong Lap Nham set out for Tokyo and the Chinese student community in Kanda ward; the students, in turn, led him to the *Min-pao* offices, where he picked up a job from the paper's editor, Chang Ping-lin.[13] Soon Luong had secured positions for two more Vietnamese; there they worked, ate, studied Japanese, and developed friendships among young T'ung-meng-hui (United League) followers.[14]

To the Vietnamese it must have seemed that the Chinese exiles, both reformers and revolutionaries, were fairly rolling in cash. This raises an important point: men like Sun Yat-sen and Liang Ch'i-ch'ao spent a good portion of their time extracting money from overseas Chinese com-munities, from the Chinese merchants of Yokohama and other Japanese cities, from those in Honolulu, Hong Kong, Singapore, and so on. This was one reason that Liang helped organize the Chinese schools in Yoko-hama and that Sun traveled so much and cultivated ties with overseas branches of secret societies. If the Chinese exiles hoped to keep free of foreign manipulation, then overseas Chinese money was essential.[15] The Vietnamese, however, had no overseas communities to speak of, and this fact conditioned the activities of their political exiles and students for some decades, either preventing them from doing many things that they deemed essential or making them overly dependent on foreigners.[16]

From the beginning, the anticolonial scholar-gentry relied on the Chinese for help in getting printed materials into Vietnam. The French colonial regime carefully monitored overt traffic in Chinese-language

13. For a biography of Chang Ping-lin (also well known as Chang T'ai-yen), see Howard L. Boorman, ed., *Biographical Dictionary of Republican China*, vol. 1 (New York, 1967), pp. 92–98. There it is indicated that Chang did not assume his *Min-pao* duties until the early summer of 1906, so it may be that Luong had initial contact with someone else.

14. NB, pp. 62–64. TP, pp. 61–63.

15. This is not to say that Sun, in particular, was necessarily adverse to taking non-Chinese money. For example, he used Akiyama Teisuke as a fund-raiser among the Japanese and even tapped the directors of the Mitsui Corporation at least once. Marius Jansen, *The Japanese and Sun Yat-sen*, pp. 79–81, 121–122.

16. A small Vietnamese community in Thailand was the minor exception. After be-ing ejected from Japan, Phan Boi Chau did try to rely on them, as we shall see. Viet-namese overseas communities would develop later in Paris, New Caledonia, Phnom Penh, and Vientiane, but they never achieved the significance of the Chinese com-munities.

materials, partly at the specific request of the Ch'ing foreign ministry.[17] French consuls in Shanghai and Canton regularly sent analyses of the Chinese press to the governor general of Indochina, on which he based his bans on specific periodicals and brochures. Nevertheless, it was relatively easy to slip materials in, providing one had the right contacts within the local Chinese communities. By mid-1908 the French authorities were complaining that, whereas the Chinese residents in Indochina had special legal status and often lived within French enclaves, thereby enjoying a security and commercial prosperity unknown in their homeland, they still for some reason chose to subsidize Chinese revolutionaries and—worse yet—to communicate revolutionary ideas to the "Annamites":

> The majority of Chinese residents in Indochina are in sympathy with the [Chinese] revolutionary party, and it is in part by means of the journals they receive, as well as their remarks and their conversations, that they contribute to the spread of new ideas among the Annamite population.[18]

With the long and approachable Vietnamese coastline, an alternative procedure was for Chinese junks to debark small packets of journals clandestinely right into the hands of the Vietnamese scholar-gentry or their associates. After that: "Thanks to their knowledge of characters, the literati recopy the articles which interest them. These are then put under their robes and smuggled to the most distant villages."[19] In the end, of course, legal niceties were no adequate protection, and by late 1909 the governor general was reporting the expulsion of Chinese nationals who had been involved in any such activities.[20] Nevertheless, during the heyday of scholar-gentry efforts, such contacts and assistance had proved extremely important.

Although the winter of 1905/1906 in Japan was harsh and food scarce, Phan Boi Chau was not one to remain idle. He studied the Japanese syllabary *(kana),* sought to make more Chinese contacts, and tried to get his student flock into schools. A member of T'ung-meng-hui named T'ang Chiao-tun[21] wrote a letter on Phan's behalf to a Ch'ing official in Kwangsi, but the reply was deeply humiliating, as the official stated that the Viet-

---

17. AOM A-80 NF 66. This dossier contains, among other things, a March 11, 1910, listing by the governor general's office of materials specifically banned. The materials were published in such diverse locations as Tokyo, Singapore, and Paris.
18. AOM A-50 NF 451, carton 32.
19. *Ibid.*
20. AOM A-50 NF 450 (1).
21. TP, p. 63. NB, p. 64, gives Yang as his surname.

namese were endowed with a hopelessly slavelike mentality. Worse yet, Phan's Chinese contact, T'ang, regarded this as a knowledgeable, definitive judgment. Liang Ch'i-ch'ao, at least, was more helpful, pointing out that many Yunnanese students were now attending Japanese military schools and advising the Vietnamese to make friends with them, on the assumption that they, too, had a special hatred of the French. As we shall see, this tactic proved very useful.[22] In January 1906 Phan visited Inukai's residence in Tokyo and arranged for the entry of three students into the Shimbu Military Academy and of one into the Dobun Shoin (Common Culture School).[23] This was also Phan's opportunity to meet General Fukushima Yasumasa, director of the Shimbu Military Academy, and to meet the rector and the chief instructor of the Dobun Shoin.

Inukai was also Phan Boi Chau's access to Sun Yat-sen, providing him a letter of introduction and remarking that his fate was probably wrapped up with that of the revolution in China. Interestingly enough, Sun had read *Viet-Nam Vong Quoc Su* before their meeting, so he opened the "brush conversation" with an attack on constitutional monarchism and a proposal that Phan and his associates all join the T'ung-meng-hui! Once the Chinese revolution was successful, he would turn his attention to helping the other oppressed peoples of Asia, and of those the Vietnamese would receive first consideration. Phan states in his autobiography that by this time he had accepted the theoretical merits of a democratic republic. But he countered Sun's strategy with a proposal that the T'ung-meng-hui first help Vietnam achieve independence and then use north Vietnam as a base for seizing Kwangsi and Kwangtung. Some days later they met again, reaching no agreement on strategy, but parting amicably. From this point on, Phan appears to have circulated more among Sun's group than Liang's, although he had not broken with the latter by any means and his working position remained monarchist.[24]

Receiving word from his comrades Dang Thai Than and Tang Bat Ho that Prince Cuong De was on the way out of Vietnam, Phan immediately left for Hong Kong, using introductions from Chinese merchant friends in Yokohama to secure an unobtrusive meeting place.[25] Nguyen Thanh, handling the Duy Tan Hoi's domestic operations, had planned originally for Cuong De merely to ask for French permission to go study in Paris and then switch ships at Singapore for the voyage to Japan. All this was

22. NB, p. 66. TP, p. 65.
23. Nagaoka Shinjiro and Kawamoto Kunie, eds., *Betonamu Bokokushi*, pp. 258–259. Phan recalled (TP, p. 40) this meeting as taking place in April 1906, but we may assume that Mr. Nagaoka had access to more precise documentation.
24. NB, pp. 67–68. TP, pp. 66–67.
25. NB, pp. 68–69. TP, pp. 67–68.

discarded, however, when they saw that Liang Ch'i-ch'ao's introduction to *Viet-Nam Vong Quoc Su* made public reference to Cuong De. Naturally, there were also money problems, which Nguyen Thanh was trying to solve by involving the Duy Tan Hoi in the formation of local commercial "fronts." At last, with a crucial assist from Ly Tue, Cuong De was hidden aboard a steamer heading from Haiphong to Hong Kong, where he arrived in March 1906.[26]

For both activists and reformists, the next two and a half years represented the high point of this generation's anticolonial efforts. Certainly Phan Boi Chau remembered them nostalgically as the only years of his life in which his plans and his works seemed to be going well.[27] Once again, he was working simultaneously on a variety of fronts. For example, in Hong Kong he saw to it that the young Cuong De met the steadfast old warhorses, Liu Yung-fu and Nguyen Thien Thuat. Phan then contacted potentially sympathetic officials in the German consulate for the first time, worked up the Duy Tan Hoi's first written platform, and encouraged Cuong De to write an initial proclamation for domestic distribution. Most important, however, was his meeting with Phan Chu Trinh, who by chance had arrived in Hong Kong at the same time, en route to seeing modern Japan for himself. Looking over Phan Boi Chau's written materials, Phan Chu Trinh apparently approved of *Khuyen Quoc Dan Tu Tro Du Hoc Van*, since he felt it essential for as many Vietnamese as possible to acquire modern educations and comprehension of modern ways. But Phan Chu Trinh did not like the Duy Tan Hoi draft platform, would not identify his name with any monarchist proposal, and expressed an overriding contempt and hatred of the entire Hue mandarinate. For him, in short, the mere restoration of an independent monarchy was not equivalent to the salvation of Vietnam.[28]

Soon the group sailed together to Yokohama, where they were at last in a position to establish a small residence-headquarters called Binh Ngo Hien (The Eaves of 1906). Okuma, Inukai, and Fukushima received Cuong De cordially but there was disappointment among the Vietnamese when it was indicated that Cuong De could not be recognized officially as a royal pretender, but only as another student on his way to the Shimbu Military Academy.[29] Phan Boi Chau at about this time also assisted Cuong De in writing several "edicts" to send back to Vietnam.[30] The gen-

26. CD, pp. 20–22.
27. NB, p. 68. TP, p. 67.
28. NB, pp. 69–70. TP, pp. 68–69.
29. CD, p. 23. TP, p. 71. NB, pp. 72–73.
30. These included "Hich Cao Quoc Dan Van" (Royal Report to the People) and "Kinh Cao Tuyen Quoc Phu Lao Van" (General announcement to the elders of Our

eral thrust of this propaganda betrayed a continuing hope of converting the royal family and mandarin collaborators to the anticolonial cause. The idea lingered that a simple description of how the French were entrenching themselves by the blood and sweat of the Vietnamese people would be sufficient to rally all to the insurgent banner.

Meanwhile, Phan Boi Chau had taken special pains to guide Phan Chu Trinh around Tokyo, visiting schools and observing general political and economic conditions. Phan Chu Trinh emerged deeply impressed, but all the more certain that the first priority for Vietnam had to be popular education, by which the people would awaken to their rights and their opportunities in the modern world. Like Liang Ch'i-ch'ao, Phan Chu Trinh warmly encouraged Phan Boi Chau to concentrate only on getting students out of Vietnam and writing for dissemination at home. Meanwhile, Phan Chu Trinh would return to Vietnam and attempt to pressure the French into undertaking major reforms, as well as trying to rouse increasing numbers of Vietnamese to participation in the modern learning process. Strictly as a tactic, Phan Boi Chau was in seeming agreement with this, but he also insisted on organizing covertly for eventual attacks against the French and on retaining monarchism as a means, if nothing else, of attracting followers and of providing popular ideological symbols for the movement. After several weeks of animated discussion, the two men apparently were unable to work out a comprehensive, coordinated strategy, and Phan Boi Chau escorted Phan Chu Trinh back to Hong Kong. Phan Chu Trinh's parting words were to the effect that the Vietnamese people were ready to follow Phan Boi Chau alone, without needing Cuong De and all the monarchist trappings.[31] This was destined to be their last meeting.

Several weeks after returning to Yokohama,[32] Phan Boi Chau sat down to write *Hai Ngoai Huyet Thu* (Overseas Book Inscribed in Blood), now employing in poetry the direct, hard-hitting approach he had used in *Viet-Nam Vong Quoc Su* in prose.[33] Again he had both Chinese and Vietnamese reading audiences in mind, although this time the emphasis

---

Country). Ly Tue again was a key man, passing batches of these materials on to Tang Bat Ho and Dang Tu Kinh in central and south Vietnam. Nguyen Hai Than left Japan temporarily to smuggle copies into the north. CD, p. 24. NB, p. 74. TP, pp. 72–73.
31. NB, pp. 72–73. TP, pp. 71–72.
32. Probably in June 1906, and escorting two new students.
33. The full poem, of 11,000 characters, is contained in *Yun-nan Tsa-chih Hsuan-chi* (Peking, 1958, Third Research Office, Scientific Research Institute), which was unavailable to me. See VT, pp. 134–154, for *quoc-ngu* translation.

was on the latter. Phan in his autobiography clearly recalled that his inspiration was Liang Ch'i-ch'ao's *I-Ta-Li Chien-kuo San-Chieh Chuan* (Biographies of the Three Heroes of the Building of Italy), dealing with Mazzini, Garibaldi, and Cavour, which he said Liang was working on when they first met.[34] Phan was entranced by Mazzini, and particularly by his argument that "education and activism must advance simultaneously." *Hai Ngoai Huyet Thu* soon was published in *Yun-nan Tsa-chih,* the editors in the preface expressing sympathy with Phan, but also some anger that all this had not been revealed twenty years earlier—before so many had to die or be enslaved. Those places "about to become Vietnams," particularly Yunnan, were instructed to take Phan's writing as a final warning.[35] Phan also ordered a large separate printing and turned batches over to several associates in Hong Kong, who later distributed them throughout Vietnam. Le Dai, a friend of Phan's, translated *Hai Ngoai Huyet Thu* into *quoc ngu* and in 1907 distributed it as part of the Dong Kinh Nghia Thuc instructional syllabus. There is no question that both versions were read and quoted, the poem becoming one of the most widely known Vietnamese anticolonial statements of the early twentieth century.

The first section of *Hai Ngoai Huyet Thu* dealt with the oppressive effects of French colonial policy. The second and more important section turned inward, trying to delineate the causes of Vietnam's "loss," calling for a sense of patriotic revenge, and pleading for mass unity. It is possible to see a subtle but definite ideological shift from the *Viet-Nam Vong Quoc Su* of the year before, which may be attributable to Phan's wider reading or to his intensive exchanges with Phan Chu Trinh. For example, there is the following famous passage:

Why was our country lost?
I submit the following:
First the monarch knew nothing of popular affairs;
Second the mandarins cared nothing for the people;
And third the people knew only of themselves.[36]
State matters to the King, other affairs to the mandarins, the people said.
Hundreds of thousands, millions together worked
To build the foundations of our country.
The bodies, the resources are from the people;
The people are in fact the country, the country is the people's.
On the throne the King had complete license
And had a long time to drowse.

34. NB, p. 75. TP, p. 73.
35. *Yun-nan Tsa-chih Hsuan-chi,* p. 701.
36. That is, they were not privy to higher or external affairs.

Within the borders his word was law,
Ten thousand people bowed low at his command.
Search back and forth over history,
Who will restore benefits and wipe out the people's misfortune?[37]

Repeatedly Phan dwelt on evidence of internal betrayal and on the court's unwillingness to accept Mencius' dictum on the people's being the basis and purpose of government (*dan vi bang ban*). He cited Japan as the model, where it was said that monarch and people lived under one roof of mutual respect, and equality was the government's byword. Sounding very much like Phan Chu Trinh, he assailed the contemporary court at Hue, accusing them of oppressing the people for selfish gain and lazing away the years in romps with the concubines.

Phan's final plea in *Hai Ngoai Huyet Thu* was for mass unity in a prolonged struggle. He specifically mentioned tax resistance and draft refusal as acceptable tactics for the moment. Once again he argued for a multi-class alliance, referring to village notables, ranking officials, scholar-gentry patriots, Catholics, soldiers, déclassé types, "delinquent youths," students, women and girls, and assorted servants of the French. He called for students to follow him overseas, spoke more feelingly of the value of propaganda in the slow process of building national unity, and cited Fukuzawa Yukichi and Jean Jacques Rousseau as the torches that should light the way for a new generation. But still dominating his thought was the fervent cry to battle:

> Blood is boiling in your heart,
> Countrymen! Draw forth your swords,
> There is Heaven, Earth, and Us.
> That is what we call true unity![38]

In another poem attributed to Phan Boi Chau and written about the same time as *Hai Ngoai Huyet Thu*, the stress was on concrete suggestions for material development.[39] People at home were urged to follow specific Japanese precedents in forming agricultural associations, savings and investment firms, and industrial and commercial corporations. To those who argued that foreign competition would quickly overwhelm such efforts, Phan countered that the China Sea was no one's private property. Hence, there was no reason why Vietnamese should not stretch out to Hong Kong, Yokohama, and Bangkok at a time when others were coming

37. HT, p. 436.
38. HT, p. 440.
39. Phan Boi Chau, "Kinh gui dong bao toan quoc," reprinted in VTCM, pp. 276–282. The poem is in 7–7–6–8 *nom* form.

to trade at Haiphong, Da-Nang, and Saigon. Local entrepreneurs were even encouraged to pool their capital with the overseas Chinese—an indication of Phan's supreme confidence, if not his comprehension of the basic problems involved, At any rate, as with all other matters, the complicated question of accumulating national wealth was for Phan ultimately reducible to cultivating grit and determination:

> There is nothing more painful than having no possessions to use,
> No possessions because there are no [skilled] people,
> No [skilled] people because their spirit is zero![40]

And lest anyone miss the point and expect to sit around waiting for the Japanese "doctor" to come and magically treat all of Vietnam's illnesses, Phan concluded with the following homily:

> One calls for the doctor out of common-sense necessity.
> But are the patient, the implements, the ingredients ready or not?
> Or are people counting on the doctor to do everything,
> From securing the medicine, building the fire and mixing,
> To providing bed and mat for the patient,
> To even asking the doctor to pay for journies back and forth?
> The sick person has little reason to hope for recovery,
> Yet the household has not thought even a little bit ahead.
> In such circumstances the doctor can hardly be expected to come over.
> Bowing and scraping to him will only compound the shame,
> Better to feel the enemy's blade and get it over with.[41]

Phan Boi Chau also wrote at least four prose articles for *Yun-nan Tsa-chih* during the rest of 1906. While we have no evidence that they were read extensively inside Vietnam, we do know that Vietnamese students arriving in Japan read them, as did the regular Chinese reading audience. The four known pieces were:

1. SOME COMMENTS AFTER READING THE INTRODUCTION OF "JAPAN'S ANNEXATION POLICY FOR CHINA": This apparently was in reference to a manuscript shown to Phan by an unidentified Japanese political figure, whereupon Phan felt the necessity in emotional terms to warn the Chinese of their future.[42]

2. AI VIET DIEU DIEN (in Chinese, Ai-yueh Tiao-tien; Sorrow for Vietnam, Condolences for Yunnan): This was phrased as a dire warning

---

40. VTCM, pp. 280–281.
41. VTCM, p. 282.
42. *Yun-nan Tsa-chih Hsuan-chi*, p. 713, as cited by Chuong Thau, "Anh huong cua Phan Boi Chau," NCLS 55: 36–37.

to the Yunnanese that they were about to "die" the same way Vietnam had. Phan reviewed the historical relations between Vietnam and Yunnan, picturing the two areas as practically inseparable in military and geographic terms. Only two things stood between the French imperialists and annexation of Yunnan, Phan argued: the absence of a complete modern rail network into Yunnan to supply French occupational forces and the agreement of the British to accept a French seizure of the territory. Phan encouraged the Yunnanese to unite behind some heroic leader to block completion of the railroad, then under way; meanwhile, the Vietnamese would try to support them, he said, perhaps by harassing the rail traffic sufficiently to render it unprofitable and to forestall an Anglo-French deal. If such tactics were unrealistic at that point, then Yunnanese anticolonialists should start an educational movement among their people and begin training a military resistance force that had popular support. Secret arrangements could be made with Vietnamese anticolonialists, so that, when all was ready, the "Yunnanese grab the French bandit's arm, and the Vietnamese grab his waist." This way, working together, the Yunnanese would preserve their independence, and the Vietnamese would come alive again. Phan concluded:

> I have cried, I have sung, laughed, spoken—but all to no avail in saving my own countrymen. [You Yunnanese should] use guns fashioned from bones, ammunition of flesh, draw swords with a roar, and cry out to heaven in one long breath.[43]

3. VIET VONG THAM TRANG (in Chinese, *Yueh-wang ts'an chuang*; Lost Vietnam's Pitiful Situation): No copy of this article is available, but it was mentioned in another *Yun-nan Tsa-chih* article by a Chinese author who pointed out that Phan was again foretelling the imminent fate of Yunnan. It apparently dealt, too, with the hardships of the Vietnamese people under French rule and cited patriots who were continuing the struggle.[44]

4. HOA LE CONG NGON (in Chinese, *Ho-li Kung-yen*, An Appeal Bathed in Tears):[45] Here Phan appeared to be directing his comments to examination candidates back home, calling for complete renunciation of the French-dominated administration and a new devotion to saving the Vietnamese people from extermination. He reviewed the traditional

43. *Yun-nan Tsa-chih Hsuan-chi*, pp. 715–719. Full *quoc-ngu* translation, NCLS 56: 38–41.
44. Cited in Chuong Thau, "Anh huong cua Phan Boi Chau," p. 38.
45. *Yun-nan Tsa-chih Hsuan-chi*, pp. 719–722. The article is signed with a pseudonym which present-day scholars, both Chinese and Vietnamese, believe to be that of Phan Boi Chau. *Quoc-ngu* translation, NCLS 56: 41–44.

attributes of scholars, including a willingness to retain honor unto death (perhaps the only justification for their status as leaders of the people). In sharp, even derogatory, tones he asked who would be around several decades hence to care whether this person was a *tien-si*, that one a *cu-nhan* or a *tu-tai*. He cited Louis Kossuth, Jean Jacques Rousseau, and the Meiji leaders Yoshida Shoin and Okuma Shigenobu as foreigners worthy of emulation. There was reference also to Patrick Henry, with his cry of "Give me liberty, or give me death!"

Specifically, Phan demanded from the educated elite emotional fervor (*nhiet-thanh*) followed by self-criticism, eloquence (to spread the word), bravery, careful preparation before action, proper timing, restraint of the overadventurous among them, technical proficiency (in sciences and engineering), and military and organizational skills that could be learned from both European and Asian sources for transmission to much larger numbers of the people.

> History creates brave men, but brave men also create history. You [the exam graduates] continue to bow your heads and work like dogs for the bandits [*giac*]. How can that ever compare with raising up your heads proudly and becoming great citizens of your fatherland?

Phan returned last of all to the meanings of country and patriotism, arguing that anyone with self-identity and a home had the responsibility to be patriotic, regardless of wealth, intelligence, age, or personality. If the examination candidates accepted this, were they not, then, aware that present-day taxes, corvée, and recruitment for plantation and railroad gangs were French techniques for killing the Vietnamese people? Why did they react like docile, fearful chickens in a coop when one of their own was taken out to be killed, instead of massing like angry bees that swarmed to the attack when threatened? It should be apparent that Phan's attack on examination degrees had by this time broadened into something of an attack on traditional social status, with the added suggestion that identification with one's class be replaced by identification with one's entire land and people.

The editor of *Yun-nan Tsa-chih*, in a comment on this article, said that he would shed no tears for a country that had lost its sovereignty, but only for a country whose people had lost heart or spirit. Such would seem to be the case among exam candidates in Vietnam, he remarked, and he wondered rhetorically if others, perhaps in Yunnan, had the same sickness.[46]

46. Quoted in Chuong Thau, "Anh huong cua Phan Boi Chau," from *Yun-nan Tsa-chih Hsuan-chi,* p. 722.

Toward the end of 1906 Phan Boi Chau was disturbed by the lack of news from inside Vietnam and dissatisfied with the meager number (fewer than twenty) of students who had reached Japan. Among the forty or more Vietnamese in Hong Kong, however, some progress in recruitment was reported, so Phan wanted to develop Hong Kong into a way-station and extend this pattern effectively into the Kwangsi and Kwangtung border areas. He had never really been convinced by Liang, Okuma, or Phan Chu Trinh that all he should do was wait in Japan, writing propaganda and nursemaiding students. So, blessed with the timely arrival of 1,000 piastres[47] from Vietnam, Phan set off for Kwangtung and a thorough scouting of the border areas, using introductions from Liu Yung-fu and Nguyen Thien Thuat to gain access to other old bandit and resistance leaders. These men provided Phan with armed escorts, geographical intelligence, and a forged Chinese passport to get himself by the French border post and aboard the train to Gia-Lam. From there he traveled up to Thai-Nguyen and a meeting with the local Chinese warlord of long standing, Liang San-ch'i (in Vietnamese, Luong Tam Ky). Phan's purpose was to persuade Liang to drop his comfortable relationship with the French, but Phan failed completely and emerged furious that not only the French imperialists but now even a minor Chinese bandit could lord it over the Vietnamese.[48]

Next, utilizing an introduction from another old Can Vuong leader, Phan gained access to De Tham (Hoang Hoa Tham), who was still holding on unobtrusively in the backlands of Yen-The. It is apparent that Phan still entertained high hopes for De Tham, considering it a victory when he persuaded the latter to join the Duy Tan Hoi, to accept Cuong De as titular leader, to provide a small camp for cadres from central Vietnam, and to agree in principle to back up future central Vietnamese uprisings. In return, De Tham was promised central suport if he himself decided to attack, some assistance in making foreign contacts, and the possibility of military supplies. From Yen-The, Phan moved back down to Bac-Ninh to smooth over growing differences between activist and reformist elements among the scholar-gentry. Dang Thai Than was made responsible for liaison between the two elements, while liaison with resistance groups overseas was tightened up by appointing one man (Dang Tu Kinh) to shuttle in and out of central Vietnam and another man (Nguyen Hai Than, alias Vu Hai Thu) to do the same in the north.[49]

---

47. The Mexican piastre and the local zinc and copper sapeques were withdrawn from circulation in Indochina in 1903. In the same year the French piastre was issued and pegged to the franc.
48. NB, pp. 77–82. TP, pp. 78–84.
49. NB, pp. 82–84. TP, pp. 84–85.

But the differences of basic approach and strategy would not be papered over by merely improving communications. The Dong Kinh Nghia Thuc educational effort was getting under way at this time in Hanoi. Ngo Duc Ke's group in Nghe An already was instituting an ambitious commercial scheme and talking publicly of the need for "revolutionary" economic and social change. Phan Chu Trinh was preaching the elimination of the monarchy and the mandarin system in favor of massive modernization under enlightened French aegis. All of these scholar-gentry, even if they did not tie themselves in with Phan Boi Chau's covert net, were in fact close friends of many members of the network and were roughly aware of its operations. Hence, Phan's most obvious fear was that their public challenge to the contemporary colonial system, even though nonviolent, would rouse French suspicions or spark other Vietnamese to premature action. Either way, the result would probably be a general French and mandarin crackdown that could not help exposing much of his covert operation. During 1906 laws had already been promulgated in northern and central Vietnam to punish fathers and elder brothers of individuals secretly leaving the country and to discipline the village leadership, as well.[50] Phan had been back in Vietnam less than a month, insufficient time really to handle these problems, when his comrades detected imminent danger for him from the police and helped him escape to Lang-Son disguised as a Chinese merchant.[51] After this, the best he could do was write a personal letter to Phan Chu Trinh, agreeing in principle to his advocacy of democracy, but imploring him to wait a few more years before spreading the doctrine:

> The Vietnamese people as compared with Western people are still far behind. . . . Now, bring out a theory that people don't really comprehend, cry out its name loudly, and it won't be difficult to secure some supporters. Beyond that, however, uniting the people is another question! On the contrary, because of clashing ideas and contradictory activities we may end up opposing each other when the external enemy is still not eliminated. Alas! for democracy [*dan-chu*]: if the "*dan*" [people] are no longer in existence, what meaning has the "*chu*" [rulership]?[52]

Phan Boi Chau did not stress it, but there appears to have been also a growing demoralization among the more militant, impatient, monarchist elements of the Duy Tan Hoi. Cuong De later pointed out that one of Phan Chu Trinh's main arguments upon returning from his single visit

50. VTCM, p. 64.
51. NB, pp. 84–86. TP, pp. 85–87.
52. Chinese transliteration, TP, pp. 210–211. *Quoc-ngu* translation, TP, pp. 212–213; also VT, pp. 155–157.

to Japan was the utter hopelessness of waiting for substantial Japanese assistance, particularly weapons. Talk like this led some wealthy people clustered around Nguyen Thanh, for example, to drop their support of his commercial "fronts," causing those money-raising schemes to fail.[53] Along with Phan Boi Chau this time Nguyen Thanh had sent two associates to discuss the situation with Cuong De in Japan and perhaps encourage him to return to help resolve this conflict. Phan Boi Chau, presumably realizing that the reformists no longer were interested in listening to a monarchist pretender, instead encouraged Cuong De to shift his prime attention to south Vietnam, where there were known to be wealthy monarchists who could solve their pressing money problems. Apparently it was at this point that Phan helped Cuong De to write *Pho Cao Luc Tinh Van* (General Proclamation to the Six Southern Provinces).[54]

By May 1907 Phan had shuttled to Hong Kong to pass along printed materials, to open a new communications link with Saigon, and to meet seven more penniless students en route to Japan. Interestingly, he now went to the trouble of having propaganda aimed at south Vietnam translated into *quoc-ngu*, since in that area *quoc-ngu* was already well on the way to becoming an acceptable mode of written expression.[55] Several southern students were already studying in Hong Kong schools. One was the son of Tran Chanh Chieu, better known as Gilbert Chieu, editor of the Saigon *quoc-ngu* paper *Luc Tinh Tan Van* (News of the Six Provinces—that is, south Vietnam) and at that time perhaps Cochinchina's most influential bourgeois intellectual. The result was a quick journey by Gilbert Chieu to Hong Kong for consultations with Phan Boi Chau and, after his return to Saigon, a substantial increase in the flow of money and students out of that part of the country. Indeed, by the end of 1907 the number of Vietnamese students in Japan had increased to at least one hundred, more than half from the south.[56]

---

53. CD, p. 23.

54. CD, p. 24. NB, p. 88, and TP, p. 88, also mention a work, written at this time by Phan and signed by Cuong De, titled "Ai Cao Nam Ky Phu Lao" (Funeral Announcement for the Elders of South Vietnam). It is possible, however, that they are talking about the same publication.

55. Besides the native Catholics, who had been somewhat familiar with *quoc-ngu* for centuries, the French regime in Cochinchina after 1861 attempted, at various times and with varying degrees of success, to institute *quoc-ngu* as the written medium in education, officialdom, and the press. Only at the end of the century, however, did it achieve some intellectual respectability—but still limited to Cochinchina.

56. NB, pp. 87–88, 92. TP, pp. 88–90, 94. Nagaoka and Kawamoto, *Betonamu*, p. 262.

Of course Phan Boi Chau was not about to give up on central and north Vietnam. In this light, it appears that an essay Phan wrote while in Hong Kong, titled *Tan Viet-Nam* (New Vietnam), represented an attempt to offset the erosion within the Duy Tan Hoi caused by reformist ideology, particularly that of Phan Chu Trinh. *Tan Viet-Nam* was visionary, at times bordering on fantasy. In addition to stealing some of the reformists' thunder in the short-term sense, Phan Boi Chau aimed to present sincerely for as large a Vietnamese audience as posssible an idea of what he and his associates were struggling for.[57] More than two-thirds was devoted to "ten great joys" that would come to Vietnam once there was "reformation" (*duy-tan*):

1. No "Protecting" Country over Vietnam:

Since France gained their protectorate they have taken over everything, even the power of life or death. The life of 10,000 "Annamese" is worth less than one French dog; the prestige of 100 mandarins is less than that of one French female. How is it that those blue-eyed, yellow-bearded people, who are not our fathers or elder brothers, can squat on our heads, defecate on us?

After reformation, Phan envisioned a steady advance in civilized pursuits, an army of three million and a navy of five hundred thousand, embassies in all the major world capitals. Japan, the United States, Germany, and England would be allies; Siam, India, and the East Indies would recognize Vietnam as their titular leader (*minh-chu*); China would be like a brother;[58] and France would be so afraid that she would be "willing to invite us as a protecting power, the flag of our Vietnam flapping over the citadel of Paris, Vietnam's colors spread across the world map."

2. No Mandarin Class That Exploits the People: Here Phan borrowed a few leaves from the book of Phan Chu Trinh. He took pains to denigrate the traditional political system imported from China, whereby a single mandarin could "suck the blood of many thousands of common people." Worse yet, the people offered themselves up as victims by the thousands, one generation after another. After reformation, the people's intellectual standards (*dan tri*) would improve, their spirits (*dan-khi*) soar, their rights (*dan-quyen*) become established, the country's destiny entering entirely into their hands. Here again we can see Phan moving gradually away from the wealthy landlords and gentry within the Duy Tan Hoi, his anger at the mandarin collaborators driving him

---

57. NB, p. 88. TP, p. 89, says he had one thousand copies printed initially.
58. Phan uses the term *anh-em*, without defining who is elder, who younger.

progressively into a more open denigration of the traditional system that had his own class at the helm.

3. NO CITIZEN WHOSE NEEDS ARE NOT SATISFIED:

French dogs, horses, women, servants can now bully anyone as they please, placing themselves in relation to others as heaven is to hell.

Once there was reformation, Phan pictured everyone, including coolies, recruits, widows, and orphans, having their problems heard by the king and solved quickly.

4. NO SOLDIER THAT IS NOT HONORED: After outlining the traditional literati bias against the martial arts, Phan demanded the elimination of the civil/military (*van/vo*) dichotomy, much in the manner of Liang Ch'i-ch'ao. The common soldier must be given his due, both during his lifetime and in death. Here Phan particularly cited Meiji precedents, for example, the Japanese emperor's semiannual pilgrimages to the sacred Yasukuni Jinja.

5. NO TAX THAT IS NOT FAIR: After again listing the oppressive colonial taxes, Phan pictured a time when a popular assembly would set rates that would be ratified by referendum before being implemented.

6. NO LAW THAT IS UNJUST: Interestingly enough, Phan here attacked only the traditional judicial system, ignoring the colonial. With reformation, Phan argued for laws patterned after those of Japan and Europe, also stressing the establishment of schools, infirmaries, and craft shops for the rehabilitation of prisoners.

7. NO EDUCATIONAL SYSTEM THAT IS ILL-CONCEIVED: Having been reared in the belief that education was central to man's existence within society, Phan not surprisingly devoted himself to this section most vigorously and precisely, writing about the future role of foreign educators (accept them eagerly; then phase them out), the structure of a public primary and secondary school system, introduction of *quoc-ngu*, civics indoctrination, specialized training in the military sciences, and the introduction of women into the skilled trades and administrative arts. Above all, however, Phan wanted education to foster patriotism and a sense of common identity:

The rivers and mountains of our country, from Ha-Tien in the south to Lang-Son in the north, are under a common roof, our roof. We are born under that roof, eat and live there, nurtured by the earth beneath and the sky above. In life we exist as countrymen together; in death we are buried under one mound. Our pulse has throbbed for more than a thousand

years, our seed is sustained, our names eternal. Who says we are like the
[ancient Chinese] states of Hu, Han, Ch'in, and Yueh, not united under
one roof?

8. NO NATURAL RESOURCE THAT IS NOT DEVELOPED: Here Phan
mentioned uncultivated lands, introduction of machinery, animal hus-
bandry, and government subsidies or technical assistance, with special
stress on the mountain regions.

9. NO INDUSTRY THAT IS NOT BEGUN: The current situation, as Phan
saw it, was not only one of complete dependence on foreign finished products, but also of French and Chinese control of the commercial establishment. After reformation, Phan envisioned trade schools in mining,
weaponry, machinery, and consumer products, turning out men and
women who could remedy these deficiencies.

10. NO COMMERCE THAT IS NOT FLOURISHING:

The hand that buys and sells is stronger than a tiger, bigger than a whale,
able to swallow down any country in the world. Say you are going to
trade but grasp in your hand a rifle, a sword, and you are able to wipe out
any people in the world. Pity the weak countries!

Accepting this situation as reality, Phan painted a future picture of Vietnamese products spreading across the globe, of commercial branch offices
in all the world capitals, "one thousand ships entering our ports every
day," and wealth rather than guns being the ultimate measure of success.

To accomplish all these wonders, not to mention achieving independence, Phan argued that six personal characteristics had to be cultivated
assiduously: an adventurous and progressive spirit; a love for one's fellow
countrymen; an active desire to seek out modern civilization; a willingness
to practice patriotism, rather than just talking about it; a willingness to
practice public virtue (*cong-duc*), that is, an individual concern for
others; and a developing consciousness of the commonweal, the benefits
and glories of common endeavor.[59]

59. The original is in Chinese. A carefully researched *quoc-ngu* translation is
in NCLS 78: 31–39. See also Chuong Thau, "An huong cua Phan Boi Chau," NCLS
55: 40–42. In the same period (1907) Phan Boi Chau also wrote the following
works: *Ky Niem Luc* (Commemorative Record), in honor of the recently deceased
Tang Bat Ho and of Vuong Thuc Quy; *Sung Bai Giai Nham* (In Honor of Exquisite
People), recalling the resistance efforts of Cao Thang and others; *Hoang Phan Thai*,
lauding a scholar executed for antidynastic activities during the reign of Tu Duc.
The latter represented a shift for Phan, now influenced by the antimonarchist
statements of Sun Yat-sen. VT, pp. 69–70.

Back in Tokyo in May 1907, Phan Boi Chau enrolled all the students who had gained some proficiency in Japanese in the Dobun Shoin, where they lived in the dormitory.[60] What sort of school were they entering? It was located in Mejiro district and was aimed mostly at the younger Chinese students but eventually also included at least sixty Vietnamese.[61] More than anything it was the personal handiwork of its organizer and secretary, Kashiwabara Buntaro. Kashiwabara was born in 1869, graduated from Dojisha School and the Tokyo Semmon Gakko (Tokyo Professional School). After that he became something of a professional Pan-Asian educator, organizing in Tokyo the Toa Shogyo Gakko (East Asia Commercial School), the Seika Gakko (Seika School), Dobun Shoin, and the Mejiro Chugakko (Mejiro Middle School). Kashiwabara was elected four times to the House of Representatives of the Diet. He died in 1936.[62] The curriculum of the Dobun Shoin seems to have been diluted middle-school fare, definitely inferior to the standard Japanese public education, at least in the opinion of Phan Boi Chau.[63] Nevertheless, Vietnamese eagerness to learn modern military skills induced at least one Dobun Shoin teacher, Naniwada Noriyoshi, a regular army major retired because of chest wounds from the Russo-Japanese War, to take them all out on Sundays to an open field for marching and basic tactical maneuvers.[64]

A few more Vietnamese also entered the Shimbu Military Academy, which was operated primarily for Chinese students under the slogan, "Asia for the Asians."[65] For all their Pan-Asian sentiments, it is signifi-

60. From this date onward the files of Japan's Interior Ministry provide rather precise information on the location and general movements of Phan Boi Chau, Cuong De, and most of the students. This was almost certainly the result of indications of official concern by the French ambassador in April and May 1907. Nagaoka and Kawamoto, *Betonamu,* p. 262.

61. Kuzuu Yoshihisa, ed., *Toa Sengaku Shishi Kiden,* p. 820, says that no recorded differentiation was made when enrolling Chinese and Vietnamese students, so most outsiders assumed that all were Chinese. NB, p. 98, and TP, p. 103, indicate that there may have been 200 Vietnamese students in all at the high point in mid-1908, but does not specify that all of them were in the Dobun Shoin. The number of 60 comes from Nagaoka and Kawamoto, *Betonamu,* p. 262, who may have drawn this from Interior Ministry records.

62. Nagaoka and Kawamoto, *Betonamu,* p. 260.

63. NB, p. 93. TP, p. 95. Inukai and others used the excuse that the Vietnamese lacked the written credentials for entry into the public schools.

64. Kuzuu Yoshihisa, *Toa Sengaku,* p. 820.

65. Vien Giac, "Truong Chan Vo o Nhat, Truong Hoang Pho o Tau voi lich su cach-mang Viet-Nam," *Duoc Tue* 76: 14, lists thirty-two "military students" in Japan at that time, but it is not at all clear that all attended the Shimbu Academy, particularly since many of the names appear on Japanese records of registrants at the Dobun Shoin. Nagaoka and Kawamoto, *Betonamu,* pp. 260, 262.

cant that the Japanese enrolled most Chinese and Vietnamese students into "special" schools, civilian and military, rather than attempting to integrate them into the nation's rigorous system of public instruction. We may presume that this was the result of extreme governmental caution, in this way circumventing official foreign objections to the presence of such students, making surveillance and control of the students more practicable, and perhaps hoping to insulate their own students and cadets from alien radicals. If things got troublesome, the government could simply shut the special schools down. Japanese chauvinists like General Fukushima, not to mention more militant types like Toyama, Uchida, and other luminaries of the Kokuryukai, hardly shared government sensitivities about diplomatic objections, but their prior theoretical advocacy of East Asian "racial equality" was even at that very moment being sullied by Uchida's deep involvement in Japan's final, ruthless subjugation of Korea.[66] Pan Asianism as a living policy alternative was fading rapidly—ironically, just when it was beginning to achieve ideological popularity among the Japanese people.

As must often be the case with politically alert émigré students, in the long run young Vietnamese in Japan learned fully as much outside school as within. Cuong De, for example, admitted that he had a poor record at the Shimbu Academy, but he remembered reading Japanese newspapers and outside books with great interest, developing special admiration for the heroes of the Meiji Restoration and the Russo-Japanese War.[67] I have already mentioned the student contacts with Sun Yat-sen's apparatus and Phan Boi Chau's arrangements with the Yunnanese. Liang Ch'i-ch'ao's "new learning" was at their fingertips. Almost all the Vietnamese were naturally impressed by Japanese advances in military and technical fields, while some soberly compared the social and ethical norms of the Japanese people with those existing among their own countrymen. Most important for the future of Vietnam, nevertheless, was the precedent they had all set by having packed up and left not only their home districts or provinces, but their entire country, in the quest for knowledge and national salvation. For a people, including the scholar-gentry, who traditionally disliked travel and suffered deep pangs of homesickness when separated from their families and villages for extended periods, this was indeed revolutionary. It was also a significant initial step for the elite in the process of fathoming Vietnam's position in a world of nation-states and colonies, which brought the elite forever out of a world of candidacy trips to Hue or occasional tributary journeys to Peking.

66. Hugh Latimer Burleson, "The Kokuryukai in Northeast Asia," pp. 73–137.
67. CD, p. 25.

By early October 1907 there were more than one hundred Vietnamese students in Japan, many having just arrived as the result of Phan Boi Chau's arrangements with Gilbert Chieu and his meeting, also in Hong Kong, with a follow-up delegation of prestigious southern gentry.[68] For arriving students the first problem was to learn Japanese, a subject that was not being taught in any accredited Japanese school. After some months of language study, consideration would then be given to enrollment and payment of tuition, if specified, in some local school. Sometime during the latter half of 1907 Phan Boi Chau again went to Inukai for help, specifically requesting that more students be allowed to enter the Shimbu Academy. On this General Fukushima, who was brought in for consultation, apparently stated that, whereas earlier Vietnamese enrollments had been accomplished on his own private initiative, he feared that further enrollments would undermine the Japanese government's position regarding foreign revolutionaries in general and its relations with France in particular. Better to limit enrollments to the Dobun Shoin, which represented "party to party" assistance and was of no legitimate business to the Japanese government. At this point in the conversation, Phan recalls that Inukai expressed some doubts about whether the Vietnamese were prepared to wait patiently in Japan until the proper opportunity arrived in their own country. Fukushima hence counseled Phan to slowly cultivate "personal dedication" among his followers, to which Phan retorted that his people lacked only the concrete means to attack the French, not the will and dedication. The outcome was the formation within the Dobun Shoin of a special curriculum for Vietnamese students, with new stress on the Japanese language and literature and on Major Naniwada's military training program.[69]

It is highly probable that Phan's increasing awareness of the limitations of Japanese friendship and overt support led him to organize all Vietnamese students into the Viet-Nam Cong Hien Hoi (Vietnam Public Offering Society) sometime in 1907.[70] Phan, in fact, spoke in his autobiography of a desire to maintain internal Vietnamese student discipline and control in the face of Japanese domination of the formal instruction program. The Cong Hien Hoi was distinct from the Duy Tan Hoi, being

68. NB, pp. 91–92. TP, p. 94.
69. NB, pp. 93–96. TP, pp. 95–98. Phan recalls the major's name as Tamba (in Vietnamese, Dan Ba), but it was almost certainly Major Naniwada Noriyoshi.
70. NTT, p. 58, identifies this organization as the Tan Viet-Nam Cong Hien (New Vietnam Contribution [Society]) and gives it something of the aura of a provisional government in exile. NTT indicates also that the society was formed in early 1907 and lasted until 1909. NB/TP implies formation in late 1907 and closure in October 1908.

limited to students in Japan and being mainly involved with fair distribution of finances, enforcing rules (both academic and personal), systematizing contacts with the Japanese and Chinese, and safeguarding group records. There was special care to distribute leadership positions among students from north, central, and south regions equally, although southerners were then dominant numerically in Japan and were providing most of the independent financing.[71] In a statement rare for a Vietnamese nationalist leader, Phan later admitted candidly that it was difficult to get students from all three regions to live and work together under Cong Hien Hoi aegis.[72] He must have appreciated that the very attempt was extraordinary; it marked the first time since the capture of King Ham Nghi—perhaps since the fall of the south in 1867—that countrywide identifications and loyalties were being serviced and nurtured on an institutional basis.

The flowering of support and participation within Cochinchina deserves special attention. I have alluded previously to historical circumstances in the decades after 1867 that produced a very small class of extremely wealthy, conservative native landowners there and have mentioned that the south played no significant role in the Can Vuong movement. Nguyen Than Hien and his associates then came into contact with Phan Boi Chau in 1903, thus reestablishing the first fragile link with the rest of Vietnam, which was followed by Prince Cuong De's written proclamation directed specifically to the south and Phan's meetings with the southern gentry in Hong Kong. In 1907 Nguyen Than Hien is said to have turned over a major portion of his financial resources to the support of overseas students, perhaps as much as 20,000 piastres.[73] He, Nguyen Quang Dieu, and others in the south founded the Khuyen Du Hoc Hoi (Society for Encouragement of Learning) primarily as a vehicle for moving southern students into the pipeline leading through Hong Kong to Tokyo. Significantly, it was only at this point that Nguyen Quang Dieu, then twenty-seven years old, decided to break off studying the *Spring and Autumn Annals* and the *Classic of Changes* (*I Ching*), apparently having concluded that clandestine fund-raising, recruitment, and distribution of propaganda held more possibility of saving his country than the most conscientious, sophisticated interpretation of the classics. Using a Buddhist temple in Cao-lanh as cover, this small group extended organizational

71. By mid-1908 Phan recalls there being about 100 southerners, plus "more than 50" from the center, and "more than 40" from north Vietnam. NB, pp. 98–99. TP, p. 103. A Sûreté agent's report lists "about three hundred students" in Japan as of August 1908. AOM A-50 NF 28(2).
72. NB, pp. 96–99. TP, pp. 98–103.
73. Nguyen Van Hau, *Chi Si Nguyen Quang Dieu*, p. 33.

contacts out to wealthy landowners, eventually reaching into every province of Cochinchina.[74]

Meanwhile, there also was significant activity in the several cities of Cochinchina. The thrust was twofold: opening new commercial ventures either to support students going abroad or to finance increased activity within clandestine societies previously existent in the area; and careful, "legitimate" expression of nationalist ideas and ideals in the local press, both French and *quoc-ngu*. In both of these Gilbert Chieu took the lead, founding the Nam-Trung hotel in Saigon, the Minh-Tan hotel in My-Tho, and the Minh-Tan industrial corporation in Cho-Lon (manufacturing soap), while simultaneously serving as editor of two newspapers published in Saigon, *Le Moniteur des Provinces* and *Luc Tinh Tan Van*.[75] The latter paper, in particular, published subtle, yet risky, articles on such matters as agricultural aid groups and popular financial cooperatives, even implying support of political insurrections if the government failed to move to alleviate rural problems.[76] When French authorities indicated their distinct displeasure, Gilbert Chieu shifted full attention to his commercial ventures and to clandestine coordination of Dong Du efforts in the south. Sometime in 1907 or 1908, Nguyen An Khuong,[77] already noted for his periodical *Nong Co Minh Dam* (Tribune of Old Agricultural People) and his *quoc-ngu* translations of Chinese novels, invested heavily in the Chieu-Nam hotel in order to hand the profits over to students leaving for Japan.[78]

While significant as profit-making institutions, these hotels in Saigon and My Tho probably were more important as centers for liaison and as purveyors of anticolonial literature. There an associate from some distant point could stop by and swap information, turn over funds for transmission to Tokyo, receive copies of essays, poetry, and proclamations, and perhaps even be presented with a signed picture and personal letter of authorization from Prince Cuong De. Along with assorted amulets, seals, banners, and brevets of more local derivation, such materials as-

74. *Ibid.*, pp. 34–36. See Georges Coulet, *Les Sociétiés secrètes en terre d'Annam,* pp. 142–191, for a discussion of the role of bonzes and their pagodas in diverse clandestine activities in Cochinchina.

75. Phuong Huu, *Phong Trao Dai Dong Du* (Saigon, 1950), pp. 28–31. A Pierre Jeantet served as manager of the latter paper, accepting legal responsibility for the political views expressed, but in actuality leaving Gilbert Chieu a free hand. CMCD–3, p. 25.

76. *Luc Tinh Tan Van,* October 17, 1907; December 12, 1907; January 13, 1908.

77. Written "Nguyen An Khang" in VNDN, pp. 158–159. Father of Nguyen An Ninh (see Chapter 10).

78. Nguyen Van Hau, *Chi Si Nguyen Quang Dieu,* p. 32.

sisted greatly in generating village support for Dong Du efforts.[79] Much of this, admittedly, would never stand the test of time, particularly after systematic repression was instituted. Yet it is striking to read from a French intelligence report, for example, that a certain Duong Minh Thanh, at a village ceremony in Tan An, chose to recite publicly and from memory an "anti-French" poem by Phan Boi Chau and then distributed copies for villagers to study on their own.[80] Clearly, Phan Boi Chau and his associates, against great odds, had established contacts in the villages of southern Vietnam.

In early 1908 another delegation of wealthy, elder supporters left Saigon with a new contingent of students, this time going all the way to Japan. Phan Boi Chau remarked that they were extremely conservative and rather out of touch with events; but he was careful to guide them around the Dobun Shoin facilities, and they left for home pledging to forward more money. These elders soon did report the availability of 200,000 piastres, but unfortunately, by means of a very careless public cable to Phan in Tokyo. The money was crucial, but compromise was almost certain, in Phan's estimate, so he asked Huang Hsing of the T'ung-meng-hui to arrange roundabout transmittal of the money through Chinese channels. Even so, Vietnamese contact men were jailed on arrival in Saigon.[81] Additionally, and unknown to Phan, a native Sûreté agent had succeeded in traveling with and gaining the confidence of two other Vietnamese visitors to Japan. He reported their turning over a sum of money to Cuong De and their receiving in exchange a picture of the prince in royal regalia, as well as some letters and brochures. The agent even managed to secure copies of the incriminating evidence, and the imprisonment and interrogation, upon his return to Saigon, of one of these indiscreet travelers provided further details about the resistance operations which led to further arrests.[82] Police raids on the suspect hotels produced stacks of literature smuggled in from Japan, and Gilbert Chieu, himself, though a French citizen, was put under arrest.[83]

Using information gathered from all these sources, in addition to that gained upon rounding up and jailing scholar-gentry figures in north and

79. Coulet, *Les Sociétiés,* pp. 49–73, 115–116, 222–229, 282–284.
80. *Ibid.,* p. 295.
81. NB, pp. 99–101. TP, pp. 104–105.
82. AOM A-50 NF 28(2). It is possible that Phan Boi Chau refers in his autobiography to this same arrest, but misconstrues the immediate causes.
83. Various detailed reports on "l'affaire Gilbert Chieu et consorts" are in AOM A-50 NF 28(2). Eventually Gilbert Chieu was released on a plea of *non-suit*; and he died of natural causes in 1913.

central Vietnam, the French authorities were able to present a specific, open-and-shut case to the Japanese government for ejection of Phan Boi Chau, Cuong De, and most of the students.[84]

While the Japanese were not prepared to comply immediately, police were sent into the Dobun Shoin to inspect the Vietnamese living area. Each student was ordered to write a letter to his parents, notifying them of his situation and whereabouts, all of which were then transmitted home via official French channels. This shifted the primary threat to families at home, most of whom had been feigning ignorance of the effort. Soon letters from the families were arriving in Tokyo by the score, especially from the south, speaking of harassment, even jailings, and generally instructing their sons, nephews, or cousins to return home immediately.[85] In truth, many of the young southern students seem to have gone to Japan either on the initiative of their families or as a nonpolitical lark, perhaps both. So, when letters of this type arrived, they immediately began asking Phan Boi Chau for funds to return home. Phan avoided supplying these for several months, but in September or October 1908 orders apparently came from the Japanese Interior Ministry to drop Vietnamese students from the rolls of the Dobun Shoin. Phan's entreaties to Inukai and Fukushima found them unable or unwilling to oppose the government on this matter. They advised that until the heat was off students should disperse to the provinces. Phan, however, found that all save five of the south Vietnamese wanted to go home. So, after more pleading, Inukai did use his "good offices" to secure one hundred steamer tickets, supposedly by courtesy of the Nippon Yusen Kaisha (Japan Mail Line).[86]

What had happened on the Japanese side to bring about this turn of events? Most obviously, there had been the Franco-Japanese Treaty, signed June 10, 1907, which included a clause of support for each other's "situation and territorial rights" on the continent of Asia.[87] Among other things, this meant full Japanese affirmation of French colonial rule in

84. AOM A-50 NF 451 carton 32.
85. Nagaoka and Kawamoto, *Betonamu*, p. 263, reports relatives jailed in and around Hanoi to the tune of 400, and more than 100 around Saigon. However, such figures probably represent indirect news in Japan of more general roundups, stemming from other serious troubles in 1908 (see Chapter 8).
86. NB, pp. 101–103. TP, pp. 106–107. Nagaoka and Kawamoto, *Betonamu*, pp. 263–264, 272–273, indicates that the majority of students had departed by December 1908, and only twenty remained by February 1909, all of whose names he lists from Interior Ministry files. However, some names apparently were aliases.
87. See L. De Reinach, comp., *Recueil des Traites conclus par la France en Extrême-Orient*, vol. 2 (Paris, 1907), for the full text of this treaty.

Indochina. The subsequent Russo-Japanese conventions (July 1907) and the Anglo-Russian entente (August 1907) tied all these powers to a resolute defense of the imperialist status quo in East Asia.[88]

Beyond this, however, it is questionable whether party politicians like Okuma and Inukai, leaders of a complex bureaucratic, capitalist, and classically liberal intellectual opposition to the oligarchy, were able or willing to defend the strictly idealistic facets of their Pan-Asianism in the face of massive historical change—and above all, Japan's military and political success within the imperialist framework.[89] With many other previously anti-oligarchic elements accepting oligarchic leadership from 1900 onward, Okuma's party (now the Kenseihonto, or Orthodox Constitutional party) found itself isolated from the sources of power. In 1905 Okuma and Inukai helped fan sharp popular anger over the "disgraceful" Portsmouth Treaty, but the oligarchs had the situation back under control by January 1906.[90] Okuma retired temporarily from active politics in 1907. Inukai at this point became only the leader of one faction of a party lacking in significant influence until the famous Taisho crisis of 1913.[91]

One of the few Japanese in early 1909 who still seriously wanted to do all he could for those Vietnamese remaining in Japan was Kashiwabara Buntaro. He took several penniless students into his own home as "part of the family"[92] and tried to intercede with the government to reverse policy trends. He wrote optimistically of future uprisings against the French and alluded in dire terms to American intentions of hopping from the Philippines into Annam:

88. The Vietnamese were by no means the first émigrés to feel the cutting edge of the altered Japanese policy: Sun Yat-sen in 1907 was discreetly induced, via the Kokuryukai leader Uchida Ryohei, to depart the country. Sun ended up on the Sino-Vietnamese border with Huang Hsing, organizing peasants, tribal minorities, and bandit groups for inconclusive attacks into China. Jansen, *The Japanese,* pp. 125–126. There is no evidence now of complicity by Vietnamese anticolonialists. On the contrary, it appears that Sun sought, and for a short while received, covert help from local French officials.

89. Scalapino, *Democracy and the Party Movement in Prewar Japan,* pp. 77–81, discusses the formation and development of Okuma's Rikken Kaishinto (Constitutional Progressive party), examining in particular their "interpretation" of nineteenth-century liberalism to fit the Japanese concept of nationalism and the emperor-centered state—not to mention the needs of the party's own capitalist backers for economic subsidies and state privileges.

90. *Ibid.,* pp. 179–189.

91. *Ibid.,* pp. 190–196. In March 1910 their party was renamed the Rikken Kokuminto (Constitutional Nationalist party).

92. Kuzuu Yoshihisa, *Toa Sengaku,* p. 821.

The Vietnamese who at great pains have become associated with Japan will now weary of us and move instead to deliver their spirits to the Americans.[93]

All of which sounds farfetched, until one appreciates that as a result of the imperialist agreements of 1907 the United States and Germany were indeed the odd men out on the East Asian mainland. For this reason, Japan had some grounds for fearing new United States challenges—perhaps, indeed, from our bases in the Philippines.

Miyazaki Torazo, a Japanese friend of decidedly more revolutionary stripe, introduced originally by Sun Yat-sen, had already helped convince Phan Boi Chau that the present generation of Japanese politicians was "strong on savage ambition and weak on chivalry." On this basis, he advised that the remaining Vietnamese students immediately shift to studying English, German, Russian, and other languages, so that they could really begin to spread the word about French oppression and perhaps gather an international group of humanistic, antiimperialist revolutionaries to assist them in their cause. Phan saw the value of building worldwide contacts and sympathy, but by now there was no money left for extensive travel. In addition, it would take time for him or the students to learn Western languages. Nevertheless, with a fortuitous gift of money from another Japanese friend, Asaba Buntaro, Phan was able to participate in the establishment of the Toa Domeikai (East Asian United League; in Vietnamese, Dong A Dong Minh Hoi), a group which included Chinese T'ung-meng-hui representatives, Korean, Indian, and Filipino members, and individuals from the Japanese Socialist party.[94]

Still trying to keep several irons in the fire, Phan had a prime role, too, in getting some Yunnan and Kwangsi émigrés to join with the remaining Vietnamese in the Que Dien Viet Lien Minh Hoi (Kwangsi-Yunnan-Viet Alliance).[95] Most of the rest of the money from Asaba went for the printing of three thousand more copies of *Hai Ngoai Huyet Thu*, each copy having *Han*, *nom*, and *quoc-ngu* versions, and for one thousand copies of a new book titled *Viet-Nam Quoc Su Khao* (A Study of Vietnam's National History).

Viet-Nam Quoc Su Khao is Phan's explanation—highly simplified— of governmental processes in the modern state. By now Phan definitely

93. Quoted in Nagaoka and Kawamoto, *Betonamu,* pp. 260–261.
94. NB, pp. 117–119. TP, pp. 120–122. I have been unable to find an Asaba Buntaro in any of the Japanese biographical dictionaries or other sources available to me. Phan recalls that he was a doctor of medicine and the son of a retired army general. Phan also names eleven other participants.
95. NB, p. 119, TP, p. 123.

equated the degree of "popular sovereignty" (*dan-quyen*) with the degree of achievement, retention, or loss of national power. Once again he probed the questions of national spirit and identity, this time, however, demonstrating much more obvious affiliation with the ideas of Sun Yat-sen. The conclusion of *Viet-Nam Quoc Su Khao* included the following moving passage:

> Listen! The Nation is every citizen's property. Common ownership requires that the people be of one heart, one strength, in common struggle. The world is being swept to its eight points by the wind and rain of the Westerners. But who are we, as a people? The land of Hong-Lac[96] must be renewed, awoken, to be again truly a thing of beauty.[97]

The time was past, however, when the Japanese government would tolerate revolutionary activities by the émigrés. Apparently acting on diplomatic requests from British, Ch'ing, and French authorities, the Japanese Interior Ministry in early 1909 disbanded both the Toa Domeikai and the Que Dien Viet Lien Minh Hoi.[98] In a raid on Phan Boi Chau's residence they captured most of the three thousand new copies of *Hai Ngoai Huyet Thu* and destroyed them, according to Phan, in a bonfire in front of the French consulate.[99] Phan and Chang Ping-lin, editor of *Min-pao,* and others were ordered deported. Before leaving, Phan paid a last visit to Asaba and gained some grim, if tardy, consolation from hearing him deride and denounce Okuma, Inukai, and other party politicians as men who exploited émigrés for their own selfish purposes.[100]

On March 8, 1909, under police surveillance, Phan departed Tokyo en route to Hong Kong.[101] In Hong Kong his depression was temporarily

96. A compound reference to the mythical dynasty of Hong-Bang (2879–258 B.C.) and its progenitor, Lac Long Quan. See Tran Trong Kim, *Viet-Nam Su-Luoc,* pp. 23–25.

97. Phan Boi Chau, *Viet-Nam Quoc Su Khao* (Hanoi, 1962), p. 168; quoted in Chuong Thau, "Anh huong cua Phan Boi Chau," NCLS 55: 42.

98. On January 14, 1909, the French made a formal request for the Japanese to "investigate" the conduct of remaining Vietnamese émigrés. On February 8 the Japanese foreign ministry replied that it was complying. Nagaoka and Kawamoto, *Betonamu,* p. 263.

99. NB, p. 120. TP, p. 124. Phan also recalled there that Kashiwabara arrived to warn him a few minutes before the raid, so he was able to escape with 150 copies of *Hai Ngoai Huyet Thu.*

100. NB, p. 121. TP, p. 125. Phan remained deeply impressed by Asaba. On returning to Japan ten years later, Phan was grieved to hear of his death and took the trouble to travel to Asaba's home village in Shizuoka perfecture to erect a stone memorial. NB, pp. 121–123. TP, pp. 125–127.

101. Nagaoka and Kawamoto, *Betonamu,* p. 264.

alleviated by news that De Tham had struck at the French with some success and that Phan's associate Pham Van Ngon[102] had moved down from the Yen-The base to open a second front in Nghe An and Ha Tinh. Phan immediately sent a messenger into Vietnam, and in about a month several key cadres showed up in Hong Kong with 2,500 piastres and a letter from Dang Thai Than. Dang painted an optimistic picture of the preparations for operations against the French and asked Phan to purchase rifles for quick smuggling into Vietnam. Relying on earlier contacts, Phan sent two men to Japan to approach a surplus-arms company; they obtained 500 rifles of Russo-Japanese War vintage, 100 for cash and 400 on credit.[103] Getting the rifles as far as a dockside warehouse in Hong Kong, Phan next traveled to Singapore to make contact with a Chinese T'ung-meng-hui cell for advice and assistance in smuggling.[104] The price for smuggling quoted by local Chinese shippers, however, was twice the original sum paid for the rifles. Moving on to Siam, Phan created something of a commotion in the local foreign office, but his manipulations proved fruitless. Back in Hong Kong by September 1909, he could only send a request into Vietnam for more money to pay the Chinese smugglers.[105]

By this time, however, Phan was already receiving steady bad news on the risings, including word of the capture of Pham Van Ngon,[106] the defeat of De Tham's forces, and the death of other important cadres. And finally, the political significance of the mass jailings and general repression of 1908 was coming into perspective for Phan, making the anti-French attacks of 1909 look more and more like ill-conceived acts of desperation. In March 1910 Phan was stunned to hear of the death of Dang Thai Than, his longtime political disciple and his last real liaison with domestic Duy Tan Hoi remnants.[107] Since the T'ung-meng-hui at

---

102. Pseudonyms, Tung Nham, Tu Ngon (from his status as *tu-tai*). Viet-yen-ha village, Duc-tho district, Ha-Tinh. After Phan Boi Chau's meeting with De Tham, Pham Van Ngon had led a small group north to set up the camp agreed upon. HT, pp. 502–503.

103. NB, pp. 126–127. TP, pp. 129–130. These were the so-called Meiji 30 rifles, with five-round clips. Another indication of lingering contacts with some Japanese was the April 8, 1909, article in *Osaka Asahi*, criticizing French operations against De Tham. AOM A-81 NF 67.

104. *Nguc Trung Thu* indicates that he went first to Bangkok, but this is not certain.

105. NB, pp. 127–128. TP, pp. 131–132.

106. Arrested March 5, 1910. Pham Van Ngon also allowed his correspondence to fall into French hands. AOM A-50 (34) carton 24.

107. NB, p. 129. TP, p. 133. According to Phan, Dang Thai Than was surprised in hiding by a combined French-native patrol, but still managed to destroy key documents and shoot one Frenchman; he then yelled that he would never try to shoot

this time was trying to engineer a series of revolts in Kwangtung and was in need of weapons, Phan reluctantly decided to turn over most of the rifles to Sun Shou-ping, Sun Yat-sen's older brother.[108] Through the spring and summer of 1910 Phan and his few remaining associates were reduced to peddling books in Canton for money to eat or sometimes to drown their discouragement in wine. Ultimately they met an elderly Chinese widow who sympathized with their cause and let them use her house as residence and headquarters.[109]

One of Phan's younger followers, Lam Duc Mau, proficient in French before leaving Vietnam and now studying Chinese and German at a "Sino-German friendship school," was used to sound out the German consulate once again. Phan also was thinking of traveling to Berlin if funds could be raised. In late 1910 money did arrive from Vietnam, but Phan used it instead to get himself and his comrades to Bangkok, where they hoped to secure land for cultivation, to reassemble scattered émigrés, and to reassess their situation.[110]

Phan had traveled to Siam first in mid-1908, using a letter of introduction from Okuma Shigenobu to gain entry to a Japanese advisor at the Siamese court. After a formal audience with the king and meetings with various courtiers, Phan had found an uncle of the king quite receptive. On this basis several students later expelled from Japan were able to settle in Siam in 1909.[111] Now, early in 1911,[112] Phan was back in Siam

those of his own race and turned his weapon upon himself. The governor general's report to the minister of colonies in Paris stated that some papers were captured, including a letter just written, destined for Phan Boi Chau and Cuong De. Interestingly, the report also commented: "We are not face to face with only acts of brigandage or localized agitation. Cuong De and Pham (sic) Boi Chau are leaders of a *mouvement de revendications nationales,* which involves more or less the whole *pays annamites,* and which has as its object the obtaining of independence for Annam." AOM A-50 (34) carton 24.

108. This would appear to refer to Sun Te-chang, although I have been unable to discover whether he used the pseudonym "Shou-ping" or was known to have been in Kwangtung at this time. NTT says that British authorities uncovered and confiscated the rifles before the delivery was complete. NB, p. 130, and TP, p. 133, have it that 480 rifles successfully reached T'ung-meng-hui hands and 20 rifles were disassembled and taken to Bangkok by Phan's group, where they were confiscated. See also Chuong Thau, "Anh huong cua Phan Boi Chau," NCLS 56: 32–33.

109. NB, pp. 130–133. TP, pp. 133–138.

110. NB, pp. 134, 136. TP, pp. 139, 141.

111. NB, pp. 125–126. TP, p. 129. See also Phan Boi Chau, "Mémoires," *France-Asie/Asia* Fall/Winter 1968, notes 120, 121, 134, and 135 for additional information on Vietnamese-Siamese contacts during these years.

112. NTT indicates a departure from Kwangtung for Siam in February 1911. NB and TP have him leaving in October 1910. Since NTT was written only three years later, it is more likely correct.

for the third time, if we include his abortive gun-running sortie. He found both his former contact, the king's uncle, and a prince in the army willing to provide the Vietnamese with plenty of land and equipment for farming, some distance from Bangkok. It was there that Phan and his student followers received their first sustained experience as "peasants," laboring along with four or five lower-class Vietnamese who had joined them in Hong Kong. While these tasks may not have moved their country much closer to independence, their spirits did remain high, and Phan's newly composed poems were set to spontaneous music in the rice fields.[113]

While he was in Siam Phan seems to have reassessed his literary efforts and found them wanting in certain respects. Up to that point he had written largely in classical Chinese, or *chu Han*. In poetry, this meant that he remained bound to laws of rhyming, balance, and tone that dated to T'ang and Sung periods. In prose, it meant a vocabulary, sentence structure, and mode of exposition quite unsuited to communicating modern political and social ideas. Like his Chinese contemporaries in Japan, Phan had already cut radically the number of hoary aphorisms, the polite circumlocutions, and the erudite innuendoes. But he must have perceived that the classical medium was being stretched to its limits and that the next step had to be complete change.

For some of Phan's younger followers the obvious solution was to switch entirely to a romanized script, to *quoc-ngu*. As will be seen, this course was hotly debated at the Dong Kinh Nghia Thuc in Hanoi and ultimately emerged triumphant throughout Vietnam. Phan Boi Chau and many of his scholar-gentry contemporaries, however, never could bring themselves to write seriously in *quoc-ngu*, although they did learn to read it and certainly encouraged their associates to translate their classical writings into it. Phan's personal solution was to write increasingly in *nom*, which was at least easier than the classical to memorize and hence was more likely to reach a popular audience beyond the scholar-gentry. It also meant that he could utilize a whole range of popular literary forms and incorporate into his writing thousands of strictly oral expressions, and even some rural colloquialisms. Indeed, one major commentator has argued that Phan Boi Chau was the first Vietnamese writer consciously to employ popular forms for patriotic, revolutionary purposes.[114] If this is true, he was still several decades ahead of his time, since the self-

113. NB, pp. 136–137. TP, pp. 142–143. "Ai Quoc Ca" (Ballad of Patriotism), "Ai Chung Ca" (Ballad of Racial Affiliation), and "Ai Quan Ca" (Ballad of Fraternity) are reprinted in VT, pp. 159–160, and VTCM, pp. 310–315.
114. VT, pp. 82–84. During these years Phan tried his hand at such diverse forms as the *dan ca, cheo, tuong, dam, phuong vai,* and *tho bon chu.*

consciously urban intelligentsia, even then emerging in Saigon and Hanoi, tended to deprecate popular Vietnamese forms in favor of frank adaptations of Western prose and poetry. Nevertheless, Phan had set a precedent, undoubtedly appreciated by the peasantry, and one eventually taken up by those members of the intelligentsia who chose later to find their way back among their own people.

One of the most interesting examples of Phan's popular literary efforts in Siam was a drama, or *tuong*, concerning the heroic Trung sisters.[115] Here Phan was much more interested in delineating a contemporary message of political struggle than in rehashing a historical narrative, to the degree that he ended the play at Trung Trac's triumphant ascension to the throne, saying nothing of the Chinese counterattacks and the double suicide of his heroines. The characters were essentially colonial and anticolonial archtypes—the hated foreign governor general, the crafty native informer, the Vietnamese subordinate-minister-turned-rebel, and the effete scholar seeking refuge behind his books. The dialogues were penetrating renditions of colloquial Vietnamese conversation among individuals of diverse rank and status.

But there is reason to believe that Phan's main purpose in writing this play was to focus on the role of Vietnamese women in the forthcoming anti-colonial struggle. Specifically, he was unobtrusively positing a situation where women were expected to act more according to the same patriotic principles that motivated their fathers, husbands, and brothers than from deference to Confucian concepts of female servitude and obligation. For example, whereas most writers continued into the twentieth century to emphasize Trung Trac's faithful desire to revenge her husband who had been executed by the Chinese governor general, Phan showed this as merely the catalyst energizing her preexistent love of country and her desire to expel the foreign invader.[116] And whereas Trung Trac's younger sister, Trung Nhi, had long been portrayed as joining the struggle out of sisterly obligation, Phan pointedly placed this motivation second to that of generalized patriotism.[117]

On the other hand, Phan did not deify the Trung sisters. Trung Trac cried pitifully when her husband's body was brought home. In adversity she temporarily lost her nerve, and her younger sister had to buck up her

115. Phan Boi Chau, *Tuong Trung Nu Vuong/Truyen Pham Hong Thai*. This version, reprinted in 1967, is said to come from one of the copies, presumably handwritten, first smuggled in from Siam after 1913. Given the nature of oral drama, many other versions have naturally developed.
116. *Ibid.*, pp. 11, 58.
117. *Ibid.*, p. 60.

courage with the following statement, "Come now, we can't give way to ordinary female emotions. We've got to get out and take care of military matters."[118] In short, like several other women in the play, Trung Trac and Trung Nhi were flesh-and-blood characters. Phan Boi Chau, born and raised amidst Confucian idealizations of female passivity, could now tell the women of Vietnam that, with their men increasingly in jail, overseas, or dead, they too would have to do their duty by their country.

While Phan Boi Chau spent his time laboring and writing in Siam, Prince Cuong De was going through a separate, somewhat more complicated scenario vis-à-vis Japanese officialdom and friends—or former friends—of Vietnamese independence. Becoming ill early in 1908 and being hospitalized for several months, Cuong De upon recovery dropped his studies at the Shimbu Academy in favor of taking classes at Waseda University.[119] In November, however, he left for Siam with some of the other students, being mindful of the historic ties between Nguyen Anh and the Siamese court and frankly hoping to secure for himself similar treatment.[120] But, finding little that was encouraging, disliking the climate, and being unable to read or speak Siamese, Cuong De went back to Tokyo in early 1909.[121] When the Japanese foreign ministry in May 1909 decided to accede to a specific French request to expell Cuong De, the police were unable to locate him until September.

Thence followed a humorous cat-and-mouse game, with Cuong De, aware that he was being followed, registering at hospitals several times (either for real illness or as a protective tactic) and generally demonstrating considerable skill in keeping one step ahead of the police. Whenever the police did catch up, they seemed eager to avoid a public scene and the bad publicity that would certainly come from throwing an Annamese royal prince out of the country like a common criminal. The chase led to Kobe, where Cuong De feigned illness and escaped out a hotel window, leaving clues that he was on his way to Nagasaki. Instead he slipped back to Tokyo, in an attempt to get help from Kashiwabara Buntaro. But Kashiwabara could only tell Cuong De that now that the affair had become a matter for the police, acting under highest orders, he could do nothing. On October 30, 1909, finally cornered, his pleas for postponement summarily refused, Cuong De was packed aboard a train for the far southern port of Moji. Two days later he was aboard the *Ijo-maru*, destined for Shanghai

118. *Ibid.*, p. 83.
119. CD, p. 25. He enrolled under a Chinese alias.
120. CD, p. 28. Cuong De claimed that 15,000 Vietnamese resided in or around Bangkok in 1908, but he admitted that many no longer spoke the language.
121. Japanese police authorities seem to have been unaware that he had left, in the first place, but they did have him listed as inquiring about a room at his former inn in February 1909. Nagaoka and Kawamoto, *Betonamu*, p. 265.

and Hong Kong, with Nguyen Sieu,[122] Tran Huu Luc,[123] and Dang Tu Man.[124]

For the Japanese, however, all was not quite over. Before being put aboard the train at Kobe, Tran Huu Luc apparently had heard rumors that the French were prepared to grab them all when the ship anchored in Shanghai. When they saw two Frenchmen aboard the *Ijo-maru*, they somehow persuaded the police to let Dang Tu Man return to Tokyo to pass on this alarming news to Kashiwabara. The latter assured Dang that the Japanese government would never permit such a thing, but Kashiwabara was concerned enough privately to telegraph certain members of the Toa Dobun Shoin within the Japanese consulate police force in Shanghai. These men on their own initiative moved to put the *Ijo-maru* under guard when it arrived November 3. The deputy consul general, Matsuoka Yosuke (foreign minister, 1940–1941), learned of it, however, and ordered the police withdrawn the next day, whereupon some Dobun Shoin members from the Furukawa Mining Company took up the watch. Either aware of definite French moves to seize Cuong De or simply wanting to pass the buck, Matsuoka advised officers of the *Ijo-maru* to take their Vietnamese passengers on to Hong Kong.

On November 5, however, Cuong De and his compatriots slipped ashore in Shanghai and found temporary refuge with some Chinese students, friends of better days in Tokyo. Furious at the Dobun Shoin's role in this affair, Matsuoka wrote a detailed report to the foreign ministry. Cuong De, donning an artificial pigtail and full Chinese garb, soon moved on secretly to Hong Kong and safety at the headquarters set up previously by Phan Boi Chau.[125] There Cuong De studied English for a while and then moved on to Singapore and Bangkok, in each place trying to raise money for the cause on the basis of his royal pedigree, if nothing else. In Bangkok, however, this immediately made the French consulate pressure the government to turn Cuong De over to them, so he was forced to ship out again, arriving back in Hong Kong early in 1911.[126]

122. Also known as Nguyen Thai Bat, long a resident at Thien Vu's house and a student at the Seijo School. NB, p. 118. TP, p. 121. Nagaoka and Kawamoto, *Betonamu*, p. 267.
123. Original name, Nguyen Thuc Dang; pseudonym, Can Kiem. He was from Dong-chu village, Nghi-loc district, Nghe An. His father was a former mandarin of Ha Tinh province. HT, pp. 512–514. AOM P-10 carton 5.
124. Dang had been attending the East Asian Commercial School in Tokyo. CD, pp. 31–34. Nagaoka and Kawamoto, *Betonamu*, pp. 265–268.
125. CD, pp. 35–43. Nagaoka and Kawamoto, *Betonamu*, pp. 269–272, includes quotes from the Matsuoka report and full particulars on the Furukawa Mining Company's involvement.
126. CD, pp. 44–49.

Chapter Seven

Suốt thân sĩ ba kỳ Nam Bắc,
Bỗng giật mình sực tỉnh cơn mê.
Học, thương xoay đủ mọi nghề,
Cái hồn ái quốc gọi về cũng mau.

Scholars from all three regions, South to North,
Suddenly are startled from their unconscious fits.
Studying, trading, mastering every kind of job,
Surely the spirit of patriotism will be called back quickly.

(*Nam thiên phong vận truyện,* 1907)

The Dong Kinh Nghia Thuc

During the time Phan Boi Chau and Nguyen Thanh were organizing the Duy Tan Hoi, recruiting Cuong De as royal pretender, and seeking weapons overseas, other scholar-gentry were considering the formation of assorted businesses, beginning to advocate specific institutional reforms, and, most important, talking about techniques for spreading "new learning" to ever-wider circles of scholar-gentry and eventually to the people at large. As I have mentioned, there was considerable overlapping in these activist and reformist efforts. The scholar-gentry involved had similar backgrounds, were generally well acquainted with each other, had read K'ang Yu-wei and Liang Ch'i-ch'ao together, and had a common, overwhelming desire to help bring Vietnam up from despair and degradation. Nevertheless, as ideas slowly matured into action, certain conceptual distinctions emerged among these men which would be important to the entire subsequent course of anticolonialism in Vietnam.

Preeminent among the reformists stood Phan Chu Trinh, although he led in ways quite different and for reasons quite different from those involved in Phan Boi Chau's domination of the Dong Du movement. Phan Chu Trinh was a loner, a proud, sensitive dealer in ideas, and not a leader of organizations. From his youthful experiences, he had developed a profound aversion to violence and, we may surmise, a ready distrust of traditional codes of behavior among the scholar-gentry; according to contemporaries, he remained bitter throughout his life about what he considered to be the unjust killing of his father by scholar-gentry associates.[1] When Dao Nguyen Pho gathered his small "Western circle" in 1904, Phan Chu Trinh was the most eager and complete reader in the group of whatever books were available.

About that time Phan Chu Trinh approached a particular court mandarin with proposals for institutional reform—probably the same mandarin to whom Phan Boi Chau had directed his *Luu Cau Huyet Le Tan Thu*.[2] Both young men had emerged empty-handed. Phan Boi Chau, although discouraged, had retained some faith in the mandarinate's ability to the see the light eventually. For Phan Chu Trinh, however, there followed an irrevocable breach with the entire Nguyen dynastic system—in effect, a declaration of lifelong warfare. He dropped his minor position at the Board of Rites in Hue and embarked on a series of trips through the provinces, hoping to rouse the scholar-gentry to the new challenges before them all. As his contemporary and perhaps his closest associate Huynh Thuc Khang later wrote:

> Previously [Phan Chu Trinh] had thought, "the time is not yet ripe for action." Now, in his heart, before his eyes, he saw clearly the road to follow and determined the means for traveling from that point onward. He often said that the poison of autocratic rule and outmoded tradition had produced an uncontrollable sickness in our country and the ideals of Western freedom and democracy were the appropriate medicine to eliminate that sickness.[3]

Just before Phan Boi Chau's first departure for Japan, the two men met for the first time. From having read *Luu Cau Huyet Le Tan Thu*, Phan Chu Trinh apparently admired Phan Boi Chau's patriotic determination but felt that he had not escaped the traditional clichés. On the other hand, Phan Boi Chau at this time approved of Phan Chu Trinh's plans for preaching the abolition of the civil exam system and the establishment of modern schools and commercial firms.[4]

Tran Quy Cap[5] and Huynh Thuc Khang, who both had just passed the court exams (second and fourth, respectively), in early 1905 joined Phan Chu Trinh in publicly breaking with the dynastic system and traveled south with him to generate support.[6] The three raised an intellectual dust

1. Ton Quang Phiet, "Phan Chu Trinh," p. 13.
2. This is the impression of Huynh Thuc Khang, *Phan Tay Ho, Tien Sinh Lich Su,* p. 17. In this case it would have been Ho Le, at that time Minister of Military Affairs (*Thuong Binh*). NB, p. 38. TP, p. 34.
3. Huynh Thuc Khang, *Phan Tay Ho,* p. 16.
4. *Ibid.,* p. 17.
5. Pseudonym, Thai Xuyen. Bat-nghi village, Quang Nam. VNDN, pp. 333–334.
6. Huynh writes that his father, who died in 1900, had aimed him only as far as

storm at each provincial center, especially in Binh Dinh, where they entered the regional exams under assumed names with more than five hundred bonafide candidates and wrote inflammatory poems in the most impeccable classical form.[7] Having themselves passed the highest exams, they had the prestige to gain a hearing among their peers as they mercilessly derided traditional studies. Scholars with any sense of honor or justice must throw off their mandarin caps, the three would urge, cast away their writing brushes, and rise up! "Why not open your ears and turn your eyes to the distance?" At times their language was indistinguishable from that of Phan Boi Chau, for example, when they recalled the glory of Vietnamese resistance to the Mongols and denounced the heavy colonial taxes for "wearing people down into skeletons without spirit or soul."[8]

Arriving in Nha Trang, the three men heard that a Russian fleet heading into battle with the Japanese had put in at nearby Cam-Ranh bay. Dressing as merchants, renting a fishing boat, and buying a supply of eggs and vegetables, they sortied into the bay to have a look at these giant iron men-of-war and perhaps to talk with the Russians.[9] The latter attempt failed for lack of a common language, but the ships made a great impression on the sensitive Vietnamese, products of a totally alien tradition, who were reaching out—almost desperately—to grasp and master the "secrets" of Western technology and power. Imagine their thoughts when word later arrived that thirty-two of those thirty-five vessels, which comprised Admiral Z. P. Rodjestvensky's Baltic fleet, had been sunk by the Japanese in May in the Tsushima straits!

The trip farther south into the Mekong delta was cut short at Phan Thiet, when Phan Chu Trinh became seriously ill. While his associates headed back north, Phan spent four months recuperating in Phan Thiet, taking the opportunity to encourage some of the local scholar-gentry to read Liang Ch'i-ch'ao, to open the Duc Thanh School for modern learning, and to organize the Lien Thanh Corporation for commercial dealings in dried fish and fish sauce (*nuoc mam*), two specialties of the area. The

---

the *tien-si*, so he felt no strong family obligation to climb the mandarin ladder. Huynh Thuc Khang, *Tu Truyen*, pp. 26–27.

7. Best known is Phan Chu Trinh's seven character, eight line, poem, written to the prescribed topic of "Chi Thanh Thong Thanh" (Absolute Sincerity Leads to Sagehood). Chinese transliterations and *quoc-ngu* translations, in HT, pp. 526–527; The Nguyen, *Phan Chu Trinh (1872–1926)*, pp. 17–18; Ngo Thanh Nhan, *Ngu Hanh Son Chi Si*, pp. 110–111.

8. These quotes are taken from the poetic essay (*phu*) by either Huynh Thuc Khang or Tran Quy Cap, written to the prescribed topic "Luong Ngoc Danh Son." *Quoc-ngu* translation in Dao Van Hoi, *Ba Nha Chi Si Ho Phan*, pp. 70–72.

9. Huynh Thuc Khang, *Tu Truyen*, pp. 27–28.

school was shut down several years later by mandarin order, but the company seems to have lasted for some time.[10] In Quang Nam, Huynh Thuc Khang soon was organizing a school, an agricultural society, and some commercial dealings in cinnamon in Faifo (Hoi-An), and on the side preaching adoption of Western dress and short haircuts. In Ha-Tinh and Hanoi, associations of scholar-gentry were beginning to pursue the same pathways, although through 1906 the prime emphasis was on raising money to send students to Japan.

Meanwhile, recovered and back in Quang Nam, Phan Chu Trinh read the letters and printed materials that Phan Boi Chau was sending home both with fascination at the descriptions of "new Japan" and with unconcealed dismay that, as he saw it, Phan Boi Chau unwittingly was leading the movement only into more death, destruction, and demoralization by his calls to armed resistance. Both reactions led Phan Chu Trinh to arrange for his own trip to Japan, meeting Phan Boi Chau en route, as I have described, and then spending some weeks in and around Tokyo and Yokohama. He almost certainly visited Keio Gijuku University in Tokyo, Fukuzawa Yukichi's proud creation, and came away impressed with the teachers, the curriculum, and the methods of instruction.[11] Phan Boi Chau, knowing that Phan Chu Trinh was his intellectual equal and not a man likely to submit to organizational discipline, tried his best to work out a mutually acceptable division of tasks toward achieving their common objective of a strong and independent Vietnam. Nevertheless, their mid-1906 leave-taking in Hong Kong marked the beginning of a definite split over strategy, and it was not long before Nguyen Thanh was sending troubled missives from Quang Nam to Phan Boi Chau pointing out the debilitating effect on the Duy Tan Hoi of Phan Chu Trinh's reformist speeches.

What exactly was Phan Chu Trinh preaching? By every account, friendly and otherwise, Phan Chu Trinh was at his best in impromptu speeches and small-group discussions, which he tended to dominate. No records of these survive, but we do have Phan's letter of this period to Governor General Paul Beau (1902–1908), which provides an apparently frank, well developed exposition of his attitudes and proposals.[12] Phan began by outlining the economic and social situation under French colonial rule, giv-

10. Chau Hai Ky, "Nhung hoat dong cach mang cua cu Phan Chau Trinh tai Binh Thuan," which draws on interviews with the wife of one local participant in these schemes. See also HT, pp. 527–528, for a poem by Phan Chu Trinh written while recuperating in Phan Thiet.
11. DKNT, p. 27.
12. Original Chinese version, *Nam Phong* 103: 24–34. *Quoc-ngu* translations: HT, pp. 528–537 (abridged); NCLS 66: 8–14 (abridged); The Nguyen, *Phan Chu Trinh,* pp. 81–100; VTCM, pp. 188–207.

ing the French some credit for the development of roads, railroads, shipping lines, and telegraph systems, but putting primary emphasis on the French failure to develop schools, hospitals, and a fair administrative and tax structure. The reason for his letter was then stated vividly:

> My countrymen's flesh and blood is being stripped away, to the extent they no longer can work for their living; people are being split up, customs corrupted, rituals [*le-nghia*] lost . . . a somewhat civilized situation degenerating into utter barbarity. Those with spirit and intelligence [*tri*] have perceived conditions, are worried about extermination of their people, and are rousing each other to seek remedies. Some courageous ones have fled overseas, crying out, lamenting, but probably not able to return. Others, timid ones, bow their heads in their home villages and act as if they are deaf and dumb, not daring to speak of the situation. Not one has yet dared to march before Protectorate officials to expose the cruel scheming of the mandarins, and the desperate plight of the people.

Phan Chu Trinh also told Beau of his travels around the country and reported bluntly that everyone believed the French were tacitly encouraging the terrible parasitism of the mandarins as a way of turning the Vietnamese people against each other, weakening them, and hence making them easier to rule. The bulk of Phan's letter was a careful delineation of three reasons that the people had come to feel this way about their French "protectors."

First, the traditional tension between local mandarins and the central court, while admittedly not entirely "fair" (*cong-bang*), at least had prevented wide-open pillaging of the people by the mandarins, since there had been severe legal punishments awaiting those who had stepped beyond all bounds of discretion. Since the establishment of the protectorate, however, progressive emasculation of the court had given local mandarins carte blanche over the people, often in covert alliance with individual court officials and aided additionally in their exploitative sorties by the countrywide degeneration of traditional values. For several decades of the French occupation it had been possible for the people to wait patiently, knowing that the establishment of any new system took time. In any event, the villagers themselves had not seen many of the French officials, as they were not active much below the central level. But now, given their increasingly desperate situation, the people were coming to wonder precisely who was responsible at the center. And so far, the people had only seen protectorate law used against them, not against the mandarins.

Second, the apparent French disgust and scorn for the Vietnamese people was leading each side to move further and further from each other. This was the most impassioned, significant section of the letter:

The French have been in Vietnam for some time, have seen the greediness of the mandarins, the ignorance of the people, the corruption of the culture, and have concluded sneeringly that the Vietnamese have no sense of national identity. So, when they print articles in their papers or talk among themselves, they all show dislike and disdain for the Vietnamese, considering them savages, comparing them with pigs and cows, unwilling to let them become equals, and even afraid that getting close will be polluting.

Phan spoke of certain French officials' taking offense at something done by Vietnamese and shaming them mercilessly, "regardless of social position or actual innocence or guilt." Persons on corvée or employed by Frenchmen had been beaten, even unto death. All this had reached an intolerable point.

Today the Vietnamese mandarins, no matter high or low, shiver and quake when they meet French officials, fearing above all that they will do something to make the Frenchmen angry. Local gentry in the villages, walking along and unexpectedly meeting a Frenchman, be he French official, French soldier, or French merchant, must bow their heads, droop their ears, and quicken their pace—simply afraid of being disgraced.

In contrast to Phan Boi Chau, Phan Chu Trinh in this letter conceded publicly to the foreigner that the mass of Vietnamese were indeed "dishonest," "greedy," and without honor. But the French seemed unaware, he said, that among twenty million people there were likely to be at least a few who could intelligently discuss the advantages and disadvantages of various policies, for the common good. Such men, however, who not too long before had resided within several hours or a day's trip from French protectorate officials were now leaving for faraway Japan:

Traditionally the Vietnamese people disliked stepping even beyond their doorways. Now they are resigning themselves to leaving the tombs of their ancestors, separating themselves from wives and children, crossing forbidden waters, arriving at a totally unfamiliar country, and openly expressing their deepest feelings—without ever once having approached the door of French officialdom. It is because the protectorate regime has been contemptuous of the Vietnamese people that this increasing distance has developed.

Third and finally, it was perversely to the advantage of the parasitic, corrupt mandarins, Phan Chu Trinh argued, to make sure that this distance between Frenchmen and Vietnamese remained, since their livelihood depended on it. Local mandarins, while oppressing the ignorant

people and keeping down the scholar-gentry patriots, spoke to French
officials in purposefully vague terms about possible uprisings and then
managed to frame their enemies or prevent honest meetings and communication on vital issues. Perhaps the French knew that the mandarins
were lying, but they let it pass, being mostly interested in regular tax re-
ceipts. It was true that more schools, improved agriculture, local agricultural fairs, smallpox inoculations, and similar advancements being proposed by concerned Vietnamese were not considered harmful by French
officials. But the local mandarins prevented communication on such potentially unsettling proposals, stepped up the taxes, increased the corvée,
ordered arbitrary fines, and harassed their countrymen back into sub-
mission:

> Among the scholar-gentry, some are proposing the study of Western lan-
> guages, others are calling for elimination of the civil exams, still others
> trying to invest in new commercial enterprises. . . . The mandarins hate
> this, considering it an open threat to their position, calling it insane, or a
> sinister plot. . . . Forgetting the question of whether or not Vietnam is in
> truth barbaric or semideveloped, it is undeniable that we have studied the
> Chinese classics for several thousand years and know that loving the peo-
> ple is meritorious [cong], while harming them is a crime [toi]. Today's
> mandarins all are literate, have all read the necessary books, yet they
> dare to use their public offices as marketplaces, to regard the people as
> morsels to be eaten, and to declare those who are concerned with the
> people insane and developmental efforts traitorous.

The concluding portion of Phan's letter was replete with specifics, beginning with a more detailed indictment of the tax and corvée systems and
ending with an offer to discuss these matters in person with the governor
general—an offer apparently never accepted. In between there were references to the dire fate of the American Indians, to the high ideals of the
French Revolution, and to the Christian concept of "loving thine enemy
as thyself." Phan averred that he had heard talk of imminent reforms, but
it had all sounded fanciful as it did not get at the most basic question of the
corrupt and outmoded mandarinate. Such reforms would be like "coaxing
a crying child with candy" or "promising starving people gold and sliver
mines in the jungle" to keep them from robbing and thieving. He reassured
the French that his people were in no condition to resort to violence
against the regime. Indeed, he professed to oppose any talk of independence at this point, since independence would only mean that within a few
years the Vietnamese would be robbing and killing each other, thus leaving
the way open for some other foreign power to move in.
    If the French would immediately direct their attention to improving the

livelihood of the people, allow the scholar-gentry freedom of expression, open newspapers to stimulate general interest, drop the civil exams, open schools, and encourage industry, then he and many others would be willing pupils to the master, children to the father, in a common effort at serious modernization. With reform under way, with the people of Vietnam happy, there would be a fear of the Frenchmen's leaving rather than a continuing hatred toward them.

> But if the Protectorate regime is still bent on a policy of persecuting the Vietnamese people, if it still intends to kill all twenty million, then punish me heavily now for high slander [*huy bang*], as a lesson to other scholar-gentry that they should continue to keep their mouths shut and remain as distant as possible.

There is no reason not to take this letter at face value. Phan Chu Trinh's subsequent life was an affirmation of the ideas expressed in it, right up to the last sentence, since he was to be jailed several times by his proposed benefactors. It seems probable that Phan had in mind as precedent K'ang Yu-wei's famous reformist petitions to the Kuang-hsu emperor in the 1890's, although with the significant difference that Phan was expressing himself to the Western overlords rather than to his own monarch, whom he considered quite impotent.[13] Governor General Beau apparently thought enough of the letter to have it printed in several Parisian papers.[14] Intellectually, Beau was more open to Phan's message than his predecessor, Paul Doumer, ever could have been, but he lacked the political and administrative authority of Doumer. His reforms were erratic and inconclusive—exactly as Phan Chu Trinh had feared.

Nevertheless, the political climate in Indochina, particularly in north Vietnam, was sufficiently ambiguous in late 1906 to allow a few scholar-gentry and wealthy merchants to take some initiatives on their own. In Hanoi in the previous twenty years the French had established eight specialized schools, enrolling about eighteen hundred students. They also had permitted at least six private schools to begin operations in and around Hanoi, mostly teaching *quoc-ngu*, French, and Chinese, with a bit of mathematics, geography, or chemistry.[15] It was within this framework that

13. Ton Quang Phiet, "Phan Chu Trinh," p. 14, brings out this precedent.
14. A French translation of an open letter by Phan Chu Trinh, dated October 1906, appears in the official publication *Bulletin l'Ecole Française d'Extrême Orient,* vol. 7, pp. 166–175. This seems almost identical to Phan's letter to Beau, dated August 1906. Paul Isoart, *Le phénomène national vietnamien,* pp. 232–233.
15. Tran Huy Lieu, ed., *Lich Su Thu Do Ha-Noi,* pp. 125–127. Several of these

the idea arose of developing a more ambitious private education program, within the letter of colonial legal restrictions yet fulfilling desires and objectives quite distinct from those which most Frenchmen and mandarin collaborators had in mind at the time.

The heart of this effort was the Dong Kinh Nghia Thuc, in the narrow sense a private school in Hanoi for four hundred to five hundred students, but in the broadest sense a popular educational and cultural movement of real significance to subsequent Vietnamese history.[16] The name was a combination of one of Hanoi's historic appellations, "Dong Kinh" (Eastern Capital), and the word selected by Fukuzawa Yukichi to symbolize his educational efforts at Keio Gijuku, "Nghia Thuc" (nontuition school). Of course, the Vietnamese scholar-gentry already understood the traditional connotations in China of *nghia-thuc* as a private school for classical studies operated by means of public donations. Fukuzawa, however, had extended it to mean "common schooling" along lines set by the English public school, an inculcation of elite values centering on social and political obligations to the larger community.[17] Phan Chu Trinh had brought back to Vietnam high praise for Keio Gijuku, Phan Boi Chau had written glowingly of Fukuzawa, and many scholar-gentry not able to travel overseas had read of Keio in contemporary Chinese sources.[18] It is interesting that while obscurantist opponents of the Dong Kinh Nghia Thuc—especially the mandarins—chose first to argue that *nghia-thuc* by definition involved study of the Confucian classics, they were not above implying later to French officials that *nghia* in the school's name meant *nghia-dang* (righteously rebellious party) or *khoi-nghia* (uprising, revolt).[19]

However, for the time being, in March 1907 the French granted permission to open the school. Apparently eight levels of instruction were available, from primary through high school, with special classes in *quoc-ngu*,

private schools appear to have been in the business of preparing the sons of mandarins and wealthy merchants for travel and study in France.

16. For those interested in making cross-cultural comparisons of early modernizing elements in Southeast Asia, William Roff, *The Origins of Malay Nationalism* (New Haven, 1967), pp. 56–67, contains a discussion of Al-Imam, a reformist group appearing in Singapore in 1906.

17. Wada Hironori, "Ajia no Kindaika to Keio Gijuku," *Shogakubu Soritsu Jushunen Kinenbi Kichi Ron Bunshu* (Tokyo, 1967), p. 7.

18. Further evidence is available that at least two founders of the Dong Kinh Nghia Thuc, Dao Nguyen Pho and Nguyen Quyen, were directly familiar with the modern connotations of the term. Dao Trinh Nhat, *Dong Kinh Nghia Thuc*, p. 15. DKNT, p. 31, also indicates that Phan Chu Trinh discussed the Keio concepts in person with most of the later Dong Kinh Nghia Thuc leaders.

19. DKNT, pp. 15, 21.

French, and Chinese, depending on the student's background and interests.[20] The French instruction, however, given in the evening by several native civil servants, was not really integrated with the rest of the program and, in contrast to all other classes, it required some tuition from the students.[21] As might be expected, science was a new item of curiosity for teachers and students, alike. There was a class in modern mathematics and geometry taught by a scholar who had the slight advantage of having read a Chinese translation of an English textbook.[22] And some attempt was made at teaching hygiene and natural sciences, although there again the lack of specialized teachers and adequate texts kept study at a rudimentary level.[23] Two women, educated daughters of scholar-gentry, were allowed the unprecedented honor of participating as teachers of Chinese and *quoc-ngu*.[24] A sports field was set up, with climbing poles and some steel shot for the shotput, but athletics failed to generate any enthusiasm among the students and were soon dropped from the curriculum.[25]

The really exciting classes were in the upper-level courses in history and literature, taught by prestigious scholar-gentry to students already proficient in written Chinese. Basic knowledge of the Four Books and Five Classics being assumed, the texts consisted mostly of extracts from contemporary Chinese books and periodicals or older literature appropriate to the aims of "new learning." For example, when studying a text on Vietnam's Tran dynasty, the word *thien-trieu* (celestial court) would immediately crop up in reference to China. The teacher would take his brush and dramatically blank out the term, for the rest of the session expostulating on traditional Chinese feelings of superiority, the resulting inferiority complexes of educated Vietnamese, the disastrous results this had had for the Ch'ing, and, finally, the alleged contrast between backward China and Vietnam, on one hand, and progressive, dynamic Japan on the other. He would culminate his discourse with a description of the Russo-Japanese War, especially the battle of Tsushima—the word *thien-trieu* having served as the springboard for all this![26]

Such pouring of new wine into old bottles was the dominant pedagogical

20. CMCD-3, p. 33.
21. DKNT, pp. 40–41.
22. DKNT, p. 40. The author transliterates the book's title as *Ky-ha tac co.*
23. VTCM, pp. 87–88, mentions that a few natural science texts from the current middle-school curriculum in China were available. Some scholars also culled pertinent information from traditional encyclopedias and the like.
24. CMCD-3, p. 31.
25. DKNT, p. 41.
26. This example is cited in DKNT, p. 42.

technique at the Dong Kinh Nghia Thuc, definitely reminiscent of the intellectual eclecticism of K'ang Yu-wei and Liang Ch'i-ch'ao but accomplished in more conscious, psychically less painful fashion, or so it would appear. When the famous Confucian passage about one's body's belonging *in absolutis* to one's parents came up among the younger students, the teacher would interpret this to mean that children should not play with knives or climb where they might injure themselves. Contrary to traditional teaching, cutting one's hair and fingernails, the teacher would say, was a way of expressing filial piety, because it kept away lice, infection, and illness. From there, the teacher might go on to a denunciation of lacquering one's teeth, of using astrology for choosing bath days, and of smoking opium. Dao Nguyen Pho, who had tried hard but failed to break his own addiction to opium, spoke feelingly on the classical phrase about the hidden dangers of passing civil exams as a youngster (*thieu nien cao khoa, nhat bat hanh gia*), since that very accomplishment had given him the leisure to seek out wine, women, and the pipe. When a few students talked of studying the old texts in preparation for the civil exams, Duong Ba Trac, who had made *cu-nhan* at the age of seventeen, would say, "You still want that useless *cu-nhan*? Here, give me a penny, and you can have mine!"[27] It was crucial that the degree system be demeaned in order to formulate a new set of social and educational values.

There was a mood of incipient nationalism at the school, which seemed to increase as the months went by. A functionary in the local bureau of cartography made a big map of Vietnam of white cloth, which he used at the school to describe the *S* shape of the country, the mountain backbone, the location of the Bach-Dang victory over the Mongols, the "former territory of the Khmer" in the Mekong delta, and so on. People are said to have come from other neighborhoods just to view that map—probably the first time that they had seen their country rendered schematically.[28] Students were encouraged to buy local products in preference to French imports. Several songs emanating from the Dong Kinh Nghia Thuc referred directly to French colonial exploitation, and several school texts on Vietnamese history openly praised the scholar-gentry resisters of the late nineteenth century. One history book ended with this rousing conclusion:

> And so now, with the sacred spirit of the country forging people's obligations, amidst these European winds and American rains, who knows but what there may be men who on behalf of their country will sweep away the fog, lift up the clouds, and create a radiant and expansive hori-

27. DKNT, pp. 37–39, 41–42.
28. DKNT, p. 39. VTCM, p. 75, also cites a geography book, *Nam Quoc Dia Du Chi* (Vietnam Geographic Annals), that was printed at the school and used in classwork.

zon for us all. . . . At that time we will write more—great books, unique books—not just this one time alone![29]

Teachers at the Dong Ninh Nghia Thuc showed a new willingness to employ *quoc-ngu* when introducing outside ideas or techniques, and they urged each student to remember to use the romanized script subsequently as a device for passing on modern knowledge to hundreds of their less literate countrymen. A contemporary poem argued:

> *Quoc-ngu* is the [saving] spirit in our country,
> We must take it out among our people.
> Books from other countries, books from China,
> Each word, each meaning must be translated clearly.[30]

It was through this translating of new concepts and simultaneous publishing in *quoc-ngu* that a number of abstract concepts entered the spoken vocabulary for the first time.[31] Some of the texts for studying *quoc-ngu* at the school were brought in from Cochinchina, which was one example of the way cultural developments in all three regions were once again influencing each other.[32]

Dong Kinh Nghia Thuc activities were divided informally into four sections, of which the school classes constituted the first, but not necessarily the most important. The other three involved fund-raising, proselytizing campaigns, and publishing. Luong Van Can, the school's principal, and Le Dai were said to be the best fund-raisers. Born in 1854 in Ha-Dong province near Hanoi, Luong really was too old to be considered part of this scholar-gentry generation.[33] Nevertheless, his connections in Hanoi as a silk merchant, his interest in general reform and commercial development, and, of course, his being older made him the natural choice for principal. Not least, he also provided a building with an adjacent lot for the school. Many other founders contributed money, but the largest per-

---

29. *Nam Quoc Vi Nhan Truyen* (Stories of Vietnam's Great Men), quoted in VTCM, p. 75.
30. Quoted in Tran Huy Lieu, *Lich su*, p. 128.
31. For example: *cach-menh* (revolution), *kinh-te* (economics), *truu-tuong* (abstract), *cu-the* (concrete), *tich-cuc* (positive, active), *tieu-cuc* (negative, passive). CMCD-3, pp. 39–40, 46–47.
32. VTCM, p. 76.
33. DKNT, p. 32. VNDN, pp. 137–138. Nhi-khe village, Thuong-phuc district, Ha-Dong. Luong became a *cu-nhan* at twenty, but turned down offers of official position, first from Hue, then from the French. He taught privately for some time; his most famous pupil may have been Nguyen Hai Than.

centage of the budget came voluntarily from parents or relatives of the students. There was also money from wealthy "sympathizers," whose names were then inscribed on plaques hung up outside the school. Each month, teachers received nominal pay of four piastres, with the remainder going for paper, ink, and the printing of textbooks and other written material.[34]

The campaign (*co-dong*) section quite simply was in the business of oral propaganda, particularly public lectures, poetry recitals, and popular dramas. Most such events were held at the school on the first and fifteenth days of each lunar month, but some of the more skillful, determined orators would venture out into the city and the six surrounding provinces, speaking whenever and wherever they could get an audience.[35] One of the earliest and most famous lectures, presented by Duong Ba Trac and Luong Truc Dam, was at the Ngoc-Son temple on beautiful Hoan-Kiem lake in central Hanoi. Just at the point when Luong was exhorting everyone to drop traditional studies and follow the Japanese example, the police appeared at the head of the bridge, the only exit from the temple. Pandemonium ensued, and Duong and Luong were detained for questioning, but the publicity seems to have helped the movement gain recognition.[36] Poetry sessions were particularly attractive to outside scholar-gentry, with the poets employing traditional forms of capping and rhyming but with new topics and messages.[37] On the other hand, less educated audiences were drawn presumably to dramatic presentations recounting the heroic legends surrounding the Trung sisters, Tran Hung Dao, and Pham Ngu Lao. As with Phan Boi Chau's efforts along similar lines, scholar-gentry authors connected with the Dong Kinh Nghia Thuc employed the *tuong*, a traditional narrative form, while their content put new stress on pride in their country, indirectly criticizing the presence of the alien French.[38]

Major lectures at the Dong Kinh Nghia Thuc were more formal affairs, although anyone could attend. Luong Van Can would chair the meetings, flanked by the principal speaker, teachers from the school, and honored guests from the outside. Men and women generally sat separately in the

34. CMCD-3, p. 31.
35. CMCD-3, p. 31.
36. DKNT, pp. 52–56.
37. CMCD-3, p. 32. Interestingly enough, a Buddhist priest from Son-Tay, Nhu Tung by name, was considered most effective in utilizing poetic forms this way.
38. Tran Huy Lieu, *Lich Su*, pp. 151–152. Particular mention is made of two works by Hoang Tang Bi, *Thu Chong No Nuoc* and *Hoa Tien Ky*. The latter incorporated northern popular singing and poetic forms, so that the average people would enjoy it even more—an innovation. *Dong A Song Phung* by Nguyen Huu Tien is also mentioned. Eventually, the *tuong* merged with the *cai-luong*, a new dramatic medium of the 1920s.

audience, with students taking up the back rows and the sides. At the time it was considered radical even to admit women to such meetings.[39] By all accounts Phan Chu Trinh was the most popular speaker, although he was spending most of his time in Quang Nam, rousing the scholar-gentry and organizing commercial enterprises. His speeches are remembered as much for the sharp give and take that ensued as for his main message. For ex-, ample, once he developed the thesis that Vietnam had fallen easy prey to the French because the Vietnamese people lacked that sense of mass enthusiasm and personal sacrifice normally supplied by religious commitment. Phan contrasted the recent defeat with the thirteenth-century victories against the Mongols, when, he asserted, Buddhism provided the unifying thrust, the sense of extrafamilial mission. There, however, Phan was challenged by a scholar named Phuong Son, who cited India as a place permeated with religious fervor, yet already "slaves of the English for several centuries." And if religion were really the crucial factor, how might Phan explain Vietnamese victories against the Ming and Ch'ing, when Buddhism was no longer flourishing?[40]

Another time Phan Chu Trinh spoke on the subject "Vietnam cannot be saved without getting rid of Chinese characters" (*Bat phe Han tu, bat tuc di cuu Nam Quoc*). To this others, including some followers of Phan Boi Chau, countered, "Vietnam cannot be saved without invigorating, improving Chinese studies" (*Bat chan Han hoc, bat tuc di cuu Nam Quoc*). Although agreeing that the civil exam system should be abolished, they still insisted that only Chinese studies could stimulate the Vietnamese people to patriotic sacrifice and bravery. One evening, in a mood of patriotic fervor, Phan Chu Trinh contradicted the implications of his normal reformist line, saying that perhaps only those who had really suffered, who had no fancy houses, no extensive property, no attractive wives or clever children—in other words, only the downtrodden—would put their lives on the line for a cause. Another scholar then tearfully quoted two powerful lines from Phan Boi Chau in agreement, and the room was said to have been filled with sobbing.

But there were times for laughter also, as when Phan Chu Trinh allegedly argued for the cutting of long hair in the following manner:

> When the Ming armies came and turned our country into Chinese prefectures and subprefectures, they also forced their customs on us, men taking the hair bun and women the split trousers. . . . Today . . . thank heavens our spirits are reviving, we are waking up, the whole country is reforming. Isn't there a great sense of elation when we quickly cut off our

39. DKNT, p. 56.
40. DKNT, pp. 56–57.

bun and can command that stupid band of parasites [a double reference to lice and the colonial regime] to leave that bit of colonial territory on top of our head and stop sucking our blood?[41]

It was after this speech that the anonymous "haircutting chant" began to circulate in Hanoi, eventually sweeping through most of the provinces, to become perhaps the most famous message of the Dong Kinh Nghia Thuc movement:

> Comb in the left hand,
> Scissors in the right,
> Snip, snip, clip, clip!
> Watch out, be careful,
> Drop stupid practices,
> Dump childish things
> Speak openly and frankly
> Study Western customs
> Don't cheat or bluff
> Don't lie
> Today we clip
> Tomorrow we shave![42]

Traditionalist scholar-gentry and mandarins soon mounted a counter-offensive, calling those who had cut their hair *dan-troc*—"bare heads" or, as a homonymic meaning, "impure, corrupt people." This prompted a clever Dong Kinh Nghia Thuc poetic rejoinder, playing on the idea of cutting one's hair to enter the "reformation monastery" and chant the "independence" prayers, with all the Buddhist implications of accepting a new regimen and changing one's attitudes decisively.[43]

Such thrusts and counterthrusts, superficially concerning the length of one's hair, in fact represented a division over the entire question of social authority. To a traditionalist choosing to interpret Confucius literally, cutting one's hair indicated grossly unfilial behavior. If one acted in that manner in relation to one's parents, how much more likely would he be to challenge monarchical or mandarin authority! Reformist scholar-gentry

41. DKNT, pp. 58–60. No source is given; we assume the above is not a literal quotation, but rather a recollection by one of the Dong Kinh Nghia Thuc participants interviewed by the author.
42. CMCD-3, p. 47. The author includes a variant verse. Also in Pham Van Son, *Viet-Nam Cach Mang Can Su, 1885–1914*, p. 396.
43. CMCD-3, pp. 47–48. DKNT, pp. 47–48. Dao Trinh Nhat, *Dong Kinh*, p. 26, has Nguyen Quyen claiming authorship of this rejoinder. HT, p. 597, also prints a portion under Nguyen Quyen's name.

were quite aware of these implications, and so the debate raged on at provincial, prefectural, and district schools. Ironically, at the same time such disputations were being raised below, authority symbols at the top were showing signs of tarnish. For example, traditionalists were truly shocked when King Thanh Thai took to having his own hair cut short, to wearing Western clothes, and to carrying a jaunty walking cane.[44] With a king like that, the argument went, it was hardly surprising that conditions were degenerating. As if to confirm traditionalist fears, poems satirizing mandarins and prospective mandarins circulated ever more widely. One poem in Nghe An and Ha Tinh parodied a prefect named Ta Thuc Dinh, who allegedly got himself a trip to France by kowtowing five times to the French governor general and then five times to the Frenchman's wife. Another poem in Thua Thien mocked the 1906 regional exam proctors and graduates, accusing them by name of nepotism, collusion, bribery, dependence on French intercession, and—most biting—securing their degrees by presenting their sisters as mistresses to French officials.[45]

The selective publication of such poems and many other materials was the responsibility of the fourth part of the informal Dong Kinh Nghia Thuc organization, compositions (*tru tac*). Naturally, one aim was to prepare study materials for the students, but a lot of the publishing seems to have made its way far beyond the school walls as part of specific reformist programs. A newspaper, *Dang Co Tung Bao* (Old Lantern Miscellany) appeared irregularly, printed half in Chinese or *nom*, and half in *quoc-ngu*. A small library at the Dong Kinh Nghia Thuc allowed outsiders to borrow books, definitely an innovation for that time. Most printing was done by simple wood-block or zinc plate techniques.[46] Nevertheless, an effort was made to use good paper, to keep printed images sharp, and to provide a reasonably good binding for the books. Often the frontispiece was a red woodcut of a jovial young Vietnamese propping up the globe—surely an appropriate symbol of the hopes of the period.[47]

Contemporary Chinese materials were sought eagerly by Dong Kinh Nghia Thuc scholars, particularly the writings of Liang Ch'i-ch'ao and his associates. Copies would pass from hand to hand, lectures would be de-

---

44. Traditionalists in Quang Nam reacted by daring to quote Mencius's condemnation of a monarch who utterly failed to live up to his role: "Vong chi bat tu nhan quan." Cited in VTCM, pp. 53–54.
45. VTCM, pp. 25–27.
46. Only a very few copies are extant. DKNT, p. 45. CMCD-3, p. 32. In Dao Trinh Nhat, *Dong Kinh*, p. 28, Nguyen Quyen recalls some sort of a printing press. It is doubtful, however, if one should take seriously his contention that some publications were printed in amounts of 20,000 or more copies.
47. VTCM, pp. 74–75.

veloped on parallel themes, and key portions would be extracted or sum-marized for republication in *Dang Co Tung Bao*. Apparently this was how famous Western works like Rousseau's *Contrat social*, Spencer's *Evolution*, and Montesquieu's *Esprit de lois* were introduced to a fairly wide audience in Vietnam.[48] At this point few, if any, of the school's main par-ticipants were familiar enough with the French language to read these works in the original, quite aside from consideration of the possible hu-miliation of asking for copies through the colonial administration. As it was, we may assume that many of the scholar-gentry found it somehow more acceptable, more satisfying psychologically, to make entry into the West via the mediating influences of the Chinese language and culture.

Such an approach had its pitfalls. Most obviously it tended to perpetu-ate and compound errors of translation originating in Peking, Canton, and Tokyo. Perhaps more serious was the phonetic confusion stemming from the fact that Vietnamese and Chinese pronunciations of specific characters often bear little or no relationship to each other. Hence, by not attempting direct transliteration of Western names and places and instead simply recopying characters that the Chinese had selected for that pur-pose, Vietnamese scholars added some enduringly nonsensical words to the national vocabulary. In this way, for example, Rousseau became known to the Vietnamese as *Lu-thoa*, Bismarck was *Ti-tu-mach*, and Gladstone ended up as *Cach-lan-tu-don*.[49]

Of even more lasting intellectual and political significance than Chinese-language efforts by Vietnamese were the translations and original creations in either *nom* or *quoc-ngu*, such as the many poems and songs aimed at the masses. Le Dai was the master of these, one of his earliest efforts being the *nom* and *quoc-ngu* translations of Phan Boi Chau's *Hai Ngoai Huyet Thu*. Eventually, through oral transmission these translations became fully as important as the original.

This willingness to print and distribute the works of Phan Boi Chau and even to utilize them in classrooms, illustrates how the Dong Kinh Nghia Thuc served as a marketplace for competing influences and ideas, rather than as the exclusive property of either reformists or activists. As I hope to show, it is important to delineate the ideas of Phan Boi Chau and Phan Chu Trinh and to establish the historical significance of the activist and reformist strategies that developed around them. But it would be inaccu-

48. In this context, DKNT, p. 44, especially mentions the efforts of Nguyen Huu Tien and Nguyen Don Phuc, scholars who later joined Pham Quynh's so-called *Nam Phong* group. CMCD-3, p. 32, lists other book titles, as does Tran Huy Lieu, *Lich Su*, p. 127.
49. VTCM, pp. 152–154, 272–273.

rate to picture the two principal figures as fully comprehending in 1907 the long-term ramifications of their diverging positions, much less to depict all the others as being divided into organized, opposing camps. The primary struggle at the Dong Kinh Nghia Thuc was not between activists and reformists, but rather for the unified development of a wide-ranging cultural and political attack on both the obscurantists and the self-denigrators inhabiting high places beyond the school walls.

The best way to appreciate this point is through short illustrations from some Dong Kinh Nghia Thuc publications and ballads:

1. "VAN MINH TAN HOC SACH" (Civilization and New Learning), anonymous:[50] With Phan Chu Trinh's letter to Beau, this essay may be considered the most careful, concise exposition of reformist ideas in the period from 1904 to 1907 that has survived to the present day. Herbert Spencer's doctrine of Social Darwinism clearly influenced the author profoundly, as did the writings of K'ang Yu-wei and Liang Ch'i-ch'ao. Nevertheless, the author demonstrated a steady determination to apply Western concepts specifically to Vietnamese rather than Chinese situations.

"Van Minh Tan Hoc Sach" was divided into sections: the diagnosis of Vietnam's ills, and the prescription leading to a cure. Borrowing from K'ang Yu-wei, the author posited a time in the past when Asia had been the source and center of science and civilization. What had happened? Briefly stated, Asians, in general, and Vietnamese, in particular, had failed to keep up in the world struggle for survival. While others had been developing scientific agriculture, state-subsidized commerce, and modern industry (mentioning James Watt and Thomas Edison with special fondness), Vietnam's obscurantist elite had been satisfying their passions for string and wind music, *dau-ho*,[51] card games, chess, poetic riddles, fortune-telling, geomancy, and witchcraft. Worse yet, was their scheming and plotting for mandarin posts:

> One of them is said to have told his associates: "if you want to become a mandarin, you'd better be careful and don't read new [modern] books or look at new periodicals." Alas! Not knowing about the existence of new books and periodicals is one thing. But knowing about them and yet sealing off, blocking out, insuring that the story is not heard or seen—that is building and preserving for oneself a fundamentally slavelike character. People of that type should really make us sick![52]

50. This probably was written in 1904, but was printed and circulated in 1907–1908. An original copy in Chinese is in the Science Library, Hanoi. Full *quoc-ngu* translation, VTCM, pp. 159–180. Abridged translation, HT, pp. 607–613.
51. A parlor game from China involving the tossing of small sticks into a vase or pot. Dao Duy Anh, *Han Viet Tu Dien*, p. 260.
52. VTCM, pp. 162–163.

In short, the author argued, Vietnamese civilization had a static (*tinh*) character, whereas Western civilization was dynamic (*dong*). This was illustrated by some devastating comparisons in the areas of ideas, education, government, national symbolism, and custom. Regarding custom, for example, the Vietnamese demonstrated a definite aversion to travel and distant adventures, whereas Westerners made much of the exploits of such wanderers as Moses, Columbus, and Matteo Ricci. Even the Chinese, the author pointed out bitterly, were better travelers than the Vietnamese.

The author of "Van Minh Tan Hoc Sach" listed four historical reasons that Vietnamese tended more toward passivity than dynamic change: a smug self-satisfaction and denigration of foreigners and hence an unwillingness even to investigate outside techniques and capabilities; a conviction that Confucius, Mencius, and so on had an eternal monopoly on truth, and hence a neglect of the advanced, specialized studies on which Western strength was founded; a rigid belief that everything old was correct, everything new inferior, and hence an ignoring of the knowledge and thinking of contemporaries; a high regard for mandarins and a contempt for the people, and hence a tendency to ignore local village conditions.

Assuming that his readers accepted the need to break away from such attitudes, the author then launched into his prescription for a cure. This was divided into six segments—language, literature, examinations, elite involvement, industry, and newspapers. There was a learned rationale, based on classical precedents, for dropping Chinese and adopting an "individual" script, in this case *quoc-ngu*. At another point the author argued (somewhat optimistically) that it was silly to spend years studying a script that had no relation to Vietnam's spoken tongue, when one could master *quoc-ngu* in six months.

Regarding literature, the author asserted that a lot of old Chinese writings were of little or no value any more. For example, some encyclopedias spent twenty or thirty thousand words expostulating on the possible location of a bronze pillar placed by General Ma Yuan, the Chinese commander of the first century A.D., only to conclude that it might well have fallen into the sea. By contrast with such materials, he saw a need to select from Vietnam's own literature, especially its history, those books that could replace Chinese texts. A major editorial effort was needed to compile new offerings from Vietnamese, Western, and Chinese sources and then to translate them into *quoc-ngu* for broad distribution.

Examination reform in "Van Minh Tan Hoc Sach" was much the same as that which Liang Ch'i-ch'ao had proposed in China and included the elimination of most arbitrary stylistic restraints and the addition of questions on mathematical and scientific subjects. Concerning elite involvement, the author cited K'ang Yu-wei to the effect that one could not "open up" the intellects of the masses until he won the scholar-gentry over. Laudatory reference was made to the colonial Quoc Hoc school in Hue, but it was pointed out that most of the graduates had not been employed. All this tied in with the author's discussion of industrialization, in which he proposed that Vietnam go so far as to place graduates of scientific studies in jobs ahead of and above regular examination graduates. There was a lengthy condemnation of reliance on foreign finished products plus several concrete ideas for rewarding inventiveness and competitive prowess. Finally, considering newspapers, the author listed wonderingly how many thousands of periodicals were published in France, Germany, England, and America and called for the immediate founding of a paper, half in Chinese, half in *quoc-ngu*, that could be disseminated throughout the provinces. In it would be news of foreign innovations and instruction in Vietnamese history, and a whole range of other subjects; in short, he described the *Dang Co Tung Bao* of the Dong Kinh Nghia Thuc.

2. "CAO HU LAU VAN" (Indictment of Corrupt Customs), authorship uncertain:[53] This poem called passionately on the scholar-gentry in the villages, still the most educated and respected figures among the people, to turn their ears to the new winds, their eyes toward the future, and help those who were sinking into despair and rouse those who were dreaming. Why could they not be the ones to steer the raft toward reality and let the drowning people get on? The author attacked those scholars who, without ever having peered much beyond the hedges surrounding their own villages, still derided K'ang Yu-wei and Liang Ch'i-ch'ao, still hauled out the ancients and borrowed their sayings in hackneyed fashion, still showed interest in ghost stories and engulfed themselves in petty love novels. Satire was employed very effectively in an imaginary confrontation with a village-bound scholar:

> Ask him which beliefs are best for today?
> He'll say, "believing in the Confucian men is enough."
> Ask him of what is he most fond?
> He'll say, "accepting the ancients as teachers."
>
> *   *   *   *   *   *   *   *
>
> Argue that "heavenly omens" bode neither good nor evil,
> He'll say, "Heaven determines all good, all evil."

53. Signed "Yen si phi ly thuan" in the original 1905 Chinese version, a term which was also used in Liang Ch'i-ch'ao's *Hsin-min ts'ung-pao* as a phoneticism for the English word "inspiration." Translated in 1907 into *nom* and *quoc-ngu* by Ngo Vi Lam, using 6–8–6–8 form, and published in *Dang Co Tung Bao*. HT, pp. 613–618. VTCM, pp. 254–258. Excerpts of a variant version are in CMCD-3, pp. 36, 44–46, under the title *Dieu Hu Nho* (Funeral Condolences for Backward Scholars).

Imply that the earth is round and moves,
He'll say, "it's square and stands as before."

Another section reflected the basic reappraisal under way among the Dong Kinh Nghia Thuc participants concerning their position, individual and cultural, in the modern world:

> Why is the roof of their [the Western] universe the broad
>   lands and skies,
> While we cower and confine ourselves to a cranny in our house?
> Why can they jump straight, leap far,
> While we shrink back and cling to each other?
> Why do they rule the world,
> While we bow our heads as slaves?
> Take up a mirror, look at yourself,
> Where on that face is there something to brag about?
> Taking steps outward, we fear what others think,
> We intend to try, but where's the ability?
> Our spirit is as cold as ash,
> Our body has the form of a shriveled tree.
> We have eyes, but they seem to be blind.
> Who will bring the lamp to light the path?
> Our ears might as well not be there.
> Who will bring the bell and ring it noisily?

3. "TINH QUOC HON CA" (A Ballad to Awaken the National Soul), Phan Chu Trinh:[54] This appears to be one of the few surviving poetic creations of Phan Chu Trinh. It employed direct, colloquial Vietnamese to propagate some of his major reform themes. It reviewed Vietnam's temporal attributes and showed an underlying faith in the country's capacity to survive and develop. Beyond this, Phan Chu Trinh appealed for individual bravery and dedication and cited Peter the Great's famous shipbuilding experience in Holland as an example of how everyone, high and low, should learn a trade. He provided coherent arguments for personal investment in new commerce and industry, incidentally reproving his own people for allowing Chinese and Indians to monopolize the Vietnamese moneylending market. All this was a reflection of Phan's practical preoccupations in Quang Nam at this time, not only his personal attempts at starting viable enterprises but also his increasing belief that the study of any kind of modern trade and specialty might help to restore a sense of

54. *Nom* poetry in 7–7–6–8 form. HT, pp. 537–545, contains about one-third of the total of 782 lines.

pride and patriotism among the Vietnamese at large, particularly as the trainees passed their skills on to ever-widening circles of peasants and townspeople.[55]

4. "THIET TIEN CA" (Iron Money Ballad), Nguyen Phan Lang:[56] This was written originally for classes at the Dong Kinh Nghia Thuc and then circulated widely outside. Essentially it was a sharply worded protest over colonial substitution of iron coinage for the former zinc and copper cash. The objection was not nostalgic, it should be pointed out, but practical, because the French authorities would not accept their own iron money for tax payments, for purchase of foreign commodities, or for train or boat tickets. From this launching point, the author then accused the French of not wanting Vietnamese to compete with them commercially, of preventing Vietnamese commerce with foreign countries, and of tricking uneducated people into handing over their savings. On colonial taxes, he lamented:

> Caught in the net, snagged from a hundred angles,
> What's left when you peel off the skin and clean the bones?

In his concluding lines, the author called on the people to wake up and resist such flagrant exploitation:

> Uncounted generations, on and on,
> Still youth, still land, still Vietnam.

5. "DE TINH QUOC DAN CA" (Ballad to Awaken Countrymen!), authorship uncertain.[57] This ballad apparently was written in 1906 and was popularized the next year through the Dong Kinh Nghia Thuc. Afterwards it circulated through most of Vietnam, developing numerous variants without maintaining strict meter and form. The common message, was outrage at having fallen prey to the foreigner, with a listing of contemporary grievances and a call to patriotic sacrifice in pursuing the recent precedents of Meiji Japan. A truly unique section of the ballad

55. CMCD-3, p. 40.
56. Pseudonym, Dam Xuyen. Tay-tuu village, Hoai-duc district, Ha-Dong. The ballad is in *nom*, 7-7-6-8 form. HT, pp. 603–606. CMCD-3, pp. 41–42, 48–51.
57. Also popularly known as the *A-te-a* (Asia) ballad, for the first word of the first line. Various sources have listed the author as Phan Boi Chau, Nguyen Thien Thuat, Tang Bat Ho, and Duong Ba Trac. Phan Boi Chau does not claim it in his autobiographies. It is *nom* poetry in the 7-7-6-8 form (with deviations, probably as a result of later oral transmission). HT, pp. 628–631. VTCM, pp. 262–270. Variant excerpt in DKNT, pp. 48–49.

listed in one angry poetic sequence at least thirty-seven colonial taxes, all enforced to the point where "nine out of ten homes have been stripped bare."

> Japan is kin, France is foe,
> Study the clever kin, take revenge on the foe.[58]
> New learning must be built up first,
> Enterprises organized together, countrywide.
> Commerce we place at the fore,
> Every skill contributes to the common effort.

6. "CAC CHU TAP BINH!" (So, You're in the Army!), anonymous.[59] This short, highly colloquial song, which originated with someone connected with the Dong Kinh Nghia Thuc, was aimed at Vietnamese serving in colonial military units:

> So you're in the Army!
> You're of Annam born,
> You're of Annam raised,
> You're plump, you're happy,
> Satisfied and content.
> You end your hitch, homeward bound,
> And you'll die of taxes and corvée.
> Your clan faces you exhausted,
> Your kith and kin in rags.
> Do you get the point yet?
> Where's thanks from the French?
> Where's love from them for you?
> The woman's bra is being used to strangle her![60]

By the summer of 1907 Dong Kinh Nghia Thuc influence was definitely being felt in the provinces surrounding Hanoi and in some areas of central Vietnam. Numerous scholar-gentry from Ha-Dong, Bac-Ninh, Son-Tay, Phuc-Yen, Hai-Duong, and Nam-Dinh either showed up at the school personally or sent messages in order to obtain materials to open up schools in their own districts or provinces. The school apparently maintained a suggestion box outside in which people could leave or forward ideas on lesson materials and on further development of the pro-

---

58. HT, p. 631, in a footnote maintains that the Sûreté spread another version of these two lines: "Japan is kin, France is *teacher*, / Study the clever kin, seek out the good teacher."
59. CMCD-3, p. 42. Pham Van Son, *Viet-Nam*, p. 406.
60. That is, Vietnamese are being used to oppress their own.

gram.[61] Dong Kinh Nghia Thuc ideas on commercial development spread within the small Vietnamese merchant class, while ballads and poems moved from person to person and began to reach the rural folk. Cutting one's hair short began among the progressive scholar-gentry, was then taken up by some of the townspeople, and at last penetrated, more slowly, to the nonscholar classes in the villages. In the generalized colonial repression of 1908, as we shall see, many people would find themselves being questioned or jailed simply because their hair was cut short.[62] Dong Kinh Nghia Thuc attacks on the traditional exam system and indeed on the entire philosophy of studying merely to pass exams and thus gain plush sinecures, seem to have put the mandarin establishment on the defensive, if only because the most persuasive attacks came from persons having the highest exam credentials. Only a *tien-si* like Phan Chu Trinh could roar forth the following lines and expect people to be impressed:

> Pallid students, lingering in the obscurantist circle,
> Of what further meaning the stone tablets [*bia*], exam
> rosters [*bang*], haughty palanquin and parasol![63]

On the subject of exams Dong Kinh Nghia Thuc participants obviously spoke with authority and complete familiarity. In the area of commerce and industry, however, their attempts to move from abstract theory into concrete application generally proved inept and abortive. It was not for lack of intent, as the following quote from *Dang Co Tung Bao* illustrates:

> How many lamps, how much oil, cloth, brocade, umbrellas, paper, stockings, and other advanced products from various countries are still being brought into our country, yet we haven't a single thing to exchange in return. More than that, we allow Chinese firms to do the buying and the selling, so that they gather in all our money, carrying it away by the wagon and trunk loads. . . . How many possessions, how much blood and sweat does our country have that we can let it all fall into Chinese bowls, until before long there is no more to be had? My god! In the whole country there isn't a single large company, a single big factory. Our people lack any specialized professions to depend on. Twenty or more million people swarm around, simply keeping jealous watch on a little bit of old, shallow paddy land. In a situation where ten people stand ready to eat that which one person has yet to finish working, is it any surprise that there is starvation when a harvest is lost?[64]

61. Tran Huy Lieu, *Lich Su*, p. 127.
62. CMCD-3, pp. 41, 43.
63. CMCD, p. 37.
64. Nghiem Xuan Quang, *Dang Co Tung Bao*, August 1, 1907, p. 56, as quoted in Tran Huy Lieu, *Lich Su*, p. 159.

Part of the blame could indeed be placed on established local Chinese competition, as well as on colonial restrictions on Vietnamese initiatives. But another real problem was the complete lack of training or experience in commercial or industrial fields among the scholar-gentry. Even Luong Van Can, Dong Kinh Nghia Thuc principal and well known silk merchant, apparently depended entirely on his wife for the sound, steady financial management of his business. When the Dong Kinh Nghia Thuc began to go into debt, it was Luong's wife who sold a store to bail the school out.[65] Do Chan Thiet,[66] reputed to be one of the best poets at the school, and who also was working clandestinely with Phan Boi Chau, had a wife who supported him by means of her prosperous goldsmithing business. When he and Phuong Son leased some boats to transport rice from Hai-Duong and Thai-Binh to Hanoi, Chinese transporters underbid them repeatedly, and lower-class Vietnamese buyers in Hanoi were frightened away by their scholar's garb, which for some reason they insisted on wearing on the job. Switching to the sale of traditional medicines, Do and Phuong found their youthfulness (both were in their twenties) a decided disadvantage; later they turned the management over to some older, properly bearded figures.[67] In the end, the only real asset of their "modern" commercial endeavors was their availability as fronts for activist operations. Of course, that was all that Nguyen Thanh and the Duy Tan Hoi had advocated from the beginning.[68]

Most other business ventures of the scholar-gentry apparently followed roughly the same pattern. For some time the enterprises of Hoang Tang Bi in Hanoi were an exception, perhaps because he not only sold varieties of tea and paper in competition with the Chinese, but also set up new weaving and dying processes for locally grown cotton. In Phuc-Yen and Hung-Yen provinces, stores set up by Phuong Son's older brother at first limited their stock to domestic wares, but soon had to include foreign goods in order to avoid financial ruin. Another Dong Kinh Nghia Thuc associate established a store in Viet-Tri, hoping to service both Son-Tay and Phu-Tho provinces. Others attempted to produce varnish, oil for paints, caulking materials, and even Western-style clothing.[69] A scholar friend of Phuong Son tried his luck at opening a plantation in Yen-Bay, while several others searched for minerals in the hills and mountains of the north. However, the plantation failed, and a coal-mining venture, under development when the Dong Kinh Nghia Thuc was shut

65. DKNT, p. 70.
66. Thinh-hao village, Ha-Dong. VNDN, pp. 60–61.
67. DKNT, pp. 72–75.
68. CMCD-3, p. 43.
69. Tran Huy Lieu, Lich Su, p. 159.

A Bastille Day parade in Indochina. The poem is a subtle scholar-gentry dig
at alien French customs. Note the Frenchman with his arm over a Vietnamese
girl (an immodest act to Vietnamese), and observe that even the unarmed
Vietnamese lantern-bearers are commanded by a "long-nosed" Frenchman.
(Reproduced courtesy of l'Ecole d'Extrême Orient, Paris.)

French men and women dancing in Vietnam in the early twentieth century.
(Reproduced courtesy of l'Ecole d'Extrême Orient, Paris.)

Phan Boi Chau in 1925.

Phan Boi Chau in about 1908. (Photograph courtesy of M. Georges Boudard.)

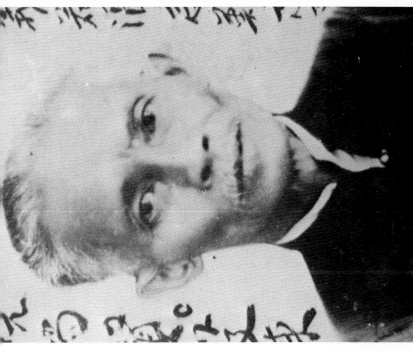

Ly Tue, an early anticolonialist liaison agent, who worked as a steward on a ship which ran between Haiphong and Hong Kong. This photograph was taken in 1938, shortly before his death.

Prince Cuong De in about 1908. (Photograph courtesy of M. Georges Boudard.)

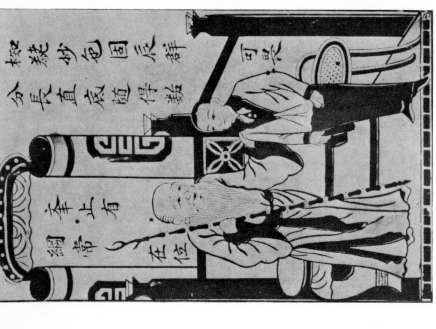

The poem reads in part, "Old and new generations, each in its own time." In the French colonial period the difference between young and old Vietnamese was evident in virtually everything from clothing and hair styles to furniture, as shown here.

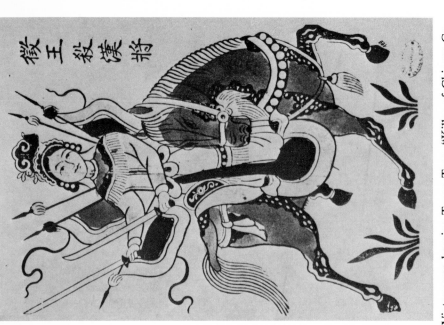

The Vietnamese heroine Trung Trac, "Killer of Chinese Generals," who led her people in the first century, A.D. (Reproduced courtesy of l'Ecole d'Extrême-Orient, Paris.)

down in 1908, had to be sold to a Chinese combine, which soon was turning a healthy profit.[70] In short, the idea of Vietnamese scholar-gentry's leading the country personally toward commercial and industrial modernity had a short, erratic trial between 1906 and 1908 and never bore fruit. More than anything, it would take time to alter centuries-old Vietnamese attitudes and practices. And time was one thing the Dong Kinh Nghia Thuc and the participating scholar-gentry were destined not to have.

Activist influence and participation in the Dong Kinh Nghia Thuc during 1907 must have become increasingly apparent to the French authorities. One obvious expression of this sentiment, of course, was the school's republication and distribution of *Hai Ngoai Huyet Thu* and other distinctly violent texts. It is significant, as well, that two sons of the Dong Kinh Nghia Thuc principal were with Phan Boi Chau in Japan; the school undoubtedly was a convenient place to observe and recruit other young men for study overseas. Do Chan Thiet and several of his school associates were storing and selling opium to raise money for the activists, besides trying to set up a small arms factory and make contacts with Yunnanese sympathizers in Hanoi, on instructions from Phan.[71] Plans also were under way for slipping firearms into Hanoi and for sending young men up to Yen-The for military training with De Tham. Because some scholar-gentry believed that these activities were directly jeopardizing the more open, nonviolent endeavors of the Dong Kinh Nghia Thuc, a meeting was held late in 1907 at which Luong Van Can proposed that those wishing to give prime attention to clandestine activities separate themselves from the school.[72] All present seem to have agreed.

At the same time the authorities opened in Hanoi what appeared to be a "counterschool" to the Dong Kinh Nghia Thuc with a prestigious scholar as principal, which planned to enroll classes up to the university level.[73] An alternative library appeared also, as did a "sponsoring association" for students wishing to go to France. Semi-official newspapers in *quoc-ngu* and Chinese reserved special space for articles on "cultural" subjects.[74] Apparently these competitive efforts proved inadequate, however, as in January 1908 the French authorities peremptorily ordered that the Dong Kinh Nghia Thuc cease functioning.

No evidence is available to indicate whether the officials were dis-

70. DKNT, pp. 75–83.
71. DKNT, pp. 87–88.
72. DKNT, pp. 89–90.
73. This was the *Hoc Quy Tan Truong* (New School for Regular Studies) mentioned in VTCM, pp. 64–65.
74. VTCM, p. 65.

turbed more by what they knew of the covert efforts or by the increasing public response to the open Dong Kinh Nghia Thuc propaganda. Perhaps by that time some Frenchmen had learned enough about anticolonial sentiments among the Vietnamese to perceive that activist and reformist efforts could serve as two edges of one sword. As we shall see, they later argued that all such activities were parts of a well coordinated plot. At any rate, the real crackdown on Dong Kinh Nghia Thuc participants did not come until some months afterward, in response to mass demonstrations against taxes in central Vietnam and De Tham's attempt at a coup in Hanoi. Well before, school leaders had destroyed the directly incriminating evidence, especially the remaining copies of patriotic ballads and works by Phan Boi Chau. When pressure intensified, they even burned most of the books in the library. But all to no avail: most of the Dong Kinh Nghia Thuc leadership, regardless of their individual reformist or activist leanings, were jailed, brought abruptly to trial, and sent to prison on Con-lon island (called Poulo Condore by the French), where they would find that Phan Chu Trinh, Huynh Thuc Khang, and others from central Vietnam had preceded them. The *Dang Co Tung Bao* was shut down in Hanoi, speeches were forbidden, and Dong Kinh Nghia Thuc printed materials found on anyone's premises were regarded as proof of rebellious intent.[75]

It should be evident that the Dong Kinh Nghia Thuc, as a vigorous but short-lived movement, was very much an anticolonial, antitraditionalist phenomenon. Its immediate political implications were soon to be clarified further by tax protests and assorted plots in 1908. But what of its long-range cultural and intellectual implications? I believe the Dong Kinh Nghia Thuc movement served several important—perhaps essential—purposes for the young men who would constitute later generations of anticolonialists. One was negative, a "chopping and clearing" exercise in which they for the first time in Vietnam put much of the official Confucian tradition on trial and found it wanting. The Dong Kinh Nghia Thuc definitely succeeded in forcing the traditionalists, the obscurantists, into a defensive posture from which they never recovered. Before 1907 the mandarinate had sought and been given political and economic shelter with their French overlords; after 1907 they would have to seek intellectual cover as well. For ironically some segments of the French administration came to encourage their archaic attitudes, to subsidize their studies, and even to profess belief in the "ultimate wisdom of the East," as delineated by these increasingly anachronistic figures.[76] Not until the

75. DKNT, pp. 91-98. CMCD-3, p. 44.
76. Nguyen Van Trung, *Chu Nghia Thuc Dan Phap o Viet-Nam (Thuc Chat va Hu-*

late 1930s—or perhaps finally in 1945—would both Vietnamese traditionalist and French quasi-traditionalist begin to appreciate just how much history had passed them by.

While Dong Kinh Nghia Thuc participants failed, on the whole, to advance a coherent alternative to traditional ideology, there were nevertheless some positive implications in their works: perhaps for the first time in Vietnam mere feeling against foreigners had been cut out of the political objections to colonialism, thus rendering large bodies of Western learning psychologically respectable. Whereas only a few years before, the stigmatic barbarian image had stood between the Vietnamese elite and Western learning, now, within the political framework of the Dong Kinh Nghia Thuc, it had become possible—indeed, it had become a patriotic duty—to master the thought of Rousseau, to speak in familiar terms of Mazzini, and to tick off the geographical characteristics of such distant places as Berlin or London.

Nowhere were the intellectual implications more obvious than in the new attraction to *quoc-ngu*. Devised originally by the foreigner and developed largely for his convenience (first for religious proselytizing, then to aid in political subjugation of the south), *quoc ngu* had come to the Dong Kinh Nghia Thuc with seemingly insurmountable colonialist and collaborationist affiliations. Yet *Dong Kinh Nghia Thuc* lecturers, essayists, and poets would refer to the romanized script as the potential saving of their culture and their country. Why? From passages I have cited, it should be evident that they saw tremendous advantages in uniting Vietnam's previously distinct oral and primary written modes of communication. Among other things, *quoc-ngu* during the next two or three decades would simplify the problems of mass education and indoctrination, bring elite and popular experiences closer together, and provide once again a common writing for the whole country—south, center, and north. Some of the imperialist's own tools for breaking into Vietnam in the first place were thus to be used against him.

In the meantime, however, it should not be a surprise that some Dong Kinh Nghia Thuc personalities ended up collaborating in one way or another with the French. Reformist attitudes toward the continuing French colonial rule were ambiguous from the start, as should be evident from Phan Chu Trinh's letter to Governor General Beau and such publications as "Van Minh Tan Hoc Sach." Hoang Tang Bi, for instance, appealing through a high-ranking in-law at court, was amnestied to Hue and later passed the very metropolitan exams that he and his compatriots

---

yen Thoai), pp. 147–167, discusses Pierre Pasquier (governor general, 1928–1934) and his idyllic pre-modern recreations.

had been condemning.[77] Nguyen Van Vinh was released from prison quickly and went on with Pham Quynh to sing the glories of French colonial rule. In an apparent effort to fill the gap left by their closing of the Dong Kinh Nghia Thuc, the French later encouraged these few scholar-gentry to publish the *Dong Duong Tap Chi* (Indochina Journal) in 1913 and *Nam Phong Tap Chi* (South Wind Journal) in 1917. In these journals the encouragement of *quoc-ngu*, the translation of Western materials, and the introduction of scientific and technical methodology was similar to Dong Kinh Nghia Thuc practice; but the intent, the objectives, and the political spirit were quite different. As Professor Dang Thai Mai has argued, among reformist and activist scholar-gentry alike "the thing most feared was not ignorance or illiteracy per se. The real worry was that under the French educational and political system the 'Annamites' would become self-serving, self-demeaning, would suffer from an inferiority complex and a sense of rootlessness, and would have no comprehension of their country and their fellow countrymen."[78] Or, as Professor Nguyen Van Trung has said, "the Dong Kinh Nghia Thuc introduced new ideas in order to encourage revolutionary sentiments; *Nam Phong* did it so that the revolution would be forgotten."[79] All in all, the course of reformism after 1908 provides an excellent example of how in such circumstances modernization or "cultural progress" can be made to serve opposing political masters.

77. DKNT, p. 96.
78. VTCM, p. 66.
79. Nguyen Van Trung, *Chu Nghia*, p. 202. A more recent student periodical describes the Dong Kinh Nghia Thuc as a time and place where Vietnamese intellectuals stood up to resist the "material and spiritual enslavement of the foreigner." Cuu Long, *Sinh Vien* 2 (September 1969), p. 5.

Chapter Eight

Làm quan người ở không cân,
Tiền bạc cướp hết của dân lúc này.
Tiền bạc ông lĩnh không biết bao cơ,
Ong làm quan giữa huyện dân có ăn nhờ chi ông.

Becoming a mandarin you treat your servants as dirt,
And steal every bit of money the people have.
Although you scoop in who knows how much money,
Do the people get any help from you, off in that
district office?

(FROM AN EARLY TWENTIETH-CENTURY
POPULAR POEM)

Nineteen-eight and the Historical Implications of Failure

The demonstrations and violence of 1908 are in many ways the climax of this story. For the history of Vietnam they represent both an end and a beginning. It is possible to view them as final outbursts in the traditional mold, the tax protests of central Vietnam in many ways resembling jac-querie or *khoi nghia* and the plots in Hanoi having definite monarchist overtones. And certainly, both efforts proved as incapable of forcing immediate change as others had in the past. This also was to be the last time that any major Vietnamese anticolonial initiative would demonstrate such an abysmal lack of planning, leadership, and conceptual orientation.

The beginning of a new era came in 1908 as a result of the progressive scholar-gentry propaganda, the spread of anticolonial poems and songs, the local attempts at commercial innovation within Vietnam, and through the links with anticolonialists overseas. All of these served to render coherent the real economic and political grievances that had been developing in the previous decade. In central Vietnam in 1908 it was of inestimable importance that, for the first time, the peasants took their grievances directly to the French résidents, after having learned to their own satisfaction that the mandarin representatives of Hue were indeed powerless, impotent. For good or for evil, the Frenchman was now ruling at the provincial level. More important, the Vietnamese people at large perceived this, began ruminating on its significance, and eventually altered their outlooks and actions accordingly.

In fact, the shift of local authority away from the mandarins in Annam and Tonkin had been under way for some time. Governor General Doumer in 1897 had eliminated King Thanh Thai's Co-Mat-Vien (Privy Council) in favor of a new royal council in which each Vietnamese member had a French counterpart and the chairman was not the king, but the French résident supérieur.[1] The next year Doumer had taken away from the court the collection of all taxes, making collaborators from the king down to the lowest mandarin paid employees of the French. Doumer's "transformation of Indochina" also had meant that new groups of Frenchmen were recruited to perform a growing number of new tasks:

> Frenchmen to enforce the production monopoly for alcohol and salt; Frenchmen to collect the customs duties; Frenchmen to fill out papers and issue or refuse permits; Frenchmen to inspect and report on the work of other Frenchmen; Frenchmen to sell postage stamps and open office doors; and finally, when the manner in which Indochina was being transformed began to have its effect on the native populations, more and more Frenchmen to watch over, apprehend, and punish malcontents.[2]

Such "beneficient" reforms required plenty of money and bodily labor—most, extracted from the Vietnamese peasantry. And there is ample evidence that by between 1906 and 1908 the peasants of the central area of the country were being hit the hardest by the French demands. The shift of tax payments from kind to money was upsetting traditional rural social patterns. There had been new surveys of ricelands, followed by hikes in the land and head taxes. But corvée appears to have hurt most of all, as the French pushed ahead on building roads into the hills for security, commercial, and recreational purposes. Laborers were required to draw from their own rice stores to survive while on corvée; and in selection of the laborers there was much shirking by the rich, so the poor were forced to go again and again. By many accounts the burden was heaviest in Quang Nam, with some people having to leave their villages as many as fifteen times a year to help clear away sandbars that prevented coal barges from traveling to the vicinity of the Nong-Son mines.[3]

Meanwhile, reformist scholar-gentry were circulating openly from village to village, most of them preaching peaceful change, it is true, but

---

1. Doumer, *Situation de l'Indo-Chine (1897–1901)*, pp. 182–192, 322.
2. Joseph Buttinger, *Viet-Nam*, pp. 35–36, citing in particular Fernand Bernard, *L'Indochine, erreurs et dangers: Un programme*, as substantiation.
3. CMCD-3, pp. 51–52.

causing excitement all the same. Schools were being opened on the Dong Kinh Nghia Thuc model, with courses in *quoc-ngu,* Vietnamese history, geography, other natural sciences, and hygiene. There were at least four such schools in Quang Nam, for example, each with seventy to eighty students, and each providing public speeches on social problems outside the normal class schedule. Huynh Thuc Khang organized one of those schools, buying numerous contemporary Chinese books and periodicals, lining up teachers for French and *quoc-ngu* language courses, and arranging special lectures on the fifteenth of every lunar month. *Quoc-ngu* instruction appears to have caught on in nearby villages, so that Huynh could write of the *ABC's* being chanted by village children just as the *Tam Tu Kinh* (Three Character Classic) had been sung previously—modern and traditional classes "competing with each other with increasing harshness."[4]

In the countryside a normal speech by a scholar-gentry propagandist would describe various commercial projects, call for the purchase of domestic rather than foreign merchandise, denounce extravagance, superstition, and long hair, and propose the exchange of mandarin garb and badges of rank in favor of modern, unadorned, domestically produced jackets. Only occasionally would the speakers try to confront the tax and corvée problems. Summaries of their talks were sometimes printed with ink-block techniques and distributed locally, along with ballads from the Dong Kinh Nghia Thuc or poems sent back from Japan by Phan Boi Chau. One particularly effective propaganda medium was the *ho gia gao* —a folk duet to be sung while working.[5] After departure of the prestigious outsider, local scholars or exam failures provided whatever impetus there might be toward establishing village industries. There were attempts, for example, to increase straw hat production, to collect and process cinnamon, and to replace small hand looms with a few more modern weaving and sewing machines.[6]

Meanwhile, for all the talk of nonviolent reform, the Duy Tan Hoi in 1907 remained quite active in central Vietnam, maintaining secret scholar-gentry cells in most provinces, trying to convince colonial soldiers to turn on the French and link up with Can Vuong remnants, and seeking ways to coordinate strategy with De Tham in north Vietnam. And in the villages, among a people increasingly distressed, public sentiment aroused by the reformists quickly swelled beyond the original intentions. By the end of February 1908 the slogan "Don't pay taxes to the French" was

4. Huynh Thuc Khang, *Tu Truyen,* p .28. CMCD-3, p. 54, lists three other schools in Quang Nam.
5. CMCD-3, p. 55.
6. CMCD-3, p. 54.

circulating quietly among the peasants of central Vietnam. The first open demonstrations occurred early in March in Phan Chu Trinh's home area, although he was in Hanoi at the time and no other scholar-gentry figures appeared to be instigating or participating in these activities.

In the first instance, on March 9, three hundred villagers of Dai-loc district in Quang Nam marched together to the district township.[7] They had come, they said, to demand that three individuals arrested for carrying "suspect propaganda" be released. They may also have brought up the corvée problem. Apparently gaining no satisfaction from the district mandarin, the crowd set off on the road to Hoi-An, the provincial seat, and reportedly marched right into the compound of the French résident. There, the prime issue definitely was corvée—not surprising, since Dai-loc was in the midst of an area where particularly heavy work was under way in connection with the Nong-Son coal mines. Specifically, the villagers requested of the résident that corvée burdens be distributed equally among all villagers; in other words, that those villagers with mandarinate influence or "pull" not be exempted or let off lightly. The résident replied by ordering the crowd to disperse and, when this failed, used local colonial troops to push them away from the building. But he did pass word that he would receive a small delegation. Six representatives were chosen, presented their grievances, received promises that the corvée situation would be investigated, and then found themselves being placed under custody. The crowd outside, which had begun to disperse, moved back toward the building and prepared for a long vigil.

Word of these events quickly spread to surrounding districts, and other groups moved on Hoi-An, many declaring taxes to be their main grievance rather than corvée. En route the villagers, having taken scissors along, would sometimes snip off the hair of passersby, willing or not. Many of those "customers" stayed inside for months afterward, either from shame or for fear of arrest.[8] In Hoi-An the résident repeatedly sent soldiers out to disperse the growing crowd, using truncheons and rifle butts when they felt it necessary. Each time, however, the crowd would slowly reassemble; it was evident at this point that neither side desired serious violence.

7. Except where otherwise indicated, information on the demonstrations in central Vietnam comes from the following sources: AOM A-20(58) carton 9, AOM A-50 NF 598, and CMCD-3, pp. 56–71.
8. Hence, the contemporary French public references to "*bande de cheveux coupes*" or "*chevaux tondus*," which generally sidestep the economic grievances expressed. AOM A-82(19) carton 28 contains a métropole newspaper cutting file concerning these 1908 "troubles" in Annam.

First indications of crowd organization may have come when small groups were sent home or to nearby villages to secure food and to increase support for the demonstration. From March 13 there were usually several thousand villagers camped around the résident's building, cooking rice and sitting passively on straw mats. Groups would normally stay two or three days and return home, with others taking their places. However, with the arrival of outside troop reinforcements some days later the résident felt confident enough to emerge and call again for dispersal, meanwhile promising to telegraph the crowd's grievances to the governor general. Someone yelled out that it wouldn't take long to receive a reply by telegraph, and much of the crowd decided to stay. At that, the résident again ordered the use of truncheons and rifle butts, this time causing injuries. There was shooting, with demonstrators lying flat in the streets to duck the bullets, troops being recalled, and the people squatting down again near the building. Eventually the résident came out in person and promised dismissal of the Dai-Loc district mandarin. Taxes could not be reduced, he said, but he did pledge that there would be no further increases.[9]

Meanwhile, however, ferment had spread throughout the Quang Nam countryside. There were many reports of tax collectors' being chased, beaten, and threatened with death. On March 20 a crowd penetrated the old Quang Nam citadel and gained entry to the residence of the provincial mandarin.[10] They induced the mandarin to mount a conveyance and travel with them to present their grievances to the résident. The next day another crowd surrounded the Dien-ban prefectural offices and followed the same routine with the prefect. However, en route to Hoi-An they were blocked by a French squad which fired on the crowd and "rescued" the prefect from his own people. Three participants are said to have fallen into the river and drowned, their martyrdom later being immortalized in poetry.[11] On March 26 there were crowds around the Thang-binh prefectural seat. In Tam-ky the prefectural headquarters was occupied for three days by a thousand demonstrators. At one point, allegedly to disengage themselves from a surrounding crowd, colonial troops fired a volley that killed one and wounded four. On April 7 a group seized and killed

9. CMCD-3, pp. 57–58, points out that this pledge was broken.
10. Located in La-qua, 11 kilometers west of Hoi-An. Here it is reported that a heated exchange took place when a prospective scholar accused the mandarin of being a useless parasite unless he interceded with the French. The mandarin replied that the man's tone was hardly in keeping with scholastic traditions. CMCD-3, pp. 65–66.
11. CMCD-3, pp. 66–68, quotes portions of one poem.

a local native official who was believed to be engaged in suppressing the movement.[12]

French army units, along with high ranking mandarins, gave top priority to blocking the spread of disturbances beyond the Quang Nam provincial borders, checking and searching every traveler over the Hai-Van pass to the north and at Ben-van in the south. Nevertheless, word did get through to the other provinces, sparking demonstrations next in Quang-Ngai. On March 28 people in Binh-hoa district[13] induced numerous village chiefs and their deputies to go to the French résident in Quang-Ngai town to request a tax reduction. Three days later more than a thousand demonstrators had gathered in front of the résident's building. There they remained, their number fluctuating, until mid-April, when two of their leaders were arrested, troop reinforcements arrived, and a serious clash resulted in the deaths of several protesters and the jailing of many others. The two leaders were then executed and some of the scholar-gentry rounded up for eventual transport to Con-lon island.[14] By this time the same thing was happening back in Quang Nam, mandarins having sent spies into selected villages to find out who the protest leadership was and passing the information on to the French, whose patrols then rounded up the suspects. In one of these actions in Dai-loc district soldiers summarily executed six persons in the Ai-nghia marketplace.

Having developed a deep distrust, or even hatred, for many reformist scholar-gentry figures, mandarins of all ranks at that point saw the repression of demonstrations as an excellent opportunity to sweep the board clean of these people. The reformist Phu-lam school and commercial buildings in Quang Nam were ordered destroyed. And among about two thousand persons jailed at Hoi-An were most of the local reformist scholar-gentry, who were generally accused of having incited the unrest with their outrageous ideas. For example, Huynh Thuc Khang, one of Phan Chu Trinh's closest associates, tells of having been in Hoi-An when the first demonstrators arrived from the countryside, "hungry, ragged, grasping small packets and bundles of food, moaning, urging each other down the road." Huynh did not involve himself, but returned to his home village fully expecting arrest; soon after, he was indeed picked up by the

12. Reported in CMCD-3, pp. 59, 70–71. This may be the same individual listed in AOM A-20(58) as a former canton chief who was seized, tortured, and drowned.
13. Now called Binh-son and located on the border of present-day Quang Tin province, which until recently was all part of Quang Nam.
14. This account is in CMCD-3, pp. 60–61. By contrast, the report in AOM A-20 (58) states that by April 13 all but about thirty demonstrators had dispersed, after apparently having been assured of special tax or corvée exemptions for the poor. The report readily admits, however, that roundups took place.

French lieutenant commanding the nearby garrison. In Tam-ky, accused before the French délégué (a subordinate of the résident) of having helped incite insurrection, Huynh replied that he had merely been publicizing a development policy expounded by high-ranking French officials. For this, Huynh would spend the next thirteen years on Con-lon.[15]

The first days of April saw a demonstrating group from Quang-Ngai trying to cross into Binh-Dinh to the south. Turned back as a body by colonial troops, many were able individually to filter across into Bong-son prefecture, and the movement soon flared up in another province. One crowd grabbed the prefect, stated its grievances on corvée and taxes, and then cut his hair short in the style of many present. Most other prefects and district mandarins hid before the arrival of demonstrators, so it was often their male secretaries and interpretors who lost their hair. By mid-April prime attention had shifted to the Binh-Dinh provincial fort, where the several thousand protesters gathered tried to scale the walls. Unsuccessful, they then camped aimlessly in the adjacent area. An attempt was made to burn several buildings around which colonial troops were camped, but this resulted in two demonstrators' being killed by rifle fire. In another direction the troops opened up on a crowd of about eight hundred, killing or wounding thirteen. In response, the demonstrators sought out and seized members of the troopers' families, as well as some policemen and couriers. Twenty of them were reported drowned. An unknown number of interpreters and tax collectors who were also seized subsequently vanished. On April 17 troops again fired directly into a crowd, that time killing or wounding about forty.

The next day two companies of the regular French infantry debarked at nearby Qui-Nhon and soon were scattering the demonstrators. In the last days of the month further gatherings were dispersed and many arrests made. May 1908 saw French-led squads of native troops moving through the villages of Binh-Dinh, with more local citizens being killed and jailed and eleven being sent to Con-lon.

In Phu-Yen, the next province to the south, propaganda leaflets appeared in April, followed by a few demonstrators from Binh-Dinh early in May. On May 11 a plot to storm the Tuy-An fortress and take firearms from the prison was foiled. There also were demonstrations in the south of Phu-Yen and encounters with colonial troops in Phu-tan and Tuy-An, which resulted in some fatalities. Just a bit farther down the coast, in Nha-Trang, Tran Quy Cap was summarily executed by order of the local mandarin. I have mentioned Tran as having scored second in the 1904 palace exams and having traveled south with Phan Chu Trinh and

15. Huynh Thuc Khang, *Tu Truyen*, pp. 29–33.

Huynh Thuc Khang in 1905. Like Phan he had been setting up schools and was completely open in his contempt for obscurantist mandarins. They in turn found the fighting an excellent opportunity to do him in, and seized upon a letter he recently had sent home to Quang Nam which expressed vague approval of the rumors he was hearing about the demonstrations against the colonial regime. Tran Quy Cap was found guilty of treason and executed by chopping him in half at the waist.[16]

In the provinces north of Quang Nam the impact of the protests appears to have been much less substantial, being limited generally to the area around Hue and to several attempts farther north by scholar-gentry leaders to generate popular support for the movement. Rumors in the first days of April spread through the villages around Hue regarding demonstrations planned in the city. Small squads of troops were sent by the French résident to warn the people against such activities. Some of the soldiers, however, were seized and put at the head of popular processions moving into the center of Hue. In one typical case a mandarin who had been dispatched with a contingent of troops to the suburb of Cong-luong was stoned. A soldier fired, killing a villager, and the people captured the mandarin and tied up several of the troopers. The next day they presented themselves at the building of the résident supérieur, with the same grievances regarding corvée and taxes that had been stated in Quang Nam and Quang Ngai. Reluctantly at their head was the official. Soldiers quickly drove the group back with batons, "rescued" the mandarin, and marched to Cong-luong to release the troops and arrest thirty villagers.

On April 11 and 12 demonstrators again gathered quietly in nearby villages and moved to surround the provincial résident's building and the homes of various mandarins, at each place demanding tax reductions. The night of the twelfth police stopped a group en route, injuring two demonstrators and arresting many. At four the next morning, a group of about a hundred followed the same route and made the same economic demands. That time, however, a detachment of regular French infantry chased the demonstrators vigorously and beat them with rifle butts. Two were badly injured, and two others were drowned after falling off a bridge in their flight.

To the north, Quang-Tri and Quang-Binh provinces apparently were not affected. In Ha-Tinh in late May a small crowd from My-duc district marched on the résident's building, calling for tax reductions. A different group tried to detain the Can-loc district mandarin to induce him to present grievances to the French, but he escaped, and a French-led unit moved in to disperse the demonstrators. Nghe-An saw a few scholar-

16. VNDN, p. 333.

gentry passing the word of Quang-Nam activities, and some slogans and leaflets in the market places; but the French jailed the scholar-gentry suspects, and nothing more developed. The same occurred in Thanh-Hoa, where at least eight scholar-gentry were shipped off to Con-lon.

Meanwhile, not directly connected with events in central Vietnam, but quite a part of the general unrest in the country, an elaborate plot was brewing in and around Hanoi that culminated in the poisoning of the French garrison there and an abortive coup d'etat against the colonial regime. The plot centered in a boarding-house/restaurant in a poor section of Hanoi, where Vietnamese colonial soldiers and cooks and servants for the French rubbed shoulders daily with associates of De Tham and with several nondescript teachers of French and Chinese. It was the teachers, apparently, who introduced materials sent home by Phan Boi Chau to this regular clientele. De Tham himself being in the distant hills of Yen-The, liaison with him was maintained through a Taoist temple in Phuc-Yen province.[17] As early as November 1907 this group developed the idea of a Hanoi coup, but its planning was indecisive, even dilatory. As I have mentioned, a number of scholar-gentry connected with the Dong Kinh Nghia Thuc were aware of such plots, the reformists among them counseling against precipitous action and the activists urging the plotters on.

Having twice postponed action, the group settled on June 27, 1908, knowing that the French were having a big military banquet that evening and that the cooks therefore would be in a position to poison their food en masse. Soldier conspirators elsewhere would spike or dismantle artillery pieces, while at least three groups of armed irregulars would move in from the suburbs to seize strategic points. De Tham himself would order a thirty-man trained unit to infiltrate and attack a key colonial camp next to the governor general's palace.

Three days before June 27 the French had vague intelligence indicating trouble. Nevertheless, the poisoning was accomplished, although apparently with an improper dosage or the wrong poison, since two hundred French artillery and infantry soldiers were taken ill but were not killed or even fully disabled. To make matters worse for the Vietnamese, one participant in the plot got cold feet immediately after dropping the poison into the food and ran to a French Catholic priest for confession. The priest immediately telephoned the authorities. With other reports of suspicious gatherings in various parts of the city coming in, the French general in charge immediately proclaimed martial law, disarmed all Vietnamese troops, sealed off the city, and dispatched street patrols to round

17. CMCD-3, pp. 71–74.

up suspects. Not having heard their attack signal from the banquet hall, insurrectionist groups in the suburbs retreated without incident. Most of the soldier and kitchen participants, however, were captured, with thirteen being executed and four receiving terms of life imprisonment.[18]

Though poorly planned and poorly led, the so-called Hanoi poison plot of 1908 did throw a decided scare into the French. In conjunction with the recently exposed activities of Gilbert Chieu in Cochinchina, which I have already discussed, it represented adequate justification for moving decisively against Phan Boi Chau, Cuong De, and the whole Dong Du movement. It was also the reason for new military moves against De Tham, who, with no more than two hundred mountain veterans had managed to keep the idea, the spirit, of resistance alive for many people in north Vietnam.[19] Throughout 1909 French colonial units worked hard at tightening the net of platoon-size forts. Several of De Tham's key subordinates surrendered or were killed, while others escaped the cordon to new hideouts. By September 1909 De Tham was reported to be down to forty gunmen; relentless pursuit allegedly reduced him to only a couple of followers by the end of the year. Still unable to catch him, the French spent considerable time and money in keeping him from recruiting a new group and in trying to have him assassinated. The latter tactic was successful in 1913, and De Tham's head was delivered to the French for a bounty and carried around for display in nearby villages.[20]

The general roundup in 1908 of scholar-gentry leaders, both reformist and activist, decisively influenced the course of Vietnamese history. Phan Chu Trinh was seized in Hanoi and transported to Hue, where he went on a hunger strike for some days before being tried by a joint French and high mandarin court. There he reputedly abused the mandarins for accepting "handouts, taken from the blood and sweat of the people." This impertinence would have rated him a quick death if it had not been for the veto of the French résident supérieur.[21] Instead, Phan was sentenced to life imprisonment and shipped to Con-lon by May 1908.

We have already followed Huynh Thuc Khang to the Hoi-An jail, where he was soon joined by Tran Cao Van, Nguyen Thanh, and many others en route to Con-lon.[22] It is ironic, yet meaningful, that Nguyen

18. CMCD-3, pp. 74–77.
19. French officials grudgingly admitted as much in AOM A-50 NF 598.
20. CMCD-2, pp. 31–47. De Tham became something of a romantic rebel to the French and occasioned a number of books: A. L. Bouchet, *Au Tonkin: La vie aventureuse de Hoang-hoa-Tham, chef pirate*; Lt. Col. E. Perez, "Le Dernier Grand Pirate," *Revue de Paris* (1907), pp. 330–421; Paul Chack, *Hoang-Tham, Pirate* (Paris, 1933).
21. Huynh Thuc Khang, *Phan Tay Ho Tien Sinh Lich Su*, pp. 23–24.
22. Huynh Thuc Khang, *Tu Truyen*, p. 33. Ngo Thanh Nhan, *Ngu Hanh Son Chi Si*,

Thanh, for a long time an active promoter of violent overthrow of the French, was sentenced only for nine years, while Huynh Thuc Khang, the advocate of nonviolent reform, was sentenced for life. By early 1909 there were on Con-lon island several score scholar-gentry representing just about every province in north and central Vietnam—the flower of Vietnamese intelligentsia.[23] They would spend their time laboring, talking politics, creating an abundance of poetry, studying some French, and just as often learning the island art of making tortoise shell trinkets. In the meantime, they were also sustaining an image of proud resistance in the minds of their countrymen.

The events of 1903 to 1908 described in this and the previous three chapters were of overriding importance in setting the direction of anticolonial developments in Vietnam, explaining in large part the abortive putschism of the next decade, the anticolonial position of the generation which emerged in the 1920s, and even the ultimate forging of the Viet-Minh between 1941 and 1945. A mere review of the activities and published works of scholar-gentry participants, however, fails to establish their crucial position in the modern history of Vietnam adequately. Therefore within the limits of available data and without getting deeply embroiled in a discussion of events of the following thirty or forty years, I shall delineate in more analytical fashion the truly significant features of that period, first by comparing Phan Boi Chau and Phan Chu Trinh as individuals and as prime representatives of the activist and reformist positions and then by asking to what degree these positions reflected major social and economic changes in Indochina in the first decade of the twentieth century.

Tran Huy Lieu, a prominent intellectual and later a leader of the Indochinese Communist Party (ICP), in his youth met both Phan Boi Chau and Phan Chu Trinh.[24] He remembered Phan Chu Trinh in 1925 when Phan was staying at a friend's house in Saigon, receiving visitors at all hours of the day in impeccable Western garb. Most of them were young people eager to find out what was happening in the world outside. Phan, however, would greet each group with the same peremptory questions

pp. 50–52. Hanh Son, *Cu Tran Cao Van*, pp. 67–69. Tran Cao Van would be held over in the Hoi-An jail for one year while they investigated his activities in Binh-Dinh; then he was sent for six years to Con-lon.

23. Of the men introduced here, the following also were sent to Con-lon at this time: Ngo Duc Ke, Nguyen Quyen, Le Dai, Dang Nguyen Can, Duong Ba Trac, and Le Van Huan. DKNT, pp. 95–98. HT, pp. 551, 585, 595, 597, 600. It should be added that many less prominent figures were sent to the penal colony at Lao-Bao, on the Viet-Lao border in Quang-Tri province.

24. Tran Huy Lieu, "Nho lai ong gia Ben Ngu."

about whether they had read *Contrat social* and *Esprit des lois*. Then he would launch into hours-long monologues on "intellectual standards of the people" (*dan-tri*), "popular sovereignty" (*dan-quyen*), "popular moral standards" (*dan-duc*), and the like. Often listeners would be unable to get a word in edgewise, yet they did enjoy his scathing, sarcastic denunciations of the Hue court and of certain intellectuals who collaborated with the French.

Some years later Tran Huy Lieu sought out Phan Boi Chau in Hue, where his first glimpse was of Phan pacing leisurely in front of his small house, wearing a Chinese-style robe. Having barely introduced himself, Tran was embraced by Phan and taken in to meet all the members of the household, many of whom were destitute former political prisoners of all classes. Emotionally, Tran says, he was won over from first contact. But in easy conversation after a spartan dinner he was disturbed by Phan's willingness to think the best of every fellow Vietnamese.[25] Of the two, he had to rate reformist Phan Chu Trinh as the keener in appraising men. Activist Phan Boi Chau still had not learned to write *quoc-ngu,* but he was trying, mostly through Chinese-language sources, to understand modern socialism. And he was still "dropping pebbles into the blue sea, hoping somehow to fill it."[26]

While admittedly taken somewhat out of their historical context, I think Tran Huy Lieu's comparative vignettes tell a lot about the two men. All other evidence also shows Phan Chu Trinh as a brilliant talker in love with words and ideas. And it is important to realize that, while he became absolutely enamored of Montesquieu and Rousseau, one never heard Phan Chu Trinh mention Robespierre or Danton. He preached ideas that had prepared the way for violent revolution in France, yet shrank from the apparent violent analogy in Vietnam. Phan Boi Chau, on the other hand, also read of and mentioned the eighteenth-century philosophers, but for him ideas always were tools to more concrete ends: the main concern of men, particularly of the scholar-gentry elite, was coping with situations by the performance of deeds. While thinking was absolutely essential in the planning stages, on other occasions such as moments of immediate danger, thinking might well stand in the way of action and prohibit instantaneous, effective response. I believe it was this attitude

25. VT, p. 95, agrees, saying that Phan Boi Chau's "faith" (*tin-tuong*) in the Vietnamese people in general often led him to optimistic, misleading judgments about groups and individuals in particular.
26. This is from a poem written in 1926 on the death of Phan Chu Trinh by Phan Boi Chau, using the classical image of a bird which continues, against all odds, to drop pebbles as a way of filling the sea and gaining its objective: "Thuong hai vi dien, tinh ve ham thach."

toward ideology that enabled Phan Boi Chau in his one lifetime to move from traditional monarchism, to constitutional monarchism, to bourgeois republicanism, and finally, it would appear, to a vague utopian socialism.[27] The fact that he never really sorted out the contradictions, instead retaining elements of all in his later thought, simply points up his overriding concern with actions rather than theory.

In contrast, Phan Chu Trinh appears to have undergone a form of spiritual conversion in his first years of contact with the positivist ideas of the Enlightenment (although reading them in Chinese, and through the interpretive veil of Chinese reformism). He never wavered, to the day he died in 1926. Unlike some less idealistic reformists, Phan Chu Trinh nurtured and sustained his conception of a progressive, rationally structured Vietnam in the face of more than one tantalizing French proposal for collaborative action. His critical intellect had no trouble perceiving that the French were interested in him primarily as a symbol and were not yet prepared to share his premises or his ultimate goals. This idealism would also lead him, as we shall see, to prefer fourteen years of semi-inactivity in France, where he felt at least he could "breathe free air and read free newspapers," rather than a life in his own country of daily harassment and disappointment, not to mention the intellectual sterility of life in prison on Con-lon island.

Having emphasized Phan Chu Trinh's commitments, we must then question just how deeply he understood what he was preaching. After all, he apparently did not learn French until after being sent to Con-lon in 1908, so many of his basic intellectual conceptions—which for him were matters of life and death—originated in inexact reformist Chinese translations and interpretations. I have noted that in his earlier traditional education Phan Chu Trinh fastened on the *Analects* and Mencius; and I believe that a careful textual study of his few writings that survive should reveal that he remained, in fact, as indebted to those works as to the works of Montesquieu, Rousseau, or any other Westerner. As with many men, Phan Chu Trinh was catholic in his initial reception of foreign ideas, seldom cross-examining himself to determine whether new inputs complemented, contradicted, or took preference over earlier conceptualizations. Since for Phan Chu Trinh the necessity for resolute action never really materialized, he never was forced into a sorting and choosing process (conscious or not) to the degree that men in subsequent generations of anticolonialists were.

The confusion occasioned by this facile cross-pollination was most

27. Chuong Thau, "Anh huong cach mang Trung Quoc doi voi su bien chuyen cua tu tuong Phan Boi Chau" discusses Phan Boi Chau's ideological shifts in some detail, basically arguing that they paralleled shifts in the Chinese revolution.

evident in Phan Chu Trinh's terminology. One example is his use of the term *Dao* (in Chinese, *Tao*; the Path, the Way). As with the majority of Chinese philosophers, Phan in his search for the Way, for historical reality, demonstrated a heavy preference for philosophical idealism, believing that it was possible truly to master the learning of the past. Thus one gained insight by the very force of men's unique understanding, reestablished some direct connection of mind with mind, and (what may be more difficult) then revealed this connection in print or in speech for others to appreciate. Therefore, like many idealists, Phan Chu Trinh abstracted ideas from their limitations of time and space, ignoring the devilish plasticity of words and concepts as they enter radically different environments. He not only confused Montesquieu with Mencius; he also tried, against all odds, to impose both on a colonized Vietnam which was entering the twentieth century.

Unfortunately, Phan Boi Chau never expressed himself clearly on such subjects, but I suspect he would have argued that creating a movement—indeed, a revolution—by the power of the mind alone was highly suspect. Would not one come to "know the *Dao*" only by acting out what one wanted to learn? In his search through Chinese, Japanese, and Western books for a guiding system, Phan Boi Chau never seems to have found satisfaction, perhaps sensing that only through action and through the historical process would a sorting and choosing take place, both for himself and for his people.

This discussion, which at first sight may seem diversionary, hopefully provides a better perspective for comparing the positions of Phan Boi Chau and Phan Chu Trinh on specific major contemporary issues. As I have stressed repeatedly, both men feared for the very existence of the Vietnamese as a people. This led them to do and say things that we Americans, in our comfortable insularity and geographic enormity, may have trouble comprehending, having yet to be driven by the fear that our communal body and spirit was in a process of ultimate disintegration and disappearance after thousands of years of proud history. Phan Boi Chau spoke up first, through his participation in forming the Duy Tan Hoi, through his herculean efforts to override regional limitations, and through his willingness to travel to Japan in search of concrete assistance for a decisive thrust against the foreign imperialists. In both of his later autobiographies Phan Boi Chau pictured his early traditional monarchism as being essentially opportunist and aimed at attracting a dedicated following. Nevertheless, apart from what I have just said about his facile leaps from one ideology to the next, there are many indications in his poems and essays that Phan Boi Chau's basic values remained traditional (as distinct from monarchist) throughout his life. Indeed his embodiment in action of selected traditional values, particularly of violent resistance to foreign domination and of an earthy, emotional exaltation of the inherent capabilities of his people, would be the most important meaning of his life in the eyes of later generations of anticolonialists. His life, for all its apparent failure, would symbolize the continuity of resistance, a savage unwillingness to be cowed.

After Phan Boi Chau had set his own personal course, Phan Chu Trinh rose to general prominence among the anticolonial scholar-gentry by publicly opposing dependence on foreign support (in this case, Japanese) and also by opposing any attempts at violent overthrow of the colonial regime. He perceived, as Phan Boi Chau did not, that with Vietnam's hopelessly inferior technology, with a demoralized and backward people, outmoded values, and a divided intelligentsia, they might sacrifice thousands—tens of thousands—of young men against the French and still not be one step closer to independence. In fact, Phan Chu Trinh feared that repeated defeats might only demoralize the people further. Even if, in some mammoth bloodbath, the French were forced to withdraw, what would prevent some other major power like Japan from moving in to exploit Vietnam's exhaustion? What would be the point, he asked, of switching one foreign master for another? Sometimes Phan Chu Trinh even declared that he would rather live under an "enlightened" colonial regime, one that was helping to modernize Vietnam, than under any independent but hopelessly backward Vietnamese regime in the traditional mold. His basic objective, which was also Phan Boi Chau's, was independence, but his concept of independence was more carefully defined than Phan Boi Chau's, probably because of his more sophisticated understanding of the components of national power and sovereignty in the modern world.

But there was a fatal flaw in Phan Chu Trinh's reasoning: What if the French refused to allow the Vietnamese to modernize their institutions effectively or to permit them real responsibilities of self-government? What if they continued indefinitely to feel that maintenance of their position in Indochina was incompatible with such ideas? Phan Boi Chau, arguing largely from traditional and emotional premises, declared flatly that the French were interested only in turning the Vietnamese into beaten-down slaves. While Phan Chu Trinh also perceived and decried their tendencies in this direction, he had chosen to identify with French Enlightment philosophers; he also thought he knew something favorable of nineteenth-century capitalist development in Europe, and he simply refused to believe that it was either the temperamental inclination or the selfish desire of France to keep the Vietnamese from progressing along paths blazed by the French themselves. We must appreciate that this was an effective intellectual posture among a scholar-gentry coterie increasingly susceptible to a Western bourgeois progressive concept of history—particularly when Governor General Beau and other high French officials were making pronouncements that seemed to confirm it. In a positivist world, what rationale could be advanced to explain active obstruction by the French of development among the Vietnamese people? Certainly Phan Boi Chau had no effective refutation. Indeed, the whole question continued to confuse and divide Vietnam's intelligentsia until Lenin's theory of imperialism came to dominate their thinking in the 1930s and 1940s.

When the Japanese turned down Phan Boi Chau's request for weapons, he reluctantly accepted the advice of Liang and Inukai—and Phan Chu Trinh—to concentrate on taking students out of Vietnam and writing anticolonial propaganda, but only as tactical preliminaries to the eventual violent confrontation. As the months and years went by, Phan Boi Chau, through his travels, his reading, and his repeated difficulties, seemed to sense more and more just how extended, how momentous, a task he had undertaken. Not the least of his problems then became the communication of a conception of the longer haul to his compatriots at home, men eager to mount attacks as soon as the first cadres and weapons were at hand. Their clandestine communications being extremely primitive, it is doubtful that many of them understood. Nevertheless, to Phan's and probably to Nguyen Thanh's credit, it should be recognized that the Duy Tan Hoi during this time did avoid overt acts of violence or retaliation. Given such discipline, the disturbing factor from their point of view became the florid statements of the reformists and the public excitement surrounding the Dong Kinh Nghia Thuc, which implied divisiveness within the resistance and, even worse, carried the risk of sweeping French repression. Their worst fears were fulfilled early in 1908 when the storm over taxes and corvée broke in Quang Nam and the French dealt all facets of the scholar-gentry endeavor a blow from which it never recovered.

How, then, can we best epitomize the two men? A set of paradoxes comes to mind. Phan Boi Chau was more the traditional aristocrat, yet he understood his people, believed in them, related to them more than Phan Chu Trinh. Popular education, democratic ideals and democratic privileges were the essence of Phan Chu Trinh's message, yet he liked to dominate conversations, had trouble making friends, and implicity disparaged the capabilities of the common people. Working from an idealized construct of modern goodness and truth, he seemed to think that his people were starting almost from zero.

Nevertheless, in the first decade of the twentieth century Phan Chu Trinh's iconoclasm was extremely important in stimulating large numbers of Vietnamese to liberate themselves from the traditional culture as defined by the mandarins, thus clearing the way for the general acceptance of modern nationalist sentiments. Phan Boi Chau, on the other hand, might have remained a mere anti-Western conservative all his life if it had not been for his increasing perception of the exploitative links between the conservative mandarins and the French colonials. Because of this perception, he came to condemn much of the old social and political order, not primarily because it inhibited Vietnam's growth and development, but because it was helping the French to sustain their presence.

If Vietnam subsequently had been induced or allowed to develop a politically conscious, dynamic native bourgeoisie, Phan Chu Trinh might well be remembered today as the godfather of some "evolutionary" approach to independence. Instead, in many ways Phan Boi Chau's attitudes and approach came to dominate an entire later generation of anticolonialists, including the communists. Although he was undoubtedly more radical in his time than Phan Boi Chau, in the ultimate paradox, Phan Chu Trinh's doctrine was appropriated decades later by the most conservative Vietnamese collaborationists.

The noted French historian Jean Chesneaux sparked an interesting polemic debate when in 1955 he wrote that events in Vietnam at the turn of the century reflected the emergence of an urban bourgeois class.[28] His periodization was then shared by one of Hanoi's most prominent historians, Tran Van Giau, who also gave some attention to the alleged advent of a small, yet "conscious" working class.[29] Since then, particularly since 1962, the tendency has been to regard the contentions of both Chesneaux and Tran Van Giau as excessively doctrinaire and as not coinciding with available data.[30] Without attempting to wade into a complex, high-voltage Marxist debate, I think it is important for us to inquire to what degree the positions of both activist and reformist scholar-gentry reflected substantial social and economic change in Vietnam. Or, to phrase it more provocatively, was there "revolution" between 1900 and 1910?

28. Jean Chesneaux, *Contribution a l'histoire de la Nation Vietnamienne*, pp. 183–205. Chesneaux, "Stages in the Development of the Vietnam National Movement 1862–1940," pp. 67–69.
29. Tran Van Giau, *Giai Cap Cong Nhan Viet-Nam* (Hanoi, 1961). Tran Van Giau, et al., *Lich Su Can Dai Viet-Nam*, vol. 3 (Hanoi, 1961).
30. See, for example, Ngo Van Hoa, "Co phai giai-cap cong-nhan Viet-Nam da hinh-thanh giai-cap 'tu-minh' tu truoc cuoc dai chien the gioi lan thu nhat hay khong?" Ho Song, NCLS 64: 39–45. Nguyen Anh, "Ban them ve nguyen nhan ra doi cua hai xu-huong cai-luong va bao-dong trong phong-trao cach-mang dau the ky XX," pp. 35–42. For a Trotskyite interpretation, see Anh Van and J. Roussel, *Mouvements Nationaux et Lutte de classes au Viet-Nam*, pp. 35–39.

Chesneaux, in his discussion of "economic dependence and social disequilibrium" between 1905 and 1930, explained how French policy speeded the decline of traditional artisan production, yet prevented the constitution of a modern industrial capacity and hindered the development of a Vietnamese industrial capitalist class.[31] In Cochinchina at that time there already had been a spectacular increase in rice production and new land relationships had developed, centering around native and French owners of vast, highly profitable plantations. However, the production of rubber, particularly in the *Terres rouges* of Cochinchina, did not begin to boom until after World War I, and the same was true to a large extent of mining operations in Tonkin. Industrial and commercial growth was not great either, and was certainly very uneven. While there were technical problems, the primary reasons for the slow development of Indochina under French aegis before World War I were political (the repression of the people and the French alliance with a backward-looking mandarinate) and financial (the relatively small amounts of international and domestic capital involved).[32] Whatever outside capital there was went for railway construction (which often proved to be of more strategic than economic value) and canal construction in Cochinchina, which was always an essential part of schemes for establishing rice plantations.

It is not surprising that when Chesneaux posited the nascence of a native bourgeois class he drew most of his examples from Cochinchina, citing particularly the native plantation owners, the native managers of plantations, and the compradores working with Western commercial firms (admitting that many of the latest were Chinese). While also granting that most existed in parasitical relationship to the French and that all lacked capability for independent action, Chesneaux insisted on speaking of them as being a distinct class from as early as 1905. Not only that, he tried to tie the political ferment of the entire period from 1905 to 1930 in tightly with the objective fate of this bourgeoisie—its successes and failures, its periods of growth or decline in influence and power.

Can the events of the first decade of the twentieth century, the formation of the Duy Tan Hoi, the Dong Du movement, and the Dong Kinh Nghia Thuc, best be understood in terms of the emergence of a new bourgeois class in Vietnam? Is that the most significant way to relate activist and reformist positions to the matrix of social and economic change? I do not believe so. On the basis of the evidence, it seems unrealistic to argue for the existence of a conscious, self-assertive bourgeois class—even a

31. Chesneaux, *Contribution*, pp. 159–182.
32. Ho Song, "Vai nhan xet," pp. 39–40, points out how little French capital went to French colonies before World War I, compared to the amount going to investment in Europe, especially in Russia.

small one—until after World War I. Before 1918, established bourgeois families in Vietnam were to be counted on one or two hands. And even those families had very limited capital, the members often having to serve as managers and salesmen in their own establishments. As I have pointed out, many supposedly capitalist enterprises were set up and funded by inexperienced scholar-gentry, and not always for economic motives.

Although it is somewhat beyond the confines of this study, reasonable arguments have been advanced that Vietnam never did develop a viable bourgeois class, as that term has been employed in the history of Western Europe. For example, even in the 1920s and 1930s the Vietnamese families in question tended to consolidate their positions not by means of a self-initiated, organized struggle against previous holders of power, but rather by making themselves directly or indirectly convenient to the dominant French capitalists and administrators. Without substantial economic independence, without real experience in political struggle, it is not surprising that the Vietnamese bourgeoisie remained insecure and subject to manipulation from various sides. Nor is it surprising that their sense of extra-class or national moral responsibility, of noblesse oblige, was hardly elaborated on a par with that of the previous elite, the scholar-gentry. Indeed, of all Vietnamese social classes in the twentieth century, the bourgeoisie had about the weakest sense of ethnic identity (*tinh than dan toc*).[33]

On the other hand, there is no question but that strong bourgeois "influences" permeated the Dong Du and Dong Kinh Nghia Thuc movements from 1904 to 1908, not because of any revolutionary changes in the economic structure, but because of the growing intellectual fascination of scholar-gentry leaders with foreign bourgeois precedents. In this respect it is not insignificant that a large proportion of the anticolonial scholar-gentry came from two areas known well before the French penetration into Vietnam for their intellectual and scholastic contributions to Vietnamese culture; Quang Nam and Nghe An/Ha Tinh. The reformists developed particular strength in Quang Nam province, which surrounded the strategic and commercial port of Da Nang (in French, Tourane). In such a relatively cosmopolitan area, they presumably were able to study foreign entrepreneurial activity not only from Chinese texts but also by personal observation. In contrast, the activists had their strongest following in Nghe An/Ha Tinh, which at that time was still barely touched by foreign entrepreneurial endeavors.

---

33. VTCM, pp. 22–24, argues along these lines, but without full-blown theoretical conclusions.

If one believes that it is possible to have a strictly intellectual revolution, that is, a changing of minds that sets certain men or certain classes marching in substantially new political and economic directions, then there was a revolution of sorts in Vietnam between 1900 and 1910. Interestingly enough, a number of Marxist historians in Hanoi have taken this position, for example, arguing that while Phan Boi Chau came from the feudal class, he was influenced by foreign bourgeois ideas to the point where he "broke radically" with the anticolonial position of the CanVuong and proceeded to fight, not for feudal-class advantages, but in direct empathic association with the mass of Vietnamese, who retained their emotional hatred of foreign domination and understood the call for armed struggle.[34] While this argument would seem to have upsetting implications for careful theoreticians of Marxism-Leninism, it does conveniently alleviate their need to explain the activities of these scholar-gentry in strictly feudal or bourgeois class and periodic confines.[35]

Without question, substantial social and economic changes were occuring in Vietnam. Nevertheless, they can better be explained in terms of a general breakdown of traditional class relationships, not by the alleged passing of leadership at that time from one class to another. I have already attempted to explain in part why that generation felt compelled at last to take on the established French regime and the collaborating mandarinate. After 1900 the social and economic situation became increasingly chaotic throughout the country, and in some places desperate, as is apparent from the tone of many of the writings introduced here.[36] Any comparison of reformist and activist positions should begin by recognizing that both were intellectual and emotional reactions to a situation they all regarded as critical.

As a generalization, it is often said that scholar-gentry activists stressed "antiimperialism," while reformists gave their prime attention

34. Nguyen Anh, "Ban them ve," pp. 35–41.
35. For example, Ton Quang Phiet, *Phan Boi Chau va Phan Chu Trinh*, pp. 133–134, had to describe Phan Boi Chau earlier as "more attached" to the feudal than the bourgeois class, whereas Phan Chu Trinh was "more bourgeois than feudal." For Ton this explains the activist-reformist split: the feudalists were losing class power and hence tended to react violently (activism); the more bourgeois types simply wanted more favorable conditions for their economic advancement (reformism). Tran Van Giau, *Giai cap*, pp. 146–147, pursues a similar line of reasoning.
36. It should be evident that I am not discussing much of the so-called modern sector of the colonial economy, which was of prime concern to the colon businessman and financier, but still of only tangential influence on the great bulk of the Vietnamese operating in the "traditional sector." Any influence at that point was largely negative—heavier taxes and corvée, the loss of public lands, the breakup of old trading patterns, and the undermining of traditional artisanry.

to "antifeudalism."[37] In other words, the reformists, while not always sure that the French would pursue a suitably enlightened program of their own volition, still maintained that success for the Vietnamese lay in pushing themselves forward educationally and then seizing the opportunities of modern technology and capital development. They saw no logical reason for the French to prevent this, but very obvious reasons that such general education would be anathema to the mandarinate. To greater or lesser degrees the reformists also perceived that some traditional or "feudal" institutions and values were downright impediments to modernization.

The activists, however, refused to believe that the foreign interloper would allow them anything but slavery. This meant for them that overthrow of the French was a prerequisite to self-government and serious modernization (insofar as they understood the implications of modernization). Success in any attempt at an overthrow also was necessarily very dependent on traditional ethnic symbols of deep meaning to the Vietnamese, and probably would require some foreign assistance. It is hardly surprising, then, that the French reacted with uniform hostility and violence toward the activists, while tending over the years to fluctuate in their attitudes toward and their treatment of the reformists.

Practically, both positions had grievous weaknesses. Activists failed to perceive that even the planning, much less the execution, of a violent overthrow, required substantial unity among various classes. Without this, they would (and they did) find themselves defeated from within their own people—not just by the native soldiers and police informers, but by their own lack of accurate intelligence, of supplies, hiding places, and recruits. Phan Boi Chau touched on this problem when he proposed a "national front" of diverse anticolonial elements; but he had no blueprint for implementation. He and other activists never got around to studying the underlying causes of the disunity which plagued Vietnamese society at that time. He and others also consistently underestimated their colonial enemy, in large part because they did not yet appreciate the wellsprings of modern military and political power.

Reformists had a somewhat better understanding of the sources of

37. This is one of the first generalizations normally made by the many historians writing on the subject for *Nghien Cuu Lich Su*. See especially Nguyen Anh, "Ban them ve," pp. 41–42, 46; Dang Viet Thanh, NCLS 25: 14–24; To Trung, NCLS 29: 53–55; Nguyen Anh, NCLS 32: 38–46; Nguyen Van Kiem, NCLS 66: 39–45, 58; To Minh Trung, NCLS 67: 29–38; Hung Ha, NCLS 68: 17–20, 24; Dang Viet Thanh, NCLS 68: 21–24; Duy Minh, NCLS 69: 15–19; Luong Khe, NCLS 69: 20–28; Nguyen Duc Su, NCLS 69: 29–33. Thanh Le, NCLS 71: 26–30; Dau Xuan Mai, NCLS 71: 31–39; Nguyen Thanh Nam, NCLS 71: 40–42, 59; Ho Song, NCLS 73: 38–43; Truong Giang, NCLS 73: 44–53; Van Tao, NCLS 76: 11–26.

French power and, indeed, wanted to share in them. As a result, much of their general propaganda served to awaken average Vietnamese to a sense of how the acquisition of modern expertise was in some vague way related to political and economic advance amidst the dire contemporary circumstances. This would be very important in legitimizing for the Vietnamese the individual acquisition of expertise, instead of continuing to condemn it outright as foreign-inspired. Nevertheless, the reformists' program as a whole was pitched at too high an intellectual level for mass comprehension, which signaled the beginning of a communications gap that grew substantially in subsequent generations. Their debunking of traditional customs was part of a necessary "demolition" job that was in large degree historically determined. In the short run, however, it really only gained them enthusiastic supporters among the small merchants, the civil servants, and the urban students. The process of reorientation among the peasantry would take several more decades and would have to occur within the larger framework of commitment to the violent overthrow of the colonial regime.

Meanwhile, as reformists made their individually appropriate breaks with tradition, cut their hair short, studied French, quoted their latest intellectual discoveries, they began to lose contact with the peasant majority and to deprecate the emotional and spiritual elements of the struggle for independence and ethnic reidentification. This can be seen even in the writings of Phan Chu Trinh, although it only assumed substantial proportions among members of the next generation, who were educated almost entirely in French or Franco-Vietnamese school systems. Eventually, contact between the classes could be restored, but only after the physical movement of the anticolonial intelligentsia into the countryside and into complete dependence on the peasantry. The result would be a surprisingly effective merging of the modern and traditional, of reformists and activists, out of which was molded the Viet-Minh and victory over the French.

What were the implications of events up to and including the outbreaks of 1908? Quite evidently, both activist and reformist causes had suffered grievously. And it is hard to argue that either group learned a great deal from its defeats. Phan Chu Trinh had been imprisoned on Con-lon island on trumped-up charges of inciting rebellion; yet he would continue to hope for some change in French policy that might permit the implementation of his programs. As an idealist, he never perceived that French colonial rule had been grounded and built up on violence and that therefore it would almost certainly take violence to alter the system substantially.

Phan Boi Chau had learned the futility of asking and waiting for aid from Japan. Yet he soon would be knocking at Chinese and German doors—with similar results. If anything, activists after 1910 became more putschist—almost nihilist—in outlook, resorting to isolated acts of terror and neglecting to develop new support among the people. By and large, this was because they still confused revolution with activism, an error that has plagued more than one militant Vietnamese party even to the present day. As Professor Nguyen Van Trung has pointed out:

> They thought that founding a party sort of required the formality of charter members choosing a name, a line, discussing, electing, etc. . . . but the real thing was getting into effective action. . . . So, action without the guidance of theory became action for itself alone. . . . The main thing was driving out the French; all other problems depended on that and could be postponed. No party had a man to sit down and define what the "French" were, what colonial imperialism was, explaining the situation, internally and outside, so that people would understand both themselves and the enemy.[38]

If the immediate scholar-gentry participants learned very little from their failures, there were still implications of tremendous significance in the more general sense. Most important perhaps was the stark revelation to ever-larger numbers of Vietnamese of mandarin impotence and the de facto control of the country by foreigners. The traditional place for villagers to take their serious grievances had always been the district magistrate's office. In the 1908 tax protests the most common pattern, as we have seen, was an attempt to corral a local mandarin and take him as spokesman to the French résident. When most of the mandarins shirked this task, the villagers tried facing the résident on their own. This was educational for them, as they finally learned with brutal clarity exactly where the power resided.

As might be expected, however, the villagers lacked the confidence and sophistication to generalize their grievances and to develop a sustained protest movement. Those scholar-gentry who had set the stage intellectually and emotionally for the tax protests apparently had stayed home and refused to lead the immediate confrontations. Although there is no evidence one way or the other, we may assume that their prestige among the people suffered accordingly. The result of the altercations of 1908, particularly in terms of the long-range psychological response, was that French and Vietnamese were forced into stark, grinding overlord-subject relationships, much like those which had occurred in Cochinchina forty

38. Nguyen Van Trung, *Chu Nghia*, p. 212.

years earlier after the flight of the mandarins and the advent of direct rule. Interestingly enough, one of the first to sense the subversive implications of the new Franco-Vietnamese continguousness was the man who had directed the repression in central Vietnam. In a confidential report, dated May 11, 1908, M. Levecque, the résident supérieur of Annam, made no effort to conceal his anger and frustration at the poor showing of the mandarinate. The reasons, he said, included mandarin sympathy with the movement, apathy, and simple incapacity or weakness. While justifying his decision to use direct French power to crush protestors in his area, out of simple necessity, if nothing else, he added the following comment:

> But I have not failed to notice the ease with which the [demonstration] ringleaders have exploited among the people resentments apparently held against the mandarins. I have ascertained as well . . . how many of the indigenous people are detaching themselves little by little from their racial representatives. Hence I have a new reason for considering that it was particularly impolitic in these conditions for us to substitute in the repression for those others [the mandarins] who ought logically and legally to do it.[39]

In subsequent years there were perfunctory attempts by the French to resuscitate the mandarinate in the eyes of the people. But that effort was doomed from the beginning, particularly as in day-to-day administration the French ignored their own prescription and relied usually on direct relationships with canton chiefs and selected village officials.[40]

The attempted coup in Hanoi had rather the same results in north Vietnam, but for different reasons. Something approaching panic swept the colon community in and around Hanoi; irrational though it was, considering the relative crudity of the plot, it nevertheless was adequate to silence for the time being those French administrators in Tonkin with inclinations toward reform.[41] The newly appointed governor general, Antoni Klobukowski, arrived in September 1908 and quickly entered into the repressive spirit by closing Beau's University of Hanoi (never

39. AOM A-50 NF 598.
40. VTCM, p. 13.
41. Three days after the poisoning, an angry crowd of colons forced the interim governor general, Gabriel Bonhours (Beau left in February 1908), to suspend normal judicial procedures in the seizure and punishment of plot participants. A sustained scare campaign was mounted in the French-language press in Hanoi, which was tied in with demands for dropping all reform proposals. Paul Isoart, *Le phénomène national vietnamien*, p. 193. Joseph Buttinger, *Viet-Nam*, pp. 64–67. Fernand Bernard, *Revue de Paris* (October 1908), as quoted in Buttinger, *Viet-Nam*, pp. 469–470.

particularly productive), abolishing the Directorate of Public Education, and dissolving several native consultative bodies in Tonkin. Subsequently he ordered military operations against De Tham that brought back memories of the ruthlessness and turmoil of a decade earlier, particularly to those unfortunate peasants who happened each time to be in the way. The veils were being torn off, and the substance of foreign domination was becoming too obvious for any man who was honest with himself to ignore.

Partly because of the events of 1908, French colonial policy veered to the right and avoided even modest experimentation with "self-rule" for at least fifteen years. If, in fact, there ever was an opportunity for the French to form a viable alliance for modernization with a respected Vietnamese elite such as the reformist scholar-gentry, it was lost somewhere between the vacant classrooms of the Dong Kinh Nghia Thuc and the festering cellblocks of Con-lon island. When French police and judicial investigators concluded in 1908 that reformists and activists were conspiring in a systematic plot to disrupt the administration of Indochina, they in effect wrote off any French chances for exploiting Vietnamese reformist inclinations toward modernizing under foreign aegis. Indeed, at least some high-ranking French officials regarded the reformists as representing the more dangerous of the two anticolonial tendencies, presumably because they had not only effectively undermined the collaborating mandarins, but had also succeeded sometimes in disseminating their visions far beyond the confines of the educated elite.[42]

The scholar-gentry failures were of great general significance for another related reason: All the organizing and propagandizing, all the demands and aspirations were cresting at a time when many leaders of anticolonial efforts of the 1920s and 1930s were between eight and eighteen years old, too young to participate fully, but old enough to be strongly influenced. Phan Boi Chau, for example, noted in his autobiography that in 1899 the nine-year-old Nguyen Ai Quoc had listened to him quoting lines of poetry which Nguyen never forgot.[43] Many heard their fathers and elder brothers talk excitedly about the Dong Du movement and the Dong Kinh Nghia Thuc, about the personalities and actions

---

42. This was the position, for example, of M. Groleau, résident supérieur of Annam, in a report dated May 29, 1909. AOM A-20(58), carton 9. See also Pierre Dabezies, *Forces Politiques au Viet-Nam*, pp. 89, 114.
43. NB, p. 30. To my knowledge, Ho Chi Minh prior to his death in 1969 had not yet published a full account of his own childhood, although he had made numerous allusions to his early spiritual debt to Phan Boi Chau and other Nghe An scholar-gentry leaders. At the moment the best work in English is Jean Lacouture, *Ho Chi Minh*.

of such giants as Phan Boi Chau and Phan Chu Trinh. Friends of the family and members of their villages would return from Japan and narrate seemingly fantastic stories. Some of the next generation, like Tran Huy Lieu, were just old enough to read anticolonial circulars, to treasure a poem by Phan Boi Chau about a local hero, and to dream of their own future resistance.[44]

It was not the objective failure of the plans that struck these young people, but the bravery and romanticism of the effort. While around them in the villages elders had probably been bowing their heads to the foreigners, proud alternatives had still been available and had reached them at an impressionable age. Scholar-gentry leaders, activist and reformist alike, were very aware of these implications. It was not for nothing that they hammered away on the themes of men's feelings (*long nguoi*; Sino-Vietnamese, *nhan tam*), popular feelings (*long dan*), and spirit (*tinh than*).[45] Hence, the French imprisonment of scores of famous scholar-gentry leaders on Con-lon only served to keep the alternatives alive, since the prisoners were seen by many Vietnamese outside as their hostages to a better fate, who never let them forget both the glories and the dangers of raising one's head high. In short, if the anticolonial effort had not been made between 1900 and 1910, it is not at all certain that the spirit of resistance could have been sustained with such startling vitality even to the present day.

In more concrete political terms, later generations in Vietnam would have adequate reason for criticizing both activists and reformists. Their conceptualizations were clouded and incomplete. Little time was spent on delineating the important philosophical questions such as identifying causes and their effects in Vietnam's contemporary plight or defining the proper values and the ultimate goals of "civilization" (*van minh*). No serious analysis of Vietnamese society had been forthcoming from that generation. Nor was there any plan for exactly how selected traditional Vietnamese patterns were to be integrated with selected Western patterns. Finally, for all their talk of uniting the people in common effort, the scholar-gentry remained fundamentally elitist. "The people" for them was still an inchoate mass, a blind, if potentially powerful, element that could be expected to follow the directions of the more enlightened.[46]

Still, the conscious decision by this last generation of scholar-gentry to take on the seemingly unbearable political burdens of their country was

44. Tran Huy Lieu, "Nho lai," p. 40.
45. VTCM, p. 86. The author points out that spirit (*tinh than*) at this time was still taken in sharp contrast to body (*vat chat*), meaning the pleasures of the flesh, the pursuit of happiness without reference to ideals, etc.
46. VTCM, pp. 69–71, 150–151.

a momentous political act in itself. There would be benefits to the nation on this basis alone. From the Can Vuong generation of the 1880s and 1890s to the anti-colonial groups of the 1920s was a vast political leap, and it was men of the turn of the century like Phan Boi Chau and Phan Chu Trinh who provided whatever bridges there were between. On the crucial subject of patriotism, for example, the century had begun with the basic imperative still being fidelity (*trung*)— that is, personal loyalty to one's king, one's family, and one's comrades. The term "love of country" (*yeu-nuoc;* Sino-Vietnamese, *ai-quoc*) certainly existed, but is was generally subsumed under fidelity. However, during the period of the Dong Du movement and the Dong Kinh Nghia Thuc, love of country achieved a new status of its own, relating to the land and the people as a whole. This concept quickly took precedence over traditional fidelity, and by the 1920s the latter term had been altered until it could effectively be subsumed under the former.[47]

Later generations did study the political positions and review the tactics of their predecessors, trying to learn from their errors. When their objective circumstances did improve, there was this reservoir of practical history to give them both sober perspective and undaunted tenacity. The fact that activist and reformist arguments had earlier been advanced, forcefully if not successfully, gave those appearing later something of an intellectual advantage. Eventually they were able to draw on the mass education and reorientation of reformism to awaken, train, and direct cadres from a variety of classes. Through bitter experience, they knew they would have to put their faith in violent overthrow; but there was an awareness, not shared by the earlier activists, that long-term political and ideological struggle had to clear the way and prepare the battlefield, if violent tactics were to have any hope of success. As Phan Boi Chau in his later years was fond of saying, in an adaptation of a Western aphorism, "defeat is the mother of victory."[48] He was right, but there would have to be many more defeats.

47. VTCM, p. 132.
48. TP, p. 16.

Chapter Nine

Chủ nhân là ai? Quốc dân ta ơi!
Đồng bào ta ơi! Dậy! Dậy! Dậy!
Who are the masters? Our people are!
Our countrymen are! Wake up! Wake up!

(PHAN BỘI CHÂU, *Hậu Trần*
Dật Sử, 1913)

Hostages

For most of the world the second decade of the twentieth century was of overriding importance, encompassing as it did the 1911 revolution in China, World War I, and the Russian Revolution, among other things. Each of those events would indirectly affect Indochina, both immediately and in time. Nevertheless, the primary impressions one gets of that era in Indochina, particularly when viewing the situation through Vietnamese eyes, are of a relative isolation, of a people temporarily in limbo, of life and death in a French colony increasingly bound by its own epochal reality, its own rules and responses to external events.[1]

During that period, in fact, the political and literary attention of most people in the cities and provincial towns of Vietnam were effectively occupied by men who took French power for granted and sought only to change the details of their situation. In northern and central Vietnam they included early graduates of the French interpreters' school in Hanoi, as well as a few reformist scholar-gentry who had chosen to accept the elimination of the Dong Kinh Nghia Thuc passively. In the south there were some anticolonial disturbances in the years from 1913 to 1916, but from 1917 to 1924 the assimilationist *Parti Constitutionaliste* was to provide virtually the sole focus of Vietnamese political attention.[2]

1. This period deserves to be investigated carefully from the side of the French colons. It seems to have been a time when they at last developed enough independent levers of power, enough organization and confidence as a colonial aristocracy, to swing policy irrevocably in their favor vis-à-vis competing and conflicting interests emanating from the métropole. It may have been this shift that was most responsible for turning the Vietnamese intelligentsia between 1920 and 1945 forever away from reformist or gradualist solutions.
2. Ralph B. Smith, "Bui Quang Chieu and the Constitutionalist Party in French Cochinchina, 1917–30," p. 136.

While the endeavors of these men who chose to work within the established colonial system are essentially outside the confines of this study, they deserve at least passing mention. Among other things, the fact that their activities went almost entirely unchallenged until 1924 demonstrates just how far anticolonial fortunes declined after 1910.

Men like Nguyen Van Vinh, Pham Quynh, and Nguyen Ba Hoc in Hanoi, and Bui Quang Chieu in Saigon were willing to work within much narrower perimeters than were most of the reformists who had been shipped to Con-lon. In return for their "moderation," they found many French administrators to be beneficent and gracious toward them, if not always understanding of their aims. Clearly, they hoped to use whatever mutual understanding did exist to promote what they conceived of as the long-term modernization of Vietnam. Their influence was particularly strong among the young Vietnamese men and women then undergoing instruction in French and Franco-Vietnamese schools.

In retrospect, however, one may conclude that these cautious modernizers always were being used far more than they were themselves using their colonial overloads. In Cochinchina this fact was often disguised by a patina of French legalism, which, for example, allowed those few Vietnamese who were fluent in French the experience of publishing newspapers with relative freedom, for each other's satisfaction. To the north, even this patina was largely missing, and hence the realities of colonial power relationships remained more obvious to all concerned. It was no accident, for example, that Louis Marty, the Frenchman who in 1917 helped Pham Quynh set up in Hanoi the most effective intellectual journal of this period, *Nam Phong* (Southern Wind), was at the same time director of the dreaded Political Service (France's operational intelligence apparatus in Indochina).[3] While Pham Quynh and his associates rephrased their reformist ideas in order to pass Marty's knowledgeable scrutiny, Marty simultaneously made certain that the more independent-minded reformist scholar-gentry remained locked up on Con-lon island. He also tried to make sure that *Nam Phong* had no significant competition from the outside, cutting off many Chinese-language periodicals on the pretext that they contained pro-German propaganda. Readers of *Nam Phong*, as well as *Dong Duong Tap Chi* (Indochina Journal)[4] and several other periodi-

3. Louis Marty was a colonial administrator fluent in both Chinese and Vietnamese, a founder of the Sûreté, and from 1934 French résident in Laos. He edited the official volumes on anticolonial movements published in 1933 and 1934: Gouvernement-General de l'Indochine, *Contribution à l'Histoire des Movements Politiques de l'Indochine* (Hanoi), 6 vol. His classified reports also appear in many AOM files.
4. *Dong Duong Tap Chi* was printed weekly in Hanoi from 1913 to 1917. *Nam Phong* appeared monthly from 1917 to 1934, but received most attention before

cals, were in reality treated only to a highly select menu of French literary and political thought. In addition, several of the contributing authors persisted in glorifying ancient Chinese values while taking pains to denigrate the changes in China after the 1911 revolution.[5]

From 1910 to 1920 educated people in the towns and cities of north and central Vietnam began seriously to imitate the small collaborating elite that had emerged in the south some decades earlier. It then became socially acceptable to scurry after French diplomas and civil service positions. With French blessing, it also was possible to write short stories, essays, newspaper articles, and the like for financial gain, rather than as a function of largely noneconomic aspirations, as in the past. More seriously, for a member of the privileged intelligentsia it was increasingly possible to conceive of a process by which one "became Western," rather than continuing to associate oneself with one's own rural, backward Vietnamese kin. Not surprisingly, all this was to become the grist of a bitter Vietnamese political debate after 1924. But, in the meantime, the initiative remained definitely in the hands of the collaborators.[6]

It would be a mistake to infer that the efforts of these educated collaborators were totally devoid of benefit to the anticolonial cause. This can be seen particularly in the way their activities advanced the growth of *quoc-ngu* as a medium of expression. Through the writings of Nguyen Van Vinh, Pham Quynh, Nguyen Ba Hoc, Pham Duy Ton, Tran Trong Kim, and others, the *quoc-ngu* vocabulary was steadily enriched, syntax became far more flexible, and many new stylistic forms were introduced.[7] Most major Vietnamese literary works in *nom* were transliterated into *quoc-ngu* and circulated in relatively inexpensive paperbound volumes. Various Chinese novels were translated into *quoc-ngu*, and, with translations of

---

1924. For a preliminary discussion of the content of these journals, see Hoang Ngoc Thanh, "The Social and Political Development of Vietnam as Seen Through the Modern Novel" (Hawaii, 1968), pp. 105–129.

5. In a message to the governor general dated December 6, 1917, the Minister of Colonies indicated his pleasure at reading *Nam Phong*. It would serve, he said, to neutralize enemy propaganda, including that appearing in the Chinese press. The latter is probably in part a reference to articles by Phan Boi Chau and other members of the Quang Phuc Hoi. AOM A-01 NF 196, carton 18.

6. VTCM, pp. 90–99.

7. Many of these changes soon produced changes in the spoken language of the urban reading public. This, in turn, probably helped to broaden the urban-rural gap, since most of the writers involved had little interest in reaching the mass of Vietnamese in the villages. Nevertheless, compared with previous cleavages between oral and written mediums, the development of *quoc-ngu* was of ultimate benefit to the villagers, since later writers and political groupings would go to great lengths to bring *quoc-ngu* and the spoken language into effective conjunction. VTCM, p. 114.

selected French novels, they provided the structural inspiration for a whole new body of Vietnamese literature of social criticism and protest which would emerge in the late twenties and thirties.

But *quoc-ngu* was merely a vehicle. What was to be its political content? The same question could be asked of the growing corps of Vietnamese journalists in Saigon, except that they would have to switch away from the French-language journals to *quoc-ngu* publications, legal or underground, before their discussions could have much impact beyond their own circles. I would argue that the imprisoned anticolonial scholar-gentry, even while they were hostages to fate, to their own limited visions, and, above all, to a thoroughly oppressive system, retained more understanding of the essential political questions of Vietnam than men like Pham Quynh, Nguyen Van Vinh, and Bui Quang Chieu ever could.

It will be remembered that Phan Boi Chau and a small group were in rural Thailand, farming, writing songs, and trying to hold themselves together for better times. That time seemed to be at hand when they received news of the Wuhan uprising in China.[8] The higher Phan's hopes rose, the deeper would be his ultimate disappointment:

> My impatient spirit shot forth without bounds, above all because I thought that, with success of the revolutionary party, the government of China naturally no longer would be corrupt and outmoded (what a mistake I made!), China thence following Japan in developing as a strong nation. If China and Japan combined their power against the Europeans, then not only our Viet-Nam, but also India and the Philippines could rise up simultaneously.[9]

Arriving in Canton, Phan met· about a score of Vietnamese activists from inside Vietnam and from scattered points in China, all having rushed to Canton with the same purpose—to capitalize on the rise to power of many of the Chinese they had befriended in Japan. Those from Vietnam claimed that news of Wuhan had revitalized the movement there, but they were not particularly specific and seemed to think that initiative for anticolonial action would have to come from the outside. In one of his autobiographical works two decades later, Phan Boi Chau admitted ruefully

8. *Nguc Trung Thu* indicates that Phan returned to China in November 1911 upon the written encouragement of Phan Ba Ngoc. TP, p. 144 and NB, pp. 138–139, recalls, on the other hand, that he first wrote a pamphlet titled "Lien A So Ngon" (Awkward Words on Asian Association) and sent it to some of his Chinese friends, wishing them success and offering to go help them. Receiving several letters in reply, he headed for Bangkok with a few followers and arrived in Canton in January 1912.
9. TP, p. 144. NB, p. 138.

that he didn't sense the fallacy in such reasoning and only in the subsequent defeat did he realize that to organize outside and to seek outside aid was useless unless the people at home were organized and prepared psychologically to move exactly when conditions were favorable.[10]

The main achievement of the gathering in Canton was to disband whatever remained of the Duy Tan Hoi, with its monarchist overtones, and instead to form the Viet-Nam Quang Phuc Hoi (Vietnam Restoration Society), unabashedly and to the smallest detail patterned after China's republican T'ung-meng-hui.[11] This was not accomplished without some bitter argument and the beginning of another ideological divergence within the anticolonial movement, this time between those activists who favored shifting immediately to republicanism and those who remained wedded in some way to traditional monarchism. Phan Boi Chau also cited Rousseau's arguments in favor of democracy and, more persuasively for the moment, pointed out that democracy was on the ascendancy in China, most obviously among those men who now might help them. He was backed up by most of the representatives from central and northern Vietnam, including the influential Nguyen Thuong Hien, who only as late as 1907 had given up his mandarin position and left the country.

Opposition came, as might be expected, from the conservative southern representatives, close followers of Cuong De, who himself apparently had chosen to be absent from these critical discussions.[12] While Phan Boi Chau

10. NB, p. 139. TP, p. 145. Interestingly enough, the Indochinese Communist Party appears to have remembered this lesson in World War II, while competing organizations, including one led by Nguyen Hai Than who had taken his in-country assessment to Phan Boi Chau in Canton in 1912, stayed idly in South China waiting for the end of the war.

11. Detailed comparison is made by Chuong Thau, NCLS 43: 18–19. For example, where the T'ung-meng-hui abbreviated platform called for overthrow of the Manchu, restoration (hui-fu) of China, and establishment of democracy, the Quang Phuc Hoi paralleled this with, "drive out the French bandits, restore Vietnam, establish a democratic republic." Nevertheless, there also was a Chinese Kuang-fu-hui, founded in 1903, led prominently by Chang Ping-lin and T'ao Ch'eng-chang. Between 1908 and 1911 it was in many ways a revolutionary competitor to the T'ung-meng-hui, particularly in Southeast Asia and in the provinces of Chekiang, Kiangsu, and Fukien. While the term "quang-phuc" (kuang-fu) was ambiguous enough to suggest either independence or restoration of a monarch, we know from Chang Ping-lin's biography that the Vietnamese could not have drawn much strictly monarchist sustenance from him. Howard L. Boorman, ed., Biographical Dictionary of Republican China, vol. 1 (New York, 1967), pp. 92–98. Finally, we may assume that in their choice of that term Phan Boi Chau and his associates also were mindful of the guerrilla exploits of Trieu Quang Phuc, who in the sixth century A.D. had helped sustain a brief period of Vietnamese independence from Chinese rule. Tran Trong Kim, Viet-Nam Su-Luoc, pp. 59–60.

12. Cuong De says he had gone to Shanghai to seek help from Huang Hsing and

simply recalled that a majority finally agreed to abandon monarchism and give Cuong De the title of "president" of the new shadow republic, it is evident that the next few months saw more and more backbiting and recriminations among participants—hardly an auspicious beginning for the Quang Phuc Hoi.[13] Among the activist group operating in Siam, for example, there developed enough dissension that Mai Lao Bang[14] was persuaded to write a poem calling for unity and an end to petty animosities. He particularly cited the manner in which Le Loi and his men four hundred years earlier had endured physical privation and each other's idiosyncrasies in the pursuit of the common objective of destroying the Ming colonial system.[15]

Characteristically, Phan Boi Chau threw himself completely into developing the new organization. This time, however, there would be less room to maneuver and less possibility of operating on multiple fronts, as had been his custom. Besides Cuong De and Phan Boi Chau as "president" and "vice-president," respectively, each subordinate "ministry" had one representative for each region—north, center, and south. Most important was the "deliberative ministry" (*binh nghi bo*), with Nguyen Thuong Hien for northern Vietnam, Phan Boi Chau for the center, and Nguyen Than Hien for the south. Several younger men undertook the various military, financial, propaganda, and other missions. Early formalities over, many participants headed back to Vietnam or to the Yunnan and Kwangsi border areas, while Phan turned his prime attention to fund-raising. Domestic sources had almost vanished. Worse yet, their key liaison on these matters, Ly Tue, had been jailed.[16] Other contact men managed to bring out 2,000 piastres (half from the south), but it was obvious that some new tack had to be tried.[17]

In April 1912 Phan Boi Chau headed for Nanking and an audience with Sun Yat-Sen. Sun received him for a few minutes and then passed him on

---

Ch'en Ch'i-mei, but his simultaneous carping at Phan Boi Chau indicates a serious difference of opinion at this time. CD, pp. 49–54. Ch'en Ch'i-mei led the *T'ung-meng-hui* capture of Shanghai in November 1911 and was military governor there until ousted by Yuan Shih-k'ai in August 1912. Yuan arranged his assassination in 1916. Boorman, *Biographical Dictionary*, vol. 1, pp. 163–165.

13. NB, p. 141. TP, p. 146. CD, pp. 53–54.

14. Pseudonym, Gia Chau. From Ha Tinh province. In 1908 he led the first group of Catholic students who arrived in Japan as part of the Dong Du effort and was with Phan Boi Chau in Siam. VNDN, p. 143. NB, pp. 115–116. TP, pp. 118–119. Poetry in HT, pp. 515–519.

15. Mai Lao Bang, "Khuyen Dong Tam," reprinted in VTCM, pp. 328–333.

16. Ly Tue was confined at Son La for nine years. He and Phan Boi Chau met again in 1938, the year Ly Tue died.

17. TP, pp. 147–148. NB, pp. 141–143.

to Huang Hsing, who, while still recognizing the principle of multi-national revolutionary assistance, yet argued frankly with Phan that it was too early to expect anything substantial from the T'ung-meng-hui. Huang instead recommended sending Vietnamese students to China for about ten years, the implication being that China might be able to do something for Vietnam by then. Having gone through much the same thing in Japan, Phan Boi Chau found this sort of response from the Chinese deeply dispiriting. Nevertheless, within the context of the T'ung-meng-hui's developing struggle with Yuan Shih-k'ai, president of the new republic, it should not have surprised him completely. Stomaching his disappointment, Phan accepted the student offer. Soon at least nine young followers were enrolled in various Peking military academies, three others in Kwangsi schools. Huang's letter of introduction for Phan also proved helpful in gaining minimal assistance from Hu Han-min and others in Kwangtung. Meanwhile, Phan headed down to Shanghai for contact with Ch'en Ch'i-mei, whom he had come to know quite well in Japan and to whom he felt he could speak more bluntly. To Ch'en's identical advice that "education of the populace" must precede attempts at violent overthrow, Phan shot back that education in Vietnam was entirely controlled by the French and therefore meant training for slavery in the government schools, the shutting down of independent efforts like the Dong Kinh Nghia Thuc, and the forbidding of overseas study. Phan even quoted Mazzini to reinforce his case, but the best he could get from Ch'en was the equivalent of 4,000 piastres and thirty explosive grenades. Phan then made the trip back to Kwangtung, sad and bitter, but increasingly enlightened about the scant prospects of T'ung-meng-hui assistance.[18]

During the summer of 1912 plans were made for the creation of a Restoration Army (Quang Phuc Quan) to be led by the young men then studying in Peking and Kwangsi. An army flag was adopted with five white stars (apparently, the three regions of Vietnam, plus Cambodia and Laos) on a red field. The white traditionally was related to metal and therefore implied destruction of the enemy; the red was related to fire—the south—and hence Vietnam. There was also a national flag, perhaps Vietnam's first: five red stars on a yellow field, the stars and the red having the same significance as in the army flag, and the yellow symbolizing the yellow race.[19] Finally, Phan Boi Chau and Hoang Trong Mau[20] together wrote

18. NB, pp. 143–145. TP, pp. 149–152. CD, pp. 50–51.
19. NB, pp. 146–147. TP, pp. 152–153. For the rich symbolism of certain colors in Vietnam and south China, dating back more than a millenium, see Edward H. Schafer, The Vermilion Bird (Berkeley, 1967), pp. 256–265.
20. Original name, Nguyen Duc Cong, pseudonym, Bao Thu. Cam-truong village (now Nghi-trung), Nghi-loc district, Nghe-An. He arrived in Japan in 1908 and later

up a training manual for the Restoration Army, dealing with everything from ideology and discipline to ranks and pay rates. While all of this never amounted to much more than fantasies on paper, it did indicate further groping efforts by the activists to incorporate modern symbolism and procedures.[21]

Indeed, although the Quang Phuc Hoi never really was able to achieve a strong domestic position, it did assert modifications in activist doctrine that in the long run profoundly influenced subsequent more sophisticated anticolonial organizations. In a proclamation written by Hoang Trong Mau for distribution inside Vietnam, the Quang Phuc Hoi flatly blamed the Nguyen monarchs for the loss of the country to the French. Clearly and uncompromisingly they declared that the Vietnamese people at large were the inheritors, the proprietors, of the country, not any single established family. If Vietnam was to be restored, it would only be through the unified efforts of the people. To that end it would certainly be necessary to establish a democratic republic (*dan-chu cong-hoa*)—the first time, apparently, that term was employed.[22] In another public statement, directed at the residents of Nghe An and Ha Tinh, the Quang Phuc Hoi called for their participation in a revolution (*cach-mang*) that would extend throughout Vietnam and asked for their assistance in forming a revolutionary army (*quan-doi cach-mang*).[23] As I have said, much of this sort of thing was still mere rhetoric, often borrowed unashamedly from the Chinese situation; nevertheless, it was rhetoric that would not be forgotten.

Still feeling that he lacked the kind of money needed to mount sustained assaults against the French, Phan had one more ploy—a combination of high-pressure salesmanship and ruse. Taking the advice of a Chinese revolutionary who had been with Sun Yat-sen in the 1907 Sino-Vietnamese border operations, he had large numbers of Quang Phuc Hoi "military bonds" printed in Hong Kong for sale inside Vietnam and in the Chinese border provinces, buyers being promised reimbursement within two years

---

studied in Chinese military schools and became closely associated with Kwangsi military leaders. He was executed by the French in 1916. TP, pp. 112–113. NB, pp. 108–110. Poetry in HT, pp. 504–511.

21. NB, pp. 147–148. TP, pp. 152–153. AOM A-50 NF 448, carton 31, mentions the formation in Hong Kong of a "Société des Martyrs" around this time, probably a reference to the Quang Phuc Hoi.

22. Hoang Trong Mau, "Loi tuyen cao cua Viet-nam Quang Phuc Hoi," reprinted in VTCM, pp. 326–327.

23. Hoang Trong Mau and Tran Huu Luc, "Thu gui dong bao Nghe-Tinh trong dip thanh lap Viet-Nam Quang Phuc Hoi," reprinted in VTCM, pp. 207–210. Both authors were from Nghi-loc district, Nghe An.

after the Quang Phuc Hoi came to power.[24] Next came formation of the Chan Hoa Hung A Hoi (Invigorate China, Revive Asia Society), essentially a friendship society and channel for selling the Quang Phuc Hoi bonds. Phan rented a big headquarters in Canton and went about energetically promoting the impression of imminent revolutionary success in Vietnam. A proclamation was printed and distributed, picturing China as the guide for all Asia and offering China a grand anti-European, anticolonial strategy, starting with evicting the French from Vietnam and perhaps ending with the freeing of India, Burma, and Korea. During the first month about two hundred Chinese signed up, and the bonds moved well. September 1912 saw some Chinese sympathizers integrated into the Quang Phuc Hoi leadership. The provincial governor and later commissioner of Kwantung, Ch'en Chiung-ming, was aware of what the Vietnamese were doing and was generally sympathetic, allowing them free rein.[25]

Phan Boi Chau knew, however, that it was built on deception behind a false front. If the momentum of financial and political support from the Chinese was to be sustained, he recognized that there was need for some domestic Vietnamese successes, quickly. With organization of the Quang Phuc Hoi inside Vietnam still infantile, after having passed public death sentences on Governor General Albert Sarraut and on several long-time collaborators like Hoang Cao Khai and Nguyen Duy Han, Phan sent teams of assassins into the three regions of the country. Their precedent almost certainly was the assassination of Ito Hirobumi, former Japanese resident general, by Korean patriots in 1909.[26] The first plot to kill Sarraut fizzled in November 1912. On April 13, 1913, they did kill Nguyen Duy Han in Thai Binh and succeeded two weeks later in blowing up two French colonels in the Hotel Hanoi. But the French used these events as grounds for rounding up 254 persons, suspect or not, of whom 7 were executed and 57 imprisoned.[27] For a while there was renewed excitement

24. Phan Boi Chau recalls the man as Su Shao-lou from Kwangtung. NB, pp. 148–149. TP, pp. 153–154. Cuong De, however, mentions a Liu Shih-fu in this role and himself takes credit for advancing the money for printing the bond issue. CD, p. 50. At any rate, he and Phan Boi Chau agree that Hoang Trong Mau carried out the job. AOM A-50 NF 28 (2), carton 8, indicates that there were two or three printings of such bonds, which may explain the confusion.
25. NB, pp. 149–154. TP, pp. 153–159. Boorman, *Biographical Dictionary*, vol. 1, pp. 173–180, for a biography of Ch'en Chiung-ming.
26. CMCD-3, pp. 80–81.
27. AOM A-50 NF 606, carton 51. Phan Boi Chau, Cuong De, and four others were also sentenced to death in absentia. AOM A-50 NF 605, carton 51, has a score or more consular telegrams attempting to detail the movements of Phan Boi Chau and others between January and May 1913. It also contains a report from the governor

among Vietnamese as regards activist anticolonial efforts, particularly in Hanoi. Nevertheless, the general effect was to destroy whatever small progress had been made in organizing a clandestine apparatus.[28]

Worse even that that, the assassinations led the French government to put heavy diplomatic pressure on the insecure Chinese government. In the short run, Phan Boi Chau countered by asking an associate to travel up to Peking and intercede with Yuan Shih-k'ai.[29] Even so, the enthusiasm of the Quang Phuc Hoi's Chinese backers was dissipating rapidly, and the bonds were no longer selling, which led Phan, like a roulette player trying to overcome mounting losses, into further frantic attempts at pulling off a startling victory. Early in 1913, following a meeting of one hundred dedicated activists, Phan Boi Chau and Mai Lao Bang stayed in Canton to try to maintain Chinese contacts and to help the forty Vietnamese students in the area, while another Quang Phuc Hoi team went to Hong Kong to set up an explosives factory, and still others went back into the three regions of Vietnam on new terrorist missions. The result was disastrous—practically a complete elimination of the Quang Phuc Hoi. The team in Hong Kong, led by Nguyen Than Hien, was captured by the British police. Other key men, from Siam to Lang-Son, were detained and turned over to the French. At this point, Phan could not help remembering the classical phrase, "happiness come singly, while misfortune arrives in droves."[30] Nevertheless, there was worse to come.

In south Vietnam about then there was a movement that achieved nothing in terms of its predetermined schemes and yet illustrates something important about religious and political traditions in that area and, indeed,

---

general to the Minister of Colonies, dated May 5, 1913, claiming that the Haiphong police had found 100 kilograms (!?) of nitroglycerin on a Chinese vessel. Vu Van Tinh, "Mot vai diem xac minh ve vu nem bom o Ha-noi nam 1913," on the basis of official French records left in Hanoi after 1954, points out that some of the people rounded up were former participants in the Dong Kinh Nghia Thuc, with the authorities apparently having used the assassinations as convenient pretext.

28. NB, pp. 154–158. TP, pp. 159–163. CMCD-3, pp. 81–82.

29. TP, p. 163. NB, p. 159, indicates that Phan Boi Chau prevailed upon Cuong De to undertake this mission. However, Cuong De almost certainly was in Singapore or south Vietnam during the period in question. Georges Boudarel believes that Nguyen Thuong Hien may have made the trip to Peking. See his note 153 in Phan Boi Chau, "Memoires," *France-Asie/Asia* Fall/Winter 1968, p. 151. Regarding results from such an intercession, we know only that the Chinese government did at least protest to France the arrest in Hanoi and Haiphong of Chinese nationals allegedly affiliated with "Annamite revolutionaries." AOM A-50 NF 451, carton 32.

30. "Phuc bat trung lai, hoa vo don chi." NB, pp. 160–161, 103–112. TP, pp. 163–164, 108–115.

it tells something about the attitudes and commitments at that time of the classes other than the scholar-gentry. It began with a very young mystic named Phan Phat Sanh, who traveled from Vietnam to Siam as a fortune-teller. By mid-1911, with two accomplices, he had founded a secret society oriented around his claimed descent from King Ham Nghi of the Can Vuong resistance period. Taking on Buddhist robes, Phan began a leisurely pilgrimage through the six provinces of the Mekong delta, while his associates installed an elderly man whom they had come upon as a "living Buddha" in a village near Cho-Lon. Soon peasants and trades-people were flocking to his residence, making silver and gold offerings ranging as high as 1,500 piastres.[31] When the "living Buddha" unex-pectedly died in February 1912, his soul was enshrined in the family altar of a prominent follower, while Phan Phat Sanh's associates declared that the old man's last words were to establish Phan as emperor. This was done in October, in a ceremonial accession to the throne, with people flocking to kowtow and contribute and word circulating that Heaven had sent Phan, who now called himself Phan Xich Long or Hong Long (both meaning Red Dragon), to drive the French out of Vietnam. By that time Phan also apparently had a letter from Prince Cuong De "confirming" his royal descent.[32]

After the ceremonies, Phan was escorted to the That-Son (Seven Mountains) area in Chau-Doc, where a temple was being built by the peasants. A small restaurant in a nearby town served as a reception center for the temple, since the latter increasingly was being used to concentrate personnel, weapons, and explosives for an uprising. Temporal aspects of the final attack plan depended on a number of bombs constructed of can-

---

31. Viet Lam, "Mot it tai-lieu ve cuoc Khoi-nghia Phan Xich Long o Nam-ky nam 1913," pp. 19–20. A register was kept of contributions.

32. *Ibid.*, p. 20. Expensive accoutrements were made for the "emperor," including: a medallion inscribed "Phan Xich Long Hoang De" (Emperor Phan Xich Long); a royal seal with a dragon's head and the characters "Dai Minh Quoc, Phan Xich Long Hoang De, Thien tu" (Greater Ming State, Emperor Phan Xich Long, Son of Heav-en), in which the "Dai Minh" was either simply borrowed from local Chinese secret-society symbolism or was advanced as an added attraction to the many Ming emi-grant families in the area—perhaps both; a sword inscribed "Tien da hon quan, hau da loan than" (First strike the debauched king, next the traitorous officials); and a ring, inscribed "Dan Cong" (Popular Tribute). A brief check of sources on Chinese secret societies does not reveal identical regalia inscriptions. It may be noted, how-ever, that the sword and seal were also central to Hung society or Triad ritual. The third and most important member of Hung palladia, the censer, apparently did not appear in Phan Xich Long's paraphernalia. See J. S. M. Ward, *The Hung Society or the Society of Heaven and Earth* (London, 1926), vol. 3, pp. 6–19.

non shot, carbon, sulphur, and saltpeter, all wrapped together under Phan's supervision, since he claimed that his background as fortune-teller, mystic, and healer made him an expert. A royal proclamation was printed with wood blocks, stating Phan's intention to strike at the French and calling on market people to flee and to convert their colonial paper money into solid copper cash. On the night of March 23/24, 1913, the bombs were taken into Saigon and placed at strategic points, with proclamations tacked up nearby. All of the bombs failed to explode, however, and the march into town of several hundred participants on March 28, all dressed in white and fortified with potions to render them invisible, was a disaster, with large numbers being captured. Before a tribunal in November 1913, leaders publicly and clearly stated their intentions of overthrowing the French colonial regime; one hundred and four men were sentenced to varying terms in prison.

Such a traditionalist outbreak might be deemed insignificant, except when we recognize that it occurred among peasants and tradespeople living in an area that had been under direct assimilationist French rule for almost fifty years. The majority of Vietnamese, the peasants largely missing from this account, who were still out of contact with modern political and intellectual developments, were yet to be reckoned with by either the native elite or the foreign authorities.[33]

During the same months of 1913, Prince Cuong De had managed to slip into south Vietnam via Singapore and then on a French steamer to Saigon. Aboard ship he had hidden in the servants' quarters, the cabin boys all coming to suspect that his head bore a healthy price, yet none turning him in.[34] In Saigon Cuong De was aided in traveling to My-Tho by the daughter of Nguyen An Khuong. She had married a Frenchman and now took her métis son along in order to get by the checkpoints without incident. Around My-Tho and Cho-Moi, Cuong De met secretly with groups of civil servants and soldiers. To the latter he made a point of re-

---

33. Viet Lam, "Mot it tai-lieu," pp. 21, 30. CMCD-3, pp. 91-92. Vuong Hong Sen, *Sai-gon Nam Xua*, p. 175. Georges Coulet, *Les Sociétiés secrètes en terre d'Annam*, pp. 49–73, 202–207, 216–217, 265–270. AOM A-50 NF 28(1), carton 8.

34. CD, pp. 55–59. Interestingly, in Singapore Cuong De broached the idea of his stowing away to a cabin boy at dockside, whom he thought he could trust because his language was well salted with Buddhist expletives. En route, however, the Catholic majority among the cabin boys was about to turn Cuong De in until they chanced to hear him consoling himself privately with patriotic poems. The Catholics were also quite conscious politically—for example, they would recite to each other the poems of Mai Lao Bang, Phan Boi Chau's Catholic associate. They met together and decided to let Cuong De off the ship without trouble.

citing "Cac Chu Tap Binh!" (So You're in the Army!), the Dong Kinh Nghia Thuc poem about the ultimate ungratefulness of their French masters. While admitting that occasionally they thought of killing their French officers and noncommissioned officers, the soldiers also said that they were held back by the depressing knowledge that there was no movement among the people to support them and no national leader to provide direction. Worse yet, they knew that killing a few French in Vietnam would not prevent the enemy from drawing on its abundant human reserves in other parts of the world to get back at them. Cuong De had no answers for these arguments.

Moving on to Vinh Long, Cuong De's subsequent contacts were limited mostly to landlords, men anxious to do their duty by their monarch pretender, but also painfully aware that the French now knew of Cuong De's presence in the south and were combing the provinces for him. Soon Cuong De found the fearful landlords placing him in almost perpetual hiding, often aboard a small sampan, where he was unable to meet anyone, much less to lead any sort of resurgence in Cochinchina. In June 1913 he paid off a local compradore in order to board a ship illegally and return to Hong Kong. It was the last time he would see his homeland.[35]

The situation in south China at that point was hardly more favorable to Vietnamese activists than in the Cochinchina Cuong De had just left. After rashly attempting to make contact with Nguyen Than Hien and his comrades in the Hong Kong jail, Cuong De himself was thrown into solitary confinement. Getting out only with the timely aid of a large sum of money from southern supporters, Cuong De decided that this was the time to take a long trip to Europe.[36] Nguyen Than Hien and the others in jail were not so fortunate, being turned over by the British to the French authorities and shipped down to the Hanoi prison, which by then was quite overcrowded with political suspects and convicts. Becoming ill, Nguyen Than Hien was ignored by the prison authorities, even when on his behalf the other inmates raised a loud ruckus and refused to eat. Only when he was almost dead did they remove him to the prison infirmary, where in January 1914 he expired. Huynh Hung eventually was transferred to Conlon island, while at least three other members of this group, including Nguyen Quang Dieu, ended up in the prison colony of French Guiana.[37]

35. CD, pp. 60–72.
36. CD, pp. 73–81. Phan Boi Chau wrote that he also had long wanted to go to Europe and had been cultivating some German contacts when Cuong De received enough funds for both to go. But Cuong De left directly from Hong Kong without notifying Phan in Canton. TP, pp. 169–170. NB, pp. 164–166.
37. Nguyen Van Hau, *Chi Si Nguyen Quang Dieu*, pp. 43–51.

Do Chan Thiet[38] had earlier been sent by the Quang Phuc Hoi to Yunnan to organize a clandestine net aimed at utilizing the Hanoi-Yunnan railway as a regular communication and liaison axis. Recruitment proceeded well among Vietnamese railway workers, interpreters, and secretaries; some money was advanced by the German consulate at Mengtzu; and once again a few soldiers in Hanoi were willing participants. But as time came for action, starting with the transportation of some weapons into Tonkin and the establishment of a bomb factory, there turned out to be a Sûreté spy within the net. The French crackdown was total: Do Chan Thiet and perhaps as many as fifty associates were killed or captured in the first sweep; three more were caught much later at the pagoda outside Hanoi that was serving as their bomb factory; and twelve were taken off the train at Lao-Cai, most eventually being executed. By late 1914—which is to say, in the crucial opening months of World War I—the ambitious Yunnan net was a thing of the past. Whether anyone had taken seriously Liang Ch'i-ch'ao's advice in 1905 about planning and organizing on the premise of another major Franco-German conflict is unknown, but it is obvious that when that situation did arise Vietnam's anticolonial elements were not in a position to exploit it.

Meanwhile, Chinese friends of the Quang Phuc Hoi in south China were also rapidly losing ground, starting with Yuan Shih-k'ai's assassination of Sung Chiao-jen in March and culminating in the short-lived "second revolution" of July and August 1913. Phan Boi Chau had traveled up to Honan to meet a Chinese contact from his days in Japan, Chang Hui-tsuan, who had become powerful in the Honan military administration. But all his promises of support evaporated as Yuan Shih-k'ai aggressively dismissed military governors from their posts and extended the control of his Peiyang clique into the south of China. Returning to Kwangtung, Phan found the new governor, Lung Chi-kuang, openly hostile. Lung ordered the disbanding of the Chan Hoa Hung A Hoi and in January 1914 had Phan and Mai Lao Bang imprisoned. Whereas in his autobiography Phan claimed that his jailing resulted from personal intervention by Governor General Sarraut, who had visited Kwangtung in mid-1913, Lung may have jailed him just as well for his close ties with the previous Kwangtung governor. Subsequently, Lung may have held Phan for simple ransom or as a pawn in his occasional attempts to get French permission to use the Hanoi-Yunnan railway for attacks against

38. Phan Boi Chau refers to him as Do Co Quang (NB, pp. 161–162) or Dau Co Quang (TP, pp. 165–166). CMCD-3, pp. 83–84, however, indicates that this was in fact Do Chan Thiet, a former participant in the Dong Kinh Nghia Thuc.

his enemies in Yunnan. At any rate, Phan was in jail until 1917, when Lung himself had to flee Kwangtung, and released Phan en route.[39]

While in prison, Phan Boi Chau managed to maintain some contact with the outside world through the sympathetic Chinese cook, but he especially resented the absence of any liquor on the premises. As usual in periods of enforced inactivity, Phan wrote profusely, particularly commemorative essays and poems for comrades recently killed and his first, short autobiography, *Nguc Trung Thu* (Prison Notes).[40] This was written shortly after he entered jail, on the assumption that it might well be his last communication with his countrymen, his final will and testament, so to speak. As one Vietnamese commentator has stated, Phan put "all his blood and tears" into this work, making it almost as significant as literature as it was as history.[41] *Nguc Trung Tu* never circulated as widely as Phan's previous works, but today it provides an invaluable comparison with his longer autobiographical effort of two decades later.[42] While the latter is more thoughtful and consistent, as a historical document, it may in some cases represent a less precise reflection of Phan Boi Chau's earlier predisposition for passionate, activist commitment.

One of Phan's short T'ang-style poems also written at that time is today recognized as a classic amidst Vietnam's ever-increasing body of "prison poetry":

> *Cam Tac Trong Nha Tu Quang Dong*
> (Impressions in a Kwangtung Prison)
> Still the patriot, still the gentleman on the move,
> With legs tired out, I come to rest in prison.
> At once the homeless guest of the four seas,
> And a wanted man on all five continents.
> Extending my arms I grasp at benefits for my people,

39. TP, pp. 166–171, 177, 187–188. NB, pp. 163–167, 173–174, 184–185. Phan in early 1919 was also able to secure Mai Lao Bang's release.
40. Phan indicates he wrote commemoratives for Dang Thai Than, Nguyen Thanh, De Tham, Tai Sinh (?), and the members of the 1908 Hanoi poison plot. I have not been able to uncover copies. Phan also received word in jail of the captures of Luong Lap Nham, Tran Huu Luc, Hoang Trong Mau, Do Chan Thiet, Lam Duc Mau, Nguyen Trong Thuong, Tran Cao Van, and Thai Phien, all of whom were executed. TP, pp. 172–174. NB, pp. 168–170.
41. Preface to excerpt from *Nguc Trung Thu*, HT, pp. 443–446.
42. Tran Minh Thu, "Tu *Nguc Trung Thu* den *Phan Boi Chau Nien Bieu*." Chuong Thau, "Ve hai tap tu truyen cua Sao Nam." Both authors compare the historical value of *Nguc Trung Thu* and *Nien Bieu* (*Tu Phan*), as well as pointing out some discrepancies between them and detailing the publication histories of the two works. Both conclude that *Nguc Trung Thu* is somewhat more reliable for chronology, while *Nien Bieu* is more carefully organized and substantial in content.

Opening my mouth I laugh to drive away resentment.
While this body remains there is work to be done,
Who's to quake at the multiple dangers.[43]

Sometime during this period Phan Boi Chau also wrote a short polemical novel, *Hau Tran Dat Su* (Strange Story of the Latter Tran Dynasty).[44] The historical setting implied by the name was the time of struggle against Ming colonial rule, but the political implications of the book were quite contemporary. In accordance with Phan's conception of a multi-class struggle, local participants in "the party" included an embittered former mandarin, a royal cousin, a farmer, a buffalo herder, a ferryman, and several independent-minded, patriotic women. Phan stated the theme of the story in the preface:

We have heard that the sovereignty of a country can go and return, can be lost and recovered—but not through the efforts of a single person. Le Loi was simply a hero famous and celebrated above others, that's all. If it were not for the millions of unsung heroes who urged him on, helped him, then he would never have assumed his heroic form.[45]

A simple but powerful speech by Tinh, one of the party cadres, represented the core political message of *Hau Tran Dat Su*. After recalling ancient Chinese justifications for individual men and women's banding together against wild animals and the elements, Tinh switched abruptly away from tradition to Spencer's concepts of Social Darwinism. He explained that countries were formed when one of these small groups or lineages achieved physical domination over other such groups.[46] In such small-scale struggles for supremacy, individual prowess and intelligence were the critical factors. However, when one reached the level of struggle between countries, between nations (*quoc-gia*), then it was no longer individual capacity, but the ability or inability of great masses of people to mobilize that provided the margin between victory and defeat. It was all desperately serious, Phan argued through his character Tinh, since "those

43. There is a second stanza, but it essentially repeats the ideas in the first. The original is in *Nom*, 7-8 structure. Copies and annotations are in: Chu Dang Son, *Luan De ve Phan Boi Chau va Phan Chu Trinh*, pp. 45–53, 125; HT, pp. 442–443; The Nguyen, *Phan Boi Chau*, pp. 32–33.
44. Also known as *Trung Quang Tam Su*. Excerpt reprinted in VTCM, pp. 211–221. Discussed in VT, pp. 88–89, and VTCM, pp. 135–136.
45. VT, p. 89.
46. Note that Phan Boi Chau consciously chose to discard the ancient Chinese rhetoric on this question, whereby it was alleged that certain "sages" were raised above others because of their *moral* preeminence.

who are defeated must die, and in death they must face ethnic extermination (*diet chung*)."

The secret of avoiding that dismal fate, however, was for each individual to realize that love of self, happiness for oneself, was really only
meaningful and possible if one loved one's fellow countrymen (*dong bao*).
The same was true for individual families and lineages, since the existence
of animosities and divisions at that level would result in the land's being
filled with a lot of half-brothers (*di bao*), not full brothers, full countrymen.[47] Once people loved their fellow countrymen, it was the same as
loving their nation, and once they loved their nation, it was easy for
them to realize that they might have to sacrifice their personal welfare—
even their lives— for the greater good:

> As individuals we may die but our country will not be lost. If we die and
> our country remains, then the product of our labors, our children and
> grandchildren, our relatives, our reputations will remain and never be
> lost. . . . On the other hand suppose that our country is lost and we re-
> main. . . . Then we will be forced to endure the destinies of servile buffalo
> and horses. The product of our labors will be seized, our children and
> grandchildren will be despised by foreigners, our lineages, our beloved
> race will gradually be wiped out. The reputation we leave behind will be
> summarized in three words: "lost-country slaves" (*vong quoc no*).[48]

With Phan Boi Chau in jail, the responsibilities of leadership, such as
they were, fell to Nguyen Thuong Hien. We know, for example, that
shortly after the outbreak of World War I Nguyen Thuong Hien wrote
and printed a passionate exhortation for distribution inside Vietnam, titled
Khuyen Nguoi Nuoc (Advice to My Countrymen).[49] There briefly he
explained the immediate opportunities provided by German battle victories on the western front in Europe in August and September 1914 and
cited the efforts of the Turks, Egyptians, and Moroccans as tactical
models for anti-Allied movements. Ridiculing his own countrymen heavily, he demanded to know why Vietnam was still lingering in the dark:

> Perhaps only the descendants of Hong Bang have skulls without brains,
> bodies without guts? . . . We still kneel down, bow our heads, kow-tow to
> the French like gods, revere them like saints, slaves to them all our lives;
> and, worse yet, we pass this on to our children and grandchildren as well.
> We're really a bunch of incurable invalids, a hoard of weird animals sel-

47. This is a play on the original meaning of *dong bao*, that is, "brothers of the same
womb," as distinct from *di bao*, "brothers of different mothers."
48. VTCM, pp. 217–218.
49. HT, pp. 478–480.

dom seen in this world! Our blood is as abundant as water, our people as numerous as trees in the forest. Will we continue to stand around and stomach this shame forever?[50]

He concluded by appealing to his countrymen at all costs to avoid French conscription and monetary levies and refuse to shed Vietnamese blood and sweat stupidly on their behalf. This appeal, too, somewhat deemphasized external assistance to the anticolonial effort, being a call to "raise Vietnam's flag in the world at this time," alone if necessary.

Nguyen Thuong Hien, however, did not heed his own advice. His contacts with German and Austrian consulates in Bangkok produced seed money of 10,000 *baht*, with promises of much more if the Vietnamese engineered something that began really to hurt the French.[51] The money was used in ill-conceived attacks on French border posts, mere petty harassments that succeeded only in creating more dissension within the dwindling ranks of the Quang Phuc Hoi.[52] In April 1915 the French executed twenty eight men involved in such efforts around Phu-Tho. The Germans remained unimpressed, membership drifted away, and the French linked up with certain Chinese warlords and bandit groups to arrange the killing or capture of the remaining leaders.[53]

During World War I there were also numerous attempted risings or coups inside Vietnam, sometimes related to efforts of the Quang Phuc Hoi overseas but in no way coordinated with them. Contrary to general historical accounts which have been based largely on official French sources, there is reason to believe that discontent among the people continued unabated. Certainly there was no groundswell of support for the tricolor in its struggle against the Reich. The French did get at least 50,000 Indochinese to fight and serve in labor brigades in Europe, but often coercion was employed in the village-level "recruitment" of these men. Also, it was often among the native troops in Vietnam that rumors about the war

---

50. HT, p. 479.
51. The 10,000 *baht* figure is from TP, p. 175, NB, p. 172. AOM P-10 NF 608, carton 5, indicates that this may have been 10,000 piastres.
52. AOM B-51 NF 992, carton 103, contains detailed French intelligence reports on Vietnamese movements in China and Siam, especially between December 1914 and March 1915.
53. Those snared included Dang Tu Kinh, Hoang Trong Mau, and Le Duong (?). CMCD-3, pp. 84–86. Hoang Nam Hung, *Nam Muoi Nam Cach Mang Hai Ngoai*, pp. 76–80, describes the abortive attack on Ta-lung border fort (Cao Bang) in March 1915. Hoang claims the initiative came from the Kwangsi governor, Lu Jung-t'ing, who was aided substantially by the Germans. When the attacks failed, Lu allegedly grabbed four minor Vietnamese participants for token recompense to the French, but they all committed suicide before being turned over.

festered and disorders brewed. Unfortunately, the scholar-gentry leaders of less than a decade earlier had been either wiped out or physically removed from the scene; and no new leadership had yet emerged to focus this discontent. Brief descriptions of some of the more interesting outbreaks follow:

MAN HIGHLAND MINORITY RISINGS of 1914–1915 in the Yen-bay area: The long-term causes included sustained Nguyen dynastic and French administrative harassment and heavy taxation. The immediate causes were a series of bad harvests (1910–1912), a smallpox epidemic in 1913, and the return of several key leaders of an earlier uprising. By September 1914 there was an organization that claimed one thousand, four hundred members in five *tong* (hill cantons) armed with swords, spears, and banana knives. However, engagements in October against French-led units were disastrous for the *Man*, their hamlets being put to the torch and the families of holdout leaders being imprisoned. By April 1915 sixty-seven participants had been executed and several hundred had been sentenced to varying terms in jail, where some were to die.[54]

RISINGS IN COCHINCHINA in February 1916: In some ways this was simply a further indication of support for the mystic Phan Phat Sanh and his efforts toward monarchy, mentioned previously. This time, however, a loose coalition of secret organizations from many Mekong delta provinces appeared to be in existence. If there was an operational center, it was the Nui Cam pagoda in Chau Doc province, from which the enigmatic priest Bay Do moved out to provide spiritual support, liaison, and minimal coordination in planning the rising. Many participants appeared to retain at least a symbolic affiliation with Prince Cuong De, although there is no evidence to support assertions that he was the leader.[55]

The crux of the plan, such as it was, involved seizing the Saigon central prison. This would bring the release of Phan Phat Sanh and many other prisoners, not to mention providing a supply of firearms to replace some of their spears and machetes. In addition, the prison was one of the most visible and hated manifestations of oppressive French rule, and so its seizure was meant to be a signal and an impetus to a general uprising in Cochinchina.

On February 14, 1916, about three hundred men landed along the Saigon waterfront and moved in groups toward the prison, yelling slogans

54. Nguyen Lien, "Phong-trao Giap-Dan, hay la cuoc dau-tranh chong Phap (1913–14) cua nhan-dan cac dan-toc Man (Yen-bai)."
55. A governor general's report to the Minister of Colonies dated March 29, 1916, argues that Cuong De was the "chef occulte" of this rising, through his "most loyal partisans and most active agents in Cochinchina." AOM A-50 NF 28(2), carton 8. In CD, however, Cuong De makes no mention of this.

as they went. Several groups, however, ran into police armed with pistols and scattered back toward the piers when fired upon. Those who did make it to the prison found the gates effectively barred, so they, too, retreated in disarray. Nevertheless, many localities in the delta went ahead with planned activities. At Bien Hoa a revolt was attempted at the provincial jail. In Thu-dau-mot (Gia Dinh) a march on Saigon was organized, but was rapidly broken up. Ben Tre saw the local archives and registers destroyed, Chinese shops burned, and a march by villagers. The last was stopped by ambuscade, after which the participants retreated and turned on any Vietnamese collaborators they could find. At Vung Tau (Cap Saint-Jacques) an armed group attempted without success to seize the military post. In Vinh Long the Nghia Hoa society led a grievance march on the office of the French administrator. A group from Can Tho which was supposed to join them was forcibly dispersed, however, before getting under way. A bomb was discovered in My Tho, while in Long Xuyen certain houses were ransacked and individuals held for ransom. Finally, in Tay Ninh a sparsely armed unit, led by "General" Vuong Van Le circulated conspicuously through several villages.[56]

The French community in Cochinchina was thoroughly shaken by these events and demanded full-scale repression. Many hundreds of Vietnamese were rounded up frantically, and summary justice was meted out by a French War Council. In the end, fifty one persons were executed and an unknown number imprisoned. There were some unfavorable reactions in metropolitan France and some bureaucratic differences of opinion in Saigon about this heavy-handed response to the situation, but the psychology of the local colons was such that their will prevailed.[57]

TRAN CAO VAN and the Duy Tan plot: As indicated earlier, the royal court at Hue from 1885 onward was an obedient if sometimes sullen instrument of French colonial rule. King Dong Khanh, who reigned from 1885 to 1889, epitomized the more tame, susceptible court elements, but he died early. His successor, Thanh Thai, did not reach maturity (eighteen) until 1897, after which he began to vaguely disturb the résident supérieur with his erratic behavior and his attitude toward a life he sensed was a gross mockery of his ancestors. There always remained a hostile minority undercurrent at court, increasingly circumscribed, yet still hoping and scheming. In September 1907 the French felt it best to replace Thanh Thai with his seven-year-old son, who took the reign name of Duy Tan.[58] By early 1916 a few anti-French scholar-gentry were cultivat-

56. Coulet, *Les Sociétiés*, pp. 158–167, 181–187, 212–215, 235–239, 315–341.
57. AOM A-50 NF 28(2), carton 8.
58. Since Duy Tan's reign name involves the same characters used in the covert organizational title of the Duy Tan Hoi, two interesting and perhaps complementary

ing the young monarch's inquisitive, independent nature for their own ends, and the stage was set for an elaborate, if ill-conceived, attempt at overthrowing the French in Thua Thien, Quang Nam, and Quang Ngai provinces.

It will be remembered that Tran Cao Van was one of the scholar-gentry leaders sent to Con-lon island after the tax demonstrations of 1908. In 1913 he was returned to Hoi-An and, through the intervention of two mandarin friends in Hue, was released just in time to be at his father's deathbed. Soon Tran was in contact with a small Quang Ngai group that maintained liaison through Siam with the Quang Phuc Hoi. The idea developed of arranging risings in central Vietnam to coincide with the planned Quang Phuc Hoi strikes along the China border, already described. Nothing really materialized in the center, however, except that Tran Cao Van, Thai Phien,[59] and a few others approached court dissidents and sought ways to tap the more general fears of Vietnamese military recruits being gathered in camps before sailing for the war in Europe. Rumors were already circulating among those men concerning torpedoed troop ships and heavy battle casualties, and the Hue camp was reported to be particularly volatile.[60]

Tran Cao Van arranged a secret meeting with Duy Tan by bribing the king's driver, thus managing to gain Duy Tan's complete agreement to a coup and even the use of the royal seal on secret orders to participants. This maneuver enabled the plotters to expand their following considerably. Small armed teams were organized to seize strategic points in Hue, Quang Nam, and Quang Ngai, the plan being for the king to flee the palace, signal assaults on the French with artillery rounds and elephant screams, and issue a royal order proclaiming a general uprising.[61] An effort was even made, apparently unsuccessfully, to cultivate the German-born commander of the Mang-ca colonial garrison in Hue. Several days before implementation of the plot, however, a mandarin in Quang Ngai who sensed trouble forced a minor participant into confessing whatever he knew. This was passed on to the résident supérieur in Hue, who then noticed an

---

hypotheses arise: (a) some high-ranking mandarin(s) sympathetic to the Duy Tan Hoi had a role in choosing the reign name; (b) the French résident supérieur and his closest Vietnamese collaborators had not uncovered, by September 1907, the actual title of the anticolonial group formed by Nguyen Thanh, Phan Boi Chau, and others.

59. Pseudonym, Nam Xuong. VNDN, p. 315.

60. Hanh Son, *Cu Tran Cao Van*, pp. 78–79. CMCD-3, pp. 96–98.

61. The go-ahead was to be passed south by means of a huge signal fire on the Hai-Van pass, a technique often used much later by the National Front for Liberation (NFL) in the same general area. There also were vague plans of setting up a resistance capital at Qui Nhon and seizing Da Nang, so that Germany could disembark supplies. Phan Boi Chau, "Mémoires," notes 145, 163.

inordinate number of soldiers' families leaving Hue for home. In Quang Nam the résident turned up rumors of planned seizures of several local forts.

The results were the immediate locking up of native troops' firearms, their confinement to barracks, and the extraction of more details from several plotters charged with arousing recruits in the Hue camp. Amazingly, Tran Cao Van and other leaders remained unaware of this abrupt turn of events and went ahead on the night of May 2/3, 1916, with spiriting Duy Tan out of the palace. Failing to hear signals setting other parts of the plan into action, most groups not already confined simply dispersed, the exception being some soldiers at Tam-Ky (Quang Nam), who killed several Frenchmen before they were overpowered by Legionnaires. Duy Tan's flight into the mountains was too slow, and the entire group was caught at a Buddhist temple south of Hue. Tran Cao Van, Thai Phien, and four others were executed; many lesser participants were sent to the Lao-bao penal colony or to assorted prisons. Duy Tan was dethroned and shipped to Réunion island in the Indian Ocean with his already deposed father Thanh Thai.[62]

The Duy Tan plot was in many ways a romantic aberration, the last strictly monarchist anticolonial effort deserving of any mention. Tran Cao Van and Thai Phien were more like the Can Vuong leaders of twenty-five years earlier than the men of their own generation who had led the Dong Du and Dong Kinh Nghia Thuc movements. Rather than pondering problems of modern technology and modern values, Tran Cao Van lived and died amidst a traditional Confucian ethos of righteousness and personal loyalty, with overtones of mysticism and fortune-telling.

Lest we forget, however, that ethos remained residually significant among the village people of Vietnam for a long time after 1916. The Duy Tan plot had nothing approaching mass participation, but, then again, that was hardly the intention of the traditionalist plotters. What impressed the people was the mere symbolic act of royal resistance, and failure. In this context it should be recognized that three of the five Vietnamese monarchs reigning between 1885 and 1926 were forcibly deposed by the French and banished overseas.[63] Duy Tan's abrupt departure in 1916 showed the people, in case it had slipped their minds, just how completely a creature of the foreigner the court and mandarinate had become. But in another, outwardly contradictory respect, I believe it also represented intimate, direct communication between king and commoner, telling the

62. Hanh Son, *Cu Tran Cao Van*, pp. 80–99. CMCD-3, pp. 98–100.
63. Ham Nghi, to Algeria; Thanh Thai and Duy Tan, to Réunion. The other two were Dong Khanh, whose collaboration with the French was apparently willing, but brief; and Khai Dinh, who reigned between 1916 and 1925.

latter that their seemingly parochial tribulations at the hands of the foreigner were part of a much larger pattern. In short, a fifteen-year-old king had made a small but spiritually significant gesture; taken together with other acts of resistance in traditional mold, it gave villagers some sense of continuing perspective and moral sustenance toward the day when all wrongs could be righted.

THE THAI NGUYEN UPRISING (August through December 1917): Objectively, this was the most serious outbreak during World War I, although it too was suppressed without significantly upsetting French military arrangements in the colony. The general Thai Nguyen area, it will be remembered, already had a tradition of resistance under such men as De Tham. In 1917 it was governed by Résident Darles, a man of particularly brutal instincts in the eyes of the native soldiers, the convicts in Thai Nguyen prison, and the people at large. The most prominent political prisoner there was Luong Lap Nham, then calling himself Luong Ngoc Quyen, son of the Dong Kinh Nghia Thuc principal, an early student at the Shimbu Military Academy in Tokyo, and a Quang Phuc Hoi activist until his capture in Hong Kong in 1915. Some time early in 1917 Luong found out that Trinh Van Can,[64] one of the Vietnamese sergeants in the local colonial garrison, possessed considerable experience operating in the Thai Nguyen terrain and for several years had been contemplating an uprising with some of his associates. Luong's impressive overseas experience, plus his assurance that Quang Phuc Hoi units in China would send substantial aid the minute even one uprising was sparked in Vietnam, turned the discussions of these soldiers from simple barracks-room fantasizing and toward active preparations.[65]

Their first plot aborted without compromising the participants in May 1917. In July they prepared to strike on the fourteenth—Bastille Day— the plan being to have a number of troopers secretly load their weapons before the parade and turn them against the small French contingent. For some reason this striking idea was dropped. Vietnamese people in town by then had wind of what was going on, but the Sûreté apparently was underdeveloped in that relatively distant district. Finally, however, the plotters were forced into resolute action by rumors that some of them were about to be transferred. On the night of August 30/31 they killed the French commander of the native garrison and his Vietnamese deputy, but not without a single ill-disciplined discharge of a weapon that tipped off the smaller, strictly French garrison down the road. They also impru-

64. Pseudonyms, Doi Can (Sergeant Can), Trinh Van Dat. Yen-nhien village, Vinh-tuong prefecture. VNDN, p. 356.
65. CMCD-3, pp. 100–105. Dao Trinh Nhat, *Luong Ngoc Quyen*, pp. 67–71.

dently neglected to inactivate the telegraph office, enabling several French soldiers to leave their posts and send a wire to Hanoi. A group of insurgents did manage anyway to move on the prison, killing the French warden and his wife and releasing all political and common criminals. Some of these were unable to walk fast or far because their legs had been deformed by the shackles or were incapacitated by their long inactivity, particularly Luong Ngoc Quyen who had been in solitary confinement.

A few Vietnamese soldiers elected to leave their weapons and head for home, but more than a hundred remained to fight. Approximately two hundred political prisoners and some local townspeople were hastily organized and armed. That night a long, confusing strategy meeting ensued, with several of De Tham's old comrades arguing for quick thrusts against posts in nearby provinces (Phuc-Yen, Bac-Giang, and Bac-Can), counting on tactical surprise to befuddle the French and inspire local troops to join them. Luong, however, favored a careful defense of Thai-Nguyen, hoping to make it a base for a prolonged struggle and perhaps actually expecting timely help from Quang Phuc Hoi remnants along the China border. Sergeant Trinh Van Can sided with Luong, which settled the debate for the troopers, but left some of the political prisoners rancorous.[66]

Hanoi had news of the revolt by two in the morning, and countermoves were under way only hours later, in particular, the mobilization of a heavily armed column to advance from Do-son against Thai Nguyen. Fighting began September 2, with heavy casualties on both sides for a few days.[67] Sergeant Trinh Van Can ordered a staged withdrawal, but many squads which did not get the word at all or got it too late, were cut down or forced to surrender. Luong was killed, and there were numerous civilian casualties in the town, as the French laid down artillery before reentering. With resistance remnants now unsettled about their next course, Trinh Van Can elected to follow De Tham's precedent and hole up in the hills. Although more than one hundred reached the temporary sanctuary of the Tam-Dao mountain spur, some enmity or treachery killed a number of others. Steadily the French moved to block likely escape routes and to pressure peasants in the lowlands to keep food away from the insurgents. Unlike De Tham before them, these resisters had few family, district, or historical ties with the local people; hence, it was not surprising that hawkers in local markets packed up and fled the minute they saw strange Vietnamese faces seeking provisions. By Septem-

66. CMCD-3, pp. 103–110. Dao Trinh Nhat, *Luong Ngoc Quyen*, pp. 76–86, has translations of two proclamations issued by the insurgents.
67. According to French reports, 107 were killed in action on the colonial side, and 56 were killed and 85 captured on the anticolonial side. Cited in CMCD-3, p. 111.

ber 19 the main remaining group was fleeing across the Hanoi-Yunnan rail line near Vinh-Yen and on south to the Red river, where they hoped to find a way across into the mountains to the southwest. But the French were ready with gunboats, and a series of engagements cut the insurgents into small groups, most of which then made it back to the Tam-Dao area and dug in for a sustained, if hopeless, defense.[68]

French authorities sought out and rounded up parents, wives, and children of the remaining insurgents, the news of which led some to surrender. With the end in sight, Trinh Van Can committed suicide in January, and two of his three remaining comrades surrendered. Apparently intent upon convincing the Vietnamese populace—and especially the colonial soldiers—that revolt was futile, the French were extremely meticulous in trying to capture or kill every single rebel soldier and political escapee; in the end they claimed that only five men had eluded their ultimate "justice." For all that, however, the legends of Sergeant Trinh Van Can's high moral leadership, of the discipline of troopers amidst terrible privation, of the hasty wedding of "Trooper 1,035" to a village chief's daughter after which both marched off, weapons in hand, to their deaths several weeks later—such emotional contributions of the Thai-Nguyen uprising also eluded French "justice," spreading among the people of north Vietnam during the next decade at about the time a new generation was coming forth to try to do successfully what their predecessors had done poorly, albeit bravely.[69]

Meanwhile, Prince Cuong De, who by his own admission was ambling without much purpose through Europe just before the war, received a letter from several Vietnamese in Peking to the effect that Tuan Ch'i-jui, Yuan Shih-k'ai's military henchman and minister of war, was open to proposals for anti-French operations. Cuong De's subsequent meeting with Tuan in the summer of 1914 did reveal the latter's at least theoretical interest in striking at the French, believing that they were the weakest of the imperialist powers threating China. Yuan Shih-k'ai himself made vague promises of a large sum of money for Cuong De in the future, but at the time he wanted nothing to disrupt his negotiations for loans from those same Frenchmen. With the outbreak of war in Europe, there was talk by Tuan of hitting the French while they were preoccupied. But then came the aggressive Japanese moves in Shantung province and, worse yet,

68. French records state that 80 got to Tam-Dao in early October; they were reduced to 40 by late November, to 29 in December, and to 4 in January 1918. Cited in CMCD-3, pp. 119-122.
69. CMCD-3, pp. 110-130. Dao Trinh Nhat, *Luong Ngoc Quyen*, pp. 73-75, 87-103. Nguyen Quynh, *Doi Can Khoi Nghia*.

Japan's comprehensive Twenty-One Demands of January 1915. All promises to Vietnam were forgotten.

So, Cuong De decided to go back to the all-powerful Japanese. There he found at least seven young Vietnamese studying under Chinese aliases at various Japanese schools, apparently with the full knowledge of Inukai, Kashiwabara, and the Interior Ministry. In a meeting with Inukai, he supposedly was told that if France was defeated in Europe, Japan would help Vietnam gain its independence. More ominously, he was told that Japan would not in any case allow Indochina to fall into the hands of a third power; specifically, Inukai counseled Cuong De not to accept German offers of assistance. Just to sweeten the pot, Inukai began subsidizing Cuong De with 100 yen per month, a practice continued regularly until the assassination of Inukai in 1932.[70]

In March 1919 Cuong De and a few students sent telegrams to the Versailles peace conference, to President Wilson, and to the French government, calling for an autonomous Indochina. They also wrote a petition for publication in a Japanese-subsidized newspaper in Peking, *Ta Kung Pao*, as well as in a local paper in Tientsin. Aside from the temporary international embarrassment of having Vietnamese publicize their displeasure at French rule, some French administrators were convinced that certain Japanese politicians were implicated in these activities, that the petition was a manifestation of a new Pan-Asian anticolonial league in China, and that it was dangerous reading for the Vietnamese members of the French military garrisons in Peking and Tientsin.[71] The result was immediate pressure on the Japanese government, including meetings of the French ambassador with the Japanese foreign minister and the dispatch to Tokyo of a ranking member of the French Political Service Bureau.

Ultimately, they worked out a mutually acceptable arrangement, whereby the French would provide information on Korean nationalists in their Shanghai settlement if the Japanese would keep Cuong De under surveillance, would prevent him from going to another country, and perhaps

70. Several years after 1915 the subsidy was increased to 150 yen. CD, pp. 88–96, 127. In 1929 Cuong De also stated that during almost a quarter century of overseas activity he had received a total of less than 30,000 piastres from supporters inside Vietnam—hardly sufficient to promote anything but the most limited of political objectives. The average high-ranking French colonial bureaucrat of that period, for example, received a salary of from 5,000 to 10,000 piastres per year. VTCM, pp. 18–19; 24.
71. A telegram from the Foreign Affairs Ministry even advocated withdrawing all "Annamites" from the "corps of occupation" in China and inspecting their baggage thoroughly upon their arrival home. It is unclear whether this was actually ordered. AOM A-50 NF28(4).

would forward periodic accounts of his activities.[72] From that point, Cuong De did little more than wait around in Tokyo for the Japanese to fulfill what he conceived to be their bargain with him. Early in 1945, when the Japanese occupation forces in Indochina finally decided to overturn the French colonial administration, it almost seemed that Cuong De's moment of triumph had arrived. But the Japanese military passed him by and chose Bao Dai as their figurehead; Cuong De died in 1951, still an exile.[73]

Phan Boi Chau, upon his release from jail in 1917, quickly went to Shanghai and then to Hangchow to avoid Sûreté agents in the Canton area and to rejoin Nguyen Thuong Hien. Receiving a letter from Tran Huu Cong in Tokyo mentioning rumors of secret talks between the German and Japanese governments, Phan traveled to Japan to see what could be done. Apparently finding nothing to put his hopes in there, he returned to China and made contact with the German consulate in Peking. But by then the tiny Quang Phuc Hoi apparatus was heavily infiltrated with Sûreté agents, so that one of the key Vietnamese involved in these contacts was grabbed in Tientsin's British concession and turned over to the French.[74] Completely disgusted with failures in Japan and China, Phan in 1918 decided to head back to Vietnam. His trip through south China, however, was badly complicated by the intense civil conflict then under way; at one point, for example, Phan was saved from summary execution by the chance intervention of a Chinese associate from the old days in Japan. Then, to his deep dismay, in Kweichow Phan read of the armistice in Europe. His plans, such as they were, had been premised on the war's continuing for several years. Demoralized and penniless, Phan turned back toward Chungking and down the river to Hangchow.[75]

Given the dismal working record of Phan Boi Chau and other activists during this period, it is at first surprising to read through the colonial archives and discover that French administrators in Indochina took all these episodes with the utmost seriousness—more so, it would seem, than they did the events of 1908. Until 1914 it is likely that this stemmed largely from their observation of developments in China, which brought the fear that Indochina might somehow get embroiled. After August 1914 this factor, while not eliminated, was certainly overshadowed by the implica-

---

72. AOM A-50 NF 28(4). Nagaoka Shinjiro and Kawamoto Kunie, *Betonamu Bo-kokushi*, pp. 275–277. The latter also provides considerable data on Cuong De's life after 1919.

73. Quoc Quang, "Gop y kien ve Cuong De." Hong Chuong, "Cuong De."

74. TP, pp. 177–179. NB, pp. 174–177. Phan names the intermediary as Le Ap Ton and says that he later died in jail. Phan also alleged that the man who betrayed him was a Yunnanese friend of Phan Ba Ngoc, who received 3,000 piastres for it.

75. TP, pp. 179–187. NB, pp. 177–183.

tions of war in Europe. Perhaps not wishing to be left out, local Frenchmen spent a great deal of time and energy maintaining surveillance over the natives, checking out all hints of German involvement in Vietnamese resistance movements, and talking about revolutionary threats to their existence. Knowing also that the metropole could provide little or no assistance if a serious threat did emerge, they reacted with particular violence and brutality against even the most inchoate indications of anticolonial sentiment.

Except for several brief trips to Japan and some journeys to Peking, Phan Boi Chau stayed in Hangchow for five years. One of his closest Chinese friends, Hu Yu-lan, was on the Chekiang governor's staff, and through him Phan secured a job writing for a local official journal, *Ping-shih Tsachih.* There Phan did something that has puzzled many Vietnamese ever since. Acting on the advice of Le Duc[76] and Phan Ba Ngoc and on their second-hand information regarding Albert Sarraut's Franco-Vietnamese collaboration policy, Phan Boi Chau wrote an essay cautiously praising the idea.[77] This was taken back by Phan Ba Ngoc to Vietnam and shown to the French authorities. The outcome was that Phan Ba Ngoc escorted to Hangchow a French representative, who allegedly offered Phan Boi Chau a high position in the court at Hue if he would publicly disavow all his previous "revolutionary doctrines." Phan rejected this in a letter to the governor general, but the French were still able to publicize his essay widely, to their definite advantage. Phan came to regret this episode deeply.[78]

---

76. Pseudonym, So Cuong. A steady writer in Pham Quynh's *Nam Phong* group. VNDN, p. 98.

77. Titled "Phap Viet De Hue Luan" (A Discussion of Franco-Vietnamese Collaboration). I have not been able to secure a copy of it.

78. TP, pp. 187–191. NB, pp. 183–188. Chuong Thau, "Anh huong cua Phan Boi Chau doi voi mot so to chuc cach mang Trung Quoc," p. 34. Nguyen Thuong Huyen, "Cu Phan Boi Chau o Hang-Chau," pp. 29–32. Phan Boi Chau cited as a partial excuse for his writing "Phap Viet De Hue Luan" the fact that Sarraut was a Radical-Socialist and clearly had said things no previous governor general dared to say. There was also Phan Ba Ngoc's "tactical" argument that writing such a conciliatory essay would alleviate French suspicions and perhaps allow members of Quang Phuc Hoi to circulate in and out of the country. By and large, communist and other activist nationalist historians in Vietnam have treated "Phap Viet De Hue Luan" either as a bad mistake or else have explained it away with elaborate, rather unconvincing theoretical discussions. On the other hand, reformists have hailed it as Phan Boi Chau's ultimate admission of the validity of Phan Chu Trinh's doctrine. Others, like Nguyen Duc Quynh, a Trotskyite leader and belated Viet-Minh participant, feel certain that Phan Boi Chau wrote this essay in painfully honest recognition of the error of his early attempts to get help from Japan, China, and Germany—all of them, countries which would prove to be as dangerous to Vietnam as France itself. Interview with Nguyen Duc Quynh in Saigon, April 24, 1967.

At the time, however, we may surmise that Phan Boi Chau's deep depression, his feeling of having accomplished absolutely nothing in more than one decade, left him open to such personal entreaties. After all, Phan Ba Ngoc was the son of the revered Phan Dinh Phung and had been with Phan Boi Chau almost from the beginning. Other Quang Phuc Hoi leaders, however, particularly Nguyen Thuong Hien and Cuong De, had been outraged by Phan Ba Ngoc's role in this and other affairs and by now considered him a traitor. In 1922 Cuong De gave a pistol to a young activist who was able to travel to Hangchow and kill Phan Ba Ngoc.[79]

In 1920, on the eve of one of his trips to Peking, Phan Boi Chau read a Japanese study of Russian communism and was so fascinated that he translated the entire work into Chinese. Through Ts'ai Yuan-p'ei, chancellor of National Peking University, Phan secured an introduction to two representatives of the Soviet Union. Asking about the possibility of Vietnamese students' going to the Soviet Union, Phan was strongly encouraged to send some on, with the frank stipulation, however, that they accept communist ideology and work for a socialist revolution and the establishment of a worker-peasant government when they returned home.[80] We have no evidence that Phan followed through on this, but someone residing with him several years later, recalls that he was intrigued by Lenin and Trotsky, reading about them through all available Chinese sources.[81] In 1924 Phan wrote in favor of a social revolution which would involve the increasingly alert workers and peasants, but led by a highly conscious elite. He spoke of a "mass ideological awakening" and cited with awe the ability of European, American, and Chinese laborers to strike en masse, their employers or government troops being able to beat down a few, but never "many millions."[82] In a publication titled *Thien Ho De Ho* (Oh Heaven! Oh God!), Phan stressed French exploitation of Christian gospel to colonize distant areas and "exterminate foreign races," giving particular attention to colonial educational and legal policies.[83] It is apparent, in short, that Phan kept in touch with contemporary intellectual currents, although his only activist contribution during this time was to provide financial sup-

79. TP, pp. 195-196. NB, pp. 192-193. CD, pp. 101-109. Cuong De may have been especially angry because he too had once been persuaded by Phan Ba Ngoc to write letters to Sarraut and Khai Dinh. See also AOM A-50 NF 28(4), carton 8.

80. TP, pp. 192-193. NB, pp. 189-190. Phan Boi Chau, "Mémoires," p. 181, n. 178.

81. Nguyen Thuong Huyen, "Cu Phan Boi Chau," p. 36.

82. Phan Boi Chau, *Tuong Trung Nu Vuong/Truyen Pham Hong Thai* (Hanoi, 1967), pp. 129-132. See Chapter 10.

83. This was printed in the French concession of Shanghai in 1923, apparently as a sort of limited-circulation petition for assistance from high Chinese sources. Japanese translation, Oiwa Makoto, *Annan Minzoku Undoshi Gaisetsu*, pp. 127-170. See also Chuong Thau, "Ve hai tap," p. 35.

port to some Vietnamese students overseas, including one in Germany to whom Phan sent regular remittances.[84]

Meanwhile, what of the many scholar-gentry who had been sent to Con-lon island in 1908 and 1909?[85] Some, like Nguyen Thanh, were doomed to die there. Others, like Huynh Thuc Khang, somehow survived the mosquitoes, the bad water, the physical neglect, and the mental torpor for ten or more years and emerged to live out the remainder of their lives in varying degrees of political and intellectual frustration. Still others indicated to the French authorities within the first few years that they had "learned their lesson" and were permitted to return to the mainland either to live under judicial surveillance in isolated towns or to collaborate in some capacity with the colonial regime. Finally there was Phan Chu Trinh, always the individualist, who, benefiting from direct intervention by the French League for the Rights of Man in 1911, left for France on the same ship as retired Governor General Klobukowski, refusing to collaborate, yet unable in fourteen years in Paris to advance his reformist proposals a single step.

What sort of island this Con-lon, turned into a prison island decades earlier by the French and destined to become a deadly symbol of anti-colonial resistance for at least three generations of Vietnamese? The tropical climate and vegetation are similar to those of the provinces of the lower Mekong delta 90 kilometers to the northwest, except that the hills on Con-lon cut off the cooling monsoon breezes from parts of the island—naturally, the places where "incorrigible" political prisoners often were forced to live and work. A generally dull diet deficient in protein was enlivened, if one was fortunate, with fish, shrimp, or turtles. Trusties (nonpolitical) were used to man small fishing boats, in charge of a French guard who was required to report directly to the prison director; the better parts of each catch were turned over to the guards, who presented the delicacies to the wardens, who in turn gave the most treasured parts to the director's cook. The director's residence was ideally placed to receive the breezes, had abundant lawns and vegetable gardens, and displayed two Louis XVI cannons out in front, which had been brought to the island more than a century earlier by the Bishop of Adran. A few Chinese and indigenous merchants were barely tolerated on the island, but the nonprison population was mainly made up of civil servants, guards, and soldiers, both French

84. Nguyen Thuong Huyen, "Cu Phan Boi Chau," pp. 29–39. The author, a nephew of Nguyen Thuong Hien, stayed with Phan in Hangchow for more than one year. He has interesting descriptions also of Phan's strict daily regimen of meditation, reading, writing, and extensive walking through the historic beauties of Hangchow.

85. VTCM, p. 124, estimates "several hundred" political prisoners on Con-lon in the period up to 1921, but does not indicate how many were scholar-gentry.

and native. Those prisoners attempting to escape had first to build rafts and then to face a profusion of sharks and perverse breezes. Their chances were not good.[86]

When the scholar-gentry first arrived on Con-lon, they were put in with the common, lower-class criminals. They soon formulated petitions, however, requesting separate quarters—understandable, given their backgrounds, but hardly in keeping with their speeches on national unity and their alignment with the downtrodden. A few of the more famous scholar-gentry, like Phan Chu Trinh, were allowed to live in huts away from the main prison compounds. In the early years, nevertheless, all had to participate in the two prime prison occupations of breaking up rocks for building roads and a jetty, and seeking out, cutting, and transporting wood of various grades for use in the charcoal, limestone, and cooking furnaces.[87] Work on the rockpile inspired one of Phan Chu Trinh's most famous poems:

> *Dap Da o Con-lon* (Breaking Rocks on Con-lon)
> As a man standing upright on Con-lon,
> I can bring mountains crashing down in pieces.
> With my hammer I shatter heap after heap,
> All my strength producing hundreds more stones,
> Day in, day out I make light of my exhausted body,
> In rain or shine my heart never fails.
> In temporary setback, those who mend the sky,
> Do not let minor things get them down![88]

Scholars on Con-lon composed such poems to pass the time, to find common solace, and to keep their sanity. There was something of a tradition of jail literature in China, and Vietnamese literature was not without precedents.[89] With the nature of prison existence and the meager amount of news filtering in from the mainland, the poems tended to repeat old views and personal commemorations rather than anything new or sub-

---

86. Tran Van Que, *Con-lon Quan Dao* (Saigon, 1961), pp. 7–68. The author was imprisoned on Con-lon during World War II. See also, Le Gouverneur General de L'Indochine, *Recueil des Arrêtés du 17 Mai 1916*, for ten decrees regulating the Indochina penal system.

87. Tran Van Que, *Con-lon Quan Dao*, pp. 68–111. The author indicates that from 1930 on, positions of "ordinary" and political prisoners began to reverse, with the latter now receiving the worst, most perverse treatment.

88. HT, p. 545. Tran Van Que, *Con-lon Quan Dao*, p. 103. The Nguyen, *Phan Chu Trinh*, pp. 30–31. Hoang Xuan, *Phan Chu Trinh Thi-tap*, p. 22. Chu Dang Son, *Luan De ve*, pp. 110–111. VTCM, p. 297.

89. VTCM, p. 117, mentions Cao Ba Nha, Doan Trung, Cao Ba Quat, and Hoang Phan Thai.

stantial.[90] But their inquisitive spirit never diminished, whether it meant debating on various Western historical figures or imagining themselves as traveling to Japan, Europe, and the United States. Sometimes they could also make effective new political statements, as when Huynh Thuc Khang wrote feelingly about three Vietnamese Catholic priests who had participated in Phan Boi Chau's activist network and had been arrested and shipped to Con-lon with the rest of them.[91]

In their spare hours many reformist scholar-gentry on Con-lon also took to studying French for the first time, both because of their continuing intellectual curiosity and, in some cases, as a step into the less rigorous prison jobs of clerks and secretaries. Activist scholar-gentry tended to deride this kind of thing, but no serious personal animosity appears to have developed because of it. For example, Nguyen Thanh, with Phan Boi Chau the very soul of activism, is known to have maintained warm relations with Huynh Thuc Khang, Dang Nguyen Can, Ngo Duc Ke, and other prominent reformist prisoners. When word came to the island that Nguyen Thanh's wife had died, they all wrote touching poems of consolation. Then came news of his daughter's death and final details on the destruction of the Dong Du movement in Japan. Deeply grieved and broken in health, Nguyen Thanh died in February 1912. Eulogies were written by many of his cellmates,[92] and Nguyen Thanh himself left behind a last, embittered poem:

> *Tuyet Menh Thi* (Poem of a Dying Man)
> Not one thing accomplished and my hair is graying,
> What right has this body to see its country again.
> Mending the sky has proven beyond my might, but talking is easy,
> Helping people I am powerless, but escaping life is also hard.
> Even if life changes as the cloud's hues, I don't mind,
> I only dread man's change of heart, as wave's ebb and flow.
> Eyes wide open, I view heaven and earth,
> Is it possible that ten years hence, the scene will be the same?[93]

Prison life for the scholar-gentry has been described in some detail by Huynh Thuc Khang.[94] Perhaps most important, each prisoner was able to

90. Twenty-four short poems and parallel sentences from Con-lon are reprinted in VTCM, pp. 296–310, 315–325, 340–343. The authors include Phan Chu Trinh, Huynh Thuc Khang, Ngo Duc Ke, Dang Nguyen Can, Dang Van Ba, Le Van Huan, Le Dai, Nguyen Thanh, and Nguyen Dinh Kien.
91. VTCM, pp. 308–310.
92. The Nguyen, "Chi Si Viet-Nam," pp. 38–43. Ngo Thanh Nhan, *Ngu Hanh Son Chi Si*, pp. 52–57.
93. HT, pp. 500–501. Ngo Thanh Nhan, *Ngu Hanh Son Chi Si*, p. 53. VTCM, p. 320.
94. Huynh Thuc Khang, *Tu Truyen*, pp. 34–41. See also VTCM, pp. 119–125.

send and receive letters once every three months, as well as occasional small packets of tobacco, tea, biscuits, paper, ink, and brushes from his family. Any money sent would be parceled out to the recipient, one piastre per month. Baths apparently were allowed only once a week. After studying French assiduously, Huynh in 1912 was given work in the director's office. During the regime of one rather clement director, he even was permitted to open a small store where political prisoners gathered to drink, gamble, and chat endlessly. In 1917, however, the lenient director was transferred, and it was back to the cellblocks for everyone.[95] In 1919 Huynh secured another office job, but was shifted back the next year to making tortoise-shell trinkets. He was released finally in 1921, along with three others. For the next few years he lived quietly at home, avoiding suspicion, turning down French offers of positions, and generally ignoring the world outside. Only in 1926 did he begin to take a small part in what the French considered the legitimate political affairs of Annam. Meanwhile, most scholar-gentry prisoners had been allowed to leave Con-lon, most of them choosing to bide their time and perhaps try to comprehend what had transpired during their long absence.[96]

Phan Chu Trinh was given preferential treatment by the French on Con-lon, perhaps because of his politics, more likely because his ideas and his reputation had reached the ears of high-level politicians back in the métropole. After the intervention of the League for the Rights of Man, Phan was called in to the prison director's office for careful questioning by the governor of Cochinchina, then on an inspection trip to Con-lon. There Phan seems to have disassociated himself again from the actions of Phan Boi Chau and to have reaffirmed his personal hopes for major reform under colonial aegis.[97] Shortly afterward he was transferred to the town of My-Tho, where he quickly protested the continuing restrictions on his activities and was allowed to leave for Paris. In Paris he apparently received a stipend from the French government (5,400 francs per year) for at least

95. The following year there was a mass attempt to overpower the guards, in which eighty-three prisoners were killed. Joseph Buttinger, *Viet-Nam*, p. 100. Since Huynh Thuc Khang makes no mention of this, we must assume that it was limited to the cellblocks of common criminals.

96. Of those men I have introduced previously in any detail, only a few really tried to pick up where they had left off. Ngo Duc Ke, returning with Huynh Thuc Khang in 1921, managed in the remaining eight years of his life to open a publishing house, edit a paper, and write extensively. See Chapter 10. Le Van Huan returned in 1917, joined the activist Phuc Viet Hoi (Restore Viet-Nam Society) in Ha Tinh and then the radical Tan Viet Cach Menh Dang (New Viet-Nam Revolutionary Party) in 1927. He was jailed again in 1929 and died soon after. HT, p. 595.

97. Huynh Thuc Khang, *Thi Tu Tung Thoai*, as quoted in The Nguyen, *Phan Chu Trinh*, pp. 31–33.

three years, or until he was thrown into Santé prison during the war as a draft resister and a possible sympathizer with Germany.[98]

While Phan Chu Trinh thus accepted some favors from the French, this never seemed to silence his independent, acidic tongue. Personal observation of bourgeois freedoms in France may indeed have made him more bitter than ever on the subject of colonial oppression in Vietnam. His prime aspiration then was to rouse public opinion in France to the vast discrepancy between French actions in Indochina and the grand French traditions of liberty, equality, and fraternity. In various articles in French periodicals Phan tried to explain the Vietnamese reformist programs of 1908 and bitterly, sarcastically attacked the colonial authorities for their ruthless reaction to the general ferment of that year. Citing a scholar who had been thrown into prison allegedly for teaching his students that "being at one with your countrymen is your first responsibility," Phan asked whether this meant that Vietnamese were not supposed to love each other, but rather to tear each other apart like dogs? And what were the implications, Phan asked, of courts punishing scholars for preaching "people's rights" (*dan quyen*)?

Why in the past have the colonial authorities always in their official speeches included resplendent promises, fancy but meaningless terms like equality, chivalry, civilizing benefits and many other flowery items? Better to speak bluntly as follows: "We conquered you people, you are our slaves, it is our convenience to use you as we desire. You have been put outside the family of humanity. You had better regard that as final."[99]

After writing of the death, starvation, and destruction meted out by the French in the wake of the 1908 tax demonstrations, Phan portrayed Vietnamese mothers praying before the altars of their husbands with tears streaming down their faces solemnly instructing their children:

You children should remember that it was the French colonial authorities that killed your father. Today is the anniversary of your father's death. You must never forget that when you grow up you also may have the same fate as your father.[100]

98. *Revue Indochinoise* (1916), p. 220. Huynh Thuc Khang, *Phan Tay Ho Tien Sinh Lich Su*, p. 28, states that the Ministry of Colonies provided the stipend. The author also infers that many former associates back on Con-lon felt that Phan had "sold out."
99. Phan Chu Trinh, "Les manifestations Annamites de 1908, une demande d'amnistie," *Bulletin Officiel de la Ligue des Droits de l'Homme*, vol. 12, no. 20, pp. 1161–1162. See also Truong Huu Ky, "Them mot so tai lieu ve cu Phan Chu Trinh," pp. 19–20.
100. Phan Chu Trinh, "Les manifestations," pp. 1171–1172.

While in Santé prison, Phan continued to write poetry and improve his French.[101] Phan's son, who had also gone to France, was allowed to visit twice a week. Once he received his baccalaureate, however, Phan instructed his son to return to Vietnam, where shortly afterward he died, probably of tuberculosis. In August 1915 Phan Chu Trinh was released from prison, apparently through the efforts of Marius Moutet, a French Socialist party leader, and a Captain Jules Roux.[102] From that point on Phan apparently received no further French stipends and lived very meagerly amidst the small Vietnamese student community, occasionally making money as a photo retoucher.[103]

Phan Chu Trinh's next significant political act was to write a vitriolic letter to King Khai Dinh, on the occasion of the latter's visit to the Marseilles Exposition in 1922. Calling it *That Dieu Thu* (Seven Point Letter), Phan charged Khai Dinh with seven "major crimes":

1. Enjoying the privileges of ruling rather than putting his subjects first, as instructed by Mencius. While Phan cited approvingly the constitutional monarchism of Meiji Japan, for Vietnam he appeared to favor the elimination of the throne. He also cited monarchs in various countries who had been overthrown and threatened Khai Dinh with execution or exile.

2. Favoritism, inequality of punishments, and rule by personal whim. Here again, Phan cited a historic case of a king who paid for such dereliction by being killed by his own people.

3. Favoring the kowtow. Phan recalled Governor General Beau's ordering the kowtow abandoned in 1906, but to no avail. Sarraut managed to have it dropped in public, but it was still used in court, as demonstrated by certain photographs, shown around the world. This publicity had caused civilized people to laugh at the Vietnamese, and for this Phan called Khai Dinh "stupid, ignorant" (*ngu*).

4. Immoral luxury. Money had been stolen from the people to provide

---

101. He had a Vietnamese cellmate, with whom he "split bread." See Phan's poem "Cam tac luc bi giam o Nguc Xang-te" (Impressions while jailed in Santé), HT, pp. 546-547. The Nguyen, *Phan Chu Trinh*, p. 39. Interestingly, most sources published in Saigon say Phan's cellmate was Nguyen Ai Quoc. However, HT, p. 547, published in Hanoi, says it was Phan Van Truong.

102. The Nguyen, *Phan Chu Trinh*, p. 40. Moutet later became Minister of Colonies in the Popular Front (1936-1939) and Minister of Overseas Territories during the crucial 1946 negotiations with Ho Chi Minh.

103. A common anecdote on Phan Chu Trinh during this period, deeply touching for all Vietnamese because of Phan's *tien-si* status, concerns his having to linger around the backs of Parisian restaurants to pick their garbage for carrot tops, turnip greens, chicken heads and entrails, etc. Hoang Xuan, *Phan Chu Trinh Thi-tap*, pp. 12-13.

the king with jewels, sumptuous clothes, furniture, etc. Here Phan labeled Khai Dinh a "pirate" of the poverty-stricken populace.

5. Clothing improper to the occasion. Here Phan denigrated Khai Dinh for some sort of outlandish East-West composite that he had worn when visiting the Tomb of the Unknown Soldier in France.

6. Inveterate wandering. This referred to Khai Dinh's travels through the Annam countryside by elephant, sedan chair, auto, and horse, all of which only created scenes and put extra burdens on the people.

7. A "fishy" trip to France. Touted as a trip to investigate France's advanced civilization, Phan said it was ridiculous for a monarch to "investigate" a democratic republic, especially when he took along mandarins who "lacked the intellectual level of a ten-year-old French child."

In conclusion, Phan wrote that Khai Dinh had only one proper recourse: "Offer governing powers as tribute back to our people, so that they may associate directly with the French people and plot their own advantage. . . . If you don't, then your head should fall to the earth, along with your savage, autocratic monarchical system." As a final thrust, Phan explained that he had purposely ignored traditional slavish usages of the Chinese when addressing the monarch; he was impelled to call Khai Dinh *Be-Ha* (Sire) only because the Chinese language gave him no alternative.[104]

From the tone of this letter, it should be evident that Phan's main purposes were to utterly humiliate Khai Dinh in Vietnamese eyes, to further upset those who still remained monarchists, and to offer a proud statement to the world at a time when Phan felt his country was a laughingstock. Nevertheless, it should be apparent that Phan's letter retained much that was traditional. His position on the potential benefits of French rule also remained unchanged. If anything, Phan showed himself to be more attached to the "free air and democratic earth" of Paris than to the disgustingly backward atmosphere of Annam. After more than fifteen years of trying to influence the French toward colonial reform, first in the colony and then in the métropole, Phan Chu Trinh still had not perceived the fundamental causes of his failure. His lifelong friend Huynh Thuc Khang tried to explain Phan's ineffectiveness by reference to "unlucky limitations" like the outbreak of World War I and the postwar political and economic turmoil inside France, both of which left the French little or no

104. Phan Chu Trinh, *Thu That Dieu* (Hue, 1958). Originally written in Chinese and sent to Khai Dinh by registered mail in 1922. Phan arranged a French translation for publication in Parisian papers. A portion of his translation into *quoc-ngu* survives and is reprinted in the 1958 edition. The remainder has been retranslated from the Chinese by Le Am, Phan Chu Trinh's son-in-law.

room for serious thought or discussion of long-range colonial policy.[105] For either of these men to have admitted that the French government was actually incapable of instituting their proposals would have been to deny and destroy all the idealistic images he had constructed over a lifetime. Like the rest of their generation, reformist and activist together, they were now hostages to a fate not of their own choosing.

105. Huynh Thuc Khang, *Phan Tay Ho*, p. 31.

Chapter Ten

Cần luôn luôn nhớ làm nhiệm vụ của người
dân mất nước

We must always remember to fulfill our
responsibilities as citizens of a lost country.

(NGUYỄN AI QUỐC, QUOTED IN 1922)

Changing the Guard

On June 18, 1924, an obscure young Vietnamese expatriate in Canton named Pham Hong Thai attempted without success to kill Governor General M. H. Merlin. The incident might have gone relatively unnoticed, as had similar attempts during World War I, except that it occurred at the beginning of a new, more promising era.

About a year later, in the same city of Canton, Nguyen Ai Quoc gathered a group of young Vietnamese whom he had come to trust and formed the Thanh Nien association, which was destined to mature into the Indochinese Communist party. At about the same time, a young southern intellectual, educated in Paris, returned to Saigon and plunged into the political ferment of that city. His name was Nguyen An Ninh, and he was fated more than any other to symbolize the anticolonial struggle in Cochinchina during the next fifteen years.

Phan Boi Chau, Phan Chu Trinh, and other aging scholar-gentry leaders had long been out of touch with month-to-month events, but they nevertheless quickly perceived a qualitative change in the political environment. Indeed, Phan Boi Chau was en route to Canton in 1925 to discuss major new organizational initiatives with Nguyen Ai Quoc when he was seized by French agents, spirited aboard a ship, and brought to trial in Hanoi. Phan Chu Trinh, long of the opinion that to reassert his ideas at home would bring only the back of the colonial hand, now had reversed himself and returned to Saigon, only to suffer a new bout of tuberculosis and die several months later. Others such as Ngo Duc Ke and Huynh Thuc Khang also returned to the fray and enjoyed transitional prominence. But each soon found that the youth of the period after 1924, the future participants in the Viet Nam Quoc Dan Dang (Vietnam National People's party), the Comintern, the Fourth International, and other such organizations, were impatient at Mencius, Montesquieu, and Spencer and were eager to move on to an operational understanding of Bakunin, Lenin, and Sun Yat-sen. In short, the stage was set for full emergence of a new anticolonial generation.

Such a change did not occur out of the blue. There had been much in the previous years to indicate that the generation of Phan Boi Chau and Phan Chu Trinh was being outpaced by events. As I have already indicated, between 1910 and 1920 activist and reformist scholar-gentry, alike, had found themselves prisoners, literally or figuratively, of situations not of their own choosing. Those activists still at large in 1915 had completely missed the implications of the war of attrition in Europe and had continued to strike out blindly for minimal gains. Their lack of strategic perspective was a function both of personal desperation and increasing ideological sterility. And the reformists had done no better. Those few not in jail had shifted into a politically questionable relationship with nonscholar collaborators. For all their compromising, they had discovered that those Frenchmen who might have been sympathetic to their cause understandably had been transfixed by events in Europe and had had little time for experimentation in Indochina. As for the volatile, insecure colons, they had come to regard almost any kind of political remonstration among the Vietnamese as potentially treasonous. This had left even those meek proponents of reform very little room for maneuver.

Nevertheless, it has sometimes been argued that the two tenures in office of Governor General Albert Sarraut (November 1911 through January 1914 and January 1917 through May 1919) had marked the opening of a new "pro-native" era in colonial policy, particularly in the fields of education and medical care and in the opening of positions for natives in the lower ranks of the administration. Leaving aside the question of Sarraut's personal intentions, which may have been lofty, it is difficult to see much merit in this interpretation of his policies.[1] Without doubt, there was a degree of liberalization in the areas mentioned above. There were also some distinct refinements in the elaborate creation myth that justified the French presence in Vietnam. With an altruism perhaps uniquely French, Sarraut based his entire argument for continued colonial rule on some "natural right" to open underdeveloped areas for the good of all humanity —in this case, the French and the native Indochinese equally. As the "elder brother" in this relationship, the French would ensure a rule of law, deliverance from disease, and modern education, not to mention protection from encroachments by third parties. As the younger brother "ma-

1. For a discussion of Sarraut's reforms, see Joseph Buttinger, *Viet-Nam*, pp. 87–100.

tured" (*slowly*), he would be allowed significant participation in colonial rule. For those recalcitrants, however, who failed to perceive the true generosity of this approach and who tried to subvert it, there could be nothing but capture and harsh punishment.[2] Hence it was that Sarraut the public benefactor could prove zealous and ruthless in sending his agents against anticolonial elements—a fact well documented in the archival records.

Having said all this, it should be freely admitted that Sarraut's published articles and public speeches created considerable interest among educated Vietnamese and were an important factor in influencing the attitudes of the young generation emerging at the time. For students now more and more strongly motivated by progressive and materialist concepts of history, there even was a certain intellectual excitement to Sarraut's arguments. If for nothing else, some would prick up their ears when they observed how furiously the established French families reacted against Sarraut's public declarations of past colonial sins in Indochina. Perhaps, they conjectured, colonial rule was not as eternal as they had been taught in the classroom. Perhaps the war, the Chinese and Russian revolutions, and the arguments of Woodrow Wilson for self-determination were indeed unsettling the French. And perhaps the logical extension of Sarraut's "enlightened" developmental theory was the inevitable obsolescence of the foreign colonial rulers and the colon class! It is hardly surprising that some perceptive and influential colons led by Pierre Pasquier (later governor general from 1928 through 1934) countered Sarraut's ideas with learned, if romantic, studies of an alleged traditional Vietnamese preference for piety, poetry, and political passivity.[3] But Pasquier was whistling a tune to which the younger Vietnamese could no longer march, while most of the older anticolonialists could see the political implications of his antimodernism and generally scorned involvement.

One scholar-gentry figure who saw things with more than average clarity at this time was Ngo Duc Ke. Released in 1921 after thirteen years on Con-lon island, he soon was editing a modest periodical in Hanoi, *Huu Thanh*. Ngo stood outside his office, watched the autos chug by, the streetcars, the women in rouge and high-heels, the students in neckties using animated slang, and likened the whole scene to a big, eye-boggling kaleidoscope. Lest readers mistake him, Ngo declared that he was all in favor of real, meaningful modern "civilization" (*van minh*). But what passed in front of him went no deeper than the rouge on the ladies' faces.

2. Sarraut speech published in *Nam Phong* 72. Albert Sarraut, *Grandeur et Servitude coloniale* (Paris, 1931). Perceptive discussion by Nguyen Van Trung, *Chu Nghia Thuc Dan Phap o Viet-Nam*, pp. 120–147.
3. Nguyen Van Trung, *Chu Nghia*, pp. 147–181.

The more such urbanites spent their time talking eagerly about salary scales, the latest watch or hat from Paris, or the best way to deceive their competitors, the more they were subjected to base enslavement.[4]

As if to illustrate his point, Ngo devoted another essay to the way that Vietnamese working for the colonial regime squabbled over petty personal status and favors. While their French overlords stood by chuckling, he said, Vietnamese mandarins demanded that their inferiors address them in humble fashion. Village officials quarreled over which one of them would get the head of the pig or chicken on festive occasions. Admittedly, much of this stemmed from traditional Confucian attention to hierarchy and decorum, but what was the purpose, Ngo asked, of studying and accepting modern civilization if not to *change* those narrow-minded fixations? If anything, Ngo declared, the situation had grown progressively more petty and ludicrous. Witness, a whole series of articles, meetings, and reports by members of the new intelligentsia on the single issue of how properly to translate into Chinese the French term *agent technique* so that it would reflect just the right degree of status—no more, no less. Since hardly any of the persons affected were knowledgeable in the Chinese language anymore, it had to be simply a question of how their descendants would inscribe their ranks on their funeral tablets![5]

In two further essays Ngo Duc Ke aggressively reopened the debate that had been initiated some fifteen years before within the Dong Kinh Nghia Thuc on the supplanting of Chinese and the various uses to which *quoc ngu* should be put. Above all, he accused Pham Quynh and the *Nam Phong* group of perverting both history and contemporary national priorities. He was highly disturbed at Pham Quynh's glorification of the poem *Truyen Kieu*.[6] While much that Ngo had to say in that connection betrayed a continuing, outmoded affinity to classical *Han* learning,[7] still, a crucial point was being raised. At a time when Pham Quynh and others spent thousands of pages praising the romantic *Truyen Kieu* as the national soul (*quoc hon*), the national essence (*quoc tuy*), of Vietnam, what was happening to the real soul of the country—the bewildered, tormented populace? Pham Quynh had the temerity to argue that if the literature of Viet-

---

4. Ngo Duc Ke, "Cam tuong trong luc bien tap," *Huu Thanh* 2, reprinted in VTCM, pp. 221–228.

5. Ngo Duc Ke, "Cai thoi ganh nhau danh vi cua nguoi Viet-Nam ta," *Huu Thanh* 15, reprinted in VTCM, pp. 228–236.

6. A long *nom* poem written by Nguyen Du about 1800, often called *Kim Van Kieu*. The debate over this poem is extensive. For a recent summary, see Jean Chesneaux and Georges Boudarel, "Le *Kim Van Kieu* et l'esprit public Vietnamien aux XIXe et XXe siecles," *Melanges sur Nguyen Du* (Paris, 1966), pp. 153–192.

7. Characterized as *chinh hoc* (upright learning) as opposed to *ta thuyet* (heresy), of which *Truyen Kieu* was a part.

nam, especially *Truyen Kieu*, survived, then the language of Vietnam would survive, and hence the country would survive. Ngo Duc Ke sharply reversed those priorities, maintaining that only if the people (*dan toc*) of Vietnam first survived, would the language survive, and hence the literature. To that end, he was prepared to see *quoc ngu* replace Chinese as the primary written medium in Vietnam. However, he believed the immediate need was not for translations of old Vietnamese literature but for the integration of Western scientific, economic, political, and legal concepts into both written *quoc ngu* and spoken Vietnamese. If this was to be accomplished, *quoc ngu* literature had to get away from the interests of a few stodgy intellectuals and into areas that the mass of the people perceived to be both concrete and purposeful.[8] Ngo in this way heralded the mass political literature and proselytization of the next anticolonial generation.

Quite obviously, most of the world had undergone momentous change by the early 1920s. First in ripples, then in waves, the impact would be felt in Vietnam. Older men like Ngo Duc Ke could see part of this, but not all. The efforts of previous anticolonial movements, of Truong Dinh, Phan Dinh Phung, De Tham, Phan Boi Chau, Phan Chu Trinh, and others, would not be forgotten, but they would be seen from a new perspective and subjected to a more critical analysis than ever before. Vietnam was possessed of a meaningful history, both in the immediate and more distant senses, but Vietnam was at this time part of world history as never before imagined.

One way to perceive some of the important, yet subtle, relationships between what we have studied in previous chapters and the events of later years is to outline the early life of the man who, more than any other, came to dominate the modern history of his country, Nguyen Ai Quoc. Today he is best known in the West by his last pseudonym, Ho Chi Minh.

Nguyen Ai Quoc was born in 1890 as Nguyen Sinh Cung, the son of Nguyen Sinh Sac. With an easy walk from either his paternal or his maternal village in Nghe An province, the younger Nguyen was able to climb a mountain from which with one sweep of the eye he could see the home regions of Nguyen Hue's ancestors, of Phan Dinh Phung, and of Phan Boi Chau. At many times much earlier than this, the Nghe An/Ha Tinh area had been deeply involved in resisting the foreigner. Before he was five or

8. Here the author used the analogy of local dike maintenance: since everyone knew the importance of the dike, knew that their village, their canton, would not exist without it, everyone, high and low, rolled up his sleeves and went to work. Ngo Duc Ke, "Nen Quoc van," *Huu Thanh* 12; and "Luan ve chinh hoc cung ta thuyet Quoc van— Kim Van Kieu—Nguyen Du," *Huu Thanh* 21. Both reprinted in VTCM, pp. 237–251.

six, we may assume that Nguyen Ai Quoc had heard of these episodes, particularly because one of his maternal aunts was a well known ballad singer of the area. Nguyen Ai Quoc's maternal great-uncle was a close friend of the son of the *tu-tai* scholar who had rallied the local people to support the Can Vuong Edict in 1885; hence, it was not surprising that this relative later fled north to join De Tham. When he returned to Nghe An to rouse new support there, he was captured and sent to Con-lon. Long after, he was released and lived with Phan Boi Chau in Hue until the latter's death in 1940.[9]

During the Le dynasty several of his ancestors had passed the examinations, but in the Nguyen period success had so far eluded his family. Nevertheless the scholastic tradition remained, so that Nguyen Ai Quoc's father, albeit the son of a concubine and lacking in wealth, demonstrated enough academic potential to be given the hand of his teacher's daughter in marriage. Such faith was not misplaced; Nguyen Sinh Sac did achieve *cu-nhan* status in 1894 and then went on to the metropolitan exams of 1901 in the same class as Phan Chu Trinh and Ngo Duc Ke and passed on the second (*pho-bang*) roster. After several years of teaching and of turning down official positions, Nguyen Ai Quoc's father accepted a place in the Ministry of Rites, apparently bowing both to village pressure (he was their most prestigious representative in some time) and increasing suspicion at court as to his political motives. In 1909 or 1910 he was appointed as a district magistrate in the uplands of Binh Dinh province. Soon he incurred the displeasure of the French résident, was removed, and rather surprisingly made the decision to travel south to Cochinchina rather than returning home. Subsequently he passed most of his time in Saigon, surviving until his death around 1930 through the prescription and sale of traditional medicines.

Nguyen Ai Quoc spent his first seven or eight years in both his mother's and his father's villages. After that the family moved to Hue so that his father could prepare for the metropolitan exams. While Nguyen Ai Quoc at this point began to study Chinese characters, his father made no special effort to prepare him for the examinations and, indeed, told other students that they should forget that routine. Perhaps as a result, Nguyen Ai Quoc was reported to spend much of his time in roaming the royal capital with his playmates, something that most of his friends back in Nghe An would never have the opportunity to do.[10]

Apparently in 1900 Nguyen Ai Quoc's father had been assigned to supervise the regional examinations in Thanh Hoa. He took with him his eldest son Khiem, even though his eldest daughter was away in Nghe An

9. Hoai Thanh, *et al., Bac Ho, Hoi Ky* (Hanoi, 1960), pp. 5–10.
10. *Ibid.,* pp. 11–15.

and his wife was about to give birth to a fourth child. This left the ten-year-old Nguyen Ai Quoc in charge. When the baby was born and his mother developed severe complications, there was a lack of medicine and adequate care. Soon Nguyen Ai Quoc's mother was dead, and we may assume that this experience affected him profoundly. The family returned to Nghe An, and the young boy's name was changed to Nguyen Tat Thanh. It was at this time that he sat with fascination at Phan Boi Chau's feet listening to him recite poetry. While his father at this time organized a more systematic study program for him, Nguyen Ai Quoc still was said to prefer the *Romance of the Three Kingdoms,* travel diaries, and other such popular writings to the Four Books and Five Classics.[11]

Another experience influencing Nguyen Ai Quoc directly at this point was the French decision to order large numbers of Nghe An villagers into the mountains to do corvée on a road construction project. Because of poor provisioning, shelter, medical care, and safety precautions, there was a high proportion of illness and injuries. No one from Nguyen Ai Quoc's family was required to go, since his father was an examination graduate, but this did not prevent the boy from ruminating on the basic injustice of the situation. Shortly afterward Phan Boi Chau or one of his associates tried to persuade the family to send Nguyen Ai Quoc and his elder brother to Japan, but his father decided that a program of French studies at the Quoc Hoc academy in Hue would be better.

This was a turning point for the fifteen-year-old boy. Among other things, it tended to focus his attention straight toward Europe instead of on Japan and China as cultural and political intermediaries, in the fashion of Phan Boi Chau, Phan Chu Trinh, and others of their generation. It might have led him ultimately into the *Nam Phong* group with Pham Quynh and Nguyen Van Vinh. However, it may have been his personal observation in April 1908 of the tax demonstrations in Hue and the subsequent repression by French troops that really prevented him from joining those moderate collaborators. Or it may have been the summary removal of his father from his position in Binh Dinh that was the critical factor. We do know that the latter event caused him to halt his studies at Quoc Hoc and travel south to Phan Thiet, where he taught French briefly at a school originally set up by associates of Phan Chu Trinh.[12]

By late 1911 Nguyen Ai Quoc was on his way to Saigon, determined to find a way to get to Europe. He accomplished this by signing on as a galley assistant on a French merchant ship, after which he spent two

11. *Ibid.*, pp. 16–20.
12. *Ibid.*, pp. 22–27. The Duc Thanh School (see Chapter 7), subsidized by a local *nuoc mam* factory and sundry shop, had been closed during the repression three years earlier. It was reopened with a less controversial curriculum.

or more years at sea, a startling but significant existence for the son of an exalted *pho-bang* graduate.[13] During the early years of World War I, he settled in London, picking up odd jobs and joining a clandestine organization of East Asian expatriots. According to one biographer, he "took an intense interest in the Irish uprising, mingled with Fabians, read books on politics," and learned the meaning of the word *revolution*.[14]

Toward the end of 1917 Nguyen Ai Quoc crossed the channel to Paris and observed the French in the midst of their desperate struggle with the Germans. He came into close contact with Phan Chu Trinh, both of them keeping alive by using their calligraphic brushes to retouch photographs. Soon he was circulating within French trade union, leftist intellectual, and pacifist circles. He had developed enough confidence in his own ideas and in his command of the French language to begin writing in *L'Humanité, Le Populaire,* and *La Révolution prolétarienne.* But this did not lead him to break his relationship with Phan Chu Trinh, since we know that the two of them, along with Phan Van Truong, spent some time together drawing up an eight-point program for the emancipation of Vietnam which they forwarded to the secretariat of the Versailles conference early in 1919. Nguyen Ai Quoc was also close to Marcel Babut, the man who had been most responsible for gaining Phan Chu Trinh's release from Con-lon prison.[15] In 1921, like Phan Chu Trinh, Nguyen Ai Quoc wrote articles bitterly criticizing King Khai Dinh's participation in the Marseilles Exposition.

By that time, however, it was obvious to politically active members of the Vietnamese community in France that Phan Chu Trinh and Nguyen Ai Quoc were pursuing different political paths. Nguyen Ai Quoc attended the December 1920 French Socialist Congress at Tours as "the delegate from Indochina" and jousted sharply with the moderates over their failure to pay enough attention to the colonial question—to imperialist oppression and exploitation in distant lands. It was on this basis that he joined the French Communist party and the Comintern, convinced that they alone were prepared to help him and other Vietnamese deliver their country from slavery.[16] Soon he was circulating his famous pamphlet, *Le Procès de la colonisation française,* and publishing, almost single-handedly, the newspaper *Le Paria.* Appointed to attend a major Comintern meeting in Moscow, Nguyen Ai Quoc arrived just in time to pay his respects at

13. Tran Dan Tien, *Nhung mau chuyen ve doi hoat dong cua Ho Chu Tich,* pp. 11–15.
14. Jean Lacouture, *Ho Chi Minh,* p. 18.
15. *Ibid.,* pp. 19–26.
16. Bernard B. Fall, ed., *Ho Chi Minh on Revolution: Selected Writings, 1920–66* (New York, 1967), pp. 3–6.

the funeral bier of Lenin.[17] As a member of the new standing committee on colonies, he soon was on his way to China with Mikhail Borodin, where he and Liao Chung-k'ai set about organizing the League of East Asian Oppressed Peoples.[18]

The alliance between the Comintern and the Chinese Kuomintang had been developing gradually since 1921. It played a significant though indirect role in delineating the course of Vietnamese anticolonial efforts. Regarding the new interest in the Soviet revolution and the Comintern, I have already mentioned Phan Boi Chau's meeting with several Russians in Peking and his passion to read whatever was available on Lenin and Trotsky. A small number of much younger activists also made their way out of Vietnam at this time on the initiative of the Quang Phuc Hoi. Not yet in contact with Nguyen Ai Quoc, they soon decided on their own that Phan Boi Chau and the Quang Phuc Hoi were too conservative, too traditionalist, in outlook. Generally coming from petit bourgeois or proletarian families, some of them formed the Tam Tam Xa (Association of Like Minds) and set about trying to recruit members in Shanghai, Hong Kong, and Tokyo. Several apparently enrolled in Whampoa Military Academy on its establishment near Canton in early June 1924 and immediately tried to put their access to explosives to good use.[19] Governor General M. H. Merlin (in office from 1923 to 1925), staying in Canton's Shameen district on his way back to Indochina from Japan, was the target of a bomb thrown by Pham Hong Thai, a member of Tam Tam Xa. The bomb killed several of Merlin's associates but failed to harm the governor general.[20]

Pham Hong Thai drowned while trying to escape, and the whole episode would have amounted to little, except that the Kuomintang chose to praise the act publicly, to curtly reject French protests, and even to

17. Hoai Thanh, *et al.*, *Bac Ho*, pp. 54–56.
18. CMCD-4, pp. 74–76.
19. To Nguyet Dinh, *Pham Hong Thai (1896–1924)*, pp. 52–53, lists Le Hong Phong and Le Hong Son as the first entries to Whampoa.
20. *Ibid.*, pp. 17–50. CMCD-4, pp. 123–124. Pham Hong Thai's gentry father had participated in Phan Dinh Phung's resistance efforts in Nghe-An and Ha-Tinh, for which the family had suffered economically. At age eight Pham went with his father to Lang-Son, where he allegedly had learned the Cantonese, *Nung*, and *Tho* languages. From 1909 to 1916 he studied at a Franco-Vietnamese school in Hanoi and after that at the Haiphong Industrial School. In 1919, however, he was turned down for the civil service and tried to make his living as an auto-repairman, quite a switch for the son of a scholar. Later he worked in a railroad repair shop, then a match factory, and finally a zinc mine. He was approached early in 1923 by a member of the Quang Phuc Hoi sent into Vietnam to raise money and recruit new students. Pham and six others followed the recruiter to China that same year.

have Pham buried with ceremony next to the famous "seventy-two martyrs" of the abortive April 1911 Canton revolt against the Ch'ing.[21] Phan
Boi Chau, reading of the incident in a Shanghai paper, traveled down to
Kwangtung and found some Kuomintang leaders newly sympathetic to
the Vietnamese anticolonials, including, by Phan's account, Liao Chung-
k'ai, Wang Ching-wei, and Hu Han-min. Phan and Nguyen Hai Than
secured a meeting with Chiang Kai-shek, then superintendent of Whampoa, and made arrangements for the entry of more young Vietnamese into
the academy.[22] The Viet-Nam Quoc Dan Dang (Vietnam National People's party), initiated by Phan Boi Chau in Canton during the summer
of 1924, not only used the name of the Kuomintang translated into Vietnamese, but also tried to pattern itself after the Kuomintang structure of
the moment. Once again, a proclamation was printed up, some copies to
be presented to Chinese sympathizers, more to be given to Ho Tung Mau
for smuggling into Vietnam.[23] Phan then returned to Hangchow. His
pamphlet *Pham Hong Thai Truyen* was in print by November 1924 and
was reviewed favorably in a Canton newspaper on the seventh anniversary of the Russian Revolution.[24]

Pham Hong Thai Truyen[25] was, in the narrow sense, simply another
emotional ode to individual patriotic commitment and initiative. More
importantly, however, it represented Phan Boi Chau's attempt in writing
to comprehend some of the new things that were happening and identify
himself with them. Phan strongly inferred that Pham Hong Thai's brief
life and violent death marked a turning point in anticolonial endeavors.
Phan called the first section of his essay "A man without a country (*mat*

---

21. The site has since become a tourist attraction for patriotic Vietnamese of widely
varying persuasions. To Nguyet Dinh, *Pham Hong Thai*, has as frontispiece a picture
of Hu Han-min, the Kwantung governor and high Kuomintang leader who was in-
strumental in Pham's honored burial.

22. TP, pp. 197–206. NB, pp. 194–201. It can also be assumed that Nguyen Ai Quoc
influenced this matter through Liao Chung-k'ai, then chief administrator of Whampoa. These early Vietnamese entries were mostly Tam Tam Xa members or unaffili-
ated, but a high proportion eventually joined the Viet-Nam Thanh Nien Cach Mang
Dong Chi Hoi (Viet-Nam Youth Revolutionary League) and then the Dong Duong
Cong San Dang (Indochinese Communist party) in 1930. Vien Giac, "Truong Chan
Vo o Nhat, Truong Hoang Pho o Tau voi lich su cach-mang Viet-Nam," *Duoc Tue*
77: 21–22. Bernard B. Fall, *The Two Viet-Nams*, pp. 93–94. Hoang Van Chi, *From
Colonialism to Communism* (New Delhi, 1966), pp. 34–36.

23. TP, pp. 206–207. NB, pp. 201–202. A Japanese translation of this is in Oiwa
Makoto, *Annan Minzoku Undoshi Gaisetsu*, pp. 171–178. Phan Boi Chau's efforts
here are not to be confused with the formation in 1927 of another party of the same
name in Hanoi.

24. Cited by Chuong Thau, NCLS 56: 36–37.

25. Phan Boi Chau, *Tuong Trung Nu Vuong/Truyen Pham Hong Thai*, pp. 108–148.

nuoc) from his mother's womb onward," then pointed out that Pham had been born just as the Can Vuong was expiring, had been educated in Franco-Vietnamese schools, and as a youth had tried to improve things peacefully within the system. After personally tasting harsh French repression, however, Pham had opted for violent solutions. In short, Pham Hong Thai had been prepared to give his life to regain for his country an independence that he himself had never experienced. Clearly this moved Phan Boi Chau. It also was a source of relief and elation for him, since he had long worried that his own generation, the last of the scholar-gentry, might also be the last generation that saw the need to fight against colonial slavery and exploitation. Born in different conditions, educated in completely different fashions, there was yet something that held the generations of Phan Boi Chau and Pham Hong Thai together and allowed them to communicate their deepest feelings to each other.

Because Pham Hong Thai had spent some time as a laborer and was part of a new group (the Tam Tam Xa) professing working-class affiliations, this essay also provided Phan Boi Chau an opportunity to grapple briefly with new questions of union organization, the mass mobilization of workers for political as well as economic objectives, and the relationship of Vietnamese anticolonial efforts to the worldwide proletarian struggle. It was a time of major strikes and urban class conflict in China. While Phan did not fathom the whole situation by any means, he was willing to learn. For example, he quoted Nguyen Ai Quoc approvingly on the need for fundamental social revolution, rather than mere tinkering with existing political institutions. He raised, too, the question of whether one went out among the workers and attempted to stimulate their revolutionary consciousness or waited until the workers developed this consciousness on their own. Either way, strikes of all kinds could serve as "laboratories for revolution," and young men like Pham Hong Thai were discovering that to initiate and sustain them was no bed of roses. Finally, regarding tactics, Phan Boi Chau denounced all attempts at "Franco-Vietnamese collaboration" and gave his sanction to further acts of individual violence along lines suggested by Pham Hong Thai. Naturally this would not be enough to alter the objective situation, but it could serve to awaken thousands to the possibilities of organizing group violence against the colonial system.[26]

By early 1925 Canton had become something of an anti-imperialist Mecca, with large numbers of dissidents arriving there from all over East

26. The latter position is criticized by Chuong Thau in his preface to the 1967 edition of *Pham Hong Thai Truyen*, p. 111. He labels it "individual terror" (*am sat ca nhan*), a misinterpretation of the role of violence in revolution, and something that the Indochinese Communist party had to struggle to overcome later.

and Southeast Asia to drink at the fountains of revolution and great ex-
pectations. Vietnamese may well have been the most numerous émigré
group;[27] by and large, they typified the generation of petit bourgeois intellectuals born after 1895 and educated in the new Franco-Vietnamese
schools. More receptive to twentieth-century intellectual currents, including socialism and Marxism-Leninism, than any of the scholar-gentry I
have dealt with so far, they regarded Phan Boi Chau and his associates
with the respect one would give a battered old warrior—as a symbol of
incredible tenacity and patriotism, rather than a provider of concrete
programs or political leadership. Nguyen Ai Quoc, older than most of the
arriving activists but much younger than Phan Boi Chau, appears to have
secured Phan's support for the Comintern-sponsored League of East
Asian Oppressed Peoples.[28]

At this point there occurs one of those murky incidents characteristic
of émigré politics. While Phan Boi Chau was out of Canton, a plot may
have developed to "sacrifice" him to the French in order to replenish
the depleted revolutionary finances (the Sûreté paid well) and to provide
a national issue that would arouse people within Vietnam to mass demonstrations and protests. At about the same time Nguyen Ai Quoc sent a
message to Phan restating his desire to consult on possible organizational
modifications in the newly formed Quoc Dan Dang.[29] Phan agreed to go
south for this purpose, wanting in addition to participate in observances
of the first anniversary of Pham Hong Thai's death. Walking out of the
Shanghai train station on the way to catch the boat for Canton, Phan was
grabbed by four Frenchmen, whisked into the French Concession, and
put aboard a ship bound for Haiphong. Either because of a poem Phan
wrote[30] and dropped off the ship which quickly was printed in the
Chinese newspapers, or because of tip-offs to the press by the plotters, if
they existed, this open French violation of Chinese territorial integrity
stirred up a hornet's nest of protests in Shanghai and Canton. In Paris,
Vietnamese nationalists fired off an angry letter to Kuomintang headquarters in Canton, accusing them of failing to help defeat the common
imperialistic enemy and of instead allowing the capture on Chinese soil of
a Vietnamese patriot.[31] If in fact someone had arranged the kidnapping of

27. Hoang Van Chi, *From Colonialism*, p. 35.

28. The Nguyen, *Phan Boi Chau*, p. 41.

29. To Minh Trung, "Gop y kien voi ong Chuong Thau ve bai 'Anh huong cach mang
Trung-quoc voi su chuyen bien tu tuong cua Phan Boi Chau," p. 58. Xxx, "Mot viec
bi mat chua ai noi ra," *Cai Tao* 25, as cited by Chuong Thau, "Phan Boi Chau qua
mot so sach bao mien Nam hien nay," p. 17.

30. Reprinted in HT, pp. 456-459; TP, pp. 208-209; NB, pp. 203-206; VT, pp.
164-168.

31. The Nguyen, *Phan Boi Chau*, p. 57. Phan Boi Chau, "Mémoires," n. 194. Most

Phan Boi Chau for political effect, his objective was well on its way to realization.

What sort of Vietnam was it that Phan Boi Chau was returning to after eighteen years of wandering? As I have already indicated, between 1909 and the end of World War I the country changed very little in any fundamental sense. But from 1920 to the Great Depression there was a rush of truly startling changes, first in the economic and then in the social realms. While serious discussion of them all is beyond this study, a few things must be said in order to understand the last years of Phan Boi Chau, Phan Chu Trinh, and other surviving members of their generation.[32]

Prewar French capital investment in Indochina had concentrated first on urban construction and easy-access mines and then shifted to communications. Postwar capital investment was much more substantial, focusing primarily on agriculture as an export industry. Rubber was the pacesetter, with the acreage used for its cultivation tripling between 1917 and 1926. Rice exports continued to expand, while the intake of rice per capita among the Vietnamese population continued to fall.[33] Imports into Vietnam from the métropole quickly (by 1922) climbed beyond any prewar levels, while local industries in general continued to be discouraged. In short, after about half a century of occupation Indochina finally was becoming a classic colony, her every economic fiber attuned to the demands of financial and industrial interests in France.

---

anti-communist writers argue that Nguyen Ai Quoc (then called Ly Thuy) was implicated in this, via his associate Lam Duc Thu. This version apparently was introduced anonymously in 1948 in *Cai Tao,* a journal published in Hanoi by Dao Trinh Nhat, and has been repeated faithfully by various English-language commentators. See for example: P. J. Honey, *North Viet-Nam Today* (New York, 1962), p. 4; Buttinger, *Viet-Nam,* pp. 155–156; Hoang Van Chi, *From Colonialism,* pp. 13–14. As for Phan Boi Chau, he believed ten years after the event that one of the students who lived with him in Hangchow, Nguyen Thuong Huyen, was paid by the French to betray him. (NB, pp. 202–203; TP, p. 207.) Nguyen Thuong Huyen has spent the rest of his life (in China and Hong Kong) denying this and blaming Nguyen Ai Quoc. Nguyen Thuong Huyen, BK 73: 39. Communist historians have also fingered Nguyen Thuong Huyen and several associates, while arguing heatedly that Phan Boi Chau subsequently often spoke highly of Nguyen Ai Quoc and received known Indochinese Communist Party members warmly in his own house. Chuong Thau, "Phan Boi Chau," pp. 17–19. Tran Huy Lieu, "Nho lai Ong gia Ben Ngu." Finally, Prince Cuong De, who hardly could be considered pro-communist, related that Nguyen Ai Quoc was not at all aware that Lam Duc Thu was secretly negotiating with the Sûreté to "sell" Phan Boi Chau. CD, pp. 120–122.

32. The most commonly cited work on economic changes: Charles Robequain, *The Economic Development of French Indo-China.* First published in French in 1939.

33. CMCD-4, pp. 8–10. Pham Cao Duong, *Thuc Trang cua gioi Nong Dan Viet-Nam duoi thoi Phap thuoc,* pp. 22–36, 174–191.

The social consequences of economic change in Indochina have yet to be analyzed in any detail, perhaps partly because of the dearth of solid data, but also because social change was by no means uniform from one region or province to another. In Cochinchina a few extremely wealthy landlords in alliance with a small but slowly increasing number of Vietnamese capitalists formed the Constitutionalist party and talked about economic modernization and administrative change within the colonial system. By 1919 or 1920 they felt confident enough to organize a boycott of Chinese commercial firms in Cochinchina, but it failed badly. In 1922 they were more successful in electing several of their members to the highly restrictive Colonial Council. With their French-language newspapers, this provided the Constitutionalists with a public sounding board and, not surprisingly, brought them into conflict with the French reactionaries who dominated the Cochinchina government.[34] With the political temperature thus heating up, the Constitutionalists found themselves being joined by a large portion of Saigon's young intellectuals and even some young maverick Frenchmen like André Malraux and the lawyer Paul Monin.[35] However, the coalition proved transitory. In brief, it appears that most of the wealthier bourgeoisie, after some initial accomplishments between 1924 and 1926, sat back to savor what they had gained personally in concessions from the French, while young radicals like Nguyen An Ninh and Tran Huy Lieu started to take their case to the local proletariat and out among the peasants and tenants in districts surrounding Saigon.[36] The days were now long past when scholar-gentry activists could depend on residual monarchist sentiments among wealthy Cochinchina landlords to support anticolonial objectives.

The postwar emergence of small native bourgeois and petit bourgeois classes in Tonkin and Annam was even more startling, since such people had been so insignificant in prewar decades. Part of their success may have resulted from the sharp reduction in imports from the métropole during the war years and the consequent temporary development of

34. Ralph B. Smith, "Bui Quang Chieu and the Constitutionalist Party in French Cochinchina, 1917–30," pp. 134–138.

35. Walter G. Langlois, *André Malraux*. Malraux, in Indochina during 1925 and early 1926, worked hard on two important periodicals: *L'Indochine* and *Indochine Enchainee*. Monin arrived in Indochina in 1919, was elected to the staid Colonial Council in 1922, and fought a running battle from that point on with old guard colon interests. Both men were involved in the formation of the semi-clandestine Jeune Annam group.

36. Le Van Thu, *Hoi Kin Nguyen An Ninh*. The author was an associate of Nguyen An Ninh, Ta Thu Thau, and others in this important South Vietnamese intellectual grouping. For a brief study of landlord-tenant relations in Cochinchina, see Pham Cao Duong, *Thuc Trang*, pp. 50–82, 108–119, 125–153.

native substitutes.[37] After the war Hanoi boasted small but respectable native firms specializing in embroidered textiles, carpets, soap, and ironwork, while other towns in north and central Vietnam developed or greatly expanded their brickmaking, pottery, lacquerware, and silk filiature, as well as their *nuoc mam* and transportation industries.[38] As in Cochinchina there was the rapid formation of business associations to protect or increase privileges and to help each other develop in competition with the foreign-owned sectors, both French and Chinese. New periodicals emerged, and a "buy native" movement was revived, only to be swamped by a steady postwar surge of French imports.

By 1925 in Tonkin and Annam it was the petit bourgeoisie, the shopkeepers, managers, civil servants, students, interpreters, professionals, and technicians, that had moved to the political forefront. Their grievances were different from those of the bourgeoisie, often centering on high taxes, the restriction of civil rights, and the lack of promotions and educational opportunities. But there was more. Knowledgeable enough about Western norms and ethics, they were deeply wounded by daily and hourly slights suffered at the hands of their French masters. Sufficiently aware of Vietnam's precolonial history and culture and the continuing undercurrent of proud anticolonial resistance, they knew that there were alternatives to their life of humiliation. It was they, much more than the bourgeoisie, who would provide leadership and ideological direction to most of the anticolonial efforts to come.

The intense literary activity of petit bourgeois groups in and around Hanoi during that period was intimately related to their need to find themselves politically and culturally. So much that was new deserved to be explored. So much that was old and a part of traditional Vietnam had to be reappraised. Sometimes the results were pathetic, as when a proponent of Franco-Vietnamese collaboration attempted to advance a writing style combining French and *quoc-ngu* expressions in a sort of linguistic mishmash.[39] At other times, however, hallowed literary forms and approaches were successfully adopted to convey modern concepts and to appeal to changing tastes.[40]

37. CMCD-4, pp. 28–29, mentions sharp drops in imports of sugar, kerosene, bottles, and textiles.
38. CMCD-4, pp. 30–36. The author also lists separately many firms with Vietnamese capital or Vietnamese partners, but still French-controlled. These Vietnamese he classes as compradores for social and political purposes, rather than as national bourgeoisie.
39. VTCM, pp. 101–102.
40. For example, the *cheo* drama was modified in style, costume, and presentation. New content, often implicitly critical of foreign rule, was provided by such authors as Nguyen Dinh Nghi. Ultimately it merged with the southern-initiated *cai luong*, a

Entire alien value systems would be loudly introduced in intellectual circles, become the objects of modish acceptance, and then often vanish as quickly as they had come. Occasionally, however, a truly resonant chord would be sounded which would have a more lasting effect on society at large, particularly as *quoc-ngu* became more important in the countryside. For example, a fascinating debate was opened on the meaning of love (*tinh-yeu, ai-tinh*) in its various manifestations, which was connected with a complete reassessment of the relationship of the individual to his family and to society. While some accepted sexual love as the ultimate good or pushed Western individualism to its logical extreme, others with equal passion advocated a platonic, abstract love that would touch all people at all times. How this related to more traditional Vietnamese patterns of affection for king, teacher, parents, children, spouse, siblings, and friends became extremely important in the formulation of new social and political norms.

One result was startling and perhaps distinctive to Vietnam. Out of the emotional self-searching, the moodiness and despair, came something that one perceptive author has characterized as revolutionary romanticism (*tinh than cach mang lanh man*), a merging of old and new psychological predilections that would drive many thousands of young men and women to devote their lives to renewing the struggle against the colonialist.[41] One youth, having left home for a life of revolutionary danger, summed up this drive in a simple parallel sentence which was forwarded to his mother's funeral:

> At a time of agony for our countrymen, we have taken Vietnam as our mother; for mourning garb we will emulate Mazzini.[42]

Finally, there was the emergence from 1919 to 1929 of a small politically conscious laboring class. Paul Isoart has calculated the existence of about 220,000 workers in Vietnam on the eve of the Depression—36.8 per cent in modern agricultural enterprises, 39.2 per cent in commerce and industry, and 24 per cent in the mines.[43] Vietnamese Marxist histo-

---

form that gained great popularity among the people. Tran Huy Lieu, *Lich Su Thu Do Ha-Noi*, pp. 136–142.

41. The term is introduced in VT, pp. 95–98, as an aspect of Phan Boi Chau's writings that was taken up in other contexts by the next generation. Unfortunately this crucial subject of value-changes after World War I is too complex and too deserving of further study to discuss in detail here. See also VTCM, pp. 104–105, 141–145.

42. VTCM, p. 143. The reference to Giuseppe Mazzini (1805–1872) is taken from the Liang Ch'i-ch'ao account of how the Italian patriot, after his mother's death, allegedly said, "I will mourn my mother at the same time as I mourn my country, until the day I die."

43. Paul Isoart, *Le phénomène national vietnamien*, p. 264.

rians accept his figures, but also emphasize the "tens of thousands" of uncounted artisans, janitors, and persons involved in cottage industries. They also point out that these figures do not reflect the extremely rapid turnover of laborers, occasioned in large part by people breaking their work contracts and escaping from the hated mines and plantations.[44] At any rate, even when we accept such marginal industry and trade categories, it is apparent that during the 1920s the laboring class in Vietnam made up no more than 2 per cent of the population. The first significant strikes among them came between 1922 and 1925, and they participated also in mass popular protests against the imprisonment of Phan Boi Chau in 1925 and 1926.[45] Soon the newly formed Thanh Nien and Tan Viet parties were attempting, in eager but highly inexperienced fashion, to recruit workers as members and to take leadership of the various strike movements.

By the time the French ship carrying Phan Boi Chau arrived in Haiphong harbor, word of his capture was circulating through Vietnam. Brought before the colonial Criminal Commission in November 1925, Phan was sentenced to life imprisonment.[46] Students and other sympathizers in various towns, however, were prepared for this and circulated amnesty petitions, passed out leaflets, and even dared to march boys and girls together in defense of a man whose exploits they had learned about only at home, never through the public media. Teachers and students of the Dong Khanh girls' school in Hue sent a telegram asking for amnesty for Phan to the governor general's office; other telegrams were sent from student groups in Paris. A group of one hundred older women reportedly knelt in front of the governor general's moving automobile to present a letter requesting Phan Boi Chau's release.[47] Even cautious bourgeois leaders like Nguyen Phan Long in Saigon wrote newspaper editorials asking for amnesty.[48]

44. CMCD–4, pp. 48–49, 56.
45. CMCD–4, pp. 61–63.
46. French charges and a summary of Phan's trial statement in The Nguyen, *Phan Boi Chau*, pp. 50–53. See also *L'Avenir du Tonkin*, November 23–25, 1925, for reports on the trial.
47. *L'Argus*, December 12, 1925. Cited in Tran Huy Lieu, *Lich Su Thu Do*, p. 171.
48. Thinh Quang Nguyen Duc Rieu, *Vu An Phan Boi Chau* (Saigon, 1926), as quoted in The Nguyen, *Phan Boi Chau*, pp. 55–62. Copies of the leaflets printed in Hanoi were supposedly sent to the League of Nations, the International Tribunal at The Hague, the French parliament, the French president, the Ministry of Colonies, the governor general of Indochina, and the Chinese ambassador in Paris. The younger generation was trying to do what Liang Ch'i-ch'ao had counseled Phan Boi Chau to do twenty years earlier, namely, mobilize international sentiments against colonial oppression. Intellectually and technically, they were much better equipped to do this than Phan. And, in addition, attitudes in certain parts of the world regarding colonialism had changed in their favor.

Alexander Varenne, who had just replaced Merlin as governor general of Indochina (he served from November 1925 through January 1928), was the first and only Socialist party leader to hold a high colonial position. At this point he wanted very much to set a liberal tone to his administration. So, to the angry consternation of the French community, Varenne paroled Phan Boi Chau in December, received him personally, and made him several offers of public office.[49] These being politely rejected, Phan was permitted to travel down to Hue, where it was understood that he would live out his life in loosely guarded "retirement." In 1928, invited by Ngo Duc Ke, Duong Ba Trac, Le Dai, and other old associates to visit them in the north, Phan rented an auto and started out, but he was stopped by French soldiers outside Hue and ordered to turn back.[50]

Phan Boi Chau did not try to make a scene about such restrictions or otherwise engage in overt political activities in Hue. This disturbed activists at the time, and it has troubled many historians, especially because his inactivity gave many collaborators and reformists-turned-collaborators a chance to crow publicly and repeatedly that Phan had finally perceived the utter futility of armed resistance and the wisdom of Franco-Vietnamese cooperation. My personal opinion here is that Phan's relative quiescence was bred of a combination of emotional exhaustion and elderly perception. He had spent twenty years moving furtively around East and Southeast Asia, searching desperately and apparently failing to find a key that might release his countrymen from bondage. While his capacity for sustained emotional commitment was extraordinary, there must be limits for every man. Returning to Vietnam for trial, Phan probably expected a martyr's death. Instead, he was allowed to live in Hue, build a small house, spend his afternoons in a small sampan on the Huong river, and chat with old cronies far into the night. For those who know the chaste atmosphere of Hue, it is possible to see how something in him found respite there, however temporary. This is also evident in the many poems

49. Reports of celebrations, parties, and financial contributions at the time of parole appeared in the newspaper *Thuc Nghiep Dan Bao,* December 30, 1925. This paper also published 15,000 copies of a book on the Phan Boi Chau trial, *Tap An Phan Boi Chau.* Cited in Tran Huy Lieu, *Lich Su Thu Do,* p. 171.

50. The Nguyen, *Phan Boi Chau,* pp. 73–74. The author maintains that Phan was in covert contact with Quoc Dan Dang elements at this time and was heading north to give them support. Nhuong Tong, a Quoc Dan Dang leader, writes in *Nguyen Thai Hoc* (Saigon, 1956), pp. 52–56, that Phan was willing in 1930 to be spirited out of the country, but the plan fell through. Other sources, however, maintain that Phan neither actively supported nor opposed any one party after 1925. Ngo Thanh Nhan, *Cu Sao Nam 15 Nam Bi Giam Long o Hue,* pp. 30–31. Tran Huy Lieu, "Nho lai," p. 43.

Phan wrote during the fifteen years before his death in 1940, poems of striking colloquial imagery, if not of major political significance.[51]

The other aspect, which I call Phan's elderly perception, is of more historical significance. Part of Phan's exhaustion stemmed from his feeling that he had failed so totally that he honestly deserved no further attention or acclaim from his countrymen. His second and last autobiography, written probably in 1937,[52] was designed in part as an apology, in part as a sharp critique of himself to help future anticolonialists know what not to do the next time.[53] Phan terminated the story abruptly at the point of his capture in Shanghai in 1925, considering the remainder of his life not to be worthy of comment. Nevertheless, there is evidence that he was honestly impressed by the eagerness and the determination of the new anticolonial generation, if a bit worried at their seeming lack of identification with tradition. Many of his poems after 1925 were directed specifically at the youth. Just about his only public political act in Hue was to give two speeches on March 17, 1926, one at the famous Quoc Hoc boys' school and the other for the girls at Dong Khanh School. While presenting nothing new in ideology, these speeches did demonstrate Phan's pride in Vietnamese history and culture and his touching desire to communicate this pride to the new generation. Once again, the emotional symbolism was most important.[54] Until the local Sûreté began to harass visitors to Phan's house, students and young civil servants came each Thursday and Sunday to listen to Phan recount his wanderings and to talk of the future. After this, not wishing to get others in trouble, Phan spent much of the time aboard his sampan in the river.[55]

In short, Phan was old enough and wise enough to sense that the torch had been passed. For good or evil, he had done what he could, what he must. If it was not his fate to die at the guillotine, then at least he could live out his life with proper decorum, refusing collaboration, providing refuge for a few homeless and elderly compatriots, and cultivating the austere simplicity so favored by all revolutionary ethics, traditional and modern. Phan died October 29, 1940, not at all a happy man.[56] But then

51. The Nguyen, *Phan Boi Chau,* pp. 107–148, 160–173. HT, pp. 464–471. Hoang Xuan, *Phan Chu Trinh Thi-tap,* pp. 36–65. Kiem Dat, *Luan De ve Phan Boi Chau,* pp. 56–133. VT, pp. 169–180, 187–195, 201–211. These late poems, part sermon in modified Confucian pattern, part Whitmanesque paean to the land and people of Vietnam, deserve future study as literature.
52. Chuong Thau, "Ve hai tap tu truyen cua Sao Nam," pp. 39–41.
53. VT, pp. 77–78.
54. These speeches appear in The Nguyen, *Phan Boi Chau,* pp. 177–195.
55. Ngo Thanh Nhan, *Co Sao Nam 15 Nam Bi Giam Long o Hue,* pp. 11–14.
56. VT, pp. 105–107.

he had never paid much due to personal happiness. Since then, it has not been the fate of his countrymen to find happiness either, but they have come to regard Phan Boi Chau as the personification of the very essence of Vietnamese resistance to foreign intervention.

The year of Phan Boi Chau's sentencing, 1925, was also the year in which, by choice, Phan Chu Trinh returned home from Paris, perhaps intrigued by new political developments in Vietnam, especially in Saigon, perhaps for reasons of health. He appears several years earlier to have requested permission to return from the Ministry of Colonies, and then to have improved his chances by accepting a role in a small "Constitutionalist Group" formed at that time in Paris. But it was almost certainly the electoral victory of the French Left in 1924 and the departure from Vietnam of Governor General Merlin in April 1925 that provided the actual opportunity.[57] Phan was preceded to Saigon by Nguyen An Ninh,[58] a young southern intellectual who had been working for his law degree in Paris and who had worked closely there with both Phan and Nguyen Ai Quoc.

Saigon was alive with political ferment, perhaps more than ever before. The prime medium was the French-language press, and the thrust, at least initially, was aimed, as I have indicated, at gaining through nonviolent means economic and political privileges for the native bourgeoisie equal to those possessed by the colons. Bui Quang Chieu and Nguyen Phan Long were generally recognized as the leaders of this effort, going up against the Lieutenant Governor of Cochinchina, M. Cognacq, the French National Assemblyman from Cochinchina, Ernest Outrey, and the editor of the newspaper L'Impartial, M. Chavigny. Issues involved such things as exploitation of the lucrative port monopoly in Saigon, alleged French efforts to corner the nuoc mam market, and the uncovering of massive

---

57. Huynh Thuc Khang, Phan Tay Ho Tien Sinh Lich Su, p. 31. The Nguyen, Phan Chu Trinh, (1872–1926), p. 49. La Tribune Indigene, January 31, 1925.

58. Nguyen An Ninh (1900–1943) was from Quan-Tre village, Hoc Mon district, Gia Dinh. I have introduced his father, Nguyen An Khuong, a scholar who translated Chinese works into quoc-ngu, participated in the Dong Du movement, and associated with Gilbert Chieu in establishing the Chieu-Nam hotel in Saigon. Nguyen An Ninh was an excellent student at the best schools in My-Tho, Saigon (Taberd and Chasseloup Laubat) and Hanoi (schools of medicine and law). Family funds were collected for his law studies in Paris, where in the years after 1918 he became involved with French anarchists, helped Nguyen Ai Quoc publish the revolutionary paper Le Paria, and yet still remained on good terms and often lived with Phan Chu Trinh. Nguyen An Ninh loved to travel, was something of a philosophical romantic, and in politics was more the intellectual loner than the organization man—which may be what he and Phan Chu Trinh had most in common. Le Van Thu, Hoi Kin Nguyen An Ninh, pp. 9–20. VNDN, p. 159.

Changing the Guard   269

land swindles in newly developed delta regions.[59] By mid-1925 the conflict, while still nonviolent, had broadened to include political issues of
overriding concern to the petit bourgeois intellectuals. There were emotional meetings protesting the ejection of northern and central Vietnamese
(classified as "protectorate" rather than "colonial" citizens) from Cochinchina, press campaigns for the easing of travel and mail restrictions, and
general condemnation of colon manipulation of the legal processes for
their own benefit.

Given his passion for idealistic debate and nonviolent reform, it is hard
to imagine Phan Chu Trinh's not being stirred by developments in Saigon.
Yet he does not seem to have participated in any day-to-day sense. In
fact, there is some evidence Phan did not really understand the passions
of the younger intellectuals, men who by 1925 were supplanting the
wealthy bourgeoisie as protagonists in the public eye. I have already cited
the personal disappointment, after listening to Phan, of Tran Huy Lieu,
who was at that time tied in with Monin's paper, *L'Indochine*.[60] More
concrete evidence of this "generation gap" are the transcripts of two
public speeches given by Phan in November 1925.

The first, "Dao Duc va Luan Ly Dong Tay" (The Morality and Ethics
of East and West), was not quite as traditionalist as the title implies. Indeed, it was an ingenious attempt by Phan to provide for the young generation a sense of pride, of respect for themselves as Vietnamese. Defining
human morality as knowing no limitations of time and space, "the same
for all systems, democratic, monarchist, even communist," Phan then
attempted to parallel Rousseau, Montesquieu, Pascal, and Voltaire with
Confucius, Mencius, and Lao-tzu, regretting only that a heavily institu-
tionalized, restrictive Confucianism had succeeded in enslaving the East
for centuries, and preventing in practice the free expression of this morality. Concerning various ethical systems, which Phan argued were temporal
and spatial in character—historically bound—he generally found the contemporary Western system superior to the Eastern and fervently advised
its gradual adoption by his people. Lest Vietnamese feel they were losing
their identity in this process, however, Phan completed the circle by
maintaining that such acceptance was in fact a return to the original pure
Eastern morality of Confucius and Mencius, a clearing away of all the
false practices built up by courts and mandarins for their own advantage,
a grand moral reconciliation of East and West. As a final qualification, he
warned that all was not good that came from the West, that the youth
gathered before him had the awesome responsibility of cutting and sorting,
with the ultimate objective being the construction of a new national ethic

59. Langlois, *André Malraux*, pp. 55–62, 71–110. CMCD–4, pp. 85–93.
60. Tran Huy Lieu, "Nho lai," p. 41.

for Vietnam, within which all Vietnamese would then know their ethical responsibilities to their country.[61]

The second speech was titled "Quan Tri Chu Nghia va Dan Tri Chu Nghia" (Monarchism and Democracy), which Phan Chu Trinh also considered, in this context, a discussion of "governments of men versus governments of laws." Here the villain clearly was Ch'in Shih Huang-ti, who, Phan argued, perverted the true teachings of Confucius and Mencius in the third century B.C. and started an autocratic tradition masquerading as Confucianism that grew worse with each succeeding dynasty. In the West, by contrast, monarchs found themselves increasingly circumscribed, particularly after the advent in the seventeenth and eighteenth centuries of the philosophy of the natural rights of man. Eastern monarchs developed elaborate ethical constructs to convince the people that they should remain passive and ignorant. This worked as long as the East was isolated. But when powerful outside forces threatened, the same monarchs found that their clever ruse had ended in the loss of their countries to foreign colonizers.

Even in 1925, Phan continued, the common people were motivated to action by appeals to personal and familial loyalties, so that when one talked about *mat nuoc* (losing one's country) they did not really fathom the predicament. The first step in correcting this weakness was the elimination of the puppet monarchy in Hue, so that the people could begin to identify directly with the image of "nation" and sense that the rights and responsibilties of this entity were theirs to share.[62] Then, after a cursory description of metropolitan France's constitution, laws, and political parties, Phan concluded that it was up to the Vietnamese people, including the young audience before him, to act, to argue, to criticize, so that they might gain whatever was rightfully theirs.[63]

Reading over these speeches and considering them together, it becomes apparent that, while Phan Chu Trinh had done a lot of reading and reflecting during his long exile in France, his position was not too different from that which he had set forth in 1906. He was not prepared, by temperament, education, or experience, to discard his philosophical idealism in favor of a more contemporary materialism. He still believed deeply in

61. The Nguyen, *Phan Chu Trinh*, pp. 128–164. Phan Chu Trinh, "Dao Duc va Luan Ly Dong Tay."
62. Phan Chu Trinh may have been led to discuss the monarchy again by the recent death of Khai Dinh. Many had hoped that the French would consider this an opportunity to reform the system in Annam. Instead, they promulgated the charter of November 6, 1925—if anything, a step backward. Paul Isoart, *Le phénomène*, pp. 239–240.
63. The Nguyen, *Phan Chu Trinh*, pp. 101–127. Phan Chu Trinh, "Bai dien thuyet ve quan-tri chu-nghia va dan-tri chu-nghia."

the reformist position on Confucius and Mencius, which of course was borrowed mostly from K'ang Yu-wei and Liang Ch'i-ch'ao. It was still very important to him that he justify the "backwardness' of the contemporary East in terms of historical villains. But, interestingly enough, whereas K'ang and Liang had retained their monarchism and in their later years had come to regard the West as morally bankrupt, Phan Chu Trinh had moved on at least to a kind of liberal eclecticism in which he roughly attempted to synthesize Western and Eastern thought. After the horrors of World War I, Phan did not react, like some of his former reformist compatriots, with a general revulsion and disgust toward Western "materialistic" civilization and talk of cultivating the rich "inner life of Eastern spiritualism." More than anything, Phan seemed acutely conscious of the vacuum left by the collapse of traditional Vietnamese ethics; he considered it of prime importance that some coherent new construct be supplied. To this he tied his long-standing opposition to the Hue court, arguing in rather original fashion that popular fixations regarding the person and position of the king were a real impediment to the development of true national affiliations. In Phan's opinion, the image of the nation could not predominate among the masses as long as a monarch stood in the way.[64]

Phan Chu Trinh's surpassing difficulty, however, lay in the fact that he was trying to influence a group of young, progressive Cochinchinese intellectuals whose direct contact with Confucius and Mencius was almost nil and who in any case were much more interested in hearing about contemporary world events, starting with the Chinese and Soviet revolutions and proceeding to the recent victory of the Left in France and the arrival in their country of the Socialist Varenne that same November. When these young men did wax philosophical, they talked not of Montesquieu and Rousseau (much less Confucius!), but of Kant, Comte, Nietzsche, and Marx. Several in their own generation, particularly Nguyen An Ninh and the group centering around his *Cloche Fêlée* newspaper in Saigon, were capable of discussing these philosophers more knowledgeably than Phan or any other member of the older generation. In any case, if this wasn't enough, there was the angry and sophisticated André Malraux, trying to promote a coherent liberal basis for Franco-Vietnamese collaboration, printing regular information on strikes and riots in China, and generally trying to spark in the local Vietnamese a sense of their own

64. In some ways I think Phan Chu Trinh resembled Ts'ai Yuan-p'ei (1867–1940), the leading liberal educator of early republican China, although Phan never had Ts'ai's opportunities to attempt to implement his ideas. Extracts of Ts'ai's works appear in Ssu-Yu Teng and John K. Fairbank, *China's Response to the West* (New York, 1963), pp. 234–239.

righteousness against the "greedy louts" of colon society.[65] In short, Phan Chu Trinh reentered Vietnam in much the same position as Phan Boi Chau—revered for what he had done, for what his life symbolized, but not really being expected or encouraged by the younger generation to provide open leadership.

Phan Chu Trinh made plans to travel north, hoping eventually to set up a printing shop and newspaper somewhere. Upon hearing of Phan Boi Chau's parole in Hue in December, he expressed a desire to meet his old friend and political rival.[66] It is not at all certain that the French authorities would have let him leave the relative freedom of Saigon for the more rigidly controlled Annam and Tonkin, particularly considering the abusive words he had directed at Khai Dinh. At any rate his plans had to be indefinitely postponed by a recurrence of tuberculosis, which sent him first to Cap St. Jacques on the coast and then to a hospital in Saigon. There Phan Chu Trinh died on March 24, 1926.

In the weeks and months after Varenne's arrival, the intelligentsia throughout Vietnam, both liberal and progressive, had been deeply disappointed by his cautiousness and his refusal to implement sweeping reforms. Malraux's paper summed up their feelings:

> Yesterday a socialist, today an outstanding conservative among prominent conservatives; another conversion under the sign of the piastre.[67]

Nguyen Phan Long, now a member of the Colonial Council, led the public discussion, trying gently to pressure Varenne into some reforms, beginning with more freedom for the *quoc-ngu* press. When that failed, young intellectuals began to urge public demonstrations as a prime tactic, often citing Mahatma Gandhi's movement in India. This meant circulating more among the coolies, drivers, and marketgoers of Saigon and giving street-corner speeches to raise mass interest and support. As a result of such actions, Nguyen An Ninh was jailed and *La Cloche Fêlée* shut down. The climax came on March 24, 1926, the day Phan Chu Trinh quietly expired in the hospital, but also the day when Bui Quang Chieu, the Constitutionalist Party leader, returned from a speaking trip in France. To the shock of Bui's moderate bourgeois associates, he was met at dockside by both a small hostile group of colons (one of whom supposedly kicked Bui) and by a large, potentially unruly crowd of petit bourgeois and lower-class Vietnamese, who wanted to march triumphantly all over town with Bui at their head. Failing that, the leaders of the crowd put heavy pressure on

65. Langlois, *André Malraux*, pp. 111–144, 163–188.
66. Huynh Thuc Khang, *Phan Tay Ho*, pp. 31–32.
67. *Indochine Enchainee 9*, as translated in Langlois, *André Malraux*, p. 178.

Bui to at least interecede with the French for the release from jail of Nguyen An Ninh.[68]

Then came news of Phan Chu Trinh's death, which spread quickly into the suburbs and countryside by word of mouth and reached Hanoi and other cities by way of the press. In Saigon a funeral committee was quickly formed, including both Constitutionalists and young progressives like Tran Huy Lieu and Phan Van Truong.[69] The result was an unprecedented surge of people into the city and an entire week of funeral observances, capped with a long procession out to the tomb which had been constructed amidst rubber trees near Tan Son Nhat. To the Vietnamese it was truly a national funeral—or certainly the closest they had ever had to such a thing.[70] Several hundred parallel-sentence banners were received, including one from Phan Boi Chau.[71] Bui Quang Chieu and Huynh Thuc Khang gave orations, the former talking comfortably of Phan's supposed advocacy of Franco-Vietnamese collaboration, the latter implicitly countering this by arguing that Phan had lived first for "overturning the regime and the coming of freedom and popular rights."[72] There was a strike by Vietnamese workers at the rice mill in Cho-Lon. Students in a number of schools wore mourning bands, and when this was prohibited and the prohibition ignored, a number of boys were expelled.[73] In Hanoi on April 4 there was a large memorial observance at the temple for the Trung sisters, and stores were closed the following day.[74] Several other towns tried to

68. CMCD-4, pp. 97–98, 101–103. Le Van Thu, *Hoi Kin*, pp. 26–37.
69. The Nguyen, *Phan Chu Trinh*, pp. 53–56, has a full list of participants, both individual and group.
70. This point is made by Huynh Thuc Khang, *Tu Truyen*, p. 47. Tran Huy Lieu, one of the organizers, estimates that 140,000 persons lined the funeral procession route; he notes with quiet glee that the police frequently lost control of the crowd. CMCD-4, p. 99.
71. The Nguyen, *Phan Chu Trinh*, pp. 68–78, lists many of these banners, forwarded to Vietnamese funerals somewhat as floral arrangements are in the West. The style and content of the parallel sentences was still largely subject to traditional prescriptions.
72. *Ibid.*, pp. 58–61. Huynh Thuc Khang himself lived on until 1947, making one attempt at collaboration with the French through his election to the Annam Popular Representative Assembly (1926–1928), withdrawing in disgust to concentrate on his Hue newspaper, *Tieng Dan*, which appeared regularly until it was shut down by the Japanese in 1943. Huynh Thuc Khang, *Tu Truyen*, pp. 47–52. In 1945 Huynh accepted a portfolio as the Minister of the Interior in the new Democratic Republic of Vietnam and then in 1946 became president of the Lien Viet Front and titular head of the government while Ho Chi Minh was in Paris.
73. Ralph B. Smith, "Bui Quang Chieu and the Constitutionalist Party in French Cochinchina, 1917–30," pp. 141–142, citing the report of the British Consul in Saigon, F. G. Gorton, April 1926.
74. CMCD-4, 99–100. Matsushita Mitsuhiro, a prominent Japanese merchant in

organize public observances but were blocked by the authorities, producing the first tentative student strikes of that generation.[75]

Conclusion

Perhaps the men studied here were merely tilting at windmills. Perhaps even their best ideas and intentions could never alter the objective conditions of the time. After all, the French had a monopoly on force. The colonizers were able to find a sufficient number of collaborators to assist them in consolidating their position. And they were not to be dislodged until 1945, when another alien power, the Japanese, upset the colonial mechanism in Indochina sufficiently to leave the way open for Nguyen Ai Quoc (by that time, Ho Chi Minh) and the Viet-Minh to move amidst revolutionary circumstances and build a truly effective anticolonial movement.

Was it worth it, then, for so many intelligent individuals to devote their lives to assaulting a colonial system that would not budge? In the most basic sense this question is irrelevant, since men throughout history have tried to alter situations that they did not, could not, fully comprehend. Even when they have believed that they understood, they have not often waited around for "objective conditions" to place prime opportunities in their laps—especially when they have conceived others to be challenging their very existence.

The anticolonial scholar-gentry of the period between 1885 and 1925, so often the recipients of French force, were not unaware of the odds against them. They also perceived that it was the Vietnamese collaborators who provided the colonial system with its day-to-day continuity, its real staying power. Without its native supporters, the system could not have survived for very long, and this truth rankled more than any other.

Yet they chose to act, in the same spirit as their ancestors had acted against Mongol, Ming, and Ch'ing invaders. When they came to understand, after much bloodshed, that the old techniques, symbols, and values were not working against this new invader, they began looking outward, beyond all their previous experiences, for alternatives. That this was an open-ended decision, full of unknown implications for themselves and their people, may not have been understood in the beginning. Even if it had been, however, most of them would have gone ahead anyway, since there was a sense of desperation in the air.

Granting the objective difficulties facing these men, I have attempted

---

Indochina, also recalls a general response among the common people of Haiphong. From a personal interview, June 2, 1967.
75. CMCD-4, p. 100.

to demonstrate that they still were successful in several ways. Most important, they succeeded in creating and re-creating resistance symbols and ideals for subsequent generations. Without this, who can say that the men who came after them would have had the sense of continuity and historical purpose to act as they did?

I have also argued that the generation coming to the fore after 1900, the generation of Phan Boi Chau and Phan Chu Trinh, succeeded in raising most of the significant questions of long-term modernization and Westernization. They were not always intellectually consistent, nor were they in complete agreement with each other, but they moved ahead with a sense of curiosity and dedication that cannot but command admiration. As I have said, too, those men set the guidelines for most later debate on anticolonial tactics, strategy, and doctrine. The next generation would be better equipped intellectually and would have the advantage of improved objective circumstances, but without having access to the experiences of their predecessors, they doubtless would have made many more errors than they did.

How have the prime personalities, Phan Chu Trinh and Phan Boi Chau, stood the test of time? It is ironic that Phan Chu Trinh, above all a man of ideas, of intellect, should today be remembered most fondly not for the substance of his thinking, although that is certainly considered important, but for his proud, stubborn refusal to compromise personally with the colonial overloads and for his sarcastic, sometimes savage, baiting of king and court. Even as he died, his reformist ideas, properly emasculated and misinterpreted, were becoming the jealously guarded "property" of one group, the wealthy burgeoisie. Having gained some advantage for themselves, these men were frightened by the upsurge of lower-class discontent: the outbreaks from 1929 through 1931 sent them into final dependent alliance with the French. Phan Chu Trinh's historical position would be sustained more accurately by others, as they recalled his slashing manner of speaking, his refusal on Con-lon to talk to the French prison director unless he was invited to sit down, and, especially, the austere conditions of his exile which reflected the scholar-gentry's traditional expression of high displeasure by abstention from state services.

Phan Boi Chau's objectives in life were simpler and more obvious than those of Phan Chu Trinh, yet, paradoxically, they have proved to be more difficult to accomplish. Phan Boi Chau wanted an end to foreign exploitation, an end to slavish bowing and scraping before alien doors. While many of Phan Chu Trinh's visions of modernization have come to fruition—and even been surpassed—Phan Boi Chau's vision of a Vietnam without foreign overlords has remained just beyond grasp, a spur to further agonizing effort—which may be the secret of why today the memory of Phan Boi Chau remains more intimate, more meaningful, to the mass of the Vietnamese people.

Phan Boi Chau's contemporary tragedy was that he defined his activism largely in terms of the target he was attacking—the French who had assaulted and colonized his country—without ever really defining himself or his movement. This led him and his followers into a blind alley of simple reaction to others' actions.

Phan Chu Trinh's tragedy was that his honest attempts to define himself anew in terms of the French Revolution and nineteenth-century European thought had led him closer to the very country whose contemporary colonial regime he and other Vietnamese patriots were pledged to overturn.

Only in this context is it possible to appreciate the raw historic symbolism of Nguyen Ai Quoc's decision to participate in the foundation of the French Communist party and become a part of the Comintern's avowed international assault on imperialism. Where else could a sensitive, engaged Vietnamese citizen of that time both openly proclaim his abhorrence of a particular France, a colonial France, and advance revolutionary social doctrines on which France in large part still held a monopoly? Where else could one relate simultaneously to the activist "anti-imperialist" traditions of Phan Boi Chau and the socially progressive "anti-feudal" ideals of Phan Chu Trinh?

The period between 1925 and 1945 saw a merging of those two intellectual streams within Vietnamese anticolonial movements. It became unmistakable that the French were not going to allow the Vietnamese to modernize their institutions effectively or to allow them any real responsibility for self-government. On the other hand, it was no longer valid simply to organize a conspiratorial group and throw hundreds—even thousands and tens of thousands—of young men and women under the sophisticated wheels of colonial repression. Given a poorly prepared populace, a hopelessly inferior technology, and a scant understanding of the international ramifications of their situation, they might all die or be imprisoned without having advanced their country one step closer to salvation.

Equally important, it was only after 1925 that the emotion-laden arguments of the fading scholar-gentry were finally brought home to the peasants and the villagers. The critical, sustained challenge to the Vietnamese identity that had affected the elite of the previous generation had at last become the apocalyptic nightmare of the millions. Economic crisis intensified the fears and torment of almost every segment of the population, lending more credence to radical social proposals. World War II demonstrated for the Vietnamese that the French, for all the myths of their invincibility which had been built up over the previous eighty years, were indeed human and vulnerable. By 1945 salvation from the foreigner was taken by the peasantry to include salvation from hunger, tenantry, and taxes—a merging of activist and reformist ambitions that fueled the deadly struggle that ended at Dien Bien Phu and that continues to motivate many in the conflict now under way.

Glossary

Complete Vietnamese readings, including diacritical marks, are provided here for all names and terms introduced in the main text and for those mentioned in the footnotes, apart from source listings. The arrangement is alphabetical, but not in standard Vietnamese fashion (i.e., broken down by diacritical markings, multiple-letter initial consonants, etc.), since this might be too confusing to some readers. Only one non-English initial consonant demands differentiation in the alphabet here: Đ (in lower case, đ), which follows D.

Á tế á

Ái Cáo Nam Kỳ Phụ Lão

Ái Chủng Ca

Ái nghĩa

Ái Quần Ca

Ái quốc

Ái Quốc Ca

Ái tỉnh

Ai Việt Điếu Điền

Ấm Ninh

Ám sát cá nhân

An Giang

An Nam

An Nam Quốc

An Nam Quốc Vương

An ninh

Án sát

Anh em

Ba Đình

Bắc Cạn

Bắc Giang

Bắc Ninh

Bạch Đằng

Bãi Sậy

Bảng

Bạo động

Bảo Lạc

Bảo Thụ

Bất chấn Hán học, bất túc
   dĩ cứu Nam Quốc

Bất nghị

Bất phế Hán tự, bất túc
   dĩ cứu Nam Quốc

Bảy Đỏ

Bệ Hạ

Bến ván

Bến Tre

Bia

Biên Hòa

Bình Dương

Bình Định

Bình Định Vương

Bình hoa

Bình Nghị Bộ

Bính Ngọ Hiên

Bỉnh sơn

Bình Tây Sát Tả Đại Tướng

Binh Thư Yếu Lược

Bỉnh Thuận

Bồng sơn

Bùi Hữu Nghĩa

Bùi Quang Chiêu

Bút đàm

Cà mâu

Các Chú Tập Bình

Cách Lan Tư Đốn

Cách mệnh

Cải lương

Cam lộ

Cam ranh

Cẩm Tác

Cẩm tác lúc bị giam ở
  Ngục Xăng tê

Cẩm tác trong Nhà Tù
  Quảng Đông

Cẩm trưởng

Cần Kiệm

Can lộc

Cần Thơ

Cần Vương

Cảnh

Cao Bá Nhạ

Cao Bá Quát

Cao Bằng

Cao Điền

Cáo Hủ Lậu Văn

Cao lãnh

Cao Thắng

Cao Văn Long

Cầu giấy

Chài Lịch

Chấn Hoa Hưng Á Hội

Châu Đốc

Chèo

Chỉ hòa

Chỉ Thành Thông Thánh

Chính học

Chính sách bế môn tỏa cảng

Chợ Lớn

Chợ mới

Chữ nho

Chữ nôm

Cờ đen

Cổ động

Cơ Mật Viện

Côn lôn

Con quỷ

Công

Công bằng

Công đức

Công Huyền Tôn Nữ Nha Trang

Công lương

Cử nhân

Cụ thể

Cung Kỳ Thao Thiên

Cường Để

Cứu quốc

Dặm

Dân

Dân ca

Dân chủ

Dân chủ cộng hòa

Dân cống

Dân đức

Dân khí

Dân quyền

Dân tộc

Dân trí

Dân trọc

Dân vi bang bản

Dị bào

Diệt chủng

Dục Thanh

Dương Bá Trạc

Dương Minh Thành

Duy tân

Duy Tân Hội

Đà

Đà Nẵng

Đại Cồ Việt

Đại lộc

Đại Minh Quốc, Phan Xích
    Long Hoàng Đế, Thiên Tử

Đại Nam

Đại Việt

Đàm Xuyên

Đan Ba

Đan Nhiễm

Đăng Cổ Tùng Báo

Đặng Nguyên Cẩn

Đặng Thái Mai

Đặng Thái Thân

Đặng Tử Kinh

Đặng Tử Mẫn

Đặng Văn Bá

Đạo

Đạo Đức và Luân Lý
    Đông Tây

Đạo Lành

Đào Nguyên Phổ

Đào Tấn

Đập đá ở Côn lôn

Đậu Cơ Quang

Đầu hồ

Đế

Đề Thám

Đề Tỉnh Quốc Dân Ca

Điện Bàn

Điện Biên Phủ

Điếu Hủ Nho

Đinh Công Tráng

Đỉnh Thần

Đỉnh Thí

Đinh Tiên Hoàng

Định Tường

Đỗ Chấn Thiết

Đỗ Cơ Quang

Đỗ Hữu Phương

Đô Sát Viện

Đồ Sơn

Đoàn Thị Điểm

Đoàn Trưng

Đốc học

Đốc Nam

Đốc Ngữ

Đội Cấn

Đồn điền	Hà Tiên
Động	Hà Tỉnh
Đông Á Đồng Minh Hội	Hai Bà
Đông Á Song Phụng	Hải côn
Đông bào	Hải Dương
Đông chủ	Hải Ngoại Huyết Thư
Đông Du	Hải Thu
Đông Dương Cộng Sản Đảng	Hải Vân
Đông Dương Tạp Chí	Hàm Nghi
Đồng Hới	Hán
Đồng Khánh	Hậu Trần Dật Sử
Đông Kinh Nghĩa Thục	Hèn
Đồng Thái	Hi Mã
Đồng Tháp Mười	Hịch Cáo Quốc Dân Văn
Đức thọ	Hồ Chí Minh
Giả Châu	Hồ giã gạo
Gia Định	Hồ Lệ
Gia Định Báo	Hồ Quý Ly
Gia lâm	Hồ Xuân Hương
Gia Long	Hỏa Lệ Cống Ngôn
Gia phả	Hoa Tiên
Giặc	Hoa Tiên Ký
Giải Huân	Hoài đức
Giải nguyên	Hoàn Kiếm
Giải Sán	Hoàng Cao Khải
Gianh	Hoàng Diệu
Giáo	Hoàng đế
Giao chỉ	Hoàng giáp
Giáo thụ	Hoàng Hoa Thám
Gò Công	Hoàng Phan Thái
Hà Đông	Hoàng Tá Viêm
Hà giang	Hoàng Tăng Bí
Hà Nội	Hoàng Trọng Mậu

Hoằng Xương

Học bánh tây sữa bò

Hốc môn

Học Quy Tân Trường

Hội An

Hội Đồng Hiến

Hội thí

Hòn gay

Hồng Bàng

Hồng Lạc

Hồng Long

Huấn đạo

Huấn Quyền

Huế

Hưng Đạo Vương

Hưng Hóa

Hưng Yên

Hương

Hương thí

Hữu Thanh

Hủy báng

Huỳnh Công Tấn

Huỳnh Hưng

Huỳnh Kim Khánh

Huỳnh Mẫn Đạt

Huỳnh Thúc Kháng

Huỳnh Tịnh Của

Khải Định

Khiêm

Khố xanh

Khởi nghĩa

Khuyến Du Học Hội

Khuyến Người Nước

Khuyến Quốc Dân Tư Trợ

  Du Học Văn

Kịch liệt

Kiến Hưng

Kim Vân Kiều

Kính Cáo Tuyền Quốc Phụ

  Lão Văn

Kính Gửi Đồng Bào Toàn Quốc

Kinh tế

Kỷ hà tắc cố

Kỷ hòa

Kỷ Niệm Lục

La qua

La Sơn

Lạc Long Quân

Lâm Đức Mậu

Lâm Đức Thụ

Lâm Ngu

Lạng Sơn

Lao bảo

Lào Cai

Lê

Lê Ấp Tốn

Lễ Bộ

Lê Dư

Lê Dương

Lê Đại

Lê Hồng Phong

Lê Hồng Sơn

Lê Lợi

Lễ nghĩa

Lê Ninh

Lê Quý Đôn

Lê Thánh Tông

Lê Thành Khôi

Lê Trực

Lê Văn Duyệt

Lê Văn Huân

Liên Á Sô Ngôn

Liên bạt

Liên Thành

Liên Việt

Linh hồn

Lô

Lồng dân

Lồng người

Long Xuyên

Lư Thoa

Luận Ngữ

Lục Nam

Lục Tỉnh

Lục Tỉnh Tân Văn

Lương

Lương Lập Nham

Lương Nghị Khanh

Lương Ngọc Danh Sơn

Lương Ngọc Quyến

Lương Tam Kỳ

Lương Trúc Đàm

Lương Văn Can

Lưu Cầu Huyết Lệ Tân Thư

Lưu Vĩnh Phúc

Lý

Lý Thường Kiệt

Lý Thụy

Lý Tuệ

Mạc

Mai Lão Bạng

Mai Sơn

Mán

Mang cá

Mất nước

Minh chủ

Minh Mạng

Minh Tân

Mính Viên

Móng Cái

Mường

Mỹ đức

Mỹ Tho

Nam Bình Vương

Nam Đàn

Nam Định

Nam Phong Tạp Chí

Nam Quốc Địa Dư Chí

Nam Quốc Vĩ Nhân Truyện

Nam Trung

Nam Việt

Nam Xương

Nga sơn

Ngàn Sâu

Nghệ An

Nghè Ôn

Nghị lộc

Nghi trung

Nghĩa

Nghĩa đảng

Nghĩa Hòa

Nghĩa quân

Nghĩa sĩ

Nghĩa thục

Ngô Đức Kế

Ngô Quang Bích

Ngô Quyền

Ngô Sĩ Liên

Ngô Vi Lâm

Ngọc Sơn

Ngu

Ngư Hải

Ngũ luân

Ngục Trung Thư

Nguyễn

Nguyễn Ái Quốc

Nguyễn An Khương

Nguyễn An Ninh

Nguyễn Ánh

Nguyễn Bá Học

Nguyễn Bỉnh Khiêm

Nguyễn Công Trứ

Nguyễn Du

Nguyễn Duy Hàn

Nguyễn Duy Hiệu

Nguyễn Điển

Nguyễn Đình Chiểu

Nguyễn Đình Kiên

Nguyễn Đình Nghị

Nguyễn Đôn Phục

Nguyễn Đức Công

Nguyễn Hải Thần

Nguyễn Hàm

Nguyễn Huệ

Nguyễn Hữu Huân

Nguyễn Hữu Tiến

Nguyễn Huy Tự

Nguyễn Khuyến

Nguyễn Lộ Trạch

Nguyễn Lữ

Nguyễn Nhạc

Nguyễn Phạm Tuân

Nguyễn Phan Lãng

Nguyễn Phan Long

Nguyễn Phúc Ánh

Nguyễn Quang Bích

Nguyễn Quang Diêu

Nguyễn Quyền

Nguyễn Siêu

Nguyễn Sinh Cung

Nguyễn Sinh Sắc

Nguyễn Tất Thành

Nguyễn Thái Bạt

Nguyễn Thân

Nguyễn Thần Hiến

Nguyễn Thành

Nguyễn Thiện Kế

Nguyễn Thiện Thuật

Nguyễn Thông

Nguyễn Thức Canh

Nguyễn Thục Đăng

Nguyễn Thức Đường

Nguyễn Thượng Hiền

Nguyễn Thượng Huyền

Nguyễn Trãi

Nguyễn Tri Phương

Nguyễn Trọng Thưởng

Nguyễn Trung Trực

Quán tre

Quân trị chủ nghĩa và
   dân trị chủ nghĩa

Quảng Bình

Quảng Nam

Quảng Ngãi

Quang Phục Quân

Quảng Tín

Quảng Trị

Quang Trung

Quảng Yên

Quế Điền Việt Liên Minh
   Hội

Qui Nhơn

Quỉ thiêng

Quốc Dân

Quốc gia

Quốc Học

Quốc hồn

Quốc ngữ

Quốc Sử Quán

Quốc túy

Rạch giá

Sa đéc

Sa Nam

Sài gòn

Sĩ phu

Sở Cuồng

Sơn La

Sơn lăng

Sơn Tây

Sử Bỉnh Tử

Sử Kinh

Sùng Bái Giai Nhân

Ta

Tả

Tạ Hiện

Tà lùng

Tạ Thúc Đỉnh

Tạ Thúc Khải

Tà thuyết

Tái Sinh

Tam đảo

Tam kỳ

Tâm Tâm Xã

Tam Tự Kinh

Tân An

Tân hỏa

Tân học

Tân sở

Tân sơn nhất

Tân Việt Cách Mệnh Đảng

Tân Việt Nam

Tân Việt Nam Cống Hiến

Tăng Bạt Hổ

Tập Xuyên

Tây Hồ

Tây Lộc

Tây Ninh

Tây Sơn

Tây tựu

Tết

Thái Bình

Thái Nguyên

Thái Phiên

Thai Sơn

Thái Thượng Hoàng

Thái Tổ

Thái Tông

Thái Xuyên

Thân sĩ

Thăng Bình

Thăng long

Thạnh Bình

Thanh cậy thế, Nghệ cậy
   thần

Thanh Hóa

Thạnh Mỹ

Thanh Niên

Thành Thái

Thánh Tông

Thất Điền

Thất sơn

Thi Kinh

Thí Sinh quân

Thiên Hộ Dương

Thiên Hồ Đế Hồ

Thiên Triều

Thiết Tiền Ca

Thiếu niên cao khoa, nhất bất
   hạnh giã

Thiệu Trị

Thịnh hào

Thổ

Thơ

Thơ bốn chữ

Thù Chồng Nợ Nước

Thủ Dầu Một

Thủ Khoa Huân

Thuận An

Thuận thành

Thượng Binh

Thương hải vị điền, tinh
   vệ hàm thạch

Thượng trì

Tỉ Tư Mạch

Tích cực

Tiên đả hôn quân, hậu đả
   loạn thần

Tiên Phước

Tiến sĩ

Tiếng Dân

Tiêu cực

Tiểu La

Tin tưởng

Tinh

Tỉnh

Tỉnh Quốc Hồn Ca

Tinh thần

Tinh thần cách mạng lãng mạn

Tinh thần dân tộc

Tỉnh yêu

Tội

Tôn Sĩ Nghị

Tôn Thất Đạm

Tôn Thất Thiệp

Tôn Thất Thuyết

Tôn Thất Toại

Tôn Thọ Tường

Tổng

Tống Duy Tân

Tổng đốc

Tổng sơn

Trẩm

Trần

Trần Bá Lộc

Trần Bá Thọ

Trần Cao Vân

Trần Chánh Chiếu

Trần Hưng Đạo

Trần Hữu Công

Trần Hữu lực

Trần Huy Liệu

Trần Nhựt Thi

Trần Quốc Tuấn

Trần Quý Cáp

Trần Thái Tông

Trần Thánh Tông

Trần Thị

Trần Thiện Chánh

Trần Trọng Kim

Trần Văn Giàu

Trần Xuân Hòa

Trảng bàng

Trảo nha

Trí

Tri huyện

Tri phủ

Triết Phu

Triệu Quang Phục

Trịnh

Trịnh Văn Cấn

Trịnh Văn Đạt

Trứ tác

Trung

Trưng

Trung Lễ

Trưng Nhị

Trùng Quang Tâm Sử

Trung Quốc

Trưng Trắc

Trương

Trương Bửu Lâm

Trương Công Định

Trương Định

Trương Quyền

Trương Vĩnh Ký

Trừu tượng

Truyện Kiều

Tự cường

Tự Đức

Tú Ngôn

Tứ phương phong động, duy
   nãi chi hưu

Tú tài

Tứ Thư Ngũ Kinh

Tự trị

Tuần phủ

Tùng Nham

Tuồng

Tuồng Trưng Nữ Vương

Tuy An

Tuyên Quang

Tuyệt Mệnh Thi

Ưng hòa

Văn minh

Văn Minh Tân Học Sách

Văn sách

Văn võ

Vật chất

Vi Văn Lý

Việt Nam

Việt Nam Cống Hiến Hội

Việt Nam Quang Phục Hội

Việt Nam Quốc Dân Đảng

Việt Nam Quốc Sử Khảo

Việt Nam Thanh Niên Cách
  Mạng Đồng Chí Hội

Việt Nam Vong Quốc Sử

Việt Trì

Việt Vong Thảm Trạng

Việt yên hạ

Vinh

Vĩnh Long

Vĩnh Yên

Võ

Vọng chi bất tự nhân quân

Vong quốc

Vong quốc nô

Vũ Hải Thu

Vụ Quang

Vua

Vũng Tàu

Vương Thúc Quý

Vương Văn Lê

Xứ

Xuân Thu

Yên bảy

Yên sĩ phi lý thuần

Yên thế

Yêu ghét

Yêu nước

Bibliography

Entries are listed in three categories: (A) Vietnamese-language sources, (B) Western-language sources, and (C) Chinese- and Japanese-language sources. I have added comments to some entries, usually more to explain a title than to attempt any full critical annotation. Many modern books issued by the government in North Vietnam are published under the names of all members of joint research committees; for the sake of brevity, I have listed these publications under the name of the principal author and have indicated the rest of the committee by "*et al.*" In addition to the abbreviations listed on page *ix*, the following appear here: NXB for *Nha Xuat Ban* (Publishing House) and XB for *Xuat Ban* (Publisher).

A. Vietnamese-language Sources

Anh Minh (Ngo Thanh Nhan). *Dat Su Cu Phan Sao Nam* (Extraordinary Activities of Phan Boi Chau). Hue: Anh Minh XB, 1950.

————. *Ky Ngoai Hau Cuong De* (Prince Cuong De). Saigon: Anh Minh XB, 1951.

————, ed. *Nguyen Lo Trach*. Hue: Anh Minh XB, 1966.

Bao Dinh Giang and Ca Van Thinh, eds. *Tho Van Yeu Nuoc Nam Bo* (Patriotic Poetry and Prose of the Southern Region). Hanoi: NXB Van Hoa, 1962.

Bao La Cu Si. "Viet-Nam tren duong giai phong" (Vietnam on the road to liberation). VHNS 50–54.

Chau Hai Ky. "Nhung hoat dong cach mang cua cu Phan Chau Trinh tai Binh Thuan" (Revolutionary activities of Phan Chau Trinh in Binh Thuan). BK 101: 117–119.

Chu Dang Son. *Luan De ve Phan Boi Chau va Phan Chu Trinh* (Topics Concerning Phan Boi Chau and Phan Chu Trinh). Saigon: Thang Long XB, 1959.

Chu Quang Tru. "Can nghiem khac len an Phan Thanh Gian" (We must severely sentence Phan Thanh Gian). NCLS 51: 35–39, 48.

———. "Tim hieu Phan Chu Trinh trong lich su can dai Viet-Nam" (Phan Chu Trinh's position in the modern history of Vietnam). NCLS 72: 50–56, 62.

Chu Quang Tru, et al. "Binh Luan ve Truong Vinh Ky" (Commentaries on Truong Vinh Ky). NCLS 62: 27–29.

Chuong Thau. "Anh huong cach mang Trung Quoc doi voi su bien chuyen cua tu tuong Phan Boi Chau" (Influence of the Chinese Revolution on changes in the thought of Phan Boi Chau). NCLS 43: 12–26, 36.

———. "Anh huong cua Phan Boi Chau doi voi mot so to chuc cach mang Trung Quoc" (Influence of Phan Boi Chau on certain Chinese revolutionary organizations). NCLS 55: 33–43, 65; 56: 32–37.

———. "Loi di chuc cua Phan Boi Chau" (The last testament of Phan Boi Chau). NCLS 79: 5–7.

———. "Mot so tai lieu va y kien ve moi quan he giua Phan Boi Chau va Cuong De" (Some data and opinions on the relationship between Phan Boi Chau and Cuong De). NCLS 45: 19–24, 32.

———. "Nguon goc chu nghia yeu nuoc cua Phan Boi Chau" (The origins of Phan Boi Chau's patriotism). NCLS 88: 21–24.

———. "Phan Boi Chau qua mot so sach bao mien nam hien nay" (Phan Boi Chau as seen in some present-day publications in south Vietnam). NCLS 67: 10–20.

———. "Ve hai tap tu truyen cua Sao Nam: *Nguc Trung Thu* va *Phan Boi Chau nien bieu*" (Regarding Sao Nam's two autobiographies). NCLS 75: 37–45. Sao Nam was one of Phan Boi Chau's pseudonyms.

——— and Minh Hong. "Luu Vinh Phuc trong cuoc khang Phap cua nhan dan Viet-Nam" (Liu Yung-fu in the Vietnamese people's anti-French endeavors). NCLS 36: 7–14, 27.

Duy Minh. "Danh gia Phan Chu Trinh" (Assessing Phan Chu Trinh). NCLS 69: 15–19.

Dam Xuan Linh. "Danh gia Luu Vinh Phuc can thay mat tich cuc la chu yeu" (We should see positive aspects as primary when assessing Liu Yung-fu). NCLS 40: 48–52.

Dan Duc Loi. "Mot so y kien ve Phan Chu Trinh" (Some views on Phan Chu Trinh). NCLS 72: 57–58.

Dang Huy Van. "Danh gia Luu Vinh Phuc va doi quan co den trong lich su can dai Viet-Nam" (Assessing Liu Yung-fu and the Black Flags in the modern history of Vietnam). NCLS 37: 15–19, 25.

———. "Them mot so tai lieu ve cuoc khoi nghia nam Giap Tuat (1874) o Nghe An va Ha Tinh" (Some further documentation concerning the 1874 rising in Nghe An and Ha Tinh). NCLS 75: 10–22.

———. "Ve cuoc khoi nghia cua Tran Tan va Dang Nhu Mai nam Giap Tuat o Nghe An va Ha Tinh" (On the 1874 rising led by Tran Tan and Dang Nhu Mai in Nghe An and Ha Tinh). NCLS 79: 15–19.

———— and Chuong Thau. "Phan Thanh Gian trong lich su can dai Viet-Nam (Phan Thanh Gian in the modern history of Vietnam). NCLS 48: 12–23.

Dang Thai Mai, *Van Tho Cach Mang Viet Nam Dau The Ky XX* (Vietnam's Revolutionary Prose and Poetry in the Early Twentieth Century). Hanoi: NXB Van Hoc, 1964. An extremely valuable work, for both the author's historical essay and the many primary materials reprinted.

————. *Van Tho Phan Boi Chau* (The Prose and Poetry of Phan Boi Chau). Hanoi: NXB Van Hoa, 1960.

Dang Viet Thanh, "Can nhan dinh va danh gia Phan Thanh Gian nhu the nao?" (How should we perceive and assess Phan Thanh Gian?). NCLS 49: 27–31.

————. "Danh gia quan diem luan ly dao duc cua cu Phan Chu Trinh" (Assessing the moral and ethical position of Phan Chu Trinh). NCLS 68: 21–24.

————. "Phong Trao Dong Kinh Nghia Thuc" (The Dong Kinh Nghia Thuc movement). NCLS 25: 14–24.

————. "Tro lai ban ve giai cap tu san mai ban nuoc ta trong thoi thuoc Phap" (Returning to a discussion of the Vietnamese compradore class during French colonial rule). NCLS 32: 15–24.

Dao Duy Anh. *Han Viet Tu Dien* (Chinese-Vietnamese Dictionary). Saigon: Truong Thi XB, 1957. First published, 1931.

————. *Viet-Nam Van Hoa Su Cuong* (An Outline History of Vietnamese Culture). Saigon: XB Bon Phuong, 1951. First published, 1938.

Dao Trinh Nhat. *Dong Kinh Nghia Thuc.* Hanoi: Mai Linh XB, 1938.

————. *Luong Ngoc Quyen.* Saigon: Tan Viet XB, 1957.

————. *Phan Dinh Phung (1847–1895).* Saigon: Tan Viet XB, 1957.

Dao Van Hoi. *Ba Nha Chi Si Ho Phan* (Three Patriots Named Phan). Saigon: n.p. 1957.

Dau Xuan Mai. "Vai tro Phan Chu Trinh trong lich su can dai Viet-Nam" (Phan Chu Trinh's role in Vietnam's modern history). NCLS 71: 31–39.

Do Thien. "Phong trao Ky-Dong nam 1897" (The Ky Dong movement of 1897). NCLS 64: 55–58.

H.H. "Gioi thieu Truong Vinh Ky" (Introducing Truong Vinh Ky). NCLS 56: 13–23.

Ha Thanh, *et al. Tu Dien Viet Han* (Vietnamese-Chinese Dictionary). Peking, 1966.

Hanh Son. *Cu Tran Cao Van.* Paris: Minh Tan XB, 1952.

Ho Huu Phuoc and Pham Thi Minh Le. "Gop them y kien ve viec danh gia Nguyen Truong To" (Contributing some opinions on the assessment of Nguyen Truong To). NCLS 31: 60–62.

Ho Huu Tuong. "Hien Tuong Truong Cong Dinh" (The Phenomenon of Truong Cong Dinh). SD 3: 115–129.

Ho Song. "Ban them ve Truong Vinh Ky" (Some more thoughts on Truong Vinh Ky). NCLS 61: 31–34.

———. "Phan Chu Trinh voi thoi dai cua ong" (Phan Chu Trinh in relation to his times). NCLS 75: 38–43.

———. "Vai nhan xet ve *Lich su can dai Viet-Nam,* Tap III" (Some observations on the *Modern History of Viet-Nam,* Vol. 3). NCLS 64: 39–45. A review of the named book written by Tran Van Giau.

Hoa Bang. "Phan Chu Trinh (1872–1926)." NCLS 72: 46–49.

———. *Quang Trung.* Saigon: NXB Bon Phuong, 1958. First published, 1944.

Hoai Nam. "Ve goc tich cua Ong De Tham" (On the origins of De Tham). NCLS 38: 35–37.

Hoai Thanh, *et al. Bac Ho, Hoi Ky* (Reminiscences About Uncle Ho). Hanoi: NXB Van Hoc, 1960.

Hoang Nam. "Danh gia vai tro Nguyen Truong To trong lich su can dai Viet-Nam" (Assessing Nguyen Truong To's role in the modern history of Vietnam). NCLS 29: 34–40.

Hoang Nam Hung. *Nam Muoi Nam Cach Mang Hai Ngoai* (Fifty Years of Overseas Revolutionary Activity). Saigon: Hong Phat, 1960.

Hoang Thuc Tram. *Quang Trung.* Saigon: n.p., 1950.

Hoang Tuan Pho. "Troi lai van de Ba-Dinh" (Returning to the question of Ba-Dinh). NCLS 81: 38–43.

———. "Ve ban do cu diem phong ngu Ba-Dinh" (Concerning a map of the Ba-Dinh defense positions). NCLS 74: 61–63.

Hoang Van Lan and Dang Huy Van. "Nhin nhan Truong Vinh Ky the nao cho dung?" (How do we correctly view Truong Vinh Ky?). NCLS 61: 16–30.

Hoang Xuan. *Phan Boi Chau Thi-tap* (The Collected Poems of Phan Boi Chau). Saigon: Anh Phuong XB, 1959.

———. *Phan Chu Trinh Thi-tap* (The Collected Poems of Phan Chu Trinh). Saigon: Anh Phuong XB, 1959.

Hoang Xuan Han. *Ly Thuong Kiet.* Saigon: Vien Dai Hoc Van Hanh, 1966.

Hong Chuong. "Cuong De: anh hung cuu nuoc hay Viet-gian ban nuoc?" (Cuong De: brave savior or high traitor to his country?). NCLS 43: 37–43.

Hung Ha. "Tu tuong quoc gia cai luong cua Phan Chu Trinh" (Reformist nationalist thought of Phan Chu Trinh). NCLS 68: 17–21, 25.

Huong Son and Thai Vu. "Nguyen Don Tiet: mot thu linh cua Phong-Trao Can-Vuong tinh Thanh-Hoa" (Nguyen Don Tiet: a commander of the Can-Vuong movement in Thanh Hoa). NCLS 92: 31–37.

Huynh Thuc Khang (Minh Vien). *Buc Thu Bi Mat* (Secret Letter). Hue: Anh Minh XB, 1957. Title assigned by publisher. Originally, a long letter to Cuong De sent March 5, 1943.

———. *Phan Tay Ho Tien Sinh Lich Su* (A Biography of Phan Chu Trinh). Hue: Anh Minh XB, 1959. Written in 1926. Perhaps the most reliable source available for data on Phan Chu Trinh, particularly for the period before 1911.

———. *Tu Truyen* (Autobiography). Hue: Anh Minh XB, 1963.

Khong Xuan Thu. *Truong Vinh Ky (1837–1898)*. Saigon: NXB Tan Viet, 1958.

Kiem Dat. *Luan De ve Phan Boi Chau* (Topics concerning Phan Boi Chau). Saigon: Khai Tri XB, 1960.

Kieu Oanh Mau. *Ban Trieu Ban Nghich Liet Truyen* (Biographies of Traitors to the Dynasty). Saigon: Bo Quoc Gia Giao Duc XB, 1963.

Le Thuoc, "Co phai day la bai *Luu Cau Huyet Le Tan Thu* cua Phan Boi Chau khong?" (Is this Phan Boi Chau's *Luu Cau Huyet Le Tan Thu?*). *Van Su Dia* 33.

―――. "Mot van kien cua cu Phan Dinh Phung vua moi phat hien" (A just-uncovered document written by Phan Dinh Phung). NCLS 71: 23–25, 30.

―――, trans. and commentator. "Viet-Nam Chinh Khi Ca" (A ballad on Vietnam's true spirit). NCLS 73: 21–29. Written c. 1900 in Chinese and *quoc-ngu* versions.

Le Van Hao. "May net ve hoi song Viet-Nam giua the ky thu XIX" (Some indications of common existence in mid-nineteenth-century Vietnam). In Truong Ba Can, *et al., Ky Niem 100 Nam Ngay Phap Chiem Nam-Ky,* pp. 59–74.

―――, ed. *Ky-Niem 100 Nam Nam-Sinh Phan Boi Chau* (Centennial Anniversary of the Birth of Phan Boi Chau). Saigon: NXB Trinh Bay, 1967.

Le Van Thu (Viet Tha). *Hoi Kin Nguyen An Ninh* (The Secret Society of Nguyen An Ninh). Saigon: NXB Me Linh, 1961. Originally published, 1949.

Luong Khe. "Gop may y kien danh gia Phan Chu Trinh" (Adding some opinions on assessment of Phan Chu Trinh). NCLS 69: 20–28.

Ly Chanh Trung. "Suy nghi ve hai chu 'mat nuoc' " (Reflections on the two words, "mat nuoc"). In Truong Ba Can, *et al., Ky Niem 100 Nam Ngay Phap Chiem Nam-ky,* pp. 220–240.

Mai Hanh. "Tim hieu thuc chat van de Truong Vinh Ky trong lich su Viet-Nam" (Understanding the real question of Truong Vinh Ky in the history of Vietnam). NCLS 58: 15–28.

Man Quoc. "Truong Vinh Ky: mot nha bac hoc tru danh da ngang nhien dong vai dac vu tinh bao lam tay sai dac luc cho giac Phap" (Truong Vinh Ky: a prominent scientist who openly gathered special intelligence as an effective lackey of the enemy). NCLS 60: 39–45.

Nam Kieu. *Tieu Su Ong Phan Chau Trinh* (Biography of Phan Chau Trinh). Saigon: n.p., 1926.

Nam Xuan Tho. *Phan Thanh Gian (1796–1867)*. Saigon: NXB Tan Viet, 1957.

NCLS, eds. "Nhung nhan dinh khac nhau ve vai tro cua Luu Vinh Phuc va Quan Co-den" (Differing assessments on the role of Liu Yung-fu and the Black Flags). NCLS 41: 8–22.

―――. "So ket cuoc thao luan ve hai nhan vat Ho Quy Ly va Nguyen Truong

To" (Tentative summing up of our discussions of Ho Quy Ly and Nguyen Truong To). NCLS 33: 8–16.

———. "Trich dang mot so bai binh luan ve Phan Chu Trinh" (Extracting from some commentaries on Phan Chu Trinh). NCLS 73: 54–61.

Ngo Thanh Nhan (Anh Minh). *Cu Sao Nam 15 Nam Bi Giam Long o Hue* (Phan Boi Chau's Fifteen Years of Detention in Hue). Hue: Anh Minh XB, 1956.

———. *Ngu Hanh Son Chi Si* (Patriots of the Ngu Hanh Mountain Area). Hue: Anh Minh XB, 1961.

Ngo Van Hoa. "Co phai giai-cap cong-nhan Viet-Nam da hinh-thanh giai-cap 'tu-minh' tu truoc cuoc dai chien the gioi lan thu nhat hay khong?" (Did the Vietnamese laboring class become "conscious" before World War I?). NCLS 38: 8–18, and 39: 48–54.

Nguyen Anh. "Ban them ve nguyen nhan ra doi cua hai xu-huong cai-luong va bao-dong trong phong-trao cach-mang dau the ky XX" (Added discussion on causes for emergence of reformist and activist tendencies in the early twentieth-century revolutionary movement). NCLS 65: 35–42, 46.

———. "Dong Kinh Nghia Thuc co phai la mot cuoc van dong cach-mang van-hoa dan-toc dan-chu hay khong?" (Was the Dong Kinh Nghia Thuc a democratic people's cultural revolutionary effort or not?). NCLS 32: 38–46.

———. "Vai y kien Truong Vinh Ky" (Some opinions on Truong Vinh Ky). NCLS 57: 17–27, 38.

———. "Ve nhan-vat lich-su Phan Thanh Gian" (On the historical personality Phan Thanh Gian). NCLS 50: 29–35.

Nguyen Ba The (The Nguyen). *Nguyen Dinh Chieu: Than The va Thi Van (1822–1888)* (The Life and Writings of Nguyen Dinh Chieu). Saigon: NXB Tan Viet, 1957.

———. *Ton Tho Tuong (1825–1877)*. Saigon: NXB Tan Viet, 1957.

Nguyen Cong Binh. "Tinh chat cuoc khoi-nghia Yen-the" (The nature of the Yen-the rising). NCLS 48: 28–43.

Nguyen Duy Hinh. *De Tham: Con Hum Yen-The* (De Tham: The Tiger of Yen-the). Saigon: Khai Tri XB, 1961.

Nguyen Duc Q. B. (Nguyen Duc Quynh). *Biet Thi Song* (To Know Is to Live). Saigon: author's mimeographed manuscript, 1967.

Nguyen Duc Su. "Chu nghia yeu nuoc cua Phan Boi Chau" (The patriotic ideology of Phan Boi Chau). NCLS 83: 28–36.

———. "Phan Chu Trinh voi nhiem vu chong de-quoc trong cach-mang Viet-Nam" (Phan Chu Trinh in relation to anti-imperialist tasks in the Vietnamese revolution). NCLS 69: 29–33.

Nguyen Hien Le. *Dong Kinh Nghia Thuc*. Saigon: published by the author, 1956.

———. "Moi tinh giua mot nha cach-mang Viet-Nam va mot nha hoc gia Trung Quoc" (Friendship between a Vietnamese revolutionary and a Chinese scholar). BK 174: 13–16. The reference is to Phan Boi Chau and Hu Shih.

Nguyen Huyen Anh. *Viet-Nam Danh Nhan Tu Dien* (Dictionary of Famous Men of Vietnam). Saigon: Hoi Van Hoa Binh Dan, 1960.

Nguyen Khac Dam. "Can nhan ro chan tuong Truong Vinh Ky de danh gia cho dung" (We must perceive the true identity of Truong Vinh Ky to evaluate him correctly). NCLS 59: 33–42, 46.

———. "Danh gia Phan Thanh Gian nhu the nao cho dung? (How do we properly evaluate Phan Thanh Gian?). NCLS 51: 29–34, 48.

———. "Nguyen Cao: mot van than yeu nuoc chong Phap" (Nguyen Cao: an anti-French patriotic scholar). NCLS 44: 27–28.

Nguyen Khac Ngu. "Nhung cuoc hanh-quan cua Phap o Trung va Nam-Ky" (Military operations of the French in central and south Vietnam). See Truong Ba Can, *et al., Ky Niem 100 Nam Ngay Phap Chiem Nam-Ky,* pp. 99–180.

———. "Nhung ly do khien Phap can thiep vao Viet-Nam" (Reasons for French intervention in Vietnam). In Truong Ba Can, *et al., Ky Niem 100 Nam Ngay Phap Chiem Nam-ky,* pp. 15–58.

Nguyen Lien. "Phong-trao Giap-Dan, hay la cuoc dau-tranh chong Phap (1913–14) cua nhan-dan cac dan-toc Man (Yen-bai)" (The Giap Dan movement, or the 1913–1914 anti-French struggle of the *Man* (Yen-bai) ethnic minority). NCLS 26: 55–65.

Nguyen Quynh. *Doi Can Khoi Nghia* (Sergeant Can's Uprising). Saigon: NXB Nam Cuong, 1956. The reference is to the 1917 Thai Nguyen rising.

Nguyen Thanh Nam. "May nhan xet ve Phan Chu Trinh" (Some observations on Phan Chu Trinh). NCLS 71: 40–42, 59.

Nguyen The Anh. *Kinh Te va Xa Hoi Viet-Nam duoi cac Vua Trieu Nguyen* (Vietnam's economy and society under the Nguyen dynasty kings). Saigon: NXB Trinh Bay, 1968.

Nguyen Thuong Huyen. "Cu Phan Boi Chau o Hong-Chau" (Phan Boi Chau in Hangchow). BK 73: 29–40.

Nguyen Van Hau. *Chi Si Nguyen Quang Dieu* (The patriot Nguyen Quang Dieu). Saigon: Xay Dung XB, 1964.

———. "Cu Phan Boi Chau va vai hoat-dong chinh-tri trong chuyen 'Nam Hanh' nam Qui Mao" (Phan Boi Chau and various political activities during his "southern travels" of 1903). BK 140: 11–14.

———. "Ly Lieu va Phong-trao Dai Dong Du" (Ly Lieu and the Dong Du movement). BK 145: 39–49.

———. "Nguyen Than Hien, mot lanh tu trong yeu trong phong-trao Dong Du Mien Nam" (Nguyen Than Hien, a key leader in the southern Dong Du movement). BK 124: 9–16 and 125: 9–14.

Nguyen Van Khon. *Viet-Anh Tu Dien* (Vietnamese-English Dictionary). Saigon: Khai Tri XB, 1966.

Nguyen Van Kiem. "Tim hieu xu huong va thuc chat cua Dong Kinh Nghia Thuc" (Understanding the tendencies and reality of the Dong Kinh Nghia Thuc). NCLS 66: 39–45, 58.

Nguyen Van Nhan. "Cuoc dieu tra ve hanh-dong cua Quan Co-den Luu Vinh

Phuc tai mot so lang thuoc ngoai thanh Ha-noi" (An investigation of the activities of Liu Yung-fu's Black Flags in a number of villages surrounding Hanoi). NCLS 42: 26–29.

Nguyen Van Trung. *Chu Nghia Thuc Dan Phap o Viet-Nam (Thuc Chat va Huyen Thoai)* (French Imperialist Ideology in Vietnam, Reality and Myth). Saigon: Nam Son XB, 1963.

Nhat Tam. *Phan Van Tri.* Saigon: NXB Tan Viet, 1956.

Nhuan Chi. "Can vach ro hon nua trach-nhiem cua Phan Thanh Gian truoc lich-su" (We must bare even more Phan Thanh Gian's responsibility before history). NCLS 52: 38–46.

Nhuong Tong. *Nguyen Thai Hoc.* Saigon: NXB Tan Viet, 1956.

Pham Cao Duong. "Mot vai chu truong cua Trieu Dinh Hue trong Hoa-Uoc Qui-Mui (25–8–1883)" (Some assumptions of the Hue Court in the 1883 Peace Settlement). SD 2: 52–60 and 4: 104–110.

————. "Mot vai khia canh dang chu y trong duong loi cai tri cua nguoi Phap o Nam-ky tu 1861 den 1867" (Some aspects worthy of attention in French approaches to governing South Vietnam, 1861–1867). In Truong Ba Can, *et al., Ky Niem 100 Nam Ngay Phap Chiem Nam-ky,* pp. 75–97.

————. *Thuc trang cua gioi Nong Dan Viet-Nam duoi thoi Phap thuoc* (The real conditions of the Vietnamese peasantry under French rule). Saigon: Khai Tri XB, 1966.

Pham Hoan Mi. "Phan Chu Trinh (1872–1926): Nguoi dung dau gio" (Phan Chu Trinh: a man standing against the wind). BK 30: 25–31.

Pham The Ngu. *Viet-Nam Van Hoc Su, Tap I* (A History of Vietnamese Literature, Vol. 1). Saigon: Quoc Hoc Tung Thu XB, 1961.

Pham Van Son. "Thai-do va hanh-dong cua nhan-si Viet-Nam trong khoang dau the ky XX" (Attitudes and activities of the Vietnamese scholar-gentry at the opening of the twentieth century). SD 6: 37–62.

————. *Viet-Nam Cach Mang Can Su, 1885–1914* (Vietnam's Modern Revolutionary History, 1885–1914). Saigon: Khai Tri XB, 1963.

————. *Viet-Nam Tranh-Dau Su* (Vietnam's History of Struggle). Hanoi: Vu Hung XB, 1951.

————. "Xet lai nguyen-nhan cua cac vu loan duoi doi Tu-Duc" (Reassessing the causes of local outbursts during Tu-Duc's reign). SD 1: 86–105.

Phan Boi Chau. "Ai Viet Dieu Dien va Hoa Le Cong Ngon" (Love for Vietnam, Condolences for Yunnan; and An Appeal Bathed in Tears). Transl., Chuong Thau. NCLS 56: 38–44. Two articles which originally appeared in *Yun-nan Tsa-chih* 6 and 7 (1906).

————. *Cao Dang Quoc Dan* (Elevating the Nation's People). Hue: Anh Minh XB, 1957. Written in 1927.

————. "Hai van-kien ngoai-giao dau tien cua Phan Boi Chau" (The first two foreign affairs letters of Phan Boi Chau). Transl. and comments, Chuong Thau. NCLS 90: 61–64.

————. *Khong Hoc Dang* (Clarifying Confucian Studies). 2 vols. Hue: NXB Anh Minh, 1957.

————. *Nguc Trung Thu* (Prison notes). Transl., Dao Trinh Nhat. Saigon: Tan Viet XB, 1950. Japanese translations in Nagaoka Shinjiro, *et al.*, *Betonamu Bokokushi*, pp. 87–156, and Oiwa Makoto, *Annam Minzoku Undoshi Gaisetsu*, pp. 81–126.

————. *Phan Boi Chau Nien Bieu* (Year to Year Activities of Phan Boi Chau). Hanoi: NXB Van Su Dia, 1957. Probably the most valuable source in preparing this book. See also *Tu Phan*, below. French translation (annotated) by Georges Boudarel in *France-Asie/Asia* vol. 22, nos. 3–4, pp. 3–210.

————. "Tan Viet-Nam" (New Vietnam). Introd. and transl. by Chuong Thau. NCLS 78: 31–39.

————. *Thien Ho De Ho* (Oh! Heaven, Oh! God). Shanghai: 1923. Japanese translation in Oiwa Makoto, *Annam Minzoku Undoshi Gaisetsu*, pp. 127–170, and Nagaoka Shinjiro, *et al.*, *Betonamu Bokokushi*, pp. 157–205.

————. *Tu Phan* (Self-judgment). Hue: Anh Minh XB, 1956. Translated from the same basic manuscript as *Phan Boi Chau Nien Bieu*, above.

————. *Tuong Trung Nu Vuong/Truyen Pham Hong Thai* (Drama of the Trung Monarch/Story of Pham Hong Thai). Introd., transl., and notes by Chuong Thau. Hanoi: NXB Van Hoc, 1967.

————. "Viet-Nam Vong Quoc Su" (History of the Loss of Vietnam). Saigon: *Dai Hoc Van Khoa* (Journal of the Faculty of Letters), 1961. Contains both the Chinese original and a Vietnamese translation by Ta Thuc Khai.

Phan Chu Trinh. "Bai dien thuyet ve quan-tri chu-nghia va dan-tri chu-nghia" (Text of a speech on monarchism and democracy). NCLS 67: 21–28. Also in The Nguyen, *Phan Chu Trinh*, pp. 101–127.

————. "Dao Duc va Luan Ly Dong Tay" (The Morality and Ethics of East and West). NCLS 66: 22–31. Abridged. Full text in The Nguyen, *Phan Chu Trinh*, pp. 128–164.

————. *That Dieu Thu* (Seven Point Letter). Hue: Anh Minh XB, 1958. Also in NCLS 66: 15–21, 31.

————. "Thu Gui Toan Quyen Beau" (A Letter to Governor General Beau). NCLS 66: 8–14. Also in The Nguyen, *Phan Chu Trinh*, pp. 81–100. Original Chinese in *Nam Phong* 103: 25–34.

Phan Khoang. "Nhung bien-chuyen dau-tien trong xa-hoi Viet-Nam khi tiep-xuc voi van-minh Au-Tay" (Early alterations in Vietnamese society upon contact with Western civilization). BK 67: 1822 and 68: 15–19.

————. "Nhung nguoi Viet-Nam co tinh-than cai-cach duy-tan khi nuoc nha moi tiep-xuc van-minh Tay-Phuong" (Vietnamese with a reformist spirit at the time our country first came in contact with Western civilization). BK 71: 19–25.

————. "Vi sao cac de-nghi duy-tan khong duoc thuc-hien?" (Why were reformist proposals not able to be enacted?). BK 12: 15–22.

————. *Viet-Nam Phap Thuoc Su* (History of Vietnam Under French Rule). Saigon: Khai Tri XB, 1960. The title is somewhat misleading, as more than half of the book deals with the period 1802–1883.

————. "Xa-hoi Viet-Nam truoc day co phai la phong-kien khong?" (Was Vietnam's earlier society feudal in character?). SD 6: 17–36.

Phan Phat Huon. *Viet-Nam Giao Su* (History of the Church in Vietnam). Vol. 1 (1533–1933). Saigon: Dong Chua Cuu The, 1958.

Phan Tran Chuc and Le Que. *Nguyen Tri Phuong*. Saigon: Chinh Ky XB, 1956.

Phuong Huu. *Phong Trao Dai Dong Du* (The Dong Du Movement). Saigon: Nam Viet XB, 1950.

Quoc Quang. "Gop y kien ve Cuong De" (Contributing an opinion on Cuong De). NCLS 48: 46–49, 56.

Son Nam and Ngoc Linh. *Nguyen Trung Truc*. Saigon: n.p., 1959.

Thai Bach. *Bon Vi Anh Hung Khang Chien Mien Nam* (Four Brave Men of the Southern Resistance). 2 vols. Saigon: Song Moi XB, 1957. Vol. 1 concerns Truong Cong Dinh and Vol. 2, Nguyen Trung Truc, Thu Khoa Huan, and Thien Ho Duong.

————. *Nguyen Dinh Chieu (1822–1888)*. Saigon: NXB Song Moi, 1957.

Thai Vu. "Tim hieu them ve cu-diem Ba-Dinh" (Understanding more on the Ba-Dinh strongpoint). NCLS 76: 61–65.

Thanh Le. "Phan Chu Trinh: mot si-phu phong-kien tu-san hoa giau long yeu nuoc" (Phan Chu Trinh: a bourgeois-influenced feudal scholar-gentry individual, rich in patriotic spirit). NCLS 71: 26–30.

Thanh Nghi. *Tu Dien Viet-Nam* (Vietnamese Dictionary). Saigon: Thoi The XB, 1958.

The Nguyen (Nguyen Ba The). "Chi Si Viet-Nam: Nguyen Thanh" (A Patriot of Vietnam: Nguyen Thanh). VHNS 66: 37–43.

————. *Phan Boi Chau*. Saigon: Tan Viet XB, 1956. Includes some of Phan's later poems.

————. *Phan Chu Trinh (1872–1926)*. Saigon: Tan Viet XB, 1956. Includes some of Phan's writings and speeches.

To Minh Trung. "Chu-nghia cai-luong Phan Chu Trinh" (The reformist ideology of Phan Chu Trinh). NCLS 67: 29–38.

————. "Gop y kien voi ong Chuong Thau ve bai 'Anh huong cach mang Trung-quoc voi su chuyen bien tu tuong cua Phan Boi Chau" (Exchanging opinions with Chuong Thau on his article "Influence of the Chinese Revolution on changes in the thought of Phan Boi Chau"). NCLS 46: 51–59.

————. "May y kien danh gia vai tro Luu Vinh Phuc trong cuoc khang Phap cua nhan dan Viet-Nam" (Some opinions on assessing the role of Liu Yung-fu in the anti-French efforts of the Vietnamese people). NCLS 38: 31–34.

————. "Truong Vinh Ky: ten tay sai dac luc dau tien cua chu nghia thuc dan Phap trong lich su nuoc ta" (Truong Vinh Ky: the first accomplished puppet of French imperialism in the history of our country). NCLS 59: 43–46.

———— and Nguyen Xuan Huy. *Binh Tay Dai Nguyen Soai Truong Dinh*

(West-subduing Marshal Truong Dinh). Hanoi: NXB Quan Doi Nhan Dan, 1965.

To Nguyet Dinh. *Pham Hong Thai (1896–1924)*. Saigon: NXB Song Moi 1957.

To Trung. "Phong trao Dong Kinh Nghia Thuc, mot cuoc van dong cai cach xa hoi dau tien" (The Dong Kinh Nghia Thuc movement, a first social reformist effort). NCLS 29: 53–55.

Ton Quang Phiet. *Phan Boi Chau va mot giai doan lich su chong Phap cua Nhan Dan Viet-Nam* (Phan Boi Chau and an anti-French historical era of the Vietnamese people). Hanoi: NXB Van Hoa, 1958.

———. *Phan Boi Chau va Phan Chu Trinh* (Phan Boi Chau and Phan Chu Trinh). Hanoi: Ban Nghien Cuu Van Su Dia XB, 1956.

———. "Phan Chu Trinh: tu cach con nguoi va chu truong chinh tri" (Phan Chu Trinh: his personal character and political position). NCLS 70: 11–18.

Tran Dan Tien. *Nhung Mau Chuyen ve Doi Hoat Dong cua Ho Chu Tich* (Various Anecdotes on Chairman Ho's Life Activities). n.p., n.d.

Tran Huy Lieu, *et al. Cach Mang Can Dai Viet Nam* (Vietnam's Modern Revolution). 12 vols. Hanoi: Ban Nghien Cuu Van Su Dia XB, 1955, and NXB Van Su Dia, 1957–1958. Vol. 1 concerns scholar-gentry resistance movements, 1885–1896. Vol. 2 concerns Yen-the (1887–1913) and minority group uprisings from 1883 to 1920. Vol. 3 concerns the Duy Tan Hoi, Dong Du, Dong Kinh Nghia Thuc, Viet-Nam Quang Phuc Hoi, and Thai Nguyen. And Vol. 4 concerns the decade after World War I.

———. "Chung ta da nhat tri ve viec nhan dinh Phan Thanh Gian" (We have reached agreement in our appraisal of Phan Thanh Gian). NCLS 55: 18–20.

———. "Cuoc khoi nghia cua Phan Dinh Phung, tieu bieu cua phong trao Van Than (1885–89)" (The uprising of Phan Dinh Phung, symbol of the scholar-gentry movement, 1885–1889). NCLS 45: 1–14.

———. "Danh gia Luu Vinh Phuc va Quan Co-den trong cuoc khang Phap o Viet-Nam" (Assessing Liu Yung-fu and the Black Flags in anti-French efforts in Vietnam). NCLS 42: 21–25, 38.

———. *Lich Su Tam Muoi Nam Chong Phap* (History of Eighty Years Against the French). 2 vols. Hanoi: NXB Su Hoc, 1961. Vol. 1 covers the history up to 1930.

———, ed. *Lich Su Thu Do Ha-Noi* (History of the Capital City of Hanoi). Hanoi: NXB Su Hoc, 1960.

———. "Nhan dinh ve Truong Vinh Ky" (A Summing-up regarding Truong Vinh Ky). NCLS 63: 29–31.

———. "Nho lai Ong gia Ben Ngu" (Memories Concerning the Elderly Gentleman of Ben Ngu). NCLS 47: 40–44. The reference is to Phan Boi Chau.

———. "Xung quanh cai chet cua Hoang Dieu va viec that thu thanh Hanoi nam 1882" (Surrounding the death of Hoang Dieu and the 1882 fall of the Hanoi fortress). NCLS 39: 1–4.

Tran Minh Thu. "Co gang tien toi thong nhat nhan dinh ve Dong Kinh Nghia

Thuc" (Endeavoring to reach unity on summing-up the Dong Kinh Nghia Thuc). NCLS 81: 31–37.

————. "Tu *Nguc Trung Thu* den *Phan Boi Chau Nien Bieu"* (From *Nguc Trung Thu* to *Phan Boi Chau Nien Bieu*). NCLS 69: 46–51, 62. A textual comparison of these two important works.

Tran Minh Tiet. *Tim Hieu Nguoi Nhat Ban* (Understanding the Japanese people). Saigon: Nhom Dan-Chu Xa-Hoi Cong Giao XB, 1954.

Tran Thanh Tam. "Mot so tai lieu bang chu viet vua moi tim duoc ve may cuoc khoi nghia o mien nui Nghe-Tinh" (Some recently uncovered handwritten documents regarding various uprisings in the Nghe-An, Ha-Tinh mountain area). NCLS 51: 49–53.

Tran Trong Kim. *Viet-Nam Su Luoc* (Outline History of Vietnam). Saigon: Tan Viet XB, 1958. Originally published, 1928. An important early modern interpretative effort.

Tran Trong Phu. "Nghi ve mot giai doan mat nuoc" (Reflections on an era when we lost our country). In Truong Ba Can, *et. al., Ky Niem 100 Nam Ngay Phap Chiem Nam-Ky*, pp. 207–219.

Tran Van Giap, ed. *Luoc Truyen Cac Tac Gia Viet-Nam* (Biographical Outlines of Vietnamese Authors). Vol. 1. Hanoi: NXB Su Hoc, 1962.

————. "Tai-lieu moi ve Truong Cong Dinh (1821–1864), vi anh-hung dan-toc mien Nam" (New documentation on Truong Cong Dinh, brave figure of the southern populace). NCLS 51: 54–57.

Tran Van Giau. *Chong Xam Lang: Lich Su Viet-Nam tu 1858 den 1898* (Opposing Invasion: History of Vietnam from 1858 to 1898). 3 vols. Hanoi: NXB Xay Dung, 1957. Vol. 1, "Nam Ky Khang Phap" (Anti-French resistance in the South), concentrates on the period 1858–1867. Vol. 2, "Bac Ky Khang Phap" (Anti-French Resistance in the North), concentrates on the period 1873–1885. And Vol. 3, "Phong Trao Can Vuong" (The Can Vuong Movement), concerns from 1885 to 1898.

Tran Van Que. *Con-Lon Quan Dao* (The Island Group of Con-lon). Saigon: Thanh Huong Tung Thu XB, 1961.

Trinh Van Thanh. *Thanh-Ngu Dien Tich Danh-Nhan Tu Dien* (Dictionary of Proverbs, Literary Allusions and Famous Men). Vol. 1. Saigon: published by the author, 1966. Includes A-M of the alphabet only.

Truong Ba Can, *et al., Ky Niem 100 Nam Ngay Phap Chiem Nam-Ky* (Centennial Anniversary of the French Seizure of South Vietnam), Saigon: Trinh Bay XB, 1967. Truong Ba Can's contribution is: "Phan Thanh Gian voi viec mat ba tinh mien Tay" (Phan Thanh Gian and the loss of the three western provinces), pp. 181–206.

Truong Ba Phat (Phu Lang). "Truong-Dinh, dong tuong huyen Tan-Hoa" (Truong Dinh, courageous commander from Tan Hoa district). SD 3: 3–80.

Truong Buu Lam. "Vai nhan xet ve thoi hien-dai trong Viet-su" (Some observations on the contemporary period in Vietnamese history). *Viet-Nam Khao Co Tap San* (Saigon) 1: 33–44.

Truong Giang. "Nhung quan diem triet hoc ve lich su cua Phan Chu Trinh"

(Some philosophical points on Phan Chu Trinh's history). NCLS 73: 44–53.

Truong Huu Ky. "Them mot so tai lieu ve cu Phan Chu Trinh" (Adding some documentation on Phan Chu Trinh). NCLS 70: 19–20, 37.

Tung Lam. *Cuoc Doi Cach Mang Cuong De* (The revolutionary life of Cuong De). Saigon: Ton That Le, 1957. Originally a 1943 interview in Japanese with Cuong De.

Van Tan. "Luu Vinh Phuc tuong Co-den va cac hanh dong cua ong o Viet-Nam" (The Black Flag general Liu Yung-fu and his activities in Vietnam). NCLS 34: 7–15.

Van Tan, *et al. Tu Dien Tieng Viet* (Vietnamese Dictionary). Hanoi: NXB Khoa Hoc Xa Hoi, 1967.

Van Tao. "Ket thuc cuoc thao luan ve Phan Chu Trinh" (Concluding the discussion on Phan Chu Trinh). NCLS 76: 11–26.

Vien Giac. "Truong Chan Vo o Nhat, Truong Hoang Pho o Tau voi lich su cach mang Viet-Nam" (Japan's Shimbu Academy and China's Whampoa Academy in the revolutionary history of Vietnam). *Duoc Tue* (Saigon) 76: 13–14, 20 and 77: 21–22.

Viet Lam. "Mot it tai-lieu ve cuoc khoi-nghia Phan Xich Long o Nam-ky nam 1913" (A little documentation on the Phan Xich Long uprising in South Vietnam, 1913). NCLS 38: 19–21, 30.

Viet-Nam Minh-tri Thu Xa. *Thanh Khi Nhe Hang* (?). Hanoi: Mai Du Lan XB, 1926. Includes short articles on Phan Boi Chau and a concluding note by Phan.

Vu Dinh Lien, *et al.,* eds. *Hop Tuyen Tho Van Viet-Nam 1858–1930* (A Collection of Vietnamese Poetry and Prose, 1858–1930). Hanoi: NXB Van Hoa, 1963. The best anthology on the writings of a variety of anticolonial leaders.

Vu Van Tinh. "Mot vai diem xac minh ve vu nem bom o Ha-noi nam 1913" (Some clarifying data on the 1913 bombing incident). NCLS 72: 59–60.

Vuong Hong Sen. *Sai-gon Nam Xua* (Saigon in Olden Days). Saigon: Tu Do XB, 1960.

B. *Western-language Sources*

Archives Nationales de France, Section Outre-Mer (AOM). The materials held here are from the former Ministère de la Marine et Colonies and Ministère des Colonies. General classification is by subject, with Series A on Political Affairs being the most important for this study. For a very useful delineation of all subject headings in this archive, see Milton Osborne, "Rule and Response: Interaction in Cambodia and Cochinchina, 1859–1905." Ph.D. dissertation, Cornell University, 1968, pp. 575–584.

Bain, Chester. "The History of Viet-Nam from the French Penetration to 1939." Ph.D. dissertation, American University, 1956. Heavy emphasis on French colonial policy.

Boudarel, Georges. "Bibliographie des Oeuvres relatives à Phan Boi Chau editées en quoc ngu à Hanoi depuis 1954." *Bulletin de l'Ecole Française d'Extrême-Orient* 56: 151–176.

———. "Phan Boi Chau: Mémoires." *France-Asie/Asia* vol. 22, no. 3/4, pp. 3–210. Translation and annotation of Phan Boi Chau, *Phan Boi Chau Nien Bieu.*

Bui Quang Tung. "La Succession de Thieu-Tri." *Bulletin de la Societe des Etudes Indochinoises* vol. 42, nos. 1 and 2, pp. 52–69.

———. "Tables Synoptiques de chronologie Vietnamienne." *Bulletin de l'Ecole Française d'Extrême Orient* January–June 1963, pp. 1–77.

Burleson, Hugh Latimer. "The Kokuryukai in Northeast Asia." Master's thesis, University of California, 1956.

Buttinger, Joseph. *The Smaller Dragon: A Political History of Viet-Nam.* New York: Praeger, 1958.

———. *Viet-Nam: A Dragon Embattled.* 2 vols. New York: Praeger, 1967.

Chabrol, Emmanuel P. G. *Opérations militaires au Tonkin.* Paris: H. Charles-Larauzelle, 1897.

Chailley-Bert, Joseph. *La colonisation de l'Indo-Chine: l'expérience anglaise.* Paris: A. Colin & cie, 1892. Translated by A. B. Brabant into English as *The Colonization of Indochina.* London: Constable, 1894.

———. *Paul Bert au Tonkin.* Paris: G. Charpentier, 1887.

Chan Hok-lam. "Chinese refugees in Annam and Champa at the end of the Sung dynasty." JSEAH vol. 7, no. 2, pp. 1–10.

Chesneaux, Jean. *Contribution à l'histoire de la Nation Vietnamienne.* Paris: Editions Sociales, 1955.

———. "French historiography and the evolution of colonial Vietnam." In D.G.E. Hall, ed. *Historians of South East Asia.* London: Oxford University Press, 1961.

———. "Stages in the Development of the Vietnam National Movement, 1862–1940." *Past and Present* 7: 63–75.

Coughlin, M., "Vietnam: In China's Shadow." JSEAH vol. 8, no. 2, pp. 240–249.

Coulet, Georges. *Les Sociétés secrètes en terre d'Annam.* Saigon: C. Ardin, 1926.

Cultru, Prosper. *Histoire de la Cochinchine française des origines a 1883.* Paris: Augustin Challamel, 1910.

Dabezies, Pierre. *Forces Politiques au Viet-Nam.* n.p., n.d. [1957?]. Apparently a *Docteur en Droit* manuscript.

Do Vang Ly. *Aggressions by China.* Delhi: Siddhartha, 1960.

Doan Thi Do. "Le journalisme au Viet-Nam et les périodiques vietnamiens de 1865 à 1944." *Bulletin d'informations de l'Association des bibliothécaires français* 25 Mars, 1958.

Doumer, Paul. *Situation de l'Indo-Chine (1897–1901).* Hanoi: F. H. Schneider, 1902.

Dumarest, Andre. *La formation de classes sociales en pays annamite.* Lyon: Imprimerie Ferréol, 1935.

Eastman, Lloyd E. *Throne and Mandarins.* Cambridge: Harvard University Press, 1967.

Fairbank, John K., Edwin O. Reischauer, and Albert M. Craig. *A History of East Asian Civilization.* 2 vols. Boston: Houghton Mifflin, 1960 and 1964.

Fall, Bernard B. *The Two Viet Nams.* New York: Praeger, 1967.

Ferry, Ferreol de. *La série d'Extrême Orient du fond des Archives coloniales conservé aux Archives nationales.* Paris: Imprimerie Nationale, 1958.

Gaultier, Marcel. *L'étrange aventure de Ham Nghi, empereur d'Annam.* Paris: la Nef de Paris, 1959.

————. *Minh Mang.* Paris: Larose, 1935.

Gosselin, Charles. *L'Empire d'Annam.* Paris: Perrin, 1904.

Gouvernement Général de l'Indochine, Directions des Affaires Politiques et de Sûreté Générale. *Contribution à l'histoire des mouvements politiques de l'Indochine française.* 6 vols. Hanoi: Imprimerie D'Extrême Orient, 1930–1933.

Le Gouverneur Général de l'Indochine. *Recueil des Arrêtes du 17 Mai 1916.* Saigon: Imprimerie Nouvelle Albert Portail, 1916. Orders dealing with the Indochina penal system.

Grandidier, Guillaume. *Gallieni.* Paris: Librairie Plon, 1931.

Hammer, Ellen J. *The Struggle for Indochina.* Stanford: Stanford University Press, 1954.

Histoire militaire de l'Indochine de 1664 à nos jours, établie par des officers de l'Etat-Major sous la direction du général Duyperoux. Hanoi: Imprimerie D'Extrême Orient, 1922.

Hoang Ngoc Thanh. "The Social and Political Development of Vietnam as Seen Through the Modern Novel." Ph.D. dissertation, University of Hawaii, 1968.

Hoang Van Chi. *From Colonialism to Communism.* New Delhi: Allied Publishers, 1966.

Honey, P. J. "Modern Vietnamese Historiography." In D.G.E. Hall, ed. *Historians of South East Asia.* London: Oxford University Press, 1961.

Ichikawa, Kenjiro, comp. *Southeast Asia Viewed From Japan: A bibliography of Japanese works on Southeast Asian Societies, 1940–1963.* Data Paper 56, Southeast Asia Program, Cornell University, 1965.

Isoart, Paul. *Le phénomène national vietnamien.* Paris: Librairie générale de Droit et Jurisprudence, 1961.

Jabouille, M. "Une page de l'Histoire du Quang-tri: Septembre 1885." *Bulletin des Amis du Vieux Hue* November/December 1923.

Jansen, Marius. *The Japanese and Sun Yat-sen.* Cambridge: Harvard University Press, 1954.

Jumper, Roy, and Nguyen Thi Hue. *Bibliography on the Political and Administrative History of Viet-Nam, 1802–1962.* Saigon (?): Michigan State University Vietnam Advisory Group, 1962.

————. *Notes on the Political and Administrative History of Viet-Nam, 1802–1962.* Saigon (?): Michigan State University Vietnam Advisory Group, 1962.

Kallgren, Joyce K. "Asian Influences on Indo-Chinese Nationalism." Master's thesis, University of California, 1955.

Lacouture, Jean. *Ho Chi Minh: A Political Biography.* New York: Vintage, 1968.

Laffey, Ella. "The content of the Sino-Vietnamese tributary relationship in the late 19th century." Paper read at the Annual Association for Asian Studies Conference, 1968, Philadelphia.

Lamb, Alastair. *The Mandarin Road to Old Hue.* London: Chatto and Windus, 1969.

Lanessan, Jean M. A. de. *La Colonisation française en Indochine.* Paris: F. Alcan, 1895.

————. *L'Indochine française.* Paris: F. Alcan, 1889.

Langlois, Walter G. *André Malraux: The Indochina Adventure.* New York: Praeger, 1966.

Le Thanh Khoi. *Le Viet-Nam, histoire et civilisation.* Paris: Les éditions de minuit, 1955.

Levenson, Joseph R. *Liang Ch'i-ch'ao and the Mind of Modern China.* Cambridge: Harvard University Press, 1959.

————. *Modern China and Its Confucian Past.* Garden City, N.Y.: Doubleday, 1964.

Malleret, L. "The position of historical studies in the countries of former French Indo-China in 1956. In D.G.E. Hall, ed., *Historians of South East Asia.* London: Oxford University Press, 1961.

Mannoni, O. *Prospero and Caliban: The Psychology of Colonization.* New York: Praeger, 1964.

Marr, David G. "Viet-Nam's Anti-colonial Movements: The Early Years (1885–1925)." Ph.D. dissertation, University of California, 1968.

Masson, André. *Histoire du Vietnam.* Paris: Presses universitaires de France, 1960.

Maybon, Charles B. *Histoire moderne du pays d'Annam.* Paris: Plon, 1920. Deals with the period 1592–1820.

———— and Russier, Henri. *Notions d'Histoire d'Annam.* Hanoi: Imprimerie d'Extrême-Orient, 1911. Includes a facing-page *quoc-ngu* translation of the text.

Murakami, Hideo. "'Viet Nam' and the question of Chinese aggression." JSEAH vol. 7, no. 2, pp. 11–26.

Nguyen Dinh Hoa. *Vietnamese-English Dictionary.* Saigon: Binh Minh, 1959.

Nguyen Phut Tan. *A Modern History of Vietnam*. Saigon: Khai Tri, 1964.

Nguyen T. Hung. *An Analysis of Money and Credit in Vietnam, 1884–1962*. Ph.D. dissertation, University of Virginia, 1965.

Nguyen The Anh. "Quelques aspects économiques et sociaux du problème du riz au Vietnam dans la première moitié du XIXᵉ siècle." *Bulletin de la Société des Etudes Indochinoises*. vol. 42, nos. 1 and 2, pp. 7–22.

Nguyen Van Thai and Nguyen Van Mung. *A Short History of Viet-Nam*. Saigon: The Times Publishing Co., 1958.

Osborne, Milton E. *The French Presence in Cochinchina and Cambodia: Rule and Response (1859–1905)*. Ithaca: Cornell University Press, 1969.

————. "Rule and Response: Interaction in Cambodia and Cochinchina (1859–1905)." Ph.D. dissertation, Cornell University, 1968.

————. "Truong Vinh Ky and Phan Thanh Gian: the problem of a Nationalist interpretation of nineteenth century Vietnamese history." Unpublished manuscript, 1969.

————. "The Vietnamese perception of the indentity of the State." *Australian Outlook*. vol. 23, no. 1, pp. 7–17.

Pallu, Leopold. *Histoire de l'expédition de Cochinchine en 1861*. Paris: Hachette, 1864.

Pasquier, Pierre. *L'Annam d'autrefois*. Paris: Challamel, 1907.

Phan Chu Trinh. An untitled letter translated by M. Ed. Huber. *Bulletin de l'Ecole française d'Extrême Orient* 7: 166–175.

Phan Chu Trinh. "Les manifestations Annamites de 1908, une demande d'amnistie." *Bulletin Officiel de la Ligue des Droits de l'Homme*. vol. 12, no. 20, pp. 1145–1172.

Phan Thien Chau. *Transitional Nationalism in Viet-Nam, 1903–31*. Ph.D. dissertation, University of Denver, 1965.

————. "Vietnamese Nationalism, 1919–40." *Chuong Viet* 146: 51–56.

Robequain, Charles. *The Economic Development of French Indo-China*. London: Oxford University Press, 1944.

Roberts, Steven H. *History of French Colonial Policy, 1870–1925*. 2 vols. London: P. S. King, 1929. For Indochina especially, see vol. 2, pp. 436–479.

Rouyer, Charles H. *Histoire militaire et politique de l'Annam et du Tonkin depuis 1799*. Paris: Lavauzelle, 1906.

Scalapino, Robert A. *Democracy and the Party Movement in Prewar Japan*. Berkeley: University of California Press, 1962.

Schreiner, Alfred. *Abrégé de l'histoire d'Annam*. Saigon: published by author, 1906.

Smail, John R. W. "On the possibility of an autonomous history of modern Southeast Asia." *JSEAH* vol. 2, no. 2, pp. 72–102.

Smith, Ralph B. "Bui Quang Chieu and the Constitutionalist Party in French Cochinchina, 1917–30." *Modern Asian Studies* vol. 3, no. 2, pp. 131–150.

————. *Viet-Nam and the West*. London: Heinemann, 1968.

Taboulet, Georges, ed. *La geste française en Indochine.* 2 vols. Paris: A. Maisonneuve, 1955 and 1956.

Teng, Ssu-yu, and Fairbank, John K. *China's Response to the West: A Documentary Survey, 1839–1923.* Cambridge: Harvard University Press, 1954.

Thomazi, Auguste A. *La conquête de l'Indochine.* Paris: Payot, 1934.

Truong Buu Lam. *Patterns of Vietnamese Response to Foreign Intervention, 1858–1900.* New Haven: Southeast Asia Studies, Yale University Monograph Series 11, 1967. Particularly valuable for the author's translation of twenty key documents.

————. "Vietnamese Nationalism from 1900 to 1918." *Chuong Viet* 146: 43–50.

Van, Anh, and Jacqueline Roussel. *Mouvements Nationaux et Lutte de classes au Viet-Nam.* Paris: Publications de la IV Internationale. 1947.

Vial Paulin. *Nos premières années au Tonkin.* 2 vols. Paris: Voiron, 1889.

————. *Les premières années de la Cochinchine, colonie française.* Paris: Challamel Aine, 1874.

Wakeman, Frederic E., Jr. *Strangers at the Gate.* Berkeley: University of California Press, 1966.

Whitmore, John W. "The Development of Le Government in Fifteenth Century Vietnam." Ph.D. dissertation, Cornell University, 1968.

Woodside, Alexander. "Vietnam and the Chinese Institutional Model: Nguyen Emperors and Their Civil Bureaucracy 1802–1847." Ph.D. dissertation, Harvard University, 1968.

————. "Vietnamese Buddhism, the Vietnamese Court, and China in the 1800's: the triangular relationship." Paper read at the Annual Association for Asian Studies Conference, 1968, Philadelphia.

C. Chinese- and Japanese-language Sources

Hsüeh Chung-san, comp. *Liang-ch'ien Nien Chung-hsi Li Tui-chao (A Sino-Western Calendar for Two Thousand Years).* Peking, 1956.

Kawamoto Kunie. *Betonamu no Shi to Rekishi* (The Poetry and History of Vietnam). Tokyo: Bungei Shunjū, 1967.

Komatsu Kiyoshi. *Betonamu* (Vietnam). Tokyo: Shinchōsha, 1954.

Kuzuu Yoshihisa, ed. *Tō A Sengaku Shishi Kiden* (Records of Pioneer Patriots of East Asia). Tokyo: Kokuryūkai, 1935.

Nagaoka Shinjiro and Kawamoto Kunie, eds. *Betonamu Bōkokushi* (History of the Loss of Vietnam). Tokyo: Heibonsha (Toyōbunko, 73), 1966. The title is taken from Phan Boi Chau's *Vietnam Vong Quoc Su,* which is translated entirely in this book. Especially valuable is the essay by Nagaoka, "Vietnamese in Japan," pp. 256–282.

Oiwa Makoto. *Annan Minzoku Undōshi Gaisetsu* (A Historical Survey of Annamese Nationalist Movements). Tokyo (?): Guroria Sosaete, 1941.

Shao Hsun-cheng. *Chung-fa Chan-cheng* (The Sino-French War). 7 vols. Shanghai: Hsin Chih-shih Ch'u-pan shih, 1955.

Takeda Ryoji. "Annan Kakyo Seido Shōkō" (A Few Thoughts on Annam's Traditional Civil Exam System). *Shigaku* vol. 37, no. 1, pp. 1–15.

————. "Genchō Kakyo Seido no Ikkōsatsu" (A Consideration of the Nguyen Dynasty's Civil Exam System). *Tohōgaku Ronshū Nukizuri* July 1, 1962.

Wada Hironori. "Ajia no Kindaika to Keiō Gijuku" (Keio University and the Modernization of Asia). *Shōgakubu sōritsu jisshūnen Kinenbi Kichiron bunshu, Betsuzuri.* Tokyo: Keio University, 1967.

————. "Matsumoto Nobuhiro Kyōju Shōrai no Betonamu Shashin Sanshū ni tsuite" (Concerning Three Texts Brought Back from Vietnam by Professor Nobuhiro Matsumoto). *Shigaku* vol. 35, no. 4, pp. 93–96.

Yamamoto Tatsurō. "Annan ga Dokuritsukoku o Keisei Shitaru Katei no kenkyū" (A Study of the Process of Forming an Independent Annam). Tokyo: Toyo Bunka Kenkyūjo Kiyō, 1943.

————. *Annanshi Kenkyū* (A Study of the History of Annam). Vol. 1. Tokyo: Yamakawa Shuppansha, 1950.

Yun-nan tsa-chih hsüan-chi (A Collection of *Yunnan Periodical*). 2 vols. Peking: K'o-hsüeh ch'u-pan she, 1958.

Index

Ai-quoc. *See* Patriotism
America: Kashiwabara fears Vietnamese shift to, 147–148
American Indians: Phan Chu Trinh recalls fate of, 162
Am Ninh. *See* Le Ninh
Annam. *See* Vietnam, central
Anti-French (term), 5
Asaba Buntaro, 148, 149
Asian, East: racial solidarity, 113, 114, 119, 140, 147, 215
A-te-A (ballad). See *De Tinh Quoc Dan Ca*

Babut, Marcel, 256
Ba-Dinh: 1886/1887 defense of, 57–59
Bai-Say: as resistance area, 71–72
Barbarians: Vietnamese and, 19n, 20, 56–57, 183
Bay Do: as activist priest, 104, 230
Beau, Governor General Paul: Phan Chu Trinh's letter to, 159–163
Ben Tre: Nguyen Dinh Chieu in, 37; 1916 disturbances in, 231
Binh Dinh province: Can Vuong in, 59; Phan Chu Trinh in, 158; 1908 demonstrations in, 191
Binh-dinh-vuong. *See* Le Loi
Binh Thuan province: Can Vuong in, 60
Binh-thu yeu-luoc, by Tran Hung Dao, 12
Black Flags. *See* Liu Yung-fu
Borodin, Mikhail, 257
Buddhism: under Ly and Tran, 11; scholar-gentry hostile to, 20n; in resistance, 104–105, 143–144, 222, 230; discussed at Dong Kinh Nghia Thuc, 169, 170
Bui Huu Nghia, 38
Bui Quang Chieu, 213, 215, 268, 272–273

Cac Chu Tap Binh! (So, You're in the Army!): short anonymous song, 178; Cuong De recites, 223–224
Cam Ba Thuoc, 64n
Canton: French consulate in, 125; Phan Boi Chau's early activities in, 151; 1912 formation of Quang Phuc Hoi in, 215–217; 1924–1925 Vietnamese in, 257–258, 259–261
Can Vuong Edict: translated, 49–51; circulated, 51, 68–69, 71; affects Nguyen Ai Quoc's home area, 254
Cao Dien, 61
Cao Hu Lau Van (Indictment of Corrupt Customs), 175–176
Cao Thang: as lieutenant of Phan Dinh Phung, 61, 63–65, 139n
Cao Van Long. *See* Bay Do
Catholicism and Vietnamese Catholics: scholar-gentry hostile to, 20n, 37; response to missionaries, 25, 26; in French repression of Can Vuong, 54, 58, 59; Can Vuong attacks, 59; Phan Dinh Phung contends with, 61–62; Phan Boi Chau on, 105, 118, 240; and Cuong De, 223n; priests jailed on Con-lon, 243
Cau Giay: 1883 battle of, 42
Chang Hui-tsuan, 225
Chang Ping-lin, 124, 149